C000214212

WHO'S WHO OF VICTORIAN CINEMA

WHO'S WHO OF VICTORIAN CINEMA

A WORLDWIDE SURVEY

Edited by
STEPHEN HERBERT AND LUKE McKERNAN

BFI PUBLISHING

First published in 1996 by the
British Film Institute
21 Stephen Street, London W1P 2LN

The British Film Institute exists to promote
appreciation, enjoyment, protection and development of
moving image culture in and throughout the whole of
the United Kingdom. Its activities include the
National Film and Television Archive; the National
Film Theatre; the Museum of the Moving Image; the
London Film Festival; the production and distribution
of film and video; funding and support for regional
activities; Library and Information Services; Stills,
Posters and Designs; Research; Publishing and Education; and
the monthly *Sight and Sound* magazine.

This book has been published as a contribution to the celebrations of the
centenary of the cinema in the United Kingdom, which are being organised
by Cinema 100 on behalf of all sectors of the industry.
Cinema 100 aims to ensure that everyone is aware of the Centenary;
that filmgoing audiences increase; that knowledge of the cinema industry's
history and culture is enhanced; and that the cinema's second century is heralded.

British Library Cataloguing in Publication Data
A catalogue record for this book is available from the
British Library

ISBN 0-85170-539-1

Front cover portrait: James Williamson.
Back cover still: Annabelle's Serpentine Dance courtesy of
the National Film and Television Archive.

Typeset in Monotype Bell by
D. R. Bungay Associates, Burghfield, Berks

Printed in Great Britain by
Page Bros Ltd, Norwich

To Gus, who came so close, but got lost along the way

CONTENTS

ACKNOWLEDGMENTS

This book was put together in less than ideal circumstances, and we are very grateful to all who assisted in its production. Wilf Stevenson initiated the project, and we are indebted to him for his support. Our thanks also go to Ed Buscombe, Roma Gibson, Dawn King and John Smoker of BFI Publishing for all their hard work, and to Imdad Hussein and Laurence McAree of the ever-reliable BFI Computer Unit. Our task was made very much easier by the translation work of Graham Melville and Robin Bishop; faultless typing and technical services were provided by Hilary and Niall McKernan.

We are especially grateful to all our contributors, each of whom responded magnificently despite the pressure of deadlines of their own. Tony Fletcher, Thomas Ganz, Alison McMahan, Clifford Shaw and Vanessa Toulmin supplied additional helpful information. Sid Brooks was a constant source of encouragement and enthusiasm; and among the contributors we would like to thank John Barnes, Stephen Bottomore and Richard Brown for having read and corrected the text during its various stages. Lastly, we are most indebted to Deac Rossell, whose overall contribution to the book at every stage has been exceptional.

The portraits appear courtesy of the Barnes Collection, BFI Stills, Posters and Designs, Les Archives du Film du C.N.C (Boleslaw Matuszewski) and private collections.

Stephen Herbert
Luke McKernan

INTRODUCTION

The confusion that existed at the birth of film to a very large extent still exists. Moving pictures did not arrive as a neat package on a specific date; those who were involved could not conceive of the phenomenon of cinema that was to come. They were scientists who saw film as an aid to their work; businessmen who hoped to exploit what they saw as the fleeting attraction of a new invention; or performers merely transferring what they normally did on stage to the new medium. Moving pictures represented just one more invention in an age of inventions, just another variety turn. What none could have foreseen was the grip that film would have on audiences, how the medium would develop and extend itself, and how the moving image would become dominant as a means of communication and entertainment in the 20th century.

One hundred years on, the birth of film retains an obvious fascination, but is a subject afflicted with rivalries (national, personal and technical), too often simplistically documented and very confusing. Who invented the cinema? No one is the sensible answer, though this debate, which arose as soon as the cinema had become established, has raged ever since and continues to do so today. What this book tries to do is to show something of the lives of the many hundreds of people worldwide who by their efforts in the closing years of the 19th century collectively invented the cinema. Scientists, entrepreneurs, doctors, sportsmen, artists, politicians, dancers, photographers, reporters, showmen, propagandists and crooks: the whole extraordinary variousness of the late Victorian era.

We have taken as our field film-making in its broadest sense, from the first glimmerings in the 1870s and 80s to the death of Queen Victoria in January 1901. Many of the names we include went on to flourish in the world of twentieth-century cinema, and these later contributions are documented. Many more slipped back into obscurity; these we have described as best we can from the few sources that remain. We have had to be selective, so this work represents a Who's Who rather

than a comprehensive biographical dictionary for the period. We have tried to keep an international balance (it would have been easy to overemphasise the British contribution, as these sources were more readily available) and to include not only those who made or acted in the films but public figures whose appearance on film helped establish its form and popularity. We have covered the major figures of the pre-cinema period whose work in sequence photography or screen projection most clearly pointed the way to cinema. We have excluded figures who made a small contribution to Victorian film but whose major contribution came later (for example, William Haggar, Ferdinand Zecca).

We have had to leave out many names, mainly because of a lack of substantial information. It is extraordinary just how little is known about so many of the Victorian filmmakers; often it consists of no more than a patent application or a few references to their activities in contemporary documents. Much information lies scattered, often in specialised journals or in works that remain unknown outside their country of origin. It was frustration at trying to piece together such information, a frustration that we knew others felt, that led to the compiling of this book. Twenty-one contributors have generously given us the benefit of their expertise to help produce what is hopefully an authoritative, international reference work.

Victorian cinema has in the past been idly and chauvinistically documented. Only today are researchers trying to look beyond much of what has been accepted for decades and arrive at something nearer the truth. This book is necessarily based on much of what has gone before (as we acknowledge in the references to each entry, together with suggestions for further reading), though, equally, there is much information that is published here for the first time. It will soon become obvious what a debt is owed to the published researches of John Barnes (Britain) and Charles Musser (USA) in particular. The early cinema histories of Britain, France and the USA have always

1

attracted researchers; today, exciting work is going on to fill out the picture in Australia, Russia, Germany and central Europe. Other areas (notably South America) still lie open, largely undiscovered.

Each entry cites the name of the person (with original name in parentheses where appropriate), the year of birth and death (where known), is initialled by the contributor and provides sources of information or background literature. Books that are included in the later select bibliography are cited in shortened form; other works are given in full. Names which have their own entries elsewhere in the text are highlighted in bold where they first appear in any one entry. Given the frequency with which the names Edison and Lumière appear, however, these are only marked in bold when the reference is to the individual rather than the firm. Japanese names are written surname first, as is the custom. The full index of names refers to many people who do not have entries on their own. A technical essay explains the most common themes and terms covered in the book.

This book is a record of what is known so far of the personalities of a particular period that attracts enthusiastic research and is in a constant state of flux. Corrections or additions are thus welcomed by the editors.

TECHNICAL ESSAY

The requirements of cinematography

To succeed, cinematography required the availability of a sufficiently sensitive photographic emulsion that would allow at least sixteen pictures to be taken in one second; a suitable medium on which to fix the photographic emulsion; and the development of suitable camera and projection mechanisms.

Panoramas, dioramas and magic lanterns

In the century preceding the introduction of cinematography, something similar to the cinema experience had been provided by huge painted panoramas and the changing pictures of the giant diorama canvas. Since the 17th century or earlier, image projection had been possible with the magic lantern, later known as the optical lantern (or in the USA, stereopticon). Projected photographic images appeared in about 1850. Late nineteenth-century versions sometimes had two (bi-unial) or three (tri-unial) lenses and optical systems, to enable a skilled lanternist to produce dissolving views and moving picture effects on the screen, sometimes by means of mechanical slides. These ranged from simple lever and slipper slides (with one or two pieces of sliding glass) to more complex rackwork slides, featuring such favourite subjects as the 'man swallowing a rat' and the twirling patterns of the chromatrope. Some of the more sophisticated slides, such as the Choreutoscope, used mechanisms similar to the Maltese cross (that would later be the prime mechanism for cinema) to produce limited animated effects with painted slides. One version of an early film projection mechanism, the Riley Kineoptoscope, simply fitted into the slide-stage of a magic lantern. Other early film projection machines had their own lenses but used a standard magic lantern as a light source.

Motion perception toys

From the 1830s, revolving optical toys such as the Phenakistiscope (disc) and Zoetrope (drum) had demonstrated the illusion of movement by viewing a succession of slightly differing images through adjacent slots.

Reynaud's Praxinoscope represented an improved arrangement using a mirror drum.

Instantaneous photography

The development of 'instantaneous' photography in the 1860s and 70s led to the possibility of exposures of 1/100 of a second and less, and the facility to engineer precision mechanisms had long existed in the clock-making and allied industries. During the 1880s and 90s inventors used their ingenuity to adapt known motion mechanisms to the particular requirements of the new art. The photographic and magic lantern industries provided the optical necessities of lenses and illuminants, and by the middle of the decade, when these various requirements had been brought together by experimenters in many parts of the world, the movies became a practical reality.

Paper movies, celluloid film and perforations

Le Prince tried shooting sequences on rolls of unperforated paper; Marey progressed from glass to paper and then celluloid, but the strips were still unperforated and were used to obtain sequences of chronophotographic images for individual analysis rather than synthesis into moving sequences on a screen. For his Parisian 'Pantomime Lumineuse' projections given from 1892 with the Théâtre Optique, Reynaud had provided registration perforations between each painted picture. From about the same time, Dickson's experiments for Edison were carried out on lengths of perforated celluloid film. He used the film manufactured for snapshot cameras. This was approximately 70mm wide, and when slit in half to provide a manageable material for the Kinetoscope, became 35mm perforated film – a standard which was to survive with minor modifications to the present day.

The Kinetograph and Kinetoscope

The Kinetograph camera moved the film intermittently by means of an unusual arrangement of a toothed disc turning at right angles to a slotted disc: a tooth on one disc entered a slot in the other, allowing the sprocket to turn one picture-height. But for viewing in the Kinetoscope peepshow the film moved continuously, a very narrow shutter aperture allowing each image to be seen for just a tiny fraction of a second, so that blurring of the moving images was minimal. To reduce flicker, a high shooting/viewing speed – around 40fps (frames per second) – was used. Fewer pictures were actually needed to give a result of good motion fidelity, and later intermittent systems, where each image could be seen for longer and the revolving shutter was less obtrusive, used only 16fps.

Continuously moving film
Experiments in non-intermittent projection were carried out in the USA by the Lathams with their Panoptikon and Eidoloscope projectors, but the very brief flash of illumination necessary to ensure that the continuously rolling images did not present a blur on the screen resulted in a very dim projected image. Early experimental cameras by C. Francis Jenkins used a revolving circle of lenses to compensate optically for the movement of the film.

Double picture bands
A double band of film was used by Proszynski and the Skladanowskys: frames from the two bands were projected alternately, ensuring that there was always an image on the screen, thereby eliminating flicker.

The Cinématographe
The Lumières, aware of the Kinetoscope and its films, created the single-unit Cinématographe camera/printer/projector. The pin (similar to the alternative claw) movement engaged in single perforations on the edges of each picture frame. The pins were attached to a shuttle (inspired by that used in sewing machines), which provided the necessary 'up-down' and 'in-out' movement. After shooting, the negative film was developed, and then run through the mechanism together with blank stock. Light from the printing lamp shone through the negative to expose the blank stock, which was in turn developed as a positive, ready for projection. The mechanism was set up in front of a lamphouse, and the lens replaced by one more suitable for projection. The Lumière films ran for less than one minute. The film passed through the picture gate and fell loosely into a chamber in the projection stand. Soon, most projectors were fitted with take-up spools as the length of the projected films increased.

Latham Loop
In the first cameras and projectors, the intermittent movement of the film in the picture gate was transmitted to the supply spool, causing it to feed the film in jerks. As films got longer the weight of the film on the spool meant that the mechanism tore the perforations. To eliminate this, most designers added a continuously rolling sprocket above the picture gate, with a loop of film (the 'Latham Loop', named after one of its inventors) between the new sprocket and the gate absorbing the intermittent jerking of the film. The length of the film that could be taken or projected was then limited only by the size of the spool.

Perforation standards
'Edison'-type perforations, with four holes on each side of the frame, were used by most producers, making it possible for the majority of films to be used in most cameras/projectors. However, small variations between one manufacturer and another in the actual size and shape of hole were a cause of picture unsteadiness, not cured until the adoption of an agreed standard in 1909.

Specialised mechanisms
As well as the Lumières' machine, some other makers' early mechanisms could be used as camera/printer/projector, but quite soon the different requirements of these three devices led to separate mechanisms being designed. Cameras generally used pin or claw movements, whereas projectors usually employed a Maltese cross or other intermittently moved sprocket design.

Maltese cross
The four-arm Maltese cross (Geneva movement) and its star-cross derivatives with five or seven arms were used early on by various inventors, including Gliewe and Messter in Germany; Carpentier and Bunzli in France. As the crank handle was turned a pin on a revolving disc entered a slot in one of the arms of the cross, moving it down before leaving the slot. The cross then remained static until the pin came round again and moved the next arm down. The cross was attached to a sprocket, which moved intermittently with it, and in turn moved the film with the required stop-start motion. An important part of the design was that the cross/sprocket (and therefore the film) were locked between movements, ensuring a steady projection of each static frame.

Beater movement

Patented in 1893, it was late 1896 before one novel arrangement, the Demenÿ 'Chronophotographe' beater movement camera/projector, appeared on the market. A rod attached to one side of a revolving disc beneath the picture gate revolved eccentrically, 'beating' the film down by the required amount (the height of one picture) with each revolution. Others made use of this mechanism (also referred to as the 'dog' movement) until about 1910, including Thomas Armat whose projector was bought by Edison and promoted as the Edison Vitascope.

Gripper-roller movement

The Mutograph and Biograph cameras used a segmented gripper-roller movement. Holes were punched in the unperforated film as it was exposed, to act as a registration guide when making the projection prints. The projectors also used gripper-rollers and frequent adjustment of the picture framing was required during projection of the unperforated print. Other ingenious mechanisms for moving film intermittently were used in the 1890s, in part to avoid patent infringements, but these gradually died away in the early years of the 20th century.

Projector development

In Britain, the first projections were produced by Birt Acres with his Kineoptikon, and Robert Paul with his Animatographe/Theatrograph. Paul made various technical improvements in the first year, abandoning his double-sprocket intermittent for a single-sprocket version, and incorporating a top-rolling sprocket and film loop to reduce film strain. With his later Century and Reliance machines, he changed his seven-arm cross to a three-arm version to increase film pulldown speed, thereby requiring only a very small shutter, and consequently reducing flicker. Similar improvements were made by many other equipment manufacturers, including those in France and Germany.

Flicker

With only one shutter blade (to block projection while the film was being pulled down to the next picture) flicker of the images was sometimes disturbing, and was often commented upon by early film viewers. In an attempt to reduce this, one method used a translucent shutter – of ground glass or oiled paper – so that some light was on the screen during the pulldown period. This was employed by Rudge in his early Phantascope multi-slide projector, and was suggested by the Lumières in their Cinématographe patent; in practice, however, it was not successful. Flicker was eventually reduced by adding a second (and later a third) blade to equalise the periods of light and dark on the screen and increase their frequency, making them less evident.

A variety of names

Most manufacturers and some showmen devised their own names for their projectors. Often derived from Greek and Latin, and usually cumbersome, they included such gems as Vever's Viviograph, Wood's Movendoscope and the Chronophotographoscope. The names of some machines introduced during this period – the Biograph, Cinématographe/Kinematograph, Bioscope – became generic terms for motion pictures. The latter term was also used by travelling fairground showmen. Film shows were also referred to as Animated Photographs and Living Pictures.

Film production

As the requirement for longer films grew, camera capacity increased from 45ft and 70ft to 400ft and more. Daylight was used to illuminate scenes, with interiors usually constructed as outdoor sets. The early Kinetoscope films were shot in a studio known as the Black Maria, a shack which could be turned to catch the light through its hatched roof. Later, some glass-roofed studios were constructed. There were no exposure meters; camera operators used their experience to judge apertures. Optical printers were not available at this time, and special effects (such as dissolves and superimpositions) were produced 'in camera', by running the same strip of film through more than once. Most companies used 35mm film, but some (Biograph/Mutograph) used film of twice the width, producing an image of much greater resolution. The original Biograph camera was huge and was driven by electric motor, but most cameras/projectors were hand-cranked. Because of this, cameras needed heavy tripods. One turn of the camera handle was geared to give eight exposures, so for the normal speed of 16fps, the cameraman cranked the handle twice a second. Camera movement was limited (there were few pan-and-tilt tripod heads), but cameras were sometimes mounted on vehicles to produce tracking effects. Especially popular were 'Phantom Rides', where the camera was mounted on the front of a train.

Mutoscopes and home movies

For arcade viewing, the Mutoscope – a development of Linnett's 1868 flip book – was introduced in 1897, with pictures on 'flip cards' printed from large-format Mutograph/Biograph camera negatives; and it soon superseded the Kinetoscope. A miniature mutoscope for amateur use, the Lumière Kinora, was the first to allow safe viewing of movies in the home; Leo Kamm's Kammatograph camera/projector, patented in 1898 and marketed from 1900, used glass discs with images arranged in a spiral, giving a maximum of forty-five seconds of motion pictures. Toy projectors by Nuremberg toymakers Bing, Plank and Carette, using oil-lamp illuminants and both star-cross and beater movements, appeared from 1897–8. These utilised 35mm films – some photographic, and others specially printed in full colour lithography. Many of the latter consisted of image sequences 'rotoscoped' (traced) from live-action films to produce short loops of repeated action (similar to the limited motion sequences of that earlier Victorian optical toy, the Zoetrope).

The professional film size was not necessary for the smaller home picture, and from 1898 manufacturers tried narrow-gauge films for economy and convenience. The Mirographe of Reulos and Goudeau used a 20mm film and an odd 'snail' movement that engaged in perforations on the outer edge of the film. Birt Acres' Birtac camera/printer/projector used film of half the normal width, and this was followed by the similarly compact Biokam from Wrench and Son, the Petite of Hughes and the Chrono de Poche of Gaumont.

Celluloid and illuminants

Nitrate-based film (nitrocellulose) was highly inflammable and could be dangerous for home use, and also in professional applications. The May 1897 Charity Bazaar fire in France led to the enforcement of regulations, and 'safety' (acetate) film was eventually produced. (This was used for all amateur formats after 1912, but would not come into general professional use until after 1950.) The main cause of the 1897 fire was the ether saturator limelight illuminant, which was eventually banned. Other forms of limelight, usually involving a mixture of hydrogen and oxygen, were still used, but were gradually superseded by electric carbon arc lamps, requiring a generator. With all of these illuminants, a glass condenser lens in the lamphouse gathered the light and concentrated it onto the small film aperture. Some machines, including the early

Lumière Cinématographe, used a water-filled glass flask as a condenser in an attempt to reduce the heat on the film.

Sound films

Recorded sound was first used with films in the Kinetophone, a special version of the Edison Kinetoscope. A cylinder player built into the machine provided loosely synchronised audio accompaniment through rubber-tube earphones. Auguste Baron produced experimental sound films in 1898, and at the Paris Exposition of 1900, Léon Gaumont showed a 'Portrait Parlant' of himself, using a cylinder phonograph mechanically coupled to a cine camera for filming, and to a Gaumont Chrono projector for the 'talkie' screening. By 1901 Ernst Ruhmer of Germany had recorded and reproduced sound on 35mm motion picture film with the Photographon, one of the very early experiments that would later lead to the optical sound-film systems still in use today.

Coloured films

One of the earliest examples of coloured film projection was by Robert Paul in London in April 1896 with an 'Eastern Dance', and the following month with a coloured film of the 1895 Derby. *The Serpentine Dance*, coloured red, blue and pale green, appeared in the first programme of the Vitascope in New York in April. By September 1896 the *British Journal of Photography* reported that coloured films were almost a matter of course. Some of Paul's colouring was carried out by Mr Doubell, formerly a slide painter to the old Royal Polytechnic Institution, who, it was said, painted only two or three frames a day, under a powerful magnifier. Normally the colouring was executed by a team of painters, usually girls, each of whom applied one colour to the print before passing it on to a colleague. Exceptionally, as many as six colours might be used, though two or three were more usual. The colouring presented great problems, since the picture was only one inch by three-quarters in size.

Natural colour films

In 1899 Edward R. Turner, financed by F. Marshall Lee, devised a system for filming and projecting a motion picture in 'natural' colour. By filming consecutive frames through red, green and blue filters, the black and white film stock contained a 'colour' record, which would then be reproduced on the screen by projection through similar colour filters. Registration of the images proved difficult, however, and the Lee and Turner projector of 1901 was unsuccessful. When Turner died the following year, Charles Urban bought the patent rights and the principle was eventually evolved by G. A. Smith into the successful Urban-Smith Kinemacolor system.

Stereoscopic moving pictures

There were several attempts at stereoscopic (3D) motion pictures from the very beginnings, with the 1861 Kinematoscope peepshow machine of Coleman Sellers in the USA, and similar devices produced by Shaw and Wheatstone. In the Victorian film period, Jenkins in the USA, Grivolas in France and Dickson in England, as well as other less well-known pioneers, experimented with and patented systems for shooting and projecting stereoscopic films, but it would be some years before there were any commercial developments.

WHO'S WHO OF VICTORIAN CINEMA

A

ABD al-AZIZ, Sultan of Morocco
(1878–1943)

One of the more unexpected enthusiasts for the cinematograph in its early days must surely have been the youthful Sultan of Morocco (ruled 1894–1908). In truth cinema was just one of many foreign-made playthings in which he was interested. Encouraged by western governments, especially Britain, he imported gadgets in large numbers: according to *The Times* correspondent these included automobiles, grand pianos, wild animals in cages, barrel-organs, hansom cabs, false hair, and even a passenger lift destined for his one-storey palace. In among these items was a large amount of camera gear, including a £2,000 camera made of gold. To operate this equipment the Sultan decided to have lessons in photography and cinematography, and some time between 1900 and 1901 the ex-Lumière operator **Gabriel Veyre** arrived on the scene. Based at the Sultan's palace in the so-called 'Cour des Amusements', surrounded by billiard tables, balloons, telephones and the other devices which had attracted the Sultan's fancy, Veyre's principal duty seems to have been to project films for the pleasure of the young ruler and his wives. But he was by no means the only film man to be so employed: in 1901 John H. Avery, one of **Charles Urban**'s cameramen, filmed the Sultan for the Warwick Trading Company, and then stayed on as his projectionist. That same year, C. Rider Noble arrived and performed the same functions for three years, later lecturing in Britain on his experiences using the films he had taken there. And by 1908 a young Charles Rosher (later Mary Pickford's cameraman) was the new resident film expert.

But by this time increasing dissatisfaction was being expressed in the country over the Sultan's extravagance and his western ways. Along with the four cinematographers in his employ, his European suite included a conjurer, a watchmaker, a German lion tamer, a French soda-water manufacturer and a Scottish piper. It was not an entourage calculated to endear him to his traditional Muslim countrymen, who considered the devices that the foreigners operated 'abominations', with particular ire being reserved for the 'boxes of Satan', as the cameras were called. One rebellion was suppressed in 1903, but in 1908 the Sultan was overthrown by his brother. He was allowed to stay in Morocco, however, where his interest in cinema continued, and in 1913 he visited Charles Urban and ordered a complete Kinemacolor installation for his residence in Algiers. (SB)

References
Gabriel Veyre, *Au Maroc: Dans l'intimité du Sultan* (Paris: Librarie Universelle, 1905).
Walter B. Harris, *Morocco That Was* (London/Edinburgh: Blackwood and Sons, 1921).

ACKERMAN, C. Fred

Cameraman, projectionist. Fred Ackerman was one of the American Mutoscope and Biograph Company's main camera operators in the Victorian period. First recorded as working for them in June 1899, he is best known for documenting his journey to China in 1900, the year of the Boxer Rebellion. Filming mostly local scenes, but also some troop movements, as well as Chinese politician **Li Hung Chang** receiving his gift of a Mutoscope, Ackerman returned the same year and toured the USA with journalist Thomas Millard, presenting a programme of films, lantern slides and commentary entitled *War in China*. Prior to his trip to China he had travelled to the Philippines to film scenes from the offshoot to the Spanish-American War which first arose in Cuba, shooting several scenes of military activity from November 1899 to March 1900. This assignment has parallels with what **W. K-L. Dickson** was doing for British Biograph in South Africa at exactly the same time, but remains little known. (LMcK)

References
Kemp Niver, *Biograph Bulletins 1896–1908* (Los Angeles: Locare Research Group, 1971).

ACRES, Birt (1852?–1918)

Inventor, film-maker. The first man successfully to take and project a 35mm film in England. Born in Richmond, Virginia, to English parents, Birt Acres was working in London as a photographer in November 1889. During 1892 he joined the large photographic materials company of Elliott and Son and became manager of their 'Dry Plate' works at Barnet, in North London. Acres had developed an interest at this time in photographing clouds, and in order to be able to reconstitute his time-lapse studies, he devised a rapid lantern slide changer, which he patented in December 1893. This would appear to represent the extent of his chronophotographic work prior to the arrival in England of Edison's Kinetoscope in October 1894. By December 1894, an electrical instrument-maker, **Robert Paul**, had begun to replicate these machines, but urgently needed an independent supply of films for them. Acres' assistant at Elliott's, **Henry Short**, was a friend of Paul, and suggested Acres to Paul as someone who had the necessary photographic knowledge required to design a workable camera, and to take and develop the films for it. The two men first met on 4 February 1895. What subsequently occurred became – and to some extent still is – a matter of controversy. According to Paul's account, he rejected Acres' idea as impractical, and designed and built the camera himself. However, since it was Paul who approached Acres, and it was Acres rather than Paul who subsequently patented the camera and claimed copyright on the films, Paul's account seems of doubtful veracity. Certainly, what is clear is that Acres' role in the enterprise was undoubtedly of considerable importance.

Rapid progress was made, and a workable camera had been completed by the middle of March. A successful test film, featuring Henry Short, was taken outside Acres' house, and on 29 March Paul sent a clip from it to **Thomas Edison**. Commercial production began on 30 March with the *Oxford and Cambridge Boat Race*, and by the beginning of June several simple comic, dramatic and actuality subjects were available. These included *The Arrest of a Pickpocket*, *The Comic Shoeblack*, *The Boxing Kangaroo*, *Performing Bears* and a film of the Derby. A photograph of Acres filming the 1895 Derby has survived, and it reveals that the camera used was relatively portable.

Unlike Paul, who was careful to retain his existing business, Acres committed himself wholly to the new enterprise and resigned from Elliott's in April 1895. This gave him the freedom to travel, and he entered negotiations with the **Stollwerck** company, who in June supported a trip to Germany, where Acres took several films of the opening of the Kiel Canal. While he was away, Paul began to advertise himself as the 'Sole European Manufacturer' of the films, and on Acres' return to England in mid-July, the association between the two men ended in acrimony and mutual recriminations.

Acres now turned his attention to achieving film projection. He claimed several times during 1896 and 1897 that he had given private demonstrations during August and September 1895. Though no documentary proof of these performances has yet been found, it seems certain that successful projection must have occurred sometime in 1895, since Acres was able to give a public performance to members of the Lyonsdown Photographic Club on Friday 10 January 1896. He presented a further showing to members of the Royal Photographic Society at 12 Hanover Square, London, on 14 January; and on 21 March commercial performances began with the 'Kineoptikon' at 2 Piccadilly Mansions, London. Admission was 6d and the films were shown from 2 p.m. to 6 p.m., and from 7.30 p.m. to 10.00 p.m. On 27 June Acres secured a film of the Prince and Princess of Wales arriving at the Cardiff Exhibition, and as a result he was asked to give the first royal command film performance at Marlborough House on 21 July.

So far Acres had enjoyed almost continual success, and by the middle of 1896 was well placed to reap substantial financial rewards, with the demand for commercial film shows, especially in music halls, rapidly increasing. But he disliked the role of showman, and though he sold his films to other exhibitors, disapproved of the use of film as simply a 'turn' inserted in a variety entertainment, believing instead that the future for cinematography lay in the photographic and educational markets. So, while Paul and others rose to the challenge of creating a new business, Acres spent much of his time between 1896 and 1899 touring the country, lecturing and giving performances to scientific and photographic societies. This brought him prestige and press coverage, but little profit, and by the end of 1897 it was clear to contemporaries that he had lost – or thrown away – the lead that he had once had. In an attempt to improve his fortunes, he introduced the Birtac, a 17.5mm combined camera and projector. Targeted at the amateur photographic market, it was available from October 1898. The Birtac was a genuine innovation, and miniaturisation represented a significant advance, both technically and conceptually, but unfortunately the instrument only had limited success, and Acres returned to 35mm film-making (until 1900), and to a film-coating, developing and printing business that he had established in July 1897.

Serious-minded and a perfectionist, Birt Acres was a clever and inventive man, undoubtedly more committed to the future of film than most of his contemporaries; but he was perhaps temperamentally unsuited to life as an entrepreneur. Though connected with the film business until his death, his later years were not successful financially, and he went bankrupt in both 1909 and 1911. Despite the number of British film 'firsts' that he could claim, Acres' reputation as a pioneer did not survive unscathed. In fact, the diminution of his reputation began in his lifetime, with the publication in 1912 of a highly inaccurate account of the origins of cinematography in England by F. A. Talbot from information supplied by Paul. Acres' own copy of Talbot's book, *Moving Pictures*, with his acerbic pencilled comments, is now in the library of the BFI. When serious interest in early film history began after the First World War, **Will Day** (the leading film historian of the time) was far more interested in promoting the nebulous claims of **William Friese Greene** than in recording the actual achievements of Acres. Many years of neglect followed, and it was not until the publication of John Barnes's *The Beginnings of the Cinema in England* in 1976 that the first detailed study of his work appeared. More sympathetic in its treatment than Barnes (who tended to follow Paul's version of events in his account of the relationship

between the two men) is Lange-Fuchs's biography, published in 1987. This work is also valuable in providing further details about Acres' activities in Germany. Now recognised as a film pioneer of outstanding importance in both England and Germany, Acres' reputation seems to be secure at last. (RB)

Note: Acres' birthdate is variously given as 1855 (from his marriage certificate), 1854 (from his headstone) and 1852 (from his death certificate). The latter has been selected as the most likely.

References

Birt Acres, 'Animated Photography', *Amateur Photographer*, 9 October 1896, p. 298.
Birt Acres, 'The Making and Exhibiting of Living Pictures', *Journal of the Camera Club*, May 1897, pp. 65–6.
Barnes, *The Beginnings of the Cinema in England* (vol. 1).
Richard Brown, 'England's First Film Shows', *British Journal of Photography*, 31 March and 7 April 1978.
Hauke Lange-Fuchs, *Birt Acres: Der erste Schleswig-Holsteinische Film Pionier* (Kiel: Walter G. Muhlau, 1987).

AKIMOV, Ivan Akimovich (?–1902/3?)

Photographer, writer, inventor. Very little is known of Akimov's life, but there are some signs of a humble origin (he may have been the illegitimate child of unknown parents). He called himself a 'retired quartermaster-sergeant'. Little too is known of his professional activities: listed as a member of the Russian Photographic Society, he was cited as an expert at the Moscow Photographic Exhibition of 1896, invented a professionally recognised photometer and was the author of *A Guide for Beginner Photographers* (*Rukovodstvo dlya nachinayushchikh fotografov*), which had passed through five editions. On 12 January 1896 Akimov received an official certificate for his invention of the Stroboscope – an apparatus designed for shooting moving photographic images on special film with a speed of 15 to 20fps. The same apparatus served for the projection of images on a screen 'transmitting original natural movement'. In his design Akimov used a German Petzvald lens, and designed an original friction clutch device for intermittent film movement. For projection he implemented a special lamp with condenser and reflector.

Akimov's apparatus was not patented until 22 August 1898, by which time the inventor had completely lost interest in his invention, overshadowed as it was by the general success of the Lumière Cinématographe. One may be sure that Akimov's Stroboscope was never used to make films, and according to some evidence only one functioning model existed, deposited in the Moscow Museum of Polytechnics, only to be destroyed in the Soviet period. Today only a technical description, a number of drafts and official papers mark the fact that it ever existed. (RY)

References
Sokolov, *Istoriya izobreteniya kinematografia* (1960).

AKKAS BASHI, Mirza Ebrahim Khan

Court photographer to the Shah of Iran, Mozaffar al-Din Shah. The Shah discovered the cinema when he saw the giant Lumière film exhibit at the Paris Exposition in July 1900. He recorded in his journal: 'They erected a very large screen in the centre of the hall, turned off all electric lights and projected the picture of cinematograph on that large screen. It was very interesting to watch. Among the pictures were Africans and Arabians travelling with camels in the African desert which was very interesting. ... We instructed Akkas Bashi to purchase all kinds of it and to bring to Teheran so that God willing he can make some there and show them to our servants.'

Akkas Bashi duly purchased the necessary equipment for the taking and projecting of film, and just one month later he was making his first films, of the Festival of Flowers in Belgium, on the Shah's visit there. On the Shah's return to Teheran the films were shown to his inner circle of family, ministers and court servants. A second trip to Europe in 1902 was also filmed. All films were kept for royal entertainment only, and the court cinematograph was thereafter used by the Persian elite to record weddings, circumcisions and other festivities. French comedy films imported from Russia were also shown. The first public film theatre opened in Iran in 1905. (LMcK)

References
M. Ali Issari, *Cinema in Iran, 1900–1979* (Metuchen, NJ/London: Scarecrow Press, 1989).

ALBERINI, Filoteo (1867–1937)

Engineer, exhibitor, film-maker. Alberini was an engineer at the Istituto Geografico Militare who on 11 November 1895 obtained an Italian patent for his Kinetografo Alberini, a combined camera, projector and printer. There is no evidence that a workable machine resulted. Alberini nevertheless went on to become an important exhibitor and film-maker on the early Italian scene. In 1897, with Anchise Cappelletti and Lionello Ganucci-Cancellieri, he produced the Cinesigrafo, which used wide film similar to the American Biograph and was first exhibited in May 1899 in Florence. In the early 1900s he opened cinemas in Florence and Rome (the Moderno), and in 1905 with Dante Santoni founded a production company for which he made Italy's first dramatic film, *La presa di Roma*. In the following year the company became Cines, and soon developed into a major and influential producer, not only in Italy but worldwide. Alberini continued to experiment with stereoscopy (the Autostereoscopio, 1911) and wide-gauge film (the Panoramico Alberini, 1914). (LMcK)

References
Bernardini, *Cinema muto italiano 1896–1904* (1980).

ALBERT I, Prince of Monaco (1848–1922)

As well as being head of state of the small principality of Monaco, Albert (reigned 1889–1922) was a pioneering oceanographer, who conducted important research in this field in the Mediterranean and North Atlantic between 1885 and 1915, and built an oceanographical museum. His interests also covered human palaeontology and technology. This latter interest would account for his surprisingly early enquiry about the Lumière Cinématographe, when, at the end of January 1896, only a month after the Grand Café premiere, the Prince wrote to his scientific collaborator Dr Jules Richard asking him to find out more about the machine. Richard went to the Paris show and wrote back that the picture was impressively realistic, though he also noted an annoying flicker. They soon discovered that the Cinématographe was not yet for sale, and spent the next year trying to obtain other machines, making enquiries in London and contacting **Eugène Pirou**. They eventually obtained a Gaumont apparatus in the summer of 1897, with which the Prince took five films in Morocco. Some of his films and cameras are preserved at the Museum Océanographique de Monaco.

Another pioneering use of cinema that took place in Monaco was the world's first ever film competition. This was organised in 1897 by the Societé des Bains de Mer of the Monte Carlo Casino, and took place as one part of a photographic competition. Press claims that this was initiated by the Prince as a way 'to encourage and develop this new art' may be exaggerated, but he at least approved of the scheme. There were three cash prizes and the overall winner, announced in March 1898, was **Clément-Maurice** with his film, *Monaco vivant par les appareils cinématographiques*. Serving on the jury was **Léon Gaumont**, and when a second competition was held in 1899 (this time exclusively for films), most of the winners were using a Gaumont camera. In this second competition there were eleven prizes totalling 30,000 francs (almost ten times that of the first). It was intended for amateurs only, and each competitor had to send in at least three previously unexhibited films, which were judged on the basis of 'originality, artistic merit and photographic quality'. The prizes were given out in February 1900 by the Prince, the first one going to Dr **Eugène-Louis Doyen** for his surgical film, *Operation du Dr Doyen: Ablation du goitre*. Prize-winning films from the Monaco competition were shown in the Monaco pavilion at the Paris Exposition of 1900; these included views of gymnastic exercises and of M. Camille Blanc's stallion in its paddock. (SB)

References
J. Carpine-Lancre, 'Le Prince Albert I de Monaco et le cinématographie', paper read at Lumière conference, Lyon 1995.
J. Carpine-Lancre, 'Prince, océanographe et "cinématographiste": Albert I de Monaco', *1895*, 1995.

AMET, Edward Hill (c.1861–1948)

Inventor of the Magniscope, an early American projector, Edward Amet was (says Ramsaye) working on weighing machines at the Chicago Scale Works, Waukegan, Illinois, when he became interested in devising a motion picture projector; Musser, however, relates that the Amet Talking Machine Company was making high-quality phonographs when his interest was taken by motion pictures. With some small financial assistance from the local Waukegan theatre manager, **George K. Spoor**, he finished his machine early in 1896. According to Ramsaye it was named the Magniscope by its distributor, **George Kleine**, then a dealer in lantern slides and related goods, and by September was on sale in the Chicago area. It was taken up by several itinerant showmen, and was also soon engaged by a number of local theatres. The following year Amet went into film production, including a re-creation, using models, of the sinking of Admiral Cervera's fleet at Santiago, which was passed off as the real thing.

Some of his productions were pirated by Edison. Amet gave up film production around 1900 and went into electrical work. (SH)

References
Musser, *The Emergence of Cinema* (1990).
Ramsaye, *A Million and One Nights* (1926).

ANDERSON, 'Professor' Phillip

Magician. Following the debut of the Lumière Cinématographe in Bombay, as presented by **Marius Sestier** on 7 July 1896, several travelling showmen visited Indian cities, having swiftly incorporated moving pictures into their act. Best known among them was the magician, **Carl Hertz**, who arrived in 1898, but he was preceded by 'Stewart's Vitograph' (which came to Bombay for a week in January 1897), an unnamed showman touring with a **W. C. Hughes** projector, and early in 1898 the magician 'Professor' Phillip Anderson, who with 'Mlle Blanche' (his wife Blanche de la Cour) had been touring India and South Asia for a decade. Anderson billed his machine, which is likely to have been a **Robert Paul** Theatrograph, as the gloriously excessive 'Andersonoscopograph'. He is not to be confused with an earlier 'Professor' Anderson, the world-famous Scottish magician, Professor (John Henry) Anderson ('The Wizard of the North'), of the mid-Victorian era, though this was doubtless the later Anderson's intention. Little else is known about him. (LMcK)

References
Barnouw, *The Magician and the Cinema* (1981).

ANNABELLE (c.1878–1961)

American skirt dancer and stage beauty. Early cinema's most prolific star, Annabelle Moore (later Annabelle Whitford, and finally Annabelle Whitford Moore Buchan) made several films for Edison and Biograph between 1894 and 1897. A follower of **Loïe Fuller**, Annabelle performed several dances at the Black Maria studio and was featured in the Kinetoscope's first London showing in October 1894. *The Serpentine Dance*, *Butterfly Dance* and *Sun Dance* were often hand-coloured, and enjoyed such popularity that they frequently wore out, necessitating many reprintings and several re-filmings. When the Biograph was launched in 1896 two of its earliest productions were Annabelle's *Butterfly Dance* and a *Flag Dance*, in which she performed draped in the colours of the American flag. The sale of her films was further boosted in December 1896 when it was revealed that she had been approached to appear naked at a private dinner party at Sherry's Restaurant, New York.

Annabelle remained the centre of public attention throughout the 90s and 1900s, starring as the Gibson Bathing Girl in the first of Ziegfeld's Follies in 1907. She continued to appear in the Follies until 1912, when she married and retired from the stage. (BA)

References

Ramsaye, *A Million and One Nights* (1926).

ANSCHUTZ, Ottomar (1846–1907)

Inventor, photographer, chronophotographer; born in Lissa, 16 May 1846. When the first movie theatre opened in Berlin in April 1896, its Kinematograph was considered in some press reports 'fundamentally an improvement on and a perfection of the Anschütz Schnellseher', a contemporary tribute to an influential and now undervalued pioneer of chronophotography. Unlike **E-J. Marey**, **Georges Demenÿ** and many other chronophotographers, Anschütz was not primarily a scientist, but rather an artistic photographer committed to the quality of the image. The son of a painter of wall decorations in homes and castles around Lissa in the (then) Prussian province of Posen, Ottomar Anschütz set up a darkroom for wet-plate photography (later switching to Monckhoven's fast dry plates when they became available in 1880) in the family home, so that he could pursue his already firm interest in photographing moving subjects.

Anschütz developed a series of fast shutters in the 80s which allowed him to take subjects at 1/1000 of a second; his deservedly famous 1884 photographs of storks in flight were a direct inspiration for aviation pioneer Otto Lilienthal's experimental gliders in the late 1880s; and he made many striking animal studies at the Breslau Zoo and elsewhere. The influential Anschütz focal plane shutter of 1888 was used in still cameras sold by the Berlin firm of C. P. Goertz for nearly thirty years. His chronophotographic camera of 1882, incorporating his fast shutter and an electrically timed release, consisted of a group of at first twelve and later twenty-four cameras of his own design, constructed with his regular collaborator, one Schneider, an organ builder and his next-door neighbour. It was used to take series photographs of horses in 1883, and beginning in 1886 Anschütz made many studies at the Military Riding Institute in Hanover with the support of the Prussian War Ministry. His adaptation of the Zoetrope, the 'Wundertrommel' or 'Schnellseher' dates from the same year. Here, photographic series pictures were mounted on the inside of a vertical or horizontal cylinder, with thin viewing slits between the images. A tabletop model was sold widely in 1891.

By March 1887 Anschütz had developed his Tachyscope, a disk of twenty-four glass 9cm x 12cm diapositives turned by a crank and intermittently illuminated by the spark from a spiral Geissler tube, which could be viewed either directly or by small groups of people. A later form of the same instrument was a long horizontal cylinder with four to six bands of series pictures, each of which could be viewed through individual ports. By 1891 a motorised and slightly smaller device called the Electrical Schnellseher was being manufactured by Siemens and Halske in Berlin as both a public coin-operated attraction and a home machine. It was displayed, among other locations, at the International Electrotechnical Exhibition in Frankfurt; on the Strand, London (1892); at the Chicago World's Fair (1893); and at the Berlin Exhibition Park (where in the summer of 1892 nearly 34,000 people paid to see it).

Two years later Anschütz developed his Projecting Electrotachyscope, which used two discs of images and a rotating shutter, all intermittently moved by a twelve-sided Maltese cross gearworks. Patented on 6 November 1894, it was used to project selections from forty series pictures on a 6m x 8m screen at the Horsaal des Postgebaudes in Berlin on 25, 29 and 30 November. From 22 February 1895 Anschütz began regular screenings with the Projecting Electrotachyscope, which was now enclosed in a soundproof booth and projected through a glass window onto the screen of a 300-seat hall in the old Reichstag building on Liepzigerstrasse in Berlin. Admission charges were 1 or 1.50 Marks; and the box-office total for March amounted to 5,400 Marks. This was the last documented use of the Anschütz apparatus. He subsequently became photographic adviser to Kaiser **Wilhelm II**'s family; accompanied the family on their trip to Palestine in 1899; opened a shop for photographic supplies and equipment at 14 Unter den Linden, Berlin; and turned to the construction of small cameras and the encouragement of amateur photography, particularly through his three-volume book, *Die Photographie im Hause*, published in 1901–2.

From 1894 to his death in Friedenau bei Berlin on 30 May 1907, Anschütz applied for twenty-six 'petty patents', or *Gebrauchsmuster*, on various photographic devices, including shutters, darkroom apparatus, film cassettes, reflex viewing screens and changing bags. With his photographs welcomed in the salons of both Europe and the USA for their outstanding quality and remarkable modernity, Anschütz was temperamentally unable to work with the less sensitive and reliable celluloid film-strips of 1894; instead he abandoned chronophotography just as his work was beginning to impress **Thomas Edison**, **Marey** and others. Though his animated projections widely excited the public and the press, the uncompromising standards of this proud innovator meant that he retreated from the field just as the cinema was born. (DR)

References
Ottomar Anschütz, *Augenblicksaufnahmen. Mappe 1 und 2* (Lissa, 1883–5).
Ottomar Anschütz, *Die Augenblicksphotographie, ihr Wesen, ihre Ziele* (Lissa, 1887).
Ottomar Anschütz, *Die Photographie im Hause*, three vols. (Berlin, 1901–2).
Hans Kocke, 'Ottomar Anschütz – ein Meister der Reihenbildner', *Bild und Ton*, Heft 11/1966.
Helmut Kummer, *Ottomar Anschütz: Ein deutscher Photopionier* (Munich, 1983)
Deac Rossell, '"Lebende Bilder": Die Chronophotographen Ottomar Anschütz und Ernst Kohlausch', in Pamela Müller (ed.), *Film in Niedersachsen* (Hannover: Historisches Museum, 1995).

APPLETON, Richard John (1856–1946)

Manufacturer, film-maker. R. J. Appleton and Co. was a long-standing Yorkshire firm of photographic and magic lantern outfitters operating from 58 Manningham Lane, Bradford.

They had been in business for some twenty years before the new field of cinematograph entertainment opened up. Appleton devised a tripartite apparatus which he called the Cieroscope, combining the functions of camera, printer and projector. First put into use in November 1896, it sold at 15 guineas, plus an extra 2 guineas with Wray's special cinematograph lens.

Appleton also produced his own films, which brought praise from **Cecil Hepworth**, writing in *Amateur Photographer*. Certainly one personal success for Appleton was his filming of **Queen Victoria**'s Jubilee procession on 22 June 1897, with the help of his local newspaper, the *Bradford Argus*. His ambitious scheme was to film the procession in London, and show the results on the same evening in Bradford. A railway van was fitted out as a darkroom, and the project – a remarkable achievement for the date – was successfully carried out. Two hundred and fifty thousand spectators are reported to have seen the films, which were projected on a giant screen beside the *Argus* building throughout the week. (RB/DG)

References
Bradford Argus, 23 and 24 June 1897.
Bradford Argus, 'Pictorial Souvenir', 8 July 1897.
Barnes, *The Beginnings of the Cinema in England* (vol. 2).

ARAI Saburo (c. 1867–?)

Showman. Arai Saburo was one of a new breed of young Japanese businessmen who had worked widely in the USA and were bringing back fresh and expansive ideas. He had designed the traditional Japanese house and garden set at the 1893 Chicago World's Fair, and in 1896 travelled to West Orange, where he purchased two Edison Vitascopes and a stock of films for $3,000. Daniel Grimm Krouse travelled with him as operator. Arai first exhibited in Osaka at the Shinmachi theatre on 22 February 1897, one week after **Inahata Shotaro** had opened in the same city with the Lumière Cinématographe, and strong competition immediately developed between the two rival machines. Moving on to Tokyo, the arrival of the Vitascope was heralded by musicians on barges proceeding down the Sanjiken Canal, while leaflets were handed out to all. Arai opened on 6 March 1897 at the Kikikan theatre, two days before **Yokota Einosuke** arrived with the Cinématographe. Both shows vied fiercely with one another, but both were hugely popular, Arai's not least because of the appeal of **Komada Koyo**, the first of the star lecturers, or *benshi*, who were to become such a prominent feature of the early Japanese cinema. Arai, unlike the populist Yokota, wanted his films to be seen by high society, and eventually succeeded in exhibiting at the prestigious Kabuki theatre, where the Crown Prince of Japan came to see the show. (LMcK)

References
Peter B. High, 'The Dawn of Cinema in Japan', *Journal of Contemporary History*, vol. 19 no. 1, January 1984.

ARMAT, Thomas J. (1866–1948)

Inventor, mechanic. Thomas J. Armat and **C. Francis Jenkins** together invented one of the most successful motion picture projectors of their day, and presented projected films for paid admission in September 1895.

Armat worked as a clerk in a hardware store for three years until he was eighteen, when he was apprenticed to a railway machine shop, leaving soon after to become a bookkeeper for the railroad's treasurer's office. He studied at the Mechanics Institute in Richmond, Virginia, and dabbled in inventing, gaining a railway-related patent in June 1894. Intrigued by the **Anschütz** Tachyscope exhibited at the Chicago World's Fair in 1893, and further prompted by a friend's glowing account of the Edison Kinetoscope, he enrolled at the Bliss School of Electricity in October 1894 to acquire the electrical knowledge necessary to handle the arc lamp that would be required for successful film projection, and in March 1895 teamed up with classmate Charles Francis Jenkins. (For an account of their work together, see Jenkins entry.) Following their shows at the Atlanta Cotton States Exposition, which were financed by Armat (who made a loss), the partners began to

argue. There ensued years of acrimonious dispute, involving not only patent litigation but also the Franklin Institute and the Smithsonian Institution.

Jenkins sold out to Armat after losing the patent case, and following negotiations with Kinetoscope agents **Raff and Gammon**, Armat sold the design of the successful 'beater' movement projector to **Thomas Edison**. At a press demonstration, **Annabelle**'s dance and other Kinetoscope films were supplemented by a copy of **Birt Acres**' 1895 *Derby*. Renamed the Edison Vitascope, the machine was used to project America's first high-profile film show at Koster and Bial's Music Hall, New York, on 23 April 1896, with Armat acting as projectionist for the first week. The first programme included *Walton and Slavin Burlesque Boxers, Umbrella Dance*, and from Britain, Acres' *Rough Sea at Dover*.

Armat continued to work on the Vitascope throughout 1896 and defended himself against not only Jenkins but, into the early years of the new century, many others whom he considered were infringing his patents. As a result, he threatened and fought various litigations against Biograph, Edison and others before eventually becoming part of the Motion Picture Patents Company. In 1947 Armat was one of a small group (**William Selig**, **Albert Smith** and **George K. Spoor**) awarded a special Academy Award for being of that 'special group of pioneers whose belief in a new medium, and whose contributions to its development, blazed the trail along which the motion picture has progressed, in their lifetime, from obscurity to worldwide fame'. (SH)

References
Musser, *The Emergence of Cinema* (1990).
Ramsaye, *A Million and One Nights* (1926).

ARMITAGE, Frederick S.

Cameraman. One of American Biograph's main cameramen, an all-purpose talent who worked on a wide variety of films from 1899 to 1905. Among the assignments he undertook was the **Jeffries**–Sharkey heavyweight boxing match at the Coney Island Sporting Club in November 1899, in which he was one of a team of four who successfully filmed a fight under artificial light for the first time; the time-lapse recording of the demolition of a building, *Demolishing and Building Up the Star Theatre* (1901), which he filmed over four weeks taking an exposure every four minutes, eight hours a day (having shown the demolition, the film was then reversed and the building reconstructed); news footage of such figures as **William McKinley**, Theodore Roosevelt and **Buffalo Bill Cody**; and a succession of delightfully titled comedies that indicate much of the appeal of the early Biograph films: *Horsewhipping an Editor* (1900), *Aunt Jane's Experience with Tabasco Sauce* (1900), *Carrie and Her Little Hatchet* (1901) and *Little Algy's Glorious Fourth of July* (1901). His last known Biograph film was the topical anarchist drama, *The Nihilists* (1905). In the summer of 1908 he was hired by Edison, where he worked with director J. Searle Dawley; in 1909 he was made head of the Edison camera department. (LMcK)

References

Kemp Niver, *Biograph Bulletins 1896–1908* (Los Angeles: Locare Research Group, 1971).

AUMONT, Charles (Charles Solomon)

Theatrical entrepreneur. 'Charles Aumont' was the stage name of Charles Solomon, a French citizen from Algeria, who from October 1891 to 1901 rented several sites in the centre of Moscow for his Théâtre–Concert Parisienne enterprise (which successfully toured throughout Russia as well). The interiors were gorgeously decorated and visitors were deeply impressed with this display of French luxury. Aumont's artistic troupe was highly professional and held in great esteem in professional circles. All of his actors were proud to participate in its shows while it opened doors to any other theatrical enterprise in Russia. But behind the front doors of Aumont's theatre was hidden its real purpose: for many years it was well known as a fashionable brothel, and it was the permanent object of sharp criticism by the defenders of public morals. Stanislavsky, for example, called it a 'den of lewdness' and demanded its immediate closure. Ironically, the founders of the Moscow Art theatre inherited Aumont's concert hall in Kamergersky Lane, but totally renovated it, in an attempt to obliterate its noxious influence.

In 1896 Aumont first introduced the Lumière Cinématographe as an attraction, and it was at an Aumont café-concert at the All-Russian Fair of Industry and Art in Nizhiny-Novogorod, which opened on 22 June 1896, that an educated and influential Russian audience first saw moving pictures, in circumstances that were inevitably controversial. Despite the atmosphere of debauchery, however, many 'respectable' people felt obliged to satisfy their curiosity about the new phenomenon. Among the visitors was **Maxim Gorky**, who wrote a famous account of his visit to Aumont's film programme and later, on learning of the attempted suicide of one of Aumont's girls, Lily Darteau, wrote a short story in which a prostitute kills herself after witnessing the unattainable domestic happiness displayed in the Lumière film, *Repas de bébé*.

Aumont continued to organise film shows as part of his package of entertainments, before quitting his business in 1901. In 1907 Aumont was due to be prosecuted for embezzlement but, it was discovered, he had sold all his property and left the country. (RY/LMcK)

References

Leyda, *Kino* (1960).
Yuri Tsivian et al., *Silent Witnesses: Russian Films 1908–1919* (London: BFI/Edizioni Biblioteca dell'Immagine, 1989).

B

BACON, John Mackenzie (1846–1904)

Scientific lecturer, aeronaut and astronomer. Educated at Cambridge, Bacon took holy orders in 1870 and worked as a curate for the next ten years before turning his attentions to scientific work. Astronomy and aeronautics had interested him from childhood, and he joined the British Astronomical Association, becoming a member of council. He was especially interested in eclipses, and in 1896 joined the expedition to observe the eclipse of the sun in Lapland.

Bacon was a friend of the magician, **J. N. Maskelyne**, and his son, Nevil (themselves descendants of astronomers), and when in 1897 they went to **Queen Victoria**'s Diamond Jubilee with a film camera, Bacon was there to assist. Subsequently, Nevil, who was to be Bacon's frequent scientific collaborator, suggested that an adapted film camera might be used to record an eclipse, capturing the movements of the solar corona. He set to work to make a 'cinematograph telescope' which could take five or six pictures a second during the minute and a half of totality, and in December 1897 Bacon set off to India with this device. The party arrived at Buxar in central India, and Bacon, after 'practising diligently' with the cinematograph for weeks, took a series of pictures of the corona. Unfortunately, the film seems to have disappeared – perhaps stolen on the voyage home – and all that remained were views of a Hindu pilgrimage and one of the Viceroy's camp. But another eclipse was predicted for May 1900 in North Carolina, and this time Nevil Maskelyne accompanied Bacon to ensure that nothing went wrong. Despite parts of the equipment failing to arrive they managed to film the eclipse, the first ever recorded (though it seems that the same eclipse had been filmed in Spain by Norman Lockyer's expedition, and a photograph of the apparatus is reproduced in *l'Illustration*).

Bacon was also a keen balloonist, crossing the Irish channel in 1902, conducting experiments in sound propagation and, with Maskelyne, in balloon inflation. He also took photographs from the balloons, and some time in 1898 experimented with taking films during a flight with his daughter, Gertrude, his frequent collaborator. Frames from this (probably the first British aerial film), showing part of the crowd watching the balloon ascend, illustrate an article he wrote in the *Strand Magazine* later that year. Bacon continued his aeronautical work, and supplemented a meagre income by giving lectures, until his death from pleurisy in 1904. (SB)

References

Gertrude Bacon, *The Record of an Aeronaut* (London: John Long, 1907).

BAMFORTH, James

Card, lantern-slide and film producer. Founded in 1870, the Bamforth firm (headed by James Bamforth) originally specialised in the production of magic lantern slides photographed in their studio at Station Road, Holmfirth, Yorkshire, England. These were mainly 'Life Model' slides, narrative sequences acted out in front of painted backcloths, illustrating a temperance or religious theme. These popular tableaux – accompanied on screen by a live 'reading' of the story – were made in a similar way to early films, except of course the players never moved. The subsequent step from lantern-slide manufacture to film production was only logical, as they already possessed the necessary costumes, backgrounds, amateur actors and experience in plot construction.

By 1898 Bamforth's were making films with **Riley** brothers of Bradford, who had been involved in the technology of the new

medium since 1896. Some of their films are of considerable significance: despite the hackneyed plots – mostly 'borrowed' from ideas previously filmed by other producers – they reveal an embryonic understanding of the potential of film cutting and simple narrative construction. In *The Kiss in the Tunnel*, for example, a long shot of a train entering a tunnel away from camera is cut to a close shot of a couple embracing in the carriage, followed by another long shot of the train moving towards the camera. *Women's Rights* (a satire on the suffrage question) contains the earliest known example of a cut to another direction within a scene with time continuity. These were innovative examples of film-making for the date, and it is fascinating to speculate what Bamforth's might have gone on to achieve. But though the films were shown locally, they were not included in the Bamforth's catalogues, and the company did not return to film-making until 1913. Their productions of this period included the popular *Winky* series.

During the First World War their production finally ceased. With the ever-increasing popularity of moving pictures at the turn of the century, the demand for lantern slides diminished, but the picture postcard was then also coming into its own, and some of the Bamforth slides were reissued as sets of coloured postcards. The firm survived into the 1990s as a manufacturer of seaside view cards, calendars and birthday cards. (RB/SH)

References

Barnes, *The Beginnings of the Cinema in England* (vols. 2–4).
John Barnes, 'A List of Magic Lantern Manufacturers and Dealers', in Dennis Crompton et al. (eds.), *Magic Images* (London: Magic Lantern Society, 1990).
Richard Brown, *Notes on the Nomenclature and Dating of Some Early Bamforth Films* (1994).
Salt, *Film Style and Technology* (1992 second ed.).

BARNETT, Henry Walter (1862?–1934)

Australian photographer. The flamboyant and self-assured Walter Barnett ran the Falk photographic studios in Sydney. Meeting up with the Frenchman, **Marius Sestier**, in August 1896 on a steamer taking Sestier and the Lumière Cinématographe to Australia, they agreed to an informal partnership. After a private screening on 18 September at Sydney's Lyceum theatre, they began to exhibit films at 237 Pitt Street. They soon started taking films as well, the first known to have been produced in Australia (for details of these, see the

Sestier entry). Though it was Sestier who did the filming and projecting, Barnett (who provided photographic facilities) promoted himself and the Cinématographe with equal vigour, and directed the films. His directorial input is particularly apparent in the celebrated films of the Melbourne Cup horse race (taken 3 November 1896), where Barnett can be seen directing the action, glancing at the camera and ensuring that the right people are seen. And at the finish of the race, Barnett is seen to run out from behind the camera urging the crowds to raise their hats.

Barnett and Sestier parted company when the latter moved on to Adelaide at the end of 1896, after which Barnett continued to operate the Lumière salon in Sydney until March 1897. He is next recorded as having filmed four scenes of the England v. Australia cricket test in Sydney in December 1897. Taken with a Cinématographe and screened in both Australia and Britain (where they were marketed by **Fuerst** brothers), one of the films survives, showing Prince Ranjitsinhji practising in the nets – the first cricket film. Barnett transferred his photography business to London in 1898, then moved to Dieppe in 1916, and died on 16 January 1934 in Nice. (CL/LMcK)

References
Chris Long, 'Local Production Begins', *Cinema Papers* 93, May 1993.

BARON, Auguste Blaise (1855–1938)

Civil engineer, musician and painter, Auguste Baron was one of the first to experiment with sound films. Born in Paris in 1855, his studies were interrupted by the Franco-Prussian War of 1870–1 and the siege of Paris. He took lessons in photography before going into military service. Working on electrical installations at the Casino de Paris in 1895, he came upon an Edison Kinetophone, and became interested in the possibilities of combining motion pictures with sound.

In 1896 he patented (with Fréderic Bureau) a system of shooting and projecting sound films, recording on a wax cylinder. In 1898 he filed a second patent for an improved arrangement and produced, with cameraman **Félix Mesguich**, several short films in a specially arranged Graphophonoscope studio at Asnières-sur-Seine. Some productions were shot on a special 50mm film, and projected on a machine with a double-lens arrangement that screened the images alternately (to reduce flicker). An electrical device on the motor-driven camera regulated the cylinder recorder to maintain synchronisation. The system was able to record a four-minute sequence, with four carbon microphones providing the signal for the electromagnetic cutting needle. Baron gave a projection demonstration to the Académie des Sciences in 1899, with a film of an actress singing, but lack of financial aid forced him to abandon further development. He took out numerous other patents in the fields of photography, film and related technologies including one in 1896 for a film-perforating machine. He died at Neuilly-sur-Seine in 1938. (SH)

References
Camille Baron, 'Mon père: Auguste Baron', and Jean Vivié, 'Le premier studio d'enregistrement de films sonores fut monté en 1898 à Asnières par A. Baron', *Bulletin de L'AFITEC* no. 30, 1970.
Harald Jossé, *Die Entstehung des Tonfilms* (Frieburg/Munich: Verlag Karl Alber, 1984).

BAUCUS, Joseph D.
See **MAGUIRE, Franck Z.**

BEARD, Robert Royou (1856–1932)

Inventor and manufacturer of a number of accoutrements important to the technology of the Victorian screen. Robert Royou Beard was born in Bermondsey, London. His family were in the wine trade, but the young Robert became apprenticed to Oakley's, a firm of brass-finishers, who were involved in the manufacture of magic lanterns. He invented an automatic regulator for high-pressure oxygen cylinders, a necessity for lantern illuminants, and set up his own company to manufacture it. His next most successful invention was the Eclipse slide carrier, which made magic lantern operation easier, and gave a primitive mix on the screen.

Beard had developed a practical interest in cinematography from its first appearance in England. In 1946 his son, Percy, recalled being taken to see the 1896 Lumière Cinématographe show at the Regent Street Polytechnic. Very soon afterwards the Beard Cinematograph (with Maltese cross intermittent) appeared on the market, and Beard projectors were produced well into the next century. The company eventually specialised in making lighting for the cinematograph industry, and was still trading in the 1980s. (SH)

References
Barnes, *The Beginnings of the Cinema in England* (vol. 2).

BEEVOR, Walter Calverley (1858–1927)

Military doctor. If Surgeon-Major Beevor were to claim pioneer status in any field, it would probably be in the area of **Röntgen** rays (X-rays) rather than in film. Educated at Edinburgh University and in the Scots Guards from 1885, he served during the Tirah campaign on the Indian North-West Frontier from 1897 to 1898. Equipped with an X-ray apparatus from Britain, Beevor became the first person to use this technology on active service. It proved a great success, and when the Scots Guards were sent to the Boer War in November 1899, Beevor was again accompanied by an X-ray machine. But he also took another piece of new technology: a film camera lent to him by the British film producer, **Robert Paul**. How Paul contacted Beevor is not clear, but prior to the Tirah campaign Beevor had been in touch with **John Le Couteur** of the Photographic Association, whose studios were equipped with both X-rays and animated photography, and who might in turn have put him in touch with Paul. As far as Paul was concerned, there were certain advantages in entrusting a camera to a combatant, who was bound to be sent to where the action was, and was also less likely to face official meddling than a journalist. Paul also lent a second camera to another military man, apparently F. A. (or Sidney) Melsom of the City Imperial Volunteers.

Beevor was quite successful with Paul's film camera, managing to take a dozen films, including the embarkation of the Scots Guards on 21 October 1899 and their entry into Bloemfontein in the spring of 1900. He filmed assorted scenes of troops, artillery and ambulances on the march and crossing the Vaal and Modder rivers, and finished his coverage in June with a film of an observation balloon. Beevor's biggest scoop, however, was to take a view of the captured Boer commander, Cronje, as he was driven off in a cart in February 1900. (Paul's catalogue notes that 'as the cart passes the camera, Cronje is seen to look out in astonishment at it'.) Beevor stayed in South Africa until 1902, seconded to the police forces. He served in India from 1902 to 1903, and during the First World War came out of retirement to work with the Territorials in a medical capacity. (SB)

References
'Bullet Wounds and X-rays in Britain's Little Wars', *Journal of the Society for Army Historical Research*, vol. 60, 1982, pp. 91–102.
'The Working of the Röntgen Ray in Warfare', *British Journal of Photography*, 27 May 1898, pp. 342–3.

BENETT-STANFORD, John Montagu ('Mad Jack') (1870–1947)

Rogue, fox-hunter, sometime war cameraman and archetypal English squire, Benett-Stanford dabbled in film-making for a short time only. Born into a Wiltshire landed family, he was educated at Eton before beginning a career in the army in 1888, seeing active service on the North-West Frontier in the Tirah campaign (as did **Walter Beevor**). His next service assignment was the Sudan expedition of 1898, where he acted as war correspondent for the *Western Morning News*, and, like **Frederic Villiers**, he was present at the battle of Omdurman. Before leaving Britain he had managed to obtain a film camera from **Prestwich**, and with this he filmed the British commander, Kitchener, as well as a view of the Grenadier Guards fixing bayonets and marching off on the day before the battle. This brief film was hugely successful, being the only film taken at Omdurman, a notable British military victory. The following year he took a couple of films on Madeira (where the family had a house) as well as a variety of farmyard and other scenes.

When the Boer War broke out, Benett-Stanford was the first man with a film camera to set off for the front, leaving Britain on 7 October 1899. By November he was at Belmont with Lord Methuen's force and filming at the Orange River; and on 8 December he filmed troops crossing the Modder River, together with other military scenes. These films were released by the Warwick Trading Company in January 1900, but in the same month Benett-Stanford's career as a camera operator seems to have ended, when **Joseph Rosenthal** took over as Warwick's principal Boer War cameraman.

After the war Benett-Stanford went back to the life of a soldier and gentleman, serving in the First World War and running the family estate in Wiltshire. In later life (apparently resembling a Colonel Blimp figure), he took up yachting and developed a penchant for practical jokes; he is also reputed to have exercised his rights of 'droit de seigneur' among the local girls. He clearly did not think that his dabblings in cinematography were of any great moment, failing to mention them either in his description of the battle of Omdurman or in his manuscript autobiography. (SB)

References
Barnes, *The Beginnings of the Cinema in England* (vols. 3 and 4).
V. W. Cook, 'The Humours of "Living Picture" Making', *Chambers' Journal*, 30 June 1900, p. 488.
Private papers from Pythouse, Wiltshire and Preston Manor, Brighton.

BERNHARDT, Sarah
(Henriette Rosine Bernard) (1844–1923)

Actress. Generally accepted as the finest actress of the late 19th century, Sarah Bernhardt made her stage debut in 1862. Her reputation was established at the Odéon theatre, Paris, between 1866 and 1872, and at the Comédie-Française from 1872 to 1880. From 1880 she toured the world with her own company, frequently appearing in her three major successes, *Phèdre*, *La Dame aux camélias* and *Adrienne Lecouvreur*. In 1897 she shocked the theatrical establishment by playing Hamlet in a new prose translation, repeating the role at the Théâtre Sarah Bernhardt, Paris, in 1899. It was in the duel scene from this production that Bernhardt made her screen debut, playing opposite Pierre Magnier in a short film made for the Phono-Cinéma-Théâtre in 1900. Under the influence of the dramatist Sardou she had developed a broad, pantomimic style of acting, much in evidence in her films, *La Dame aux camélias* (1911) and *Les Amours de la Reine Elisabeth* (1912). The scene from *Hamlet* was part of an extensive series of primitive sound films which provided a surprisingly wide coverage of the French entertainment world at the turn of the century.

Opening on 8 June 1900 as an attraction in the Paris Exposition, the Phono-Cinéma-Théâtre in the rue de Paris was the brainchild of **Clément-Maurice** and Henri Lioret. Many well-known actors and actresses, opera singers, dancers and music hall performers were persuaded to appear in short films which were synchronised with phonograph recordings, though in some cases the accompaniment consisted of sound effects or music rather than dialogue. Among the celebrities to be filmed were the famous French baritone, Victor Maurel (1848–1923), singing arias from *Don Juan* and *Falstaff*; the ballerinas, Rosita Mauri and Zambelli; Gabriella Réjane (1857–1920) from the Comédie-Française; the comic-opera star, Mariette Sully; and the dancer and courtesan, Cléo de Mérode. The leading French actor, Benoît-Constant Coquelin (1841–1909), appeared in the duel scene from Rostand's *Cyrano de Bergerac*, a role that he had created in 1897. Among the variety performers to be included in the programme were the patriotic singer, Polin; the internationally famous clowns, **Footit and Chocolat**; and the English music hall performer, **Little Tich**. After the Exposition closed, the films were taken on a European tour by **Félix Mesguich**, and in 1901 exhibited by the **Isola** brothers at the Olympia, Paris. Rediscovered in 1930, a selection was reissued as *Cinéma Parlant 1900* (1952). (BA)

References
Robert Hamilton Ball, *Shakespeare on Silent Film* (London: George Allen and Unwin, 1968).
Sadoul, *Histoire générale du cinéma: Part 2* (1948).

BERTOLDI, Ena (c.1878–?)

Music hall contortionist and early performer for Edison's Kinetoscope. Born into a family of acrobats, Ena Bertoldi (or Bertholdi) made her stage debut at the age of eight, touring Europe and the USA throughout the late 80s and 90s. The films, *Bertholdi (Mouth Support)* and *Bertholdi (Table Contortion)*, taken at the Black Maria studio, West Orange, were among the first selection to be exhibited at the original Kinetoscope parlour, Broadway, New York, from 14 April 1894. An illustrated article in *The Royal Magazine* shows that the acrobatic feats were the mainstay of her act, stating that 'Bertoldi places every reliance upon the strength of a magnificently perfect set of teeth and, of course, her powers of equipoise'.

Among the many other acrobats, dancers and variety turns performing for the Kinetoscope between 1893 and 1895 (of whom very little else is known except that they had usually appeared at New York's Koster and Bial's Music Hall) were voluptuous Spanish dancer Carmencita; French dancer Armand d'Ary (real name Marthe Armandary); Mexican tightrope dancer Juan Caicedo; comic boxers the Glenroy brothers, Walton (Charles F.) and

Slavin (John C.); genuine boxers Mike Leonard and Jack Cushing; Spanish contortionist Louis Martinelli; Gaiety Girls Lucy Murray and May Lucas; the Rixfords troupe of acrobats; Robetta and Doretto in a Chinese laundry; Princess Ali with her Dance du Ventre (belly dance); George Layman (the original 'man with a thousand faces'); several artists from Buffalo Bill Cody's Wild West show; casts of shows such as Charles Hoyt's *A Milk White Flag*; and numerous performing animals. (See individual entries for some of the performers: **Eugen Sandow, Fred Ott, Jim Corbett, Annabelle, Buffalo Bill Cody, Joe Rastus** and others (*The Pickaninnies*) and **Ruth St Denis**.) (BA/LMcK)

References

H. J. Holmes, 'A Queen of Contortionists', *Royal Magazine*, May 1899, pp. 77–80.
Musser, *Before the Rapid Firing Kinetograph* (1996).

BHATVADEKAR, Harishchandra Sakharam ('Save Dada') (1868-1958)

Indian film-maker. Present at the first demonstration of the Lumière Cinématographe by **Marius Sestier** in India (Bombay, 7 July 1896) was a photographer from Maharastra, H. S. Bhatvadekar (more commonly known as Save Dada). He had established a photographic studio in Bombay in 1880, and was so captivated by the Lumière show that he ordered a camera from **Riley** brothers of England, at a price of 21 guineas. Bhatvadekar's first film, of a wrestling match at the Hanging Gardens in Bombay, was taken in November 1899 and then sent back to London for processing. While awaiting the film's return Bhatvadekar secured a projector and began touring with imported films, adding the wrestling film on its return, together with his second film, showing the training of circus monkeys. He filmed local scenes and one particular occurrence which has gone down as the first Indian news film, the return to India from Cambridge in December 1901 of acclaimed mathematics student R. P. Paranjype, an event with considerable resonance for both Indian and British communities.

Bhatvadekar went on to film the 1902–3 Delhi durbar celebrating Edward VII's coronation, before turning to exhibition, becoming manager of the Gaiety theatre in Bombay and ending up a wealthy man. He died while cracking a joke with a friend. (LMcK)

References

Indian Documentary, vol. 4, nos. 3–4, 1958, p. 14.

BITZER, Johann Gottlob Wilhelm ('Billy') (1872–1944)

Cameraman. The most celebrated cameraman of the earliest years of American cinema, chiefly through his association with D. W. Griffith. Born in Roxbury, Massachusetts, Billy Bitzer worked as a silversmith before an interest in magic led him to join **Elias Koopman**'s Magic Introduction Company in 1894, marketing various novelties. Koopman was one of the four founders of the Mutoscope and Biograph Syndicate, and in 1897 the young Bitzer found himself working as **W. K-L. Dickson**'s assistant on some of the earliest Biograph films. After Dickson had left for England Bitzer became a full-time camera operator for Biograph, and filmed news and actuality subjects, including a period in Cuba during the Spanish-American War of 1898, as well as innumerable short fiction films.

Bitzer was still with the company in 1908 when he began his long association with director D. W. Griffith, working as cameraman on virtually all of Griffith's Biograph output, including such notable titles as *The New York Hat, A Corner in Wheat, The Lonedale Operator* and *Man's Genesis*. And he followed Griffith when he broke away from Biograph to film the cornerstones of American silent cinema, *The Birth of a Nation* (1914) and *Intolerance* (1916).

Bitzer's association with Griffith produced many of the classic technical devices of cinema, from the close-up to the iris out, and it was Bitzer's technical ingenuity that made Griffith's ideas and dreams workable. He continued to work with Griffith, photographing *Broken Blossoms* (1919), *Way Down East* (1920) and others, but by 1920 Griffith was using Bitzer in association with other cameramen, and their partnership ended after *America* (1924). Bitzer, like his longtime associate, now isolated by the growth and advance of the film industry, went into virtual retirement. Through the 1930s he annotated the Biograph records at the Museum of Modern Art's Department of Film with Katharine Stone White, and then worked on his memoirs, which were published posthumously. (LMcK)

References

G. W. Bitzer, *Billy Bitzer: His Story* (New York: Farrar, Straus & Giroux, 1973).
Eileen Bowser, *The Transformation of Cinema, 1907–1915* (New York: Charles Scribner's Sons, 1990).

BLACK, Alexander (1859–1940)

Photographer, who in 1894 produced an innovative ninety-minute 'photoplay', *Miss Jerry*, using lantern slides of actors and live commentary. Alexander Black was a 'Kodak fiend' in the early 90s, writing press articles on the new snapshot photography. Lecturing in the eastern USA with *Life through a Detective Camera* or *Ourselves as Others See Us*, illustrated with slides produced by himself and other amateurs, he recognised the possibilities of developing a screen narrative. Using professional actors he shot the exteriors for *Miss Jerry*, the adventures of a female reporter, in New York, and the interiors at the Carbon Studio at 5 West 16th Street. With a double lantern dissolving the slides every fifteen seconds, by using a fixed background the actors appeared to 'move' between key positions within the scene. Black himself spoke all the different parts, changing his voice for each character. In the spring of 1896 it toured the lyceum stages throughout the East, just as the Edison Vitascope was making its screen debut.

Miss Jerry was followed by the even more ambitious *A Capital Courtship*, featuring specially taken shots of Grover Cleveland and President **William McKinley**. In January 1897 Black presented his lecture, *Ourselves as Others See Us*, at the Brooklyn Institute, 'illustrated by Cinematographe, Chromograph and Stereopticon'. He stayed away from vaudeville theatres, believing that the 'low-brow' audiences would not have the attention span for his presentation medium, which he later referred to as the 'slow movie'. He became a novelist, and editor of graphic items for Hearst's Newspaper Feature Service syndicate. (SH)

References

Alexander Black, *Miss Jerry* (New York: Charles Scribner's Sons, 1897).
Alexander Black, *Photography Indoors and Out: A Book for Amateurs* (Boston: Houghton Mifflin Company, 1893).
Alexander Black, 'Photography in Fiction', *Scribners*, xviii, September 1895, pp. 348–60.
Musser, *The Emergence of Cinema* (1990).

BLACKTON, James Stuart (1875–1941)

Cartoonist, conjurer, actor, director, writer, producer. J. Stuart Blackton was born in Sheffield on 5 January 1875; his parents emigrated to the USA when James was ten. A natural talent for drawing secured him a place on the staff of the *New York World*, writing and drawing a regular illustrated feature on personalities in

the news. At this time Blackton was making regular stage appearances as a cartoonist in the company of conjurer **Albert Smith**, and in the summer of 1896 the Edison company visited a *New York World* Sick Baby Fund concert at which they were performing. Blackton was the hit of the concert, and in August 1896 he was hired to make three 150ft films in Edison's Black Maria studio: *Humorous Cartoon, Political Cartoon* (caricaturing **William McKinley** and President Grover Cleveland) and *Sketching Mr Edison*, which was also released as *Edison Drawn by World Artist*. The romantic story that he went to sketch **Thomas Edison** for the *World* and so impressed the inventor that he was chosen for filming is untrue. The three films were first shown at Proctor's Pleasure Palace on 12 September 1896, and the film of Edison, in particular, brought Blackton fame and encouraged his entry into the film business. Blackton returned to cartoon films with *The Enchanted Drawing* (1906), *Humorous Phases of Funny Faces* (1906), *Lightning Sketches* (1907) and *The Magic Fountain Pen* (1909). Each film featured himself on screen as the cartoonist, and used various animation styles from stop–camera techniques to under-cranking.

Apart from fathering the American animated cartoon, in 1897 Blackton co-founded (with Albert Smith) the film production company, Vitagraph (for details, see Smith entry), playing the lead in *The Burglar on the Roof* (1897) and devising the topical short, *Tearing Down the Spanish Flag* (1898). He supervised the construction of the first enclosed glass studio in Flatbush, where he directed such famous titles as *Raffles the Amateur Cracksman* (1905). At Vitagraph, which after 1905 became the major American film production company, Blackton was in the van of serials, series and feature film production, and in the 1920s returned to Britain to produce and direct the colour feature film, *The Glorious Adventure* (1922), starring Lady Diana Manners. He subsequently lost his fortune, being declared bankrupt in 1931, and died in an automobile accident. (DG)

References
Charles Musser, 'The American Vitagraph, 1897–1901: Survival and Success in Competitive Industry', in Fell, *Film Before Griffith* (1983).
Anthony Slide, *The Big V: A History of the Vitagraph Company* (Metuchen NJ/London: Scarecrow Press, 1987 rev. ed.).
Marian Blackton Trimble, *J. Stuart Blackton: A Personal Biography by his Daughter* (Metuchen NJ/London: Scarecrow Press, 1985).

BLAIR, Thomas Henry (1855–1919)

Inventor, photographer, manufacturer, executive. In the 90s, the various firms associated with Thomas Henry Blair represented the major competitor to **George Eastman**'s photographic company for the popular amateur market in the USA, and a primary supplier of flexible celluloid film-strips to the new cinema industry.

Leaving farming to become a travelling ferrotype (or tintype) worker, Blair emigrated from Nova Scotia, Canada, to south-western Massachusetts in 1873. In 1877 he incorporated in Connecticut as the Blair Tourograph Company to produce a portable system for wet collodion photography. He moved to Boston in 1881, and an investment by a Pawtucket, Rhode Island textile magnate, Darius L. Goff, capitalised the firm and facilitated the production of the Kamaret roll camera in 1891, a daylight-loading camera in 1892, as well as a complete line of photographic dry plates, supplies and accessories, as Blair consciously imitated the vertical integration of the Eastman firm by opening agencies in Philadelphia, New York, Chicago, Cincinnati and elsewhere.

The decade also saw a series of long patent fights between the Blair and Eastman companies. Blair began the commercial production of celluloid roll film in Boston in 1891, using a frosted celluloid support particularly suited for direct viewing by transmitted light purchased from the Celluloid Company of New Jersey. In November 1891 **W. K-L. Dickson** began purchasing Blair film for the Edison laboratory after experiencing difficulties with both the quality and reliability of Eastman stock (until September 1896 almost all film used by Edison was purchased from Blair, including all film for Kinetoscope productions). For parts of 1892 and 1893, Blair was the sole supplier of flexible celluloid film, as Eastman experienced serious production problems.

The financial Panic of 1893, the loss of important patent suits to Eastman, and arguments among the financiers of the company (now including the photographic manufacturers E. and H. T. Anthony) led to Blair's removal from management in the USA and he moved to England, where he established the European Blair Camera Company, with offices in Holborn and manufacturing facilities in St. Mary Cray, Kent. This replicated the American company's range of photographic products and supplied celluloid film to **Birt Acres**, **Robert Paul**, **G. A. Smith**, Lumière, **Charles Urban** and other pioneer film-makers. In 1896, when film with a clear base suitable for projection was needed, the American Blair company had difficulty producing the new stock, and the field was left to Eastman, who ultimately purchased the entire Blair operation and merged it into the new Eastman Kodak Company. Blair died at Northboro, Massachusetts, on 4 April 1919. (DR)

References
Reese V. Jenkins, *Images and Enterprise. Technology and the American Photographic Industry, 1839 to 1925* (Baltimore/London: John Hopkins University Press, 1975).
Musser, *Before the Nickelodeon* (1991).

BLOW, Mark

Australian photographer and film-maker. Born in Portsmouth, England, Blow came to Sydney and established a photographic business in 1888. He adapted one of his studios to incorporate Edison Kinetoscopes, **Röntgen** rays (X-rays) and other optical novelties, and bought a projector, probably a **Wrench** Cinematograph, in 1897. He began filming in August 1897, and moved his exhibition business from the photographic studio to a special hall. Known as the Sydney Polytechnic, in imitation of the London home of popular scientific displays and the site of the first Lumière presentation in Britain, it presented a mixed programme of music, live acts and films. Blow realised the pulling power of locally filmed scenes, particularly horse races, and was an active film-maker from 1897 to 1901, though the Polytechnic itself closed in 1899 after a fire and some poor attendances. (CL/LMcK)

References
Chris Long, 'Indigenous Production Begins', *Cinema Papers 95*, October 1993.

BONINE, Robert Kates (1862–1923)

Cameraman, photographer. Bonine came from Altoona, Pennsylvania, and was a noted photographer of ten years' experience when he first worked for Edison in 1898. In June 1899 he was hired again by the Edison company, which had done a deal with the Klondike Exposition Company for the exploitation of films depicting the Alaskan gold rush. Bonine left for Alaska in the company of Klondike entrepreneur Thomas Crahan, and took a number of films. Returning in October, it was discovered that faulty registration had rendered the results quite unwatchable. Crahan was unable to use the films as promotions for the region at the Paris Exposition as he had intended, and both Edison and the Klondike Exposition Company lost heavily on the deal.

Bonine moved over to Biograph, filming in Japan and China in the summer of 1901, then settling as chief cameraman at Biograph until 1903, during which time he also travelled to England to film the coronation of Edward VII in 1902. He rejoined Edison in January 1905, where he specialised in travel scenes, notably the aftermath of the San Francisco earthquake, Hawaii and the Panama Canal (then under construction). He continued to take still photographs for himself as well as Edison films, and subsequently gave illustrated lectures on his travels. Feeling isolated by the growth in popularity of fiction films and the declining market value of the actuality film, the disillusioned Bonine left Edison in May 1907 and was not replaced. After a photographic world tour he settled in his much-loved Hawaii, where he continued as a film-maker and photographer. (LMcK)

References
Musser, *Before the Nickelodeon* (1991).

BOOTH, Herbert Henry (1862–1926)

Evangelist. Herbert Booth was the son of William Booth, founder of the Salvation Army, and was as charismatic a figure as his father, but also wilful and independent. In September 1896 he arrived in Australia as the new Salvation Army commandant for Australasia, and swiftly saw that the new moving pictures could be added to the already existing lantern-slide projections of the Army's Limelight department (run by **Joseph Perry**) to reinforce the Army's message and to serve as a valuable source of funds. Film projections were gradually introduced into Perry's programmes

throughout 1897, and following the first tentative experiments at shooting films of his own, the Salvation Army went into film production seriously in 1898. A glass-walled studio was constructed in Melbourne for the production of films and life-model slides.

The first Army films were exhibited in February 1898, but only as a prelude to a major accompaniment to Booth's social work lecture, premiered at the Sydney Town Hall, 11 July 1898. Known first as *The Commandant's Limelight Lecture*, then as *The Salvation Army's Social Work in Australasia*, it was most commonly known as *Social Salvation*. The two-and-a-half-hour show, as it became in the years that it toured, eventually comprised 275 lantern slides, twenty-five one-minute films shot by Perry with a Lumière Cinématographe, hymns, scriptural readings and instrumental solos. Individual stories featured throughout, in slide and film form, showing how people who had fallen by the wayside were rescued by the Salvation Army. Films of slum dwellings were employed to challenge the audience to rise to the problems faced, a radical use of the new invention, which until then had been seen by most as merely a passing diversion.

Social Salvation led the way to a second production, *Soldiers of the Cross*. Sometimes mistakenly described as the world's first feature film, this was another 'multimedia' presentation of songs, slides, films and scripture on the theme of Christian martyrdom. The impetus was the Limelight department's earlier successful presentation of the Lumière Passion play films, *La Vie et la Passion de Jésus-Christ* (1897), filmed by **Georges Hatot**. Booth wrote out his lecture, with descriptions of the slides and films he required, and a cast of 150 (recruited entirely from Army members) acted out the scenes. However, much of *Soldiers of the Cross* employed material reused from earlier exhibitions, including some of the Hatot films. Those films made by the Army were directed by Booth and photographed by Perry during 1899–1900, and the premiere took place on 13 September 1900 at Melbourne Town Hall. The show lasted just over two hours, three-quarters of which was occupied by lantern slides, interspersed with fifteen ninety-second films. Further film scenes were added as the production toured and the Limelight department acquired Warwick Bioscope cameras and projectors with greater film capacity in 1901.

Booth delivered the lecture for the debut presentation, but illness meant that he gave

27

only one further presentation in 1900. A tour was relaunched in 1901, but Booth's ill health and souring relations with the Salvation Army's command in London, which he felt to be autocratic and restrictive, led to his request to leave his post. As a result, *Soldiers of the Cross* enjoyed a somewhat infrequent exhibition schedule, despite much popular acclaim.

Booth left for Western Australia in September 1901, taking *Soldiers of the Cross* for its final Australian tour, and in February 1902 resigned completely from the Salvation Army. Booth and his family left for San Francisco in August, with the Army shattered at the departure of its founder's son and one of its most brilliant representatives. Booth continued to tour as a lecturer throughout the USA, still giving his *Soldiers of the Cross* lecture. He toured Europe, South Africa and Canada, and returned with it to Australia in 1919–20, by which time the film inserts had been dropped. He died from heart disease in New York on 25 September 1926. (CL/LMcK)

References
Chris Long, 'Screening the Salvation Army', *Cinema Papers* 97/98, April 1994.
Chris Long and Clive Sowry, '"Soldiers of the Cross": Milestones and Myths', *Cinema Papers* 99, June 1994.
Ford C. Ottman, *Herbert Booth* (New York: Doubleday, 1928).

BOOTH, Walter Robert (1869–1938)

Cartoonist, conjurer, producer, director, screenwriter, animator, W. R. Booth was born on 12 July 1869, the son of a china painter. Apprenticed as a painter to the Royal Worcester Porcelain factory (1882), he worked there until 1890. A keen amateur magician, he joined the company of **J. N. Maskelyne** and **David Devant** at the Egyptian Hall in London. Booth began devising and stage-managing (the term then used for directing) short trick films for **Robert Paul**, beginning with *The Miser's Doom* and *Upside Down; or the Human Flies* (1899) in which, by turning the camera upside down, he made his actors perform on the ceiling. Many of his early films were based on conjuring tricks (*Hindoo Jugglers, Chinese Magic*, both 1900), and with *The Devil in the Studio* (1901) he began to introduce effects involving cartoon-type artwork. Later that year his *Artistic Creation* employed rudimentary animation, while his *Political Favourites* (1903) featured Booth rapidly drawing caricatures of Lord Rosebery, Joseph Chamberlain and other politicians of the day.

By 1906 Booth had joined the **Charles Urban** organisation and made *The Hand of the Artist*, the first British animated cartoon film, clearly inspired by **J. Stuart Blackton**'s *Humorous Phases of Funny Faces* of a few weeks earlier. Booth constructed his own outdoor studio in the back garden of Neville Lodge, Woodlands, Isleworth, London, and here, with F. Harold Bastick as his cameraman, he produced and directed a large number of films for Urban. At least fifteen films a year were made up to 1915, after which he entered the publicity film market, producing advertising shorts for Cadbury's cocoa and chocolate, including *A Cure for Cross Words*. He also invented an advertising method called 'Flashing Film Ads': 'Unique colour effects in light and movement'. (DG)

References
Denis Gifford, *British Animated Films: 1895–1985* (Jefferson/London: McFarland and Company, 1987).

BOULY, Leon-Guillaume (1872–1932)

We know little about this early experimenter in chronophotography. On 12 February 1892, he deposited a patent for a sequence camera called a Cinématographe (the Lumières later took up the term without fear of a lawsuit, as Bouly had not paid the annuities on his patent), and intended 'to obtain automatically and without interruption a series of analytical negatives of movement'. In the Bouly Cinématographe, the film is driven by a segmental roller, and stopped intermittently by a pressure pad. On 27 December 1893, Bouly deposited a second patent for a machine said to be capable of both filming and projecting. The Bouly bands were not perforated, and would not have given a steady projection. At least three Bouly Cinématographes were made: two are conserved at the Conservatoire Nationale des Arts et Métiers, Paris, and the third at George Eastman House, Rochester, New York. (SH)

References
Mannoni, *Le grand art de la lumière et de l'ombre* (1994).

BRADY, William Aloysius (1863–1950)

American theatrical entrepreneur and boxing promoter. Brady's position as manager of **James Corbett** brought him into contact with films as early as 1894 when he acted as timekeeper in the Corbett–Courtney contest held in Edison's Black Maria studio. Brady was also involved with the filming of the Corbett–**Fitzsimmons** title fight in 1897 and the **Jeffries**–Sharkey contest in 1899. As well as producing over 250 plays, he retained an interest in motion pictures, running the Hale's Tours shows in the 1900s and opening the Unique cinema, Manhattan, in 1907. In 1914 he became a founder member of World Film Corporation (with their famous slogan, 'World Pictures – Brady Made'). He served as president of the National Assembly of the Motion Picture Industry between 1915 and 1920, and, in 1917, was appointed chairman of a committee to organise the American film industry for the First World War. His daughter Alice Brady (1892–1939) was a well-known stage and film actress. (BA)

References
Ramsaye, *A Million and One Nights* (1926).

BROMHEAD, Alfred Claude
(1876–1963)

Producer. Born 25 July 1876 at Southsea. The Bromhead brothers, Alfred Claude (always referred to as A. C.) and his younger brother Reginald, established the British end of the Gaumont company, which had been set up as a branch of the French firm in 1898 by **John Le Couteur**, originally A. C. Bromhead's employer. A.C. soon took over, and built up an important position for himself and the company he managed within the British film industry. His brother joined the company in 1903. Though originally an agency for French Gaumont films and machinery, British Gaumont swiftly became a successful outfit in its own right, its fiction film production programme in turn influencing the work of the French parent company. The director of these films was music hall comedian and producer, Alfred Collins. Many of the productions were actuality and topical items, which led to his foundation of an early newsreel, *Gaumont Graphic*, in 1910. The firm's newsgathering profited from the worldwide reach of the French parent company, as it also benefited from Gaumont innovations in synchronised sound films (Chronophone) and colour (Chronochrome).

Bromhead toured the world on behalf of Gaumont, opening branches in Australia, Canada, Malta and New York. In 1912 he opened a large factory in Shepherd's Bush, which supplied the majority of positive prints of American and foreign films for the British market. During the First World War he attained the rank of lieutenant colonel and led a British film propaganda mission to Russia (1916–17), for which he was awarded the CBE. In 1922 the Bromheads bought out the French interests, making the former agency an entirely British firm, with studios at Shepherd's Bush. A. C. remained prominent in the Gaumont organisation, becoming chairman of the Gaumont British Picture Corporation in 1927. (DG/LMcK)

References
'Chats with Trade Leaders: no. 3 – Mr A. C. Bromhead', *The Optical Lantern and Cinematograph Journal*, February 1904, pp. 85–9.
A. C. Bromhead, 'Reminiscences of the British Film Trade', *Proceedings of the British Kinematograph Society*, no. 21 (London: BKS, 1933).

BULL, Lucien Georges (1876–1972)

Chronophotographer. Assistant and successor to **E-J. Marey**, Bull was destined to have a profound influence on many branches of scientific research, and in particular on applications of spark illumination in photography and high-speed cinematography. Born on 5 January 1876 in Dublin, to a British merchant/carpenter father and French mother, a large part of his life was spent in France. His brother was the cartoonist and photographer, René Bull.

In 1895, through his skills as an amateur photographer, he became an assistant to, and student of, the scientist whom he described affectionately sixty years later as 'Mon Maitre Marey'. His duties included developing and printing the chronophotographic negatives. Bull, attired completely in white, was himself the subject of at least one of Marey's physiological studies, jumping a hurdle. He later recalled being 'sent out into the streets of Paris, to photograph ... scenes ... with the early Chronophotographe. Marey was content to study the negatives. Selected frames were printed. Marey understood the importance of it, and we very often took negatives that had no real scientific interest at all, just to show what could be done with non-perforated film.' Marey had failed to achieve successful projection with the non-perforated film-strips, but Bull claimed in one version of his reminiscences to have later achieved a few shaky projections when his master was not present.

When Marey died in 1904, Bull was able to concentrate on his own work, including high-speed studies of insect flight (some stereoscopic), producing a stream of research papers. He later became sub-director of the

Institut Marey (the director being an absent political nominee). A craftsman in wood and metal, he constructed much of his own apparatus. During the First World War he developed sound-ranging equipment (adopted by the British army) for the location of enemy gun batteries, and produced high-speed photographic analyses of ballistics. By 1924, he was able to report to the Royal Institution in London filming speeds of 100,000 images per second. His activities in acoustics, physiology and optics continued unabated, and in the 1950s he was still publishing papers on high-speed cinematography. Bull, described by his friend Stanley Bowler (one-time editor of the *British Journal of Photography*) as a 'tiny, bird-like, lovable figure, with an irrepressible sense of humour, and an ability to bring pleasure to those around him', received numerous honours from the French and British, and was still receiving visitors to tea in his Paris flat in 1971, aged ninety-five. He died on 25 August 1972. (SH)

References
Lucien Bull, *La Cinématographie* (Paris: Armand Collin, 1928).
Lucien Bull, 'Quelques souvenirs personnels de mon maitre Et.-J. Marey', *Bulletin de l'Association Française des Ingénieurs et Technicians du Cinéma*, 1954, no. H.S.
Stanley Bowler, 'Tribute to a Pioneer', *British Journal of Photography*, 7 January 1966.
Jean Vivié, *Lucien Bull* (Brussels: Hayez, 1967).

C

CALCINA, Vittorio (1847–1916)

Italian cinema pioneer. Already long established as a photographer in Turin, Calcina became the Lumières' Italian representative, and from 1896 made numerous films for the parent company. Late in 1896 he and a partner opened the first public cinema in the former premises of a charity hospital in via Po, Turin. In November of the same year he was permitted to film the King and Queen of Italy at Monza, and subsequently was appointed official cinematographer to King Umberto. In 1899, still with the same partner, Calcina opened a cinema at 25 via Maria Vittoria. In 1901 Calcina filmed the Duke of Abruzzi's ship, *Stella Polare*, and in 1905 the Calabria earthquake. Between 1908 and 1911 he worked on the development of the Cine Parvus, which used 17.5mm film and comprised camera, printer, perforator and projector in one machine. Calcina's efforts to develop the apparatus commercially were frustrated, however, and finally came to an end with the outbreak of the First World War and Calcina's own death. The prototype of the Parvus is preserved in the Museo Nazionale del Cinema, in Calcina's native Turin. (DRB)

References
Bernardini, *Cinema muto italiano 1896–1904* (1980).

CARPENTIER, Jules (1851–1921)

Inventor. Jules Carpentier enrolled in 1871 at the École Polytechnique in Paris, and, when his studies were completed, bought the workshop of the physicist Ruhmkorff (inventor of the induction coil) at 20 rue Delambre. There he manufactured precision instruments and electrical and optical machines. His main outlet in 1895 was **Léon Gaumont**'s Comptoir Général de Photographie. On 22 March 1895, Carpentier was present at **Louis Lumière**'s cinematographic demonstration at the Société d'Encouragement. At the end of the lecture, Lumière suggested that Carpentier should manufacture this new camera/projector. However, only eight days later, Carpentier filed his own patent for a camera called the Cynégraphe which used perforated film and incorporated a ramp system (*système à rampe*) to provide the intermittent movement. But Carpentier, like **Max Skladanowsky** in Germany, chose two linked projectors which projected alternate frames. This impractical system was soon abandoned.

At the end of October 1895, Carpentier began to manufacture Lumière's Cinématographe (the first model had been built at Lyon). The machine travelled to and fro between Lyon and Paris, as the final delicate adjustments were made. The definitive model was eventually completed by the end of the year, at which point Lumière asked Carpentier to make 200 of them. Carpentier continued to work with Lumière: at least 700 or 800 Cinématographes were eventually made, followed by the Carpentier-Lumière for films 400m long, for use with 75mm cameras and projectors (1900). In 1909, he brought out, still in collaboration with Lumière, the Cinématolabe camera using 35mm film.

Jules Carpentier seems to have been the first to file a patent for a Maltese cross projector (28 March 1896). The mechanism was also used by Victor Continsouza (patent filed 28 April 1896), and then used worldwide in almost all cinema projection. Carpentier died in 1921, following a car accident. (LM)

References
Mannoni, *Le grand art de la lumière et de l'ombre* (1994).

CARRE, André Desiré

Cameraman. An operator for the Lumières, André Carré gave his first film show in Belgrade, assisted by the mechanic Jules Guérin, and under the guidance of A. Velhora, a Lyon businessman who had also arrived in Belgrade at the same time and was probably the Lumière concessionaire for the region. Following the usual pattern for a travelling Lumière showman, Carré gave a press screening for journalists on 5 June 1896, opened to the public in the hall 'Aux Croix d'Or' of a former restaurant on 6 June, and on 16 June demonstrated the Cinématographe for King Alexander and Queen Mother Natalia, who expressed astonishment at the show. Carré and Guérin closed in Belgrade on 18 June, after which Carré is lost to history for half a year.

In February 1897 he was back in Belgrade at the Grand Hotel, and on 6 March made the first films in the area, showing King Alexander leaving his palace for the cathedral. Carré also travelled through Zagreb and Zemun, becoming a part of the band of travelling showmen who opened up the further regions of the Austro-Hungarian Empire and the Balkans: these included, in Sarajevo, Angelo Curiel with a programme of Lumière films on 17 July 1897; in Karlovy Vary, the **Eugène Dupont** agent Goldschmidt with a Lumière Cinématographe

programme in July 1896; the showman Charles Crassé with unidentified equipment in Celje, Ljubljana and Maribor (all Slovenia) in autumn 1896; and the Oeser brothers, whose travelling show added motion pictures in late autumn 1896 for their regular tour of the markets and fairs in Czech districts. (DR)

References
Rittaud-Hutinet, *Le Cinéma des origines* (1985).
Dejan Kosanovic, *Il cinema muto in Jugoslavia 1896–1932* (Belgrade: Instituto Per il Cinema, 1988).
Zdenek Stabla, 'The First Cinema Shows in the Czech Lands', *Film History*, vol. 3 no. 3, 1989.

CASLER, Herman (1867–1939)

Mechanical engineer, inventor. Casler was the co-founder with **Elias Koopman**, **Harry Marvin** and **W. K-L. Dickson** of the KMCD group, which subsequently became the American Mutoscope and Biograph Company. Following an initial suggestion from Dickson, Casler developed the Mutoscope – a viewing device which used radially mounted photographs flicked over in rapid sequence to give an illusion of movement. This instrument, which was ready by the autumn of 1894, was originally intended as a competitor to the Edison Kinetoscope. Casler next worked on the development of a camera, the Mutograph, to provide subjects for it, and by June 1895 a prototype had been successfully tested with film.

In the meantime, it had become clear that it was projected film rather than the Kinetoscope that offered the most potential for a long-term business, and so Casler set about designing the Biograph projector. Electrically driven, and using wide-gauge unperforated film, it was intended, like the camera, to be as different as possible from anything that had been patented by Edison. Dickson's knowledge of the development work done at West Orange makes it very likely that he was involved with Casler, at least at the design stage, but officially it was Casler who was cited as the inventor in both patent specifications and theatre announcements. The high-quality mechanical work done by both Casler and Marvin laid the foundation for the later success of the Biograph group. Both camera and projector produced outstandingly good results, enabling the company quickly to gain a reputation for high quality, and helping it to differentiate its products from the many competitors it faced. It was by using Casler's patents as security for loans that the group was able to raise the considerable amount of capital required to begin international expansion during the 90s. (RB)

References
Hendricks, *Beginnings of the Biograph* (1964).
Musser, *The Emergence of Cinema* (1990).

CHAPUIS, Marius (c.1879–?), Pierre (1879–1900) and Lucie (?–?)

Lumière operators. These two teenage brothers and their sister came from Lyon, and all three started working with the Lumière Cinématographe in 1896. Lucie seems to have been the least significant figure (except that she is probably the world's first camerawoman), taking occasional views in the Lyon region in 1896, whereas the brothers were sent further afield for longer assignments. Pierre went to Italy in June 1896, showing films in Milan, Turin and Venice in collaboration with the Lumière concessionaires **Vittorio Calcina** and Genty, and also filming scenes such as the wedding celebrations of the Prince of Naples and the Princess of Montenegro. He returned to Lyon at the beginning of 1897.

Of the three Chapuis siblings, Marius had the most daunting task, travelling to Russia in May 1896 and staying there for almost a year and a half. The standard Lumière practice was to send a Cinématographe to a territory with two operators who were supervised by the local concessionaire; Marius Chapuis first worked with an operator called Curtillet, until the latter returned to France due to illness, and then with Paul Decorps (the name of Camille Cerf is also mentioned). The concessionaires in Russia were the Grünewald brothers, with Arthur Grünewald taking the prominent role. Marius and his colleagues travelled to towns and cities all over the Russian empire, including Odessa, St Petersburg, Kiev and Tiflis, and showed films to audiences who were mostly seeing them for the first time.

The Chapuises seem to have been a close-knit family, and part of the reason that we know so much about their activities (in contrast to several other Lumière operators) is the voluminous correspondence that they exchanged during this period and which has been preserved. (SB)

References
Bulletin du Congrès Lumière, no. 3, 1995.
Rittaud-Hutinet, *Le Cinéma des origines* (1985).

CHEETHAM, Arthur (1864–1936)

Film-maker, cinema proprietor. The first Welsh-based film-maker, Arthur Cheetham made his debut movie (of children playing on Rhyl sands) in January 1898, a year after first showing films in the town and two years after **Birt Acres** had first filmed in Cardiff. Cheetham, a burly, charismatic showman and insatiable gadgeteer, was born in Derby but settled in Wales from the 80s. He made films until at least 1912, but was particularly active before 1900, and much of his output (about thirty shorts) dates from 1898–9, which he featured in his own programmes, hiring halls throughout north and mid-Wales. At least eight of Cheetham's films survive, including his 1903 record of **Buffalo Bill Cody**'s visit to Rhyl and *Royal Visit to Conway* (1899). His *Blackburn Rovers v. West Bromwich Albion* footage from 1899 is the earliest known surviving British soccer film, and *E. H. Williams and his Merrie Men* (1899) is an invaluable record of a Rhyl popular stage entertainment (a minstrel show).

Cheetham's early film titles are self-explanatory, including *Rhyl May Day Procession*, *Mailboat Munster Arriving at Holyhead*, *Irish Mail Train Going through Rhyl Station* and *Ladies Boating at Aberystwyth Bay* (all 1898). Cheetham took the first film to many rural communities, opening Rhyl's first all-year-round cinema entertainment in 1906 and Colwyn Bay's first cinema in 1908. Programmes published for the public hall screenings and cinemas he ran in Wales and the Manchester area in the early 1900s and up to the 1920s supply a detailed, colourful insight into his early cinema practices. (DB)

References
David Berry, *Wales and Cinema: The First Hundred Years* (Cardiff: University of Wales Press/BFI, 1994).

CHINNOCK, Charles E. (1845–1915)

Producer. Chinnock saw the Edison Kinetoscope soon after its launch in 1894, and engaged engineer Frank D. Maltby to build a motion picture camera with friction-roller movement. Chinnock's interest in challenging Edison's device may have been more than commercial: a couple of years previously he had been involved in patent litigation (relating to electric lighting) with Edison, and had unfairly lost the case due to false testimony given in Edison's favour by **W. K-L. Dickson**.

The Chinnock Kinetoscope viewing machine was a development of the Zoetrope, but with a spiral of photographs mounted on a canvas band, rather than a circle of drawings. Before Christmas 1894, the camera was being used to produce subjects for the Chinnock

Kinetoscope. The first subject was probably a boxing match, shot on the roof of a building at the rear of 1729 St Marks Avenue, Brooklyn. Later films were processed in a laboratory beneath the stage, and included the *Caflin Sisters* (skirt dancers), *A Cock Fight*, *Casey at the Bat*, a blacksmith shop scene and a dance by Ruth Dennis (**Ruth St Denis**). The Chinnock Kinetoscopes were placed in bars and cafés in New York and elsewhere in the eastern USA.

Chinnock made other cameras and other 'Kinetoscopes', continuing production possibly until the end of August 1895. In May 1895 he made an agreement with **Michel Werner** in France and James Edward Hough in England, and claimed to have sent them both cameras, the latter in June 1895. (Werner was the first Paris agent for the Edison Kinetoscope, and with Hough had been involved in producing counterfeit 'Edison' Kinetoscopes.) On 18 May 1895 Hough patented a viewer similar to the Chinnock Kinetoscope. There does not, however, seem to have been any commercial exploitation of the Chinnock devices in Europe. (SH)

References
Hendricks, *The Edison Motion Picture Myth* (1961).
Hendricks, *The Kinetoscope* (1966).

CHIRGWIN, George H. (1854–1922)

Music hall entertainer. The striking appearance adopted by performers to distinguish themselves in the competitive world of music hall provided film-makers with an attractive subject for their brief productions. There was no mistaking G. H. Chirgwin when he appeared in two of **Robert Paul**'s earliest films. Billed as 'The White Eyed Kaffir', Chirgwin had appeared as a blackface minstrel from childhood, evolving an act that mixed sentimental songs, wisecracking comedy and a bizarre costume and make-up consisting of tight black body-suit, extravagantly tall hat and a white diamond painted over his right eye. A Filoscope flip book preserves the opening of *Chirgwin in his Humorous Business* (1896), while a frame illustration from *Chirgwin Plays a Scotch Reel* (1896) shows that he used clay pipes in the same way that Chaplin employed bread rolls for the famous dance in *The Gold Rush*. Chirgwin also featured in a synchronised sound version of his tear-jerking song 'The Blind Boy' for **Walter Gibbons**'s Phono-Bio-Tableaux in 1900, and a 1917 feature film based loosely on the song. (BA)

References
Barry Anthony, 'Chirgwin Continued', *Music Hall*, August 1981, pp. 32–43.
George Chirgwin, *Chirgwin's Chirrup: Being the Life and Reminiscences of George Chirgwin, the 'White Eyed Musical Kaffir'* (London: J. and J. Bennett, 1912).

CHOCOLAT *See* FOOTIT, George

CHURCHILL, Sir Winston Leonard Spencer (1874–1965)

British statesman and writer. While almost every aspect of the career of Churchill has been examined in detail, his contacts with the cinema have been rather overlooked, yet he had considerable interest in the new medium. In 1895, when cinema first appeared on the scene, Churchill enlisted in the army, seeing service on the North-West Frontier and joining up with Lord Kitchener's Nile Expeditionary Force in 1898. Both **Frederic Villiers** and **John Benett-Stanford** brought film cameras to this campaign, a fact which did not escape the young Churchill, who wrote of war correspondents arriving 'equipped with ice machines, typewriters, cameras, and even cinematographs'. The cinema had evidently entered Churchill's consciousness by this point: he took part in the famous charge of the 21st Lancers at the battle of Omdurman, and interestingly uses a filmic image to describe his impressions of the experience: 'The whole scene flickered exactly like a cinematograph picture; and, besides, I remember no sound, the event seemed to pass in absolute silence.'

The following year the Boer War broke out, and Churchill soon made his name as a daring war correspondent. What is less well known is that he had planned to film the war. A joint venture with his friend Murray Guthrie (MP), each was to pay half the expenses, estimated as not more than £700 in total, including an operator. But Churchill was booked on the same ship to South Africa (the *Dunottar Castle*) as **W. K-L. Dickson**, departing 14 October, and before he embarked Churchill wrote a note to Guthrie warning of the competition from the 'American Biograph Co.'. He maintained nevertheless that 'I have no doubt that, barring accidents, I can obtain some very strange pictures. My only fear is that all the Theatres will be pledged to the American Company. But even then I might make a lecturing tour.' (He did indeed lecture after the war, but using lantern slides rather than films.) On board the *Dunottar Castle* Churchill noted the presence of Dickson's 'party of cinematographers', but also saw that their machine was 'cumbrous' and slow to prepare. Probably the first film to be taken of Churchill was at a Boer War celebration polo match, filmed in 1901 by the Warwick Trading Company as *Polo Match between the London Polo Club and the Trekkers* (Churchill was one of the Trekkers).

In subsequent years Churchill's relations with the cinema blossomed: he became a short-lived 'star' as Home Secretary, when he was notoriously filmed by newsreel cameras at the siege of Sidney Street in 1910. He was a great admirer of Charlie Chaplin, wrote a laudatory article about him in *Collier's* in 1935, and spoke at the premiere of *City Lights* (1931), though his favourite film was *That Hamilton Woman* (1941), for which he was even rumoured to have written a speech. In 1934 he had been employed by the latter film's producer, Alexander Korda, to write scripts, including a feature film on the life of King George V, though nothing came of this. Churchill was also one of the most frequently portrayed figures on the screen, and some sixteen roles have been based on his persona. (SB)

References

Randolph S. Churchill, *Winston S. Churchill: Companion to Volume 1* (London: William Heinemann, 1966).
D. J. Wenden and K. R. M. Short, 'Winston S. Churchill: Film Fan', *Historical Journal of Film, Radio and Television*, 11/3, 1991.

CLARKE, H. Spencer

Exhibitor of the film shows sponsored by Messrs Lever and Nestlé during a nationwide advertising campaign undertaken in 1897–8. Equipped with Lumière apparatus, Spencer Clarke was responsible for a great number of performances throughout Britain, and at one time employed as assistant the future British film producer, **Cecil Hepworth**. Clarke was also a capable cinematographer in his own right, and some of the films he shot were included in the shows. William Hesketh Lever, the first Lord Leverhulme and founder of Port Sunlight where the famous soap was manufactured, was one of the first industrialists to realise the value of the cinematograph as an advertising medium, and, in association with the Nestlé milk company, recruited Clarke to undertake the task of promoting their products by means of popular film shows at greatly reduced prices. A Swiss by the name of **Henri Lavanchy-Clarke** is also known to have been associated with Lumière and to have reached an agreement to exploit the Cinématographe in Switzerland for one year, with a preference

right for Lever and Nestlé in England. Whether or not Spencer Clarke was related in some way to Lavanchy-Clarke has not been determined. Hepworth recalls that no fewer than twelve complete Lumière projection outfits were purchased, indicating that the Lever–Nestlé undertaking was on quite a considerable scale.

In 1897 a series of Cinématographe performances were given throughout the country, featuring **Queen Victoria**'s Diamond Jubilee procession. All persons presenting Nestlé Milk or Sunlight Soap wrappers were admitted at half price to all seats, the normal price of admission being 6d. Among the films which Clarke himself shot were four scenes of the Oxford and Cambridge University boat race (26 March 1898), which was taken from the coach's launch and included a 'Moving Panorama of the River Bank'. By 1900, Spencer Clarke had already severed his connection with Nestlé and Lever, and also with Lumière, and though he continued to function as an exhibitor, his performances were now billed under the name of 'Clarke's Royal Bioscope', which seems to suggest that he was operating a Warwick machine. (JB)

References

Barnes, *The Beginnings of the Cinema in England* (vols. 3–5).
Cecil M. Hepworth, *Came the Dawn: Memories of a Film Pioneer* (London: Phoenix House, 1951).

CLEMENT-MAURICE
(**Clément Maurice Gratioulet**) (1853–?)

Photographer, camera operator, and the 'first' cinema manager. Clément Maurice Gratioulet (always referred to as Clément-Maurice) was born at Aiguillon (Lot-et-Garonne), France in 1853. He worked for several years at the Lumière photographic factory at Monplaisir, where he became a friend of **Antoine Lumière** and his sons, following with interest their work in the new photographic processes. He became a professional photographer with a studio at 8 boulevard des Italiens, Paris. It was Clément-Maurice who arranged the rental of the Salon Indien, at the Grand Café, for the first public Lumière show on 28 December 1895, and who took charge of the till for the first performances. He later recalled how the owner had, unwisely, rejected the offer of a percentage of the takings for a fixed daily rent of 30 francs.

Clément-Maurice continued to manage the Lumière programme at the Grand Café for some time, and remained an active figure in the burgeoning Paris film scene. In 1898 he acted as camera operator, with the assistance of his teenage son Leopold and the operator **Ambroise-François Parnaland**, in the filming of operations conducted by the surgeon **Eugène-Louis Doyen**. In March 1898 he won first prize in the world's first film competition, held in Monaco, for his film *Monaco vivant par les appareils cinématographiques*. In 1900 he devised, with Henri Lioret, the Phono-Cinéma-Théâtre for the Paris Exposition, where simple synchronised sound films were made of **Sarah Bernhardt**, **Little Tich** and many others. (SH)

References

Coissac, *Histoire du Cinématographe* (1925).
Emmanuelle Toulet, 'Cinema at the Universal Exposition, Paris, 1900', *Persistence of Vision*, no. 9, 1991.

CODY, William Frederick ('Buffalo Bill') (1846-1917)

American frontiersman, showman, star of the first cowboy film and a perennial inspiration to Western movie-makers. Cody's daring exploits as a Pony Express rider, army scout and buffalo hunter inspired a series of sensational dime novels and a play, *Scouts of the Plains*, in which he appeared under the enduring sobriquet of 'Buffalo Bill'. In 1894 he featured in a number of Kinetoscope films, together with performers from his Wild West show, founded in 1883. Cody was a popular subject with newsreel cameramen, also appearing as himself in *The Life of Buffalo Bill* (1909); *Buffalo Bill's Far West and Pawnee Bill's Far East* (1910); *The Indian Wars Refought* (1913); *Sitting Bull – The Hostile Indian Chief* (1914); and *Patsy of the Circus* (1915). Annie Oakley (1860–1926), the 'Little Sure Shot' of his Wild West show, also performed for the Kinetoscope in 1894. (BA)

References

Kevin Brownlow, *The War, the West and the Wilderness* (London: Secker & Warburg, 1979).

COLLINGS, Arthur Esmé

Film-maker, photographer, painter. Esmé Collings was a notable Brighton portrait photographer. At one time he had studios in London, Brighton, Liverpool and Manchester. In the 80s he had been in partnership with **William Friese Greene**, and it was probably through him that he became interested in the photography of movement. In 1896, with apparatus probably supplied by **Alfred Darling**, he made a number of films, of which only three are known to have survived. Yet, from a surviving stock list and other sources, it is clear that he made at least nineteen films during his first year of production. Among the titles listed are *Boys Scrambling for Pennies under the West Pier, Brighton*, as well as other local views. One of his most notable productions depicted the actor/musician Auguste van Biene in a scene from a Victorian play called *Broken Melody*, in which the 'servant persuades the cellist to play, and the errant wife returns'. He also made *Woman Undressing*, which must have been one of the first erotic films in British cinema. In 1897, he was enlisted by **Lewis Sealy** to photograph three scenes based on the popular song 'Simon the Cellarer' which were intended to be shown in unison with live singers present on the stage.

Soon afterwards he seems to have abandoned films to devote himself to painting, and an exhibition in London of his miniatures was very well received. However, his chief claim to fame is as one of the first of that small band of south-coast film-makers whom the French film historian Georges Sadoul labelled the 'Brighton School'. (JB)

References

Barnes, *The Beginnings of the Cinema in England* (vol. 1).

CORBETT, James J. (1866–1933)

Boxer, actor. One of twelve children of a San Francisco family of Irish descent, 'Gentleman Jim' Corbett worked as a bank clerk before turning to professional boxing. To the often disreputable and dangerous world of boxing Corbett brought a new professionalism and a scientific approach, and with it an increasing social acceptability. He became world heavy-weight champion in 1892 after defeating John L. Sullivan, and held on to the title (apart from a brief period of retirement when he offered the title to Peter Maher) until his 1897 bout with **Bob Fitzsimmons**. Prior to that, while appearing in the play *Gentleman Jack*, on 7 September 1894 Corbett met Peter Courtney in a bout specially arranged for filming in the Edison Black Maria studio. The second boxing contest to be filmed for the Kinetoscope (after the Cushing–Leonard fight), each round lasted a minute (which was all the film the camera could hold) with rest periods while the film was changed. Corbett's manager **William Brady** acted as timekeeper. The fight was staged so that Corbett would win by a knockout in the sixth round. He was paid $5,000 and a royalty on films exhibited; Courtney was paid $1,000.

Corbett's open-air contest with Fitzsimmons, held in Carson City, Nevada, on 17 March 1897, was filmed in its fourteen-round entirety by **Enoch Rector** for the Veriscope company in a specially devised 63mm format. Corbett was knocked out. The large sums involved (a $10,000 purse) were a direct result of the motion picture interest and exploitation, and began the process which turned boxing into a hugely profitable business. The finished film, taken from a single position, was an extraordinary 11,000ft long, and though arousing much controversy, it played successfully all over the USA and abroad.

Corbett came close to regaining his title from **James Jeffries** in 1900, retiring from the ring in 1903 to concentrate on his acting career. This resulted in a number of roles in American feature films: *The Man from the Golden West* (1913), *The Burglar and the Lady* (1914), *The Other Girl* (1916), *The Prince from Avenue A* (1920), *The Beauty Shop* (1922), *Broadway After Dark* (1924) and *Happy Days* (1929). (LMcK)

References
Nat Fleischer and Sam Andre, *A Pictorial History of Boxing* (Secaucus, NJ: Castle Books, 1975 rev. ed.).
Musser, *The Emergence of Cinema* (1990).

CRICKS, George Howard (1861–1936)

Producer. G. H. Cricks was the producer of many comedy and crime films during the new century, with his name linked to several well-known companies. His main trademark was the head of a roaring lion – 'Lion's Head Films' – predating MGM by many years. A keen amateur photographer, by 1895 he was the assistant honorary secretary of the Leytonstone Camera Club. He was employed by George Harrison and Co., a firm of stationers, and when they opened a photographic section, Cricks was the natural man to run it. He made his first films in the late 90s using a Moy camera on the roof of premises in Camden Town. Cricks then moved to a managerial position at **Robert Paul**'s Animatograph works, running the London office in Holborn. In 1904 he teamed up with Henry Martin Sharp as Cricks and Sharp, film producers. In 1908 the firm became Cricks and Martin (with John Howard Martin – another former Robert Paul employee – the new partner), and specialised in trick films. Martin departed in 1912, and Cricks entered the harder world of crime series and feature films. Lack of financial resources eventually led to the closure of his company, after which he managed the Croydon Film Company for some years, eventually becoming manager of the film printing department of Gaumont. (DG)

References
Low and Manvell, *The History of the British Film 1896–1906* (1948).

CROWTHER, T. P.

Cameraman, showman. T. P. Crowther was an employee of the Co-operative Wholesale Society (CWS) towards the end of the 19th century. Photography was his hobby, and with the arrival of cinematography he persuaded his employers to purchase a camera and projector to assist in the promotion of the CWS. He made his first short film (50ft) for the Co-op in 1899, and soon had taken a series of industrials showing views of the CWS soap, starch and candle factory at Irlam, followed by their biscuit factory at Crumpsall and the tea warehouses in London. The films were incorporated into a roadshow consisting of an hour's programme made up from actuality and entertainment films purchased through agencies of the day. The show was toured by Crowther until 1903. A new Gaumont camera/projector was then purchased, and fresh films taken. Crowther accompanied his films with an explanatory lecture, preceded by warnings of what to do if the films caught fire. He continued making and showing CWS advertising films through to the sound period, and was still in harness in 1936. (DG)

References
Sydney Box, 'Britain's First Advertising Films were Shown in 1899', *The Commercial Film*, March 1936, p. 6.

D

D'ALCY, Jehanne (Charlotte-Stephanie Faes) (1865–1956)

Actress. A performer at the Théâtre Robert-Houdin from 1888, when it was reopened by **Georges Méliès**, Jehanne d'Alcy (also known as Fanny Manieux) later became Méliès' mistress and appeared in a number of his films, including the first of his risqué productions, *Après le bal - le tub* (1897). Méliès' first wife Eugenie died in May 1913, and in 1925 he married d'Alcy. Her concession of a toy stall at the Gare Montparnasse, Paris, manned by Georges, provided their only income for several years. In 1932 they moved into an apartment at a home for cinema veterans. After Méliès' death, d'Alcy appeared in the poignant framing sequences of Georges Franju's short dramatisation of his life, *Le grand Méliès* (1952), with Méliès' son André playing his father. Jehanne d'Alcy died on 14 October 1956 at Versailles, aged ninety-two. (SH)

References

David Robinson, *Georges Méliès: Father of Film Fantasy* (London: BFI/MOMI, 1993).
Georges Sadoul, *Georges Méliès* (Paris: Cinéma d'aujourd'hui/Seghers, 1970).

DANJURO IX (1838–1903)

Actor. Ichikawa Danjuro IX was a legendary figure of the Kabuki theatre, ninth and last in an unbroken line that started with Danjuro I (1660–1774). Thought of as perhaps the greatest of all Japanese actors, he was a consummate master of his art who also did much to elevate the status of his profession, in 1887 becoming the first Kabuki actor to perform before the Emperor. At the peak of his profession in 1897, Danjuro had nothing but contempt for the suggestion made by **Arai Saburo** that films be shown at the theatre, sneering at the very idea of the 'ship-brought' thing. However, Arai eventually got to exhibit at the Kabuki, and associates of Danjuro tried to persuade the actor that a cinematograph record of his act would be an important gift to posterity. Eventually he agreed, on the understanding that the film would remain part of his personal collection and would not be seen by anyone until after his death.

A reel was shot of the Noh drama, *Momiji-gari* (*Maple Leaf Hunters* or *Viewing Scarlet Maple Leaves*), in which Danjuro, acting opposite Onoe Kikugoro V (1844–1903), played an ogress who has disguised herself as the Princess Sarashina. Filmed by **Shibata Tsunekichi** in the open air on a windy day in November 1899, Danjuro would allow only the one take, so that when his fan blew away in mid-performance the scene had to stay. The film re-emerged at the Kikikan theatre in 1907 where it proved a great success, inspiring a wave of fiction film-making based on traditional Japanese narratives. The film has indeed been handed down to posterity. (LMcK)

References

Peter B. High, 'The Dawn of Cinema in Japan', *Journal of Contemporary History*, vol. 19 no. 1, January 1984.

DARLING, Alfred (1862–1931)

Engineer. Originally from London, in 1894 Alfred Darling started a small engineering shop in a back room of his house at 47 Chester Terrace, Brighton. Success forced a move to larger premises at 25 Ditchling Road, which he occupied until 1926. Here he undertook the manufacture of all manner of light-engineering products. Coming into contact with that small group of Brighton film pioneers, he began to specialise in cinematographic equipment, and **Esmé Collings, G. A. Smith** and **James Williamson** were among his first customers. He also encouraged them in their pioneering work, and was able to render valuable technical assistance whenever it was needed.

In 1897, he was associated with the firm of J. Wrench and Son, and in July of that year took out a patent, with **Alfred Wrench**, for a claw-operated cine camera with a variable shutter. In the following year, he was employed by **Charles Urban** to make the mechanism for the Biokam, a small-gauge cinematograph for amateur use. He was later to make a wide range of standard 35mm cine cameras that found a favourable market, not only in England but throughout the world. Other equipment manufactured by Darling included printers, winders, measurers, tripods and projectors. His customers included many of the top names of the industry. Alfred Darling died on 24 July 1931, aged sixty-nine, and is buried in Hove cemetery. (JB)

References

Barnes, *The Beginnings of the Cinema in England* (vols. 1–5).

37

DAY, Will (Wilfred Ernest Lytton Day) (1873–1936)

Collector, historian, showman and dealer in film equipment. One of the best-known figures in the early British film community, Will Day's contacts with the screen began early, when his father instructed him in magic lantern projection before he was ten. By the 90s, as well as being a keen cyclist, Will Day was an 'elocutionist', performing recitations in halls in the London region. He saw some of the first film shows at the Empire and Alhambra music halls, and, through a cycling colleague, Teddy Tulk, obtained a **Robert Paul** projector, with which they gave their first show in December 1896 at the Castle, Woodford. Day was able to operate independently after he purchased a **Wrench** projector, which he used to show films at the Assembly Rooms, Wood Green, in early 1899. In 1907, at some expense, he opened his own picture theatre at Wood Green's old Liberal Club, and the following year was giving weekly shows at Alexandra Palace, under the title, 'The Kynograph Company'.

Over the next two years Day tried his hand at scriptwriting – *The Sisters of the Hospital* was one effort – but none of his work appears to have reached the screen, and at this point he began work as a film equipment dealer, an activity which he continued for the rest of his life. His first post was with the Tyler Apparatus Company; then in early 1912 he started Jury's Kine Supplies Ltd, and the following year opened his own shop, 'Will Day Kinutilities', which remained in business for many years. He was also involved in film production at this time, producing a Will Evans comedy, *Whitewashing the Ceiling*, in 1913, and a couple of educational films the following year. During the First World War he made thousands of propaganda lantern slides.

Day's interests included magic, inventing, motoring, freemasonry and royalty, but his greatest love was in documenting the history of the cinema. He began collecting items – films, apparatus and documents – in the first years of the century, and by 1914 was planning to write a history of the cinema, which he finally achieved in the early 1930s with *25,000 Years to Trap a Shadow*. But Day failed to interest a publisher and the work never appeared. A similar disappointment greeted his attempts in the 1920s and 30s to find a permanent home for his large collection. Eventually, having been displayed at London's Science Museum for many years, it was bought by the Cinémathèque Française in 1959, where it is now held.

Day knew many of the pioneers personally and, though only a mediocre historian (**William Friese Greene**'s former reputation as 'the inventor of kinematography' stemmed very largely from Day's uncritical championing of his cause) he used his contacts to collect many unique items and reminiscences of the early cinema. In an age before cinematheques and film museums existed he recognised the importance of this work, and today's film historians have much to thank him for. (SB)

References

Laurent Mannoni, '"Whither wilt thou lead me?": en suivant l'ombre de Will Day', *Cinémathèque*, no. 6, Autumn 1994, pp. 166–77.
Will Day, 'The Joys of Operating Twenty Years Ago', *Kinematograph and Lantern Weekly*, 1 March 1917, pp. 11–12.
Will Day, *25,000 Years to Trap a Shadow* (unpublished).

DE BEDTS, George William

The first person in France to patent and market a combination camera/projector. Nothing is known of the origins or the dates of birth and death of George William de Bedts, who was, however, one of the most important pioneers of French cinema. His work was almost totally unknown until the recent discovery of some archive material and equipment. At the end of 1892, de Bedts opened a shop, the 'Anglo-American Photo-Import Office', at 368 rue Saint-Honoré, Paris, where he had the exclusive French concession for film and photographic equipment manufactured by the European Blair Camera Company (London). From 1895 de Bedts stocked rolls of high-speed film in his shop. Late in 1894, he met **Georges Demenÿ**, who asked him to retail the Phonoscope glass disc projector and Chronophotographe (with beater movement). The two machines were put on sale sometime in November 1894, but without much success. Demenÿ introduced **Léon Gaumont** to de Bedts's shop, and in September 1895 Gaumont bought a stock of unperforated 60mm celluloid negatives for the Biographe camera that he proposed to market with Demenÿ.

De Bedts, in close contact with Demenÿ, **Henri Joly**, Edison and the Blair Camera Company, quickly realised that the future lay in the projection of films. In 1895 he developed a camera for perforated 35mm films which doubled as a projector. This machine, the Chronos (later Kinétographe), alarmed

Louis Lumière in November 1895 (concerned about a possible rival that would upstage the Cinématographe before its first public show), but it was not in fact marketed until 1896 – the first camera/projector sold in France. De Bedts also created, in January 1896, the first French financial company set up to exploit the cinema. He opened a shop at 65 Chancery Lane, London (there was also an agency, the Kinétographe Company, at Herne Hill), built a number of machines and made his first films. In 1897 his catalogue contained 310 short films, including remakes of Edison and Lumière productions and original works by de Bedts and his assistant Arthur Roussel. Late in 1896, de Bedts marketed a simplified version of his Kinétographe, aimed at amateurs. With the retirement of partner Guillaume Sabatier, finance became a problem, and the firm went bankrupt in July 1898. The last record of de Bedts is in 1902. (LM)

References
Barnes, *The Beginnings of the Cinema in England* (vol. 1).
Mannoni, *Le grand art de la lumière et de l'ombre* (1994).

DE GRANDSAIGNES D'HAUTERIVES, Vicomte Henry (?–?) and Comtesse Marie-Anne (1840–?)

Exhibitors. French citizens from Brittany, Henry and his mother Marie-Anne came to Quebec in October 1897 to give film exhibitions, apparently as part of an attempt to rebuild the family fortune he had squandered. They baptised their show the 'Historiographe', because they concentrated on showing historical subjects: the life of Jesus Christ, of Napoleon, the history of Great Britain, and so on. The couple made some ten trips to Canada, presenting their films every day in schools and churches, both in urban and rural areas, and often being the first to introduce the cinema in the localities they visited. They also toured their show extensively in the USA, appearing, for example, at the 1904 World's Fair.

In their early days most of the films shown were Lumière subjects, but their programme soon started to include **Georges Méliès** trick films and, later, Pathé melodramas. Their biggest success was reserved for various versions of the Crucifixion, presented with a rousing commentary by Henry (but which earned the ire of certain clergymen). They ceased their Quebec tours in 1906, partly due to competition from the Ouimetoscope shows mounted by Ernest Ouimet in Montreal and elsewhere,

and thereafter the pair continued their film exhibition in various locations in the USA as 'Parisian Mimodramas'. They visited Bermuda at this time, but on the eve of the First World War, unable to compete with the mushrooming of permanent cinemas in the USA, Marie-Anne returned penniless to France, where she was reduced to renting out rooms and selling Breton lace to tourists. (SB)

References
Germain Lacasse and Serge Duigou,
'L'Historiographe', *Dossiers de la Cinémathèque*, no. 15 (Montreal: Cinémathèque Quebecoise, 1985).
Germain Lacasse, 'Cultural Amnesia and the Birth of Film in Canada', *Cinema Canada*, vol. 3 no. 108, June 1984.

DEMENY, Georges Emile Joseph (1850–1917)

Inventor, chronophotographer, film-maker, promoter of physical education. Demenÿ devised the first apparatus to show chronophotographic views on the screen and invented the 'beater movement' mechanism, of great importance to early film projection.

Georges Demenÿ was born at Douai in 1850. In 1874, after studying at Douai and Lille, he reached Paris and enrolled in the physiology course of **E-J. Marey**, quickly becoming one of the scientist's closest associates. Together they established a programme of research that was to lead to the creation of the 'Station Physiologique', which opened in 1882 in the Bois de Boulogne. Demenÿ worked as Marey's assistant there, and the two researchers produced a considerable body of work, photographing human and animal movement using sequential photography, that is, chronophotography (a camera with fixed plate, and later moving plate, 1882–8).

The 'film' career of Marey and Demenÿ really began in 1888, when Marey's camera recorded on a sensitised paper strip several series of images. From 1890 they were using celluloid film. Several hundred film-strips (90mm wide and about 1.20m long) were made at the Station, at Joinville and at Naples (where Marey, often away from Paris, owned a house). On 3 March 1892, Demenÿ filed a patent for the Phonoscope, an apparatus for glass discs (42cm diameter) with a series of chronophotographic images on their circumference which could be projected using a powerful Molteni lantern. After the Phonoscope was successfully presented at the Exposition Internationale de Photographie de Paris (1892), Demenÿ dreamed of commercialising chronophotography, and pushed Marey to order the manufacture of six cameras intended for sale. Relations between them soured when, in December 1892, Demenÿ formed the Société de Phonoscope. Marey refused to co-operate in this enterprise, so Demenÿ devised his own camera, inventing the 'beater' mechanism – used in many later projectors – to move the film.

In 1894 Demenÿ was dismissed from the Station Physiologique. He installed himself at Levallois-Perret, rue Chaptal, where he produced about a hundred very diverse Phonoscope scenes: *Danseuse de French-Cancan*, *Premiers pas de bébé*, and *Passage du train*. In December 1894, **Louis Lumière** visited Demenÿ, who showed him a design of a cam-and-claw mechanism for moving film (the fascinating sketches for which have been rediscovered recently), but Lumière did not seem interested. On 22 August 1895 Demenÿ and sleeping partner **Léon Gaumont** signed their first contract, and in November the Phonoscope (renamed Bioscope) was offered for sale. Early in 1896, the Biographe camera, using 60mm unperforated film, was also available. Projection by means of Phonoscope/Bioscope discs allowed for only very brief entertainment. The Biographe camera was already archaic in 1896, in contrast to those of Lumière or **de Bedts**, and Demenÿ's machines were a financial failure. However, Gaumont exploited Demenÿ's principle of the beater movement with great success, and Demenÿ entrusted him with the financial battle of cinematography, returning to his first passion, gymnastics.

In 1909 he published a brochure, *Les Origines du cinématographe*, describing in a clumsy fashion his part in the invention of cinema, but his claims were always rejected by the Lumièristes' and the friends of Marey. Only today is it possible to understand the pioneer role played by Demenÿ in the commercialisation of chronophotography. From 1892 his 'movies' encompassed a wide variety of subjects, and the glowing and lively images of the Phonoscope already represented the true concept of cinema. (LM)

References
Georges Demenÿ, *Les Origines du cinématographe* (Paris: Henry Pailin, 1909).
Mannoni, *Le grand art de la lumière et de l'ombre* (1994).
Sadoul, *Histoire générale du cinéma*, vol. 1 (1948).

DEPUE, Oscar B.
See **HOLMES, E. Burton**

DEVANT, David (David Wighton) (1868–1941)

Magician, shadowgraphist and film exhibitor. Early on in his career he became a member of the famous company of Maskelyne and Cook, performing regularly at the Egyptian Hall, Piccadilly. He eventually became such a part of the organisation that in 1905 he was taken into partnership with **John Nevil Maskelyne** himself. Devant was personally responsible for introducing **Robert Paul**'s Theatrograph into the programmes. In fact, he took the initiative in acquiring one of the first projectors Paul made, paying for it out of his own pocket, as Maskelyne at first had no faith in the new 'animated photographs'. The Theatrograph was introduced at 'England's Home of Mystery' on 19 March 1896, two days before Paul himself began his first commercial performances at Olympia. Maskelyne must soon have warmed to the idea of including films in his repertoire, for he took it upon himself to introduce each picture and comment upon it in a most lively and entertaining manner. The films were accompanied on the piano by F. J. Cramer.

In July, or thereabouts, Devant extended his film activities by giving performances at private homes for a fee of 25 guineas, still maintaining his association with Maskelyne at the Hall in Piccadilly. He also toured Britain with a magical troupe, incorporating the Theatrograph into the act. The films were projected by an experienced lanternist, C. W. Locke, who was well known in the lantern world for his numerous innovations in optical projection.

Devant also performed in some of Paul's early films, including *The Mysterious Rabbit*, *The Egg-Laying Man* and *Objects Produced from Paper*, all made in 1896. Short sequences from the first two films are still to be seen in **Short**'s Filoscope and the **Casler**-Lumière Kinora, devices based on the principle of the simple flip books which were then so popular. Devant was also filmed performing in one of his magic acts by **Georges Méliès** (*D. Devant, prestidigitation*; cat. no. 101). The two men had known each other in London and also in Paris, to where Devant made regular trips in quest of new French films, then acknowledged to be among the best in the world. He subsequently sold a Paul Theatrograph to Méliès in 1896. Devant attempted film-making himself, and was the author of several manuals on conjuring. (JB)

References
David Devant, *My Magic Life* (London: Hutchinson, 1931).
Barnes, *The Beginnings of the Cinema in England* (vols. 1–5).

DICKSON, William Kennedy-Laurie
(1860–1935)

W. K-L. Dickson is a key figure in the practical development of cinematography. He was born in France of English and Scottish parents, and emigrated to the USA in 1879. Joining **Thomas Edison** in 1883, he quickly rose to become one of his senior associates. Work on motion pictures began in 1888, and continued – with many interruptions – for several years. Dickson and his assistants were influenced in their perception of the problem and its solution by the ideas of Edison himself, **Muybridge**, **Anschütz** and particularly **E-J. Marey**, whom Edison visited in Paris in August 1889. After experiments involving microphotographs, a Tachyscope and a horizontal-feed camera, the final form of a vertically fed 35mm camera utilising celluloid strips with a double row of perforations had been realised by October 1892. The famous Black Maria revolving film studio was designed by Dickson, and had been completed by February 1893, but work on the viewing device – the Kinetoscope – delayed the start of regular film production until January 1894. A wide variety of subjects, many featuring athletes (an idea probably suggested by Muybridge's work) and popular entertainers, was produced at this studio. The first Kinetoscope parlour was opened in New York in April 1894, and by the end of the year news of the machine had spread throughout the world. Though crude in both appearance and effect, it was a successful and practical device, and it provided the inspiration for many later attempts to achieve film projection.

By 1894 Dickson had reached the height of his reputation with Edison, and in that year he and his sister wrote a biography of the pioneer, in which they discussed and illustrated the early film work at West Orange. But this same year also marked the time when Dickson's loyalty to his employer was compromised as he became covertly involved with the **Lathams** in their film enterprises. **W. E. Gilmore**, Edison's newly appointed general manager, discovered this deception and reported it to Edison. Perhaps overconfident of the security of his position, Dickson challenged Edison to choose between himself and Gilmore. The result was that he left West Orange at the beginning of April 1895. It marked a rather sad end to an often brilliant career, and he never subsequently regained the prestige he had enjoyed there.

Working with the Lathams proved to be uncongenial – they had little money and Dickson soon found that their hedonistic lifestyle was not to his taste. He therefore turned his attention to development work for the KMCD group (**Koopman**, **Marvin**, **Casler**, Dickson), which he and three friends had set up at the end of 1894. This eventually became the American Mutoscope and Biograph Company, and represented a formidable rival to Edison's own film interests. (The Biograph was a projector using wide-gauge 68mm film, and the Mutoscope was a viewing device utilising bromide prints in a 'flip-book' principle.)

Dickson was not offered a senior management position with the company when the development work ended, and instead became a travelling cameraman, an occupation he followed for the next five years. During 1896 and the early part of 1897 he filmed in various parts of the USA, and in May 1897 came to England to take up an appointment as technical manager and cameraman for the newly formed British Mutoscope and Biograph. Using London as his base, he travelled widely throughout Britain and Europe, providing a steady stream of product for the British company and the international group.

In October 1899 he went to South Africa to cover the Boer War, and despite many difficulties and dangers managed to obtain a number of successful scenes of war damage, troop movements and camp life. During this campaign he kept a diary, which was later published on his return to England as *The Biograph in Battle*. A unique and valuable account, it was the first book to be published by a film cameraman, and remains of exceptional interest and veracity, having been compiled on the spot while the events were taking place. Dickson left British Biograph in about 1903, and by 1906 had established himself in London as an electrical engineer.

Assessments of the relative contribution of Dickson and Edison in the important work done at West Orange between 1888 and 1894 have varied widely. In his old age Edison, perhaps not surprisingly, regarded Dickson as disloyal and refused to have anything to do with him, even though Dickson tried to re-establish contact. Inevitably, Edison's attitude affected accounts such as Ramsaye's, which were written in the inventor's lifetime. A completely different perspective was offered by Gordon Hendricks in the 1960s. Making extensive use of the Edison archive, Hendricks argued that Dickson had been a victim of Edison's ruthlessness and love of fame, and that his true contributions had been overlooked or even suppressed. More recently it has been suggested by Charles Musser that

Hendricks's criticism of Edison lacks objectivity, and that his conclusions are suspect. Utilising an approach which he terms 'critical sympathy', Musser has carefully re-examined the evidence, but it seems unlikely that a definitive judgment of Dickson has yet been achieved.

A concentration on the personalities of either Dickson or Edison is in any case misleading, for the motion picture work carried out at West Orange was essentially a co-operative team effort rather than the result of individual inspiration. In common with both the Lumière and Biograph organisations, successful product development emerged from the background of a well-capitalised and large-scale industrial manufacturing environment, and the final result represented a synthesis of previous work by other pioneers rather than one all-important 'invention' made by a sole worker – however brilliant. While company employees such as Dickson may have done much of the day-to-day work, what they achieved was only possible because of the first-class facilities available, together with Edison's willingness to spend considerable sums of money on his research and development function. W. K-L. Dickson died of cancer at Twickenham, London, on 28 September 1935. He was twice married and had one (adopted) son. (RB)

References

W. K-L. and Antonia Dickson, *The Life and Inventions of Thomas Alva Edison* (New York: Thomas Y. Crowell, 1894).
W. K-L. and Antonia Dickson, *History of the Kinetograph, Kinetoscope and Kinetophonograph* (New York: Albert Bunn, 1895; reprinted Arno 1970).
W. K-L. Dickson, *The Biograph in Battle: Its Story in the South African War* (London: T. Fisher Unwin, 1901; Flick Books reprint 1995).
Fielding, *A Technological History of Motion Pictures and Television* (1967) [contains a reprint of an important late account by Dickson, 'A Brief History of the Kinetograph, the Kinetoscope and the Kinetophonograph' (1933)].
Hendricks, *Origins of the American Film* (1972).
Musser, *The Emergence of Cinema* (1990).
Ramsaye, *A Million and One Nights* (1926).

DONISTHORPE, Wordsworth
(1848–1914)

English barrister who spent over twenty years developing experimental motion picture apparatus. His first (provisional) patent of 9 November 1876 described a camera in which photographic plates could be exposed in rapid succession. The resulting pictures were to be printed on a continuous strip which, when viewed intermittently, would give an animated picture. On 24 January 1878 in *Nature*, he proposed a combination of this Kinesigraph apparatus with **Thomas Edison**'s newly invented Phonograph as a means of recording and reproducing dramatic performances.

On 12 August 1889, with W. C. Crofts (a draftsman who made the working drawings), he patented an ingenious new design, using roll film for sequence pictures. The film was moved at a constant speed from reel to reel on an oscillating carriage. During the upward movement the carriage speed matched that of the downward-moving film, keeping it stationary in relation to the lens, and an exposure was made. During the downward movement of the carriage, the film moved on sufficiently to clear the previous exposure. The apparatus, both a camera and projector, gave quite good results, which is demonstrated by a few frames of surviving celluloid film of Trafalgar Square, London, exposed in 1890. Donisthorpe was, however, unable to find a sponsor to develop the idea, a committee of experts appointed by Sir **George Newnes** having turned down the concept of moving pictures as impractical, and it was never commercially exploited. (BC)

References

Brian Coe, 'William Friese Greene and the Origins of Cinematography 111', *Screen*, vol. 10 nos. 4/5 July/October 1969.
Brian Coe, *The History of Movie Photography* (1981).

DOUBLIER, Francis (1878–1948)

Lumière operator. Doublier was born crippled, and his father Edouard determined that he would train for an occupation that did not require him to walk much; ironically, Doublier was destined to travel the world over promoting the Lumière Cinématographe. His father was killed in an accident when Francis was twelve; the children of the family (two boys and two girls), resident in Lyon, were then all found employment by **Antoine Lumière** in his factory (Francis's brother Gabriel subsequently worked on colour photography for the Lumières). Doublier was thus present at much of the very first Lumière film activity: he claimed to be in the first Lumière film, *Sortie des usines*, riding on a bicycle and wearing a straw hat.

Doublier's first major trip abroad was with **Charles Moisson** to introduce the Cinématographe to Russia (having passed first through Amsterdam, where he established a Lumière show). On 17 May 1896 films were shown for the first time in Russia when Doublier presented a Lumière programme in St Petersburg that included such titles as *Partie d'écarté* and *Arrivée d'un train*. However, the first film show was held after the first filming, as an equally important reason for the trip was to film the coronation of Tsar **Nikolas II** on 14 May. Special permission had to be sought by the French embassy from a suspicious Russian government before it was possible to set up a stand, from where Doublier and Moisson recorded the first moving pictures in Russia. They were also there two days later to record the presentation of the Tsar to his people, when a stand gave way, panic ensued and thousands were trampled to death. Doublier and Moisson's cameras faithfully recorded the scene, but the films were confiscated.

Moisson returned to Paris and Doublier went on to Schwerin in Germany, but came back to Moscow in September 1896, and under the direction of the newly appointed Lumière concessionaires, Arthur and Ivan Grünewald, set up a salon in the same month. Doublier, accompanied by his assistant Swatton, then toured Russia extensively for the next two years. Among the anecdotes he told, the best known concerns his appearance in southern Russia, when he presented combined stock film of troops, buildings and a warship with appropriate commentary as a record of the **Dreyfus** case, to the great interest of the local Jewish population.

His subsequent journeys were many, though difficult to date. Certainly he visited the Netherlands, Spain, Germany and Hungary, and in 1899 alone travelled to Greece, Bulgaria, Romania, Turkey, Egypt, Greece, India, China and Japan. He also visited Indo-China and Java, filming and exhibiting each time. In 1900 he returned to France to assist at the Lumière exhibit at the Paris Exposition. In 1902 he went to the USA to work at the Lumière North American Company plant in Burlington, Vermont, before moving to Fort Lee, New Jersey, where he was to remain, continuing to work as a film laboratory technician. (LMcK)

References

Deutelbaum, *'Image' on the Art and Evolution of the Film* (1979).
Leyda, *Kino* (1960).
Rittaud-Hutinet, *Le Cinéma des origines* (1985).

DOYEN, Dr Eugène-Louis (1859–1916)

French surgeon. Of all those of the medical profession who took an early interest in the arrival of moving pictures, none was more enthusiastic or bolder in his use of the new medium than Eugène-Louis Doyen. Struck at an early Lumière show by the possibilities of film as a means of recording his work for educational purposes and of publicising it, he employed **Clément-Maurice**, organiser of the very first Lumière shows at the Grand Café, and **Ambroise-François Parnaland** to film and photograph some of his surgical operations. Clément-Maurice had to modify a Cinématographe for the extended filming required, and recommended that Doyen operate on a cadaver in the open air. The doctor refused, and the operations were filmed under moderate artificial light, with success. Encountering hostility towards his plans in France, Doyen presented the results in Edinburgh to the British Medical Society in July 1898. The exhibition of these films (including a craniectomy and an abdominal hysterectomy) upset many of Doyen's French colleagues, who felt that the integrity of their profession had been violated, but he had much success abroad showing his films at medical conferences.

He produced about ten films per year, and in 1902 filmed *La Séparation de Doodica-Radica*, an operation to separate Siamese twins (it was successful, though both Doodica and Radica died within a year). Doyen found himself at the centre of further controversy when it was discovered that some of his films were being secretly distributed by Parnaland, with copies turning up at fairground shows. Doyen successfully prosecuted Parnaland (marking an important legal step in recognising film as an artefact meriting legal protection). In 1911 Doyen's collection of films was bought by the Eclipse company, which sold it on to Gaumont after the First World War.

Frequently the object of satire, Doyen was a celebrated figure who courted both controversy and fame, had a wealthy clientele and a taste for duels. However, his interest in the educational power of the cinema was genuine, and included experimentation with stereoscopic film (1903), microcinematography (1911) and colour film (1912). His surgical films were parodied by **Georges Méliès** and others. (LMcK)

References

Robert Didier, *Le Docteur Doyen: Chirurgien de la Belle Époque* (Paris: Librairie Maloine S. A., 1962).

Thierry Lefebvre, 'Le Cas étrange du Dr Doyen', *Archives* 29, February 1990.
Tosi, *Il cinema prima di Lumière* (1984).

DREYFUS, Alfred (1859–1935)

Artillery captain, celebrated prisoner and martyr to anti-Semitism. The Dreyfus Affair, as it came to be called, began in 1894, when the French military discovered that someone had been passing defence secrets to the Germans. Captain Alfred Dreyfus, a Jew, was arrested for the crime and sentenced to life imprisonment. Over the next few years, as the doubtful evidence was publicly re-examined, France divided into two opposed and sometimes violent camps: 'Dreyfusards' who believed that he was innocent and had been made into a scapegoat because he was Jewish, and the frequently anti-Semitic 'anti-Dreyfusards', who refused to countenance any questioning of military justice. The affair was the biggest news story of its time, and, taking place at the same time as the birth of cinema itself, it became one of the first major news events to be tackled by the infant film medium, though with varying degrees of accuracy. One filmic representation exhibited outright deception, when **Francis Doublier**, touring the Jewish districts of Russia in the late 90s, showed selected shots of buildings and scenery, while a lecturer mendaciously declared them as the very places where Dreyfus had been tried and imprisoned. However, a genuine attempt to record Dreyfus on film took place when the prisoner was brought back from Devil's Island in July 1899 to face a second trial in France. This event, which took place in Rennes, became a great media circus, with scores of journalists and photographers descending on the town. Among them was a certain Monsieur Orde, equipped with a huge Biograph camera, and, despite the protests of the Dreyfus family, trying to record anything connected with the affair. He managed to film Mme Dreyfus on one of her visits to the prison and, by renting a house across from the prison yard and biding his time, succeeded in obtaining a shot of the prisoner himself on one of his daily walks.

The next step in the screen portrayal of Dreyfus was dramatisation, and two film versions of the affair were made in 1899. **Georges Méliès** began work on his version in August: consisting of some twelve separate scenes, it followed Dreyfus (played by an ironworker) from his arrest, through his degradation and imprisonment, to the trial in Rennes. A Pathé version, in six scenes including the trial, was in production at about the same time, and both were on the market by the autumn of 1899. Méliès was a passionate Dreyfusard, and his portrayal of the prisoner reflects the filmmaker's sympathies; though this was not to everyone's taste: the first screening provoked fighting between pro- and anti-Dreyfusards, and Méliès' version was apparently banned by the French government, the first instance of political film censorship. A restriction on showing films about the Dreyfus affair was only finally lifted in 1950. The affair had clearly demonstrated, even in this very early period, that the cinema could tackle burning contemporary events in both factual and dramatised formats. (SB)

References

Stephen Bottomore, 'Dreyfus and Documentary', *Sight and Sound* vol. 53, no. 4, Autumn 1984.
Stephen Bottomore, '"Zischen und Murren": Die Dreyfus-Affäre und das frühe Kino', *KINtop*, no. 2, 1993.
Madeleine Malthête-Méliès, 'L'Affaire Dreyfus de Georges Méliès', *Cahiers de la Cinémathèque*, nos. 35–6, Autumn 1982.

DUPONT, Eugène J.

Exhibitor, Lumière agent. Dupont seems to have been one of the most wide-ranging of the Lumière concessionaires. It is not known just what limits applied to his representation of the Cinématographe, but certainly he is identified closely with exhibitions throughout central Europe. His main base of operations was Austria, where the Lyon-born businessman had been active in 1894–5 promoting a variety of French goods. Returning to Vienna in March 1896, he gave a private showing of the Lumière Cinématographe at the K. K. Lehr- und Versuchsanstalt für Photographie on the 20th, before giving a further demonstration at the French embassy and opening to the public in the mezzanine of a house at Kartnerstrasse 45 on the 27th, where Kaiser Franz Joseph I visited the shows on 17 April. His agent, Goldschmidt, opened the Cinématographe at the Casino in Karlovy Vary on 15 July, and another agent, Hermann Arlet, demonstrated the apparatus at the court of the Saxony Hotel in Prague on 2 October, opening to the public the next day. Dupont is himself reported to be the operator for an opening at the town theatre in Cracow, which began on 14 November and continued for four weeks.

Though the exploitation of the Cinématographe in Germany was the exclusive right of the **Stollwerck** company, Dupont is also reported as having supplied a machine and operator, after first refusing, to Carl Gabriel in Munich in July 1896. Dupont is a subject for further research; his wide-ranging activities in Austria, the Czech lands, France, Germany and Poland indicate an informality, and perhaps a looseness of definition in the Lumière territorial system that requires further examination. (LMcK/DR)

References

Walter Fritz, *Kino in Österreich 1896–1930: Der Stummfilm* (Wien: Osterreichischer Bundesverlag, 1981).
Rossell, 'The New Thing with the Long Name', *Film History*, vol. 7 no. 2, Summer 1995.
Zdenek Stabla, 'The First Cinema Shows in the Czech Lands', *Film History*, vol. 3 no. 3, 1989.

DUSSAUD, François (or Franz) (1870–1953)

Inventor. The Geneva-born François Dussaud was a pupil of Professor Emile Yung, and, at the early age of twenty-three, held the chair of physics and chemistry at the Ecole de Mécanique in Geneva. He was one of Europe's first researchers in the synchronising of sound and the cinematographic image, along with the Frenchmen **Auguste Baron**, **Henri Joly**, **Clément-Maurice** and Henri Lioret. Dussaud's approach was based on his own invention, the microphonograph (December 1896, Faculté de Médecine, Paris), a system for electrically recording and reproducing sound, combined initially with mechanical amplification and, later, with acoustic amplification, which he constructed with the clockmaker **Casimir Sivan**.

Dussaud always maintained his ties with his native city, but from the summer of 1898 he pursued his work in Paris. He was associated with Georges Jaubert, professor of physics at the Ecole Polytechnique, and Berthon, engineer and administrator of the Société Industrielle des Téléphones. On 13 June 1897, Dussaud, Jaubert and Pereire, director of the Compagnie Générale Transatlantique, formed the Société du Phonorama, named after an audiovisual system which was publicly presented at the Musée Oller, 28 boulevard des Capucines, from April to July 1899.

The Exposition Universelle of 1900 marked an important stage in Dussaud's career. His inventions were presented in the setting of the Swiss Village, in conjunction with the Pathé Phonograph. At the same time, his company's pavilion housed the Phonorama, though with

45

how much success is not known. This system of synchronised projection involved a battery of a dozen microphonograph rolls corresponding to as many filmed *scènes*, the sound being conveyed through individual ear pieces. The hand-coloured films, made by **Félix Mesguich**, were of two kinds – the 'scènes de la vie parisienne' and a series of 'cris de Paris' – in contrast to the spoken or sung numbers that constituted the repertoire of other systems.

Dussaud had earlier (1898) invented a Phenakistiscope for the blind (the microphonograph had been intended mainly to relieve certain forms of deafness), and was equally interested in reproducing colour. On 7 April 1904, sponsored by the popular daily, *Le Petit Journal* (Paris), he presented his Dussaudscope, based on a process as yet unidentified. Some Pathé colour films, such as *L'Antre infernal* (1905) or *L'Arête malencontreuse* (1905), could have been made using this system as well as open-air subjects. At the time, the inventor was close to **Charles Pathé** and his brother Emile. He worked as consulting engineer for the Pathé firm from its refounding in 1900. In addition, the Société Dussaud, one of the companies formed to distribute Pathé's films, was responsible for nine *départements* in northern France and for all of Switzerland, an enterprise in which Dussaud's brother-in-law, Charles Ackerman, was also involved.

During the First World War he remained in France, taking part in the war effort as a scientific research assistant. In the early 1930s, his research in the field of 'endomechanics' has led some historians to claim him as a cybernetics pioneer. What remained of the inventor's personal archive was deposited in 1994 at the Geneva public and university library (Papiers Dussaud). (RC)

References
This article owes much to the research of Jean-Marie Pastor (Geneva).
Harald Jossé, *Die Entstehung des Tonfilms* (Frieburg/Munich: Verlag Karl Alber, 1984).

DYER, Frank Lewis (1870–1941)

Lawyer, executive. The combative and articulate Frank L. Dyer had an immense influence on the structure of the emerging American film industry. A patent lawyer, who also became **Thomas Edison**'s personal lawyer, he and his partner W. H. Seeley engaged in protracted negotiation and argumentation with the US Patent Office (between 1891 and 1897) over the wording of Edison's first three motion picture patents, which ultimately resulted in establishing very broad claims that gave the Edison organisation the legal grounds to pursue competitors in the new medium, a policy which the company implemented energetically. Moving to the Edison Manufacturing Company in 1903, from where he commanded both an in-house patents staff and the services of corresponding lawyers in cities across the country, Dyer later replaced **William E. Gilmore** as vice-president and general manager in June 1908, and was a leading organiser in December that same year of the Motion Picture Patents Company. As its first president he attempted to rationalise and monopolise the film business, and was appointed president of the parallel distribution combine, the General Film Company (1912–14).

For Edison, Dyer greatly expanded film production in the summer of 1908 to increase the company's market share; personally screened and approved all film releases; and reorganised the film department again in January 1909, introducing a director/unit system. He may have been the first American film executive to replace an experienced film-maker with a sales-oriented employee, when he demoted **Edwin S. Porter** as a manager of film production in February 1909, replacing him first with salesman John Pelzer and then with carpet dealer Horace G. Plimpton. In October 1914 he formed the Dyreda Art Film Corporation with J. Parker Read, Jr. and J. Searle Dawley, but the company lasted only a year before being sold to a division of Metro Pictures. (DR)

References
Frank Lewis Dyer and Thomas Commerford Martin, *Edison: His Life and Inventions* (New York/London: Harper & Brothers, 1910).
B. M. Wood (ed.), *Who's Who in the Motion Picture World* (New York, n.d. [c.1915]).
Musser, *Before the Nickelodeon* (1991).

E

EASTMAN, George (1854–1932)

Manufacturer. Born on 12 July 1854 at Waterville, New York, Eastman became a clerk/bookkeeper in the Rochester Savings Bank, Rochester, New York. He took up photography in 1877 and experimented in coating new gelatine dry-plate emulsions onto glass plates. He was soon so successful that he decided to go into commercial production. He devised a machine to simplify the coating of plates, and travelled to England in July 1879 to patent it. In April 1880 he began manufacture, and formed the Eastman Dry Plate Company on 1 January 1881. In 1884 the company became a corporation, the Eastman Dry Plate and Film Company, and Eastman, with the camera maker William H. Walker, designed a roll-holder suitable for most plate cameras, in which the heavy glass plates were replaced by a roll of emulsion-coated paper. Eastman designed and patented a coating machine for the large-scale production of the paper film, bringing costs down dramatically. The roll-holders were acclaimed by photographers worldwide, and the flexible paper film was welcomed by experimenters in sequence photography. The Kodak camera was launched in June 1888, holding paper film sufficient for 100 exposures, and bought ready loaded. After the film had been exposed, the camera was returned to Eastman's factory where the film was developed and printed. The Kodak camera put photography into the hands of the countless thousands who wanted photographs without complications. Eastman's marketing slogan neatly summed up the advantage: 'You Press the Button, We Do the Rest'.

The Kodak camera was the last product in which Eastman was personally involved in the design. His company grew rapidly, and he acquired the most talented scientists and technicians available. New products emerged regularly – notably the first commercially produced celluloid roll film for the Kodak cameras in 1889. Celluloid – a new plastic material in search of useful applications – had been proposed as a photographic medium by the Revd Hannibal Goodwin (1822–1900) in 1886. This key innovation made possible the introduction of cinematography a few years later.

Over the years the Eastman Kodak Company grew into a giant multinational corporation with manufacturing and marketing organisations throughout the world, responsible for many major advances in photography. Eastman continued to guide the company, pursuing an enlightened policy of employee welfare and profit-sharing decades before this was common in the industry, and made massive donations to many educational concerns. He withdrew from the day-to-day control of the company in 1925, and on 14 March 1932, suffering from a painful terminal cancer, he tidied up his affairs and shot himself through the heart, leaving a note: 'To my friends: My work is done. Why wait?' (BC)

References

Brian Coe, *George Eastman and the Early Photographers* (Hove: Wayland, 1973).

EDISON, Thomas Alva (1847–1931)

More than any other single figure, Thomas Edison was responsible for making moving pictures a practical and commercial business. His Kinetoscope, launched in 1894, became the first moving picture apparatus offered for sale, and provided the inspiration for the leading European inventors, **Robert Paul** and the **Lumière** brothers.

Moving pictures were not, however, Edison's main concern. He was above all an inventor of all things modern, with a worldwide reputation for solving every problem that he tackled. After minimal schooling, he started work as a railway telegraphist and (at least according to legend) set up his first laboratory in a railroad wagon. A device for automating telegraphic sending provided the first of the prodigious number of patents which brought him fame and wealth. Known as 'the Wizard of Menlo Park' after the site of his first laboratory, Edison was from the start involved with electricity and its widening field of applications. He developed the light bulb, the storage battery and a large-scale distribution system, and boasted that he had made invention an industrial process. His work on recording began with the carbon microphone in 1877, which improved Alexander Graham Bell's telephone and led to Edison's Phonograph, the first successful sound-recording device. Edison was already a master of public relations, and his speculations about a combination of the telephone and some form of visual transmission inspired a *Punch* cartoon of 1879, which shows a couple in contact with their distant children by means of a 'Telephonoscope [which] transmits light as well as sound'.

After a meeting with **Eadweard Muybridge** and a demonstration of his Zoöpraxiscope in 1888, Edison announced that he envisaged 'an instrument which does for the Eye what the phonograph does for the Ear', and first used the term 'Kinetoscope'. However, his early attempts to record images on a phonograph-style cylinder proved unsuccessful, until an encounter with **E-J. Marey** in Paris in 1889 pointed the way towards sequential images recorded on a strip moved intermittently in front of a single lens. The team that Edison assigned to work on this project was headed by **W. K-L. Dickson** and included Charles A. Brown, **William Heise** and occasionally **Frederick Ott** and **Eugène Lauste**.

Exactly when the Kinetoscope first emerged, and who played the most important part in developing it, have been matters of controversy ever since Dickson abruptly left Edison's employment in April 1895. That Edison set the goal and supported the research until its successful conclusion is not in dispute, even if it was his custom to claim a personal role in all inventions carried out in his organisation for patent reasons. The Kinetoscope, a peephole viewing machine which showed a film loop lit by electricity and activated by an electric motor, made its debut on 20 May 1891, demonstrated by Edison himself to a meeting of the National Federation of Women's Clubs hosted by his wife. But frames still appeared side by side on a narrow strip with a single row of perforations.

By 1892 Dickson and his team had produced a camera, the Kinetograph, which used 35mm film-strips with two rows of perforations and vertical alignment of frames, and a Kinetoscope to match. In December of the same year Dickson supervised construction of a special building at the West Orange site to facilitate efficient production of subjects for the new system. This revolving structure, made of tarred paper and with a movable shutter to control the entry of light, was soon known informally as the Black Maria – the world's first film studio. The first public demonstration, using subjects taken in the Black Maria including *Blacksmith Scene*, took place at the Brooklyn Institute on 9 May 1893, and a contract for the manufacture of twenty-five machines was signed in June. But these did not materialise until March of the following year, which prevented a planned promotion at the World's Columbian Exposition in Chicago.

After nearly a year of delays, commercial exploitation of the Kinetoscope began in earnest in April 1894. A group of new demonstration subjects had been hurriedly filmed, including such vaudeville acts as the dancers **Annabelle** and Carmencita, the strong man **Eugen Sandow**, and miniature dramas like *Bar Room Scene*. At first Edison sold Kinetoscopes and films to all who wished to buy them, but the business was soon channelled through three groups, which each took responsibility for different territories: **Raff and Gammon**, the **Lathams**' Kinetoscope Exhibition Company and **Maguire and Baucus**'s Continental Commerce Company. Kinetoscope parlours spread quickly throughout the USA and Europe in 1894–5, until the public appearance of the Lumière Cinématographe at the beginning of 1896 offered a superior image quality and the attraction of group viewing. Faced with this competition, Edison arranged to license **Thomas Armat**'s projector, which he renamed the Edison Vitascope, and held his first public screening – with as much publicity flair as ever – on 23 April 1896 at Koster and Bial's Music Hall on Broadway.

Over the next five years Edison seems to have taken little personal interest in his moving picture business; and in 1900 he was on the brink of selling it to his rivals, American Mutoscope and Biograph, before cancelling the deal at the last moment. However, the arrival of **Edwin S. Porter** at the Kinetograph department in 1900 led to a rise in the quality and ambition of Edison's production, culminating in such landmarks as *The Life of an American Fireman* (1902), *The Great Train Robbery* (1903) and *The Dream of a Rarebit Fiend* (1906). But for the most part Edison's output appeared oldfashioned. While his rivals invested in longer and more spectacular films, Edison stubbornly tried to defend his claim to hold all the important USA motion picture patents, ruthlessly prosecuting newcomers to the business.

In 1908 he adopted a different tactic and invited his competitors to form a cartel, the Motion Picture Patents Company, which would resist newcomers. Despite this truce, Edison production and equipment sales remained sluggish, and he chose to invest in developing a Home Projecting Kinetoscope in 1911 rather than venture into the new longer films. After the Company's monopoly was legally overthrown in 1915, it was only a matter of three years before Edison sold all his remaining motion picture interests, though his interest in new media remained strong to the end of his life. (IC)

References

Ian Christie, 'The Wizard of Oz', *Sight and Sound*, vol. 5 no. 5, May 1995.
Musser, *Before the Nickelodeon* (1991).
Hendricks, *The Edison Motion Picture Myth* (1961).
Ramsaye, *A Million and One Nights* (1926).

ELFELT, Peter (1866–1931)

Danish photographer. Impressed by what he saw of the Lumière show at the Grand Café in 1896, Danish court photographer Peter Elfelt tried unsuccessfully to buy a Cinématographe. However, he befriended **Jules Carpentier**, constructor of the first Cinématographes, and saw enough of the works to be able to take detailed plans back to Denmark, where a camera was constructed for him by engineer Jens Poul Andersen (1844–1935). With this camera Elfelt shot the first Danish film, *Kørsel Med Grønlandske Hunde* (*Driving with Greenland Dogs*), some time between December 1896 and January 1897. Despite its title the film was produced in a Copenhagen park.

Over the next fifteen years Elfelt made over 200 films and for the first ten of those years he was solely responsible for all Danish film production. Elfelt chiefly produced filmed records of the famous, from royalty and politicians to sportsmen and composers, but also produced advertising and ballet films and his only (and Denmark's first) dramatic film, *Henrettelsen (The Execution)*, in 1903. However, the production of film always remained secondary to his main work as a photographer. (LMcK)

References
Ole Brage (ed.), *Danmarks Radio Praesenterer Elfelt Film* (Copenhagen: Danmarks Radio, 1975).
Marguerite Engberg, *Dansk Stumfilm I* (Copenhagen: Rhodos Forlag, 1977).

ERLANGER, Abraham Lincoln (1860–1930)

Theatrical agent, producer. With his theatrical booking partner Marc Klaw, Abraham Lincoln Erlanger had an uneasy relationship with the new medium of motion pictures throughout a career that was dominated by a ruthless commercial instinct. The two men purchased a small New York booking agency in 1886, becoming formal partners in 1888. In August 1896 they joined the Theatrical Syndicate, which rationalised the booking of shows to minimise travel expenses and layoff days while maximising performances and income. Under Erlanger's obsessive and autocratic control, this centralised system became the most powerful commercial monopoly in the American theatrical world. At this time Klaw and Erlanger, on their own behalf, contracted with Charles Smith Hurd to produce a film of the Horitz Passion play. The elaborate ninety-minute production (filmed by **Charles Webster** and the International Film Company), which included lantern slides, hymns sung by a chorus and a tightly scripted spoken commentary, opened at the Philadelphia Academy of Music on 22 November 1897, subsequently touring their theatrical circuit for several years as a special presentation.

In 1907 Klaw and Erlanger joined a successful lawsuit against the Kalem film company over its unauthorised film of one of the company's most enduring and commercially successful plays, an adaptation of Lew Wallace's novel *Ben Hur*, which set an important legal precedent on film copyrights. By November 1909, as motion pictures continued to erode the income from their vaudeville bookings, Klaw and Erlanger forbade their contracted actors from appearing in films. Four years later, in June 1913, however, they had contracted with the Biograph Company to produce two feature productions per week from the theatrical properties they owned; D. W. Griffith was to supervise the productions for Biograph, which continued to deny his own aspirations to make longer pictures, and he left Biograph in October.

By the 1920s Erlanger, no longer in partnership with Klaw, continued to book productions, and finally made an arrangement with Metro Pictures for a film version of his personally owned theatrical property, *Ben Hur*, which repeated its spectacular theatrical career on the movie screen in 1926. Erlanger remained a financial power in the theatre, and was preparing elaborate plans to expand his activities when he died on 7 March 1930. (DR)

References

William Danforth, 'Abraham Lincoln Erlanger', *The Green Book Album*, March 1909.

Eileen Bowser, *The Transformation of Cinema, 1907–1915* (New York: Charles Scribner's Sons, 1990).

F

FITZSIMMONS, Robert (1862–1917)

Boxer. Born at Helston, Cornwall, the distinctively freckled Bob Fitzsimmons moved to New Zealand as a boy. His first fights were in New Zealand and Australia, but he moved to the USA in 1890, defeating Jack 'Nonpareil' Dempsey to become world middleweight champion in 1891. He worked his way up to heavyweight bouts, knocking out Peter Maher – briefly **Jim Corbett**'s successor as world champion – in the first round on 21 February 1896 (dark skies and rain had already ruined **Enoch Rector**'s attempt to film the fight), before challenging Corbett for the world championship at Carson City, Nevada, on 17 March 1897. The film of this match, covering all fourteen rounds before Fitzsimmons knocked out Corbett, was taken by Enoch Rector for the Veriscope Company and aroused considerable interest and controversy, being shown widely throughout the USA and abroad. For two years after his victory Fitzsimmons controversially fought no one, but instead toured the country with his theatre company. When he returned to the ring it was to lose to **James Jeffries** in 1899. Fitzsimmons fought on, becoming world light heavyweight champion in 1903, and later fighting Jack Johnson, before retiring and returning to the stage. (LMcK)

References

Musser, *The Emergence of Cinema* (1990).

FEDETSKY, A. (?) Konstantinovich

Ukrainian photographer, cameraman. Fedetsky was a professional photographer of renown, who owned a large studio in the centre of Kharkov. Since the late 80s he had been experimenting with the Edison Phonograph, trying to achieve better results in the quality of recording, and even experimenting with stereophonic sound. In the summer of 1896, while travelling abroad, he noted the success of 'the living photography', and bought a **Georges Demenÿ** 60mm Biographe camera directly from Gaumont, apparently signing a concessionary contract. After a short period of training, he calculated that he could become the permanent correspondent of the French company in southern Russia, and from September 1896 his activities are well recorded in the local press.

On 19 September he filmed *The Religious Procession Carrying over the Miraculous Icon of the Virgin in the Kharkov Kuryazh Monastery*, and within a fortnight had shot *The Fancy Riding of the 1st Orenburg Kossack Regiment*. His third film, *The Sight of the Kharkov Railway Station at the Moment of a Train's Departure with the Command at the Platform*, was produced in October and transferred the most famous of Lumière subjects to Russian soil. At the beginning of 1897 Fedetsky is known to have shot *Skating at Red Square, Kharkov* and *Public Outdoor Fête at Mews Square, Kharkov*. Though Fedetsky would undoubtedly have taken more films than these, the documentary evidence is missing. Fedetsky had no technical facilities, and it is obvious that he had to use the Gaumont laboratories. Thus, one may presume that most or even all of his films were designed for release in France as well, though there is no definite evidence of this.

The first public screening of Fedetsky's films took place on 2 November 1896 at the Kharkov Opera House during a pause in *The Barber of Seville*, and consisted of a mixed programme of his own and Gaumont productions. This and later shows brought Fedetsky both acclaim and financial success. He also organised several charity screenings to benefit the poor of Kharkov, and toured throughout the Ukraine. On 20–25 November 1897, for instance, he put on film shows at Kiev's Bergonier theatre, alternating with dramatic plays by Ukrainian actors. In February 1898 he signed a contract with Kiev's Solovtsov theatre during his great tour throughout the Volga region and Siberia, but there are no indications as to the success of this enterprise, and there were by now a number of competitors for the Fedetsky film shows. It would appear that commercial failure during 1898 led to the breaking of the contract with Gaumont and the end of Fedetsky's career as a filmmaker. Nothing is known of him in the following years. (RY)

References

S. Ginsburg, *Cinematography of Pre-Revolutionary Russia* (Moscow, 1963).

FLAMMARION, Nicolas Camille
(1842–1925)

French astronomer, writer. Having originally studied for the priesthood, Camille Flammarion became first an engraver then an astronomer, popularising the subject in a number of works for a general audience that gained him a wide fame. He founded the French Astronomical Society and edited its bulletin, established the journal *L'Astronomie* in 1883 and held positions at the Paris Observatory (1858–62 and 1867) and Juvisy, near Paris (from 1882), where he studied the moon, Mars and double stars. To illustrate his observations, in 1898 he turned to cinematography, making films that simulated the apparent motions of the planets and depicted how the earth would appear from the moon. More controversially, he was also interested in mysticism and psychical research.

Flammarion was well known for his fictional writings, and Terry Ramsaye quotes from a perceptive (but undated) *St Louis Post Dispatch* review of the Kinetoscope, where the writer compares the Kinetoscope's ability to reverse time by playing the film backwards to Flammarion's speculative work, *Lumen* (1887). Here, omniscient beings view the passing of time as a ray of light, and are able to move freely along that ray and hence to view events at all times and in any direction. Flammarion's most outstanding work, his science fiction novel, *La Fin du monde*, was filmed by Abel Gance in 1930. (LMcK)

References

Amateur Photographer, 25 February 1898, p. 142.
Ramsaye, *A Million and One Nights* (1926).

FLORMAN, Carl Ernest Oliver
(1862–1952)

Photographer, film-maker. The aristocratic Ernest Florman was Sweden's pioneering filmmaker, who began shooting fiction films of the unusual length of 60m in 1897. The son of an army officer who resigned his commission to devote himself to his great passion for photography and both founded a photographic studio and became court photographer to King Oscar II, Ernest Florman was educated in Stockholm and ran his father's branch studio in Göteborg from 1885. He helped his friend and fellow-photographer **C. V. Roikjer** establish a film theatre at the 1897 exhibition in Stockholm in honour of the King's Silver Jubilee, and received additional instruction in cinematography from **Alexandre Promio**, the Lumière operator who filmed King Oscar's arrival at the opening of the exhibition on 15 May 1897, and other local scenes.

In July 1897, Florman began to make his own films, produced by **Numa Peterson**, with actualities like *A Game of Lawn Tennis* and *Gate of the Castle in Old Stockholm*, as well as his first fiction film, *Slagsmål i Gamla Stockholm* (*A Battle in Old Stockholm*), using seventeenth-century costumes and settings in the re-creation of old Stockholm at the Jubilee exhibition, where it premiered on 14 August 1897. A second comic farce, *An Acrobat Has Bad Luck*, opened at the exhibition in September. In 1898 Florman became manager for K. E. Ståhlberg's fashionable photographic studio in Helsinki; Ståhlberg was later to become Finland's pioneering film exhibitor and producer. Florman returned to Stockholm upon the death of his father in 1900, taking over the family photographic business until it closed in 1933, and also becoming the official court photographer. (DR).

References

Bengt Idestam-Almquist, *När Filmen kom till Sverige* (Stockholm, 1959).
Rune Waldekranz, *Levende Bilder: De första biograferna* (Stockholm, 1955) [reprinted as 'La nascita del cinema in Scandanavia' in Paolo Cherchi Usai (ed.), *Schiave bianche allo specchio* (Pordenone: Edizioni Studio Tesi, 1986)].

FOERSTERLING, Hermann O.

Manufacturer, promoter. A small-time manufacturer of advertising novelties in Berlin, the firm of H. O. Foersterling and Co. was one of several companies in Germany (George Bartling Co., **Gliewe** and Kugler, Ed. Liesegang and Co., **Oskar Messter**) to begin making cinema apparatus in the first half of 1896. Foersterling's projector was taken from a design by Victor Continsouza in Paris, and sold for 1,250 Marks at a time when Messter was selling his first equipment for 2,000 Marks. By the end of the year, Foersterling equipment was being used in Germany, Holland, Poland, Czechoslovakia and Switzerland. Not merely only a cut-price manufacturer, Foersterling devised a clever scheme to promote his apparatus and associate it with the inventions of **Thomas Edison**, the Lumière brothers and, later, Oskar Messter, invariably identifying it as 'Edison's Ideal' – the invention of A. and L. Lumière'. At a time well before the nomenclature of the cinema had been resolved in any language, he established a consistent advertising campaign of designs and slogans which was provided for travelling showmen using his equipment across Europe. (DR)

References
Deac Rossell, 'Showmanship and Deception: the Case of H. O. Foersterling', in Thomas Elsaesser (ed.), *German Cinema: The First Two Decades* (Amsterdam: Amsterdam University Press, 1996).

FOOTIT, George (1864–1921)

English clown who, with his partner Chocolat, appeared in a number of early French films. Footit trained as an equestrian acrobat with his father's circus and, by 1880, his appearances with Sanger's Circus established him as a leading horseback clown. His double, Cuban Raphaël Padilla, known as Chocolat (1868–1917), began at the Cirque Médrano in 1886, flourishing throughout the 90s and early 1900s at the most fashionable Parisian circus, the Nouveau Cirque. Their slapstick antics, in which Chocolat was the perennial victim of the violent but impassive Footit, were popular with all levels of society, attracting the attention of many intellectuals and artists. A Photoscenograph film of their sketch, *Guillaume Tell*, provided the basis for a picture band projected at **Emile Reynaud**'s Théâtre Optique in August 1896, while their act was also filmed by the Lumière Cinématographe by **Georges Hatot** and for the Phono-Cinéma-Théâtre in 1900. Following the breakup of the partnership in the 1900s, Footit appeared on the stage and for a brief time ran his own circus. (BA)

References
Maurice Willson-Disher, *Clowns and Pantomimes* (London: Constable, 1925).

FRANCIS, George

Lecturer, cameraman. The connection between music hall and early cinema in England was a strong one, and George Francis, the 'lecturer' at the first performances of Lumière's Cinématographe at the Polytechnic in Regent Street, London, had previously been associated with the 'Royal Standard' music hall. Later replaced by M. Pochet, he became an exhibitor for the Lumières, and from July 1897 to the end of 1898 demonstrated their Triograph. At the beginning of 1901 he was working for the Warwick Trading Company and was responsible for organising their coverage of the Queen's funeral. By June 1902 he was filming for **Robert Paul**, and clips from two films he shot at Marlborough House survive in the English copyright records. (RB)

References
The Entr'acte, 7 March 1896, p. 6.
Barnes, *The Beginnings of the Cinema in England* (vol. 2).

FREER, James S.

The first Canadian film-maker. James Freer was an English printer from Bristol who emigrated to Manitoba in 1888, where he became a farmer. In the autumn of 1897, having purchased some Edison equipment, he began to take films of farming and railways in Manitoba, with the encouragement of the Canadian Pacific Railway (CPR) Company. The company subsequently sponsored Freer's touring show, *Ten Years in Manitoba*, which visited Britain in April 1898. As with the films of **Frederick Wills** in Australia (but here with positive official backing), Freer's programme of films and lectures was intended to encourage emigration, emphasising Canada's agricultural riches and the availability of land. The CPR was to become a significant sponsor of film at this period, notably with the 'phantom ride' railway films of the American Mutoscope and Biograph Company and travel films shot for **Charles Urban** by **Joseph Rosenthal**. Freer's programme included such titles as *Six Binders at Work in Hundred Acre Wheatfield*, *Harvesting Scene, with Trains Passing By* and *Arrival of CPR Express at Winnipeg*. He may also have taken film in Britain during his travels. Press reports of Freer's successful British tours indicate that at least one film showed his own home and family as a model of what potential emigrants could expect.

He returned to Manitoba in the spring of 1899, making a film of his journey from Liverpool to Quebec. Though he continued to tour with his existing films, he found that the amateur was being squeezed out of the film market and was forced to purchase further films of Canadian events from Edison. Freer's second tour to Britain in 1901 was not so successful, and the CPR turned to the professional Charles Urban Trading Company. Freer went back to his farm, though he continued to give the occasional film show locally. (LMcK)

References
Morris, *Embattled Shadows* (1978).

FREGOLI, Leopoldo (1867–1936)

Mimic, magician. Fregoli was from an early age blessed with a remarkable gift for mimicry and impersonation, readily able to turn his voice or face into almost any character, and with such lightning changes that he left audiences dumbstruck. Learning conjuring as well, and specialising in the impersonation of noted figures from politics and the arts, a typical show-stopping display included a routine in which he impersonated an entire trial – judge, jury, prosecutor, advocate and defendant – with instantaneous shifts of character.

He was already an immensely popular performer when he acquired a Lumière Cinématographe (**Louis Lumière** was a fan) in 1898 after a visit to Lyon, and began to present films on what he renamed the Fregoligraph as part of his stage act. The films were no more than records of his various sketches, though he soon learned the possibilities of film trickery and began to employ surprise cuts and reverses. Among his Italian films were *Maestri di musica*, in which Fregoli impersonated a variety of composers (Verdi, Wagner, Rossini and others), *Fregoli illusionista, Impressioni di Ermete Novelli* (a noted Italian actor and later film star), *Fregoli, danza serpentina* and *Fregoli dietro le scene*. Films of his acts were also offered by **Robert Paul**, whose *Fregoli, the Protean Artiste, in his Impersonation of Famous Composers* (1898), though based on the same act as *Maestri di musica*, was recorded during a different performance when Fregoli was appearing at the Alhambra; and **Georges Méliès**, in whose *l'Homme-Protée* (1899) Fregoli played twenty different characters. His filming was, however, only a brief interlude in an international stage career that lasted many years. Fregoli was a dazzling entertainer whose exuberance and agility are readily apparent from the surviving films. (LMcK)

References
Bernardini, *Cinema muto italiano 1896–1904* (1980).
Leopoldo Fregoli, *Fregoli racontato da Fregoli* (Milan: Rizzoli, 1936).
Jean Nohain, *Frégoli, 1867–1936: Sa Vie et ses sécrets* (Paris: Jeune Parque, 1968).

FRIESE GREENE, William (1855–1921)

Photographer, experimenter. An inscription on the monument to Friese Greene in Highgate cemetery calls him 'The Inventor of Kinematography', and it is possibly this posthumous compliment that has led his achievements to be first glorified then damned. He was the subject of a romantic and unreliable biography, *Friese Greene, Close-up of an Inventor*, which was then turned into an even more misleading film, *The Magic Box* (1951).

Born William Edward Green, the son of a Bristol metalworker, he changed his name when he married Helena Friese in 1874. Leaving school at fourteen he was apprenticed to a local photographer, Maurice Guttenberg, and proved a fast learner with a special knack for portrait work. Within a few years they had parted company and Friese Greene had set up his own studio in Bath. He was very successful, so much so that by 1877 he also had two shops in Bristol and one in Plymouth. Sometime in 1880 he met **J. A. R. Rudge**, a Bath instrument maker who had devised a number of novel adaptations of the magic lantern to create an illusion of movement. Friese Greene was fascinated by the idea and worked with Rudge, producing photographs, suggesting improvements and later demonstrating the lanterns at photographic societies and elsewhere.

In 1885 he moved to London, opening two shops in partnership with **Esmé Collings**. Once again, Friese Greene's photographic talents proved both popular and fashionable, and a number of other London shops were added over the next few years. In 1889 Friese Greene and civil engineer Mortimer Evans designed a sequence camera using 'a roll of any convenient length of sensitised paper or the like', capable of taking four or five pictures a second. There is no record of a successful film projection at this time; the claimed demonstration at the Chester Photographic Convention in 1890 was a failure. That same year Friese Greene used a stereoscopic sequence camera made by Frederick Varley, but once again there is no record of successful projection.

In 1891 he was made bankrupt, an event which led to the sale of almost all his equipment and considerable social disgrace. Various patents followed over the next ten years. In 1893, he patented a camera/projector almost identical to Varley's stereoscopic model, but by this time **E.-J. Marey** and **Le Prince** had both achieved success in recording sequences of images at rates in excess of those that any of these cameras were capable of. By the time projected motion picture films had achieved any commercial application, Friese Greene had abandoned the field. At the time when the first films were being shown in Britain, he was demonstrating X-rays.

In 1896, Friese Greene teamed up with **John Alfred Prestwich** to make a camera and twin-lens projector, intended to eradicate flicker. 1898 was the beginning of his obsession with colour photography, albeit with a rather impractical patent for stills. In 1905, however, he took out a patent for colour moving pictures which predated **G. A. Smith**, and he later challenged **Charles Urban** in court over the similar Urban/Smith Kinemacolor process. He continued to develop colour processes throughout the rest of his life, with his son Claude carrying on his work and becoming a leading colour cinematographer.

Aside from moving pictures, Friese Greene was a prolific inventor, who took out over seventy patents. Some were impractical, some were workable but before their time (for example, phototypesetting), while others were commercially exploited (for example, rapid photographic printing for cigarette cards and reproducing photographs in magazines). The cost of his obsessive inventing and the chaotic handling of his business affairs led to imprisonment, a further bankruptcy and separation from his second wife. Nonetheless, he enjoyed periods of wealth and success, and throughout it all appeared to remain optimistic about the future. His death at a film industry meeting in 1921 sparked a pang of guilt in a cinema world that had outgrown and largely abandoned those who had witnessed its birth, and it attempted to make amends with his tombstone inscription and a lavish funeral wreath – a floral projector and screen with blooms spelling out 'The End'. (PC/SH)

References

Ray Allister, *Friese Greene, Close-up of an Inventor* (London: Marsland, 1948).
Michael Chanan, *The Dream that Kicks* (Routledge & Kegan Paul, 1980).
Brian Coe, 'William Friese Greene and the Origins of Cinematography', *Screen* vol. 10 nos. 2–4, 1969.
Hendricks, *The Edison Motion Picture Myth* (1961).
Hopwood, *Living Pictures* (1899).

FUERST, Jules

Chemist, photographer and cameraman. Fuerst brothers of 17 Philpot Lane, London, were dealers in 'oils, chemicals, drugs, herbs, abstracts, drysalteries, photographic plates and chemicals'. In August 1894 it was reported that they had the agency for Lumière's orthochromatic film plates, which connection naturally led them to become selling agents for the Lumière Cinématographe and films. They were taking orders for these goods in June 1897. Though Fuerst advertised themselves as sole agents, in fact others also handled the Lumière products in England, including **Philipp Wolff**, **Maguire and Baucus** and **Jasper Redfern**.

Jules Fuerst was responsible for the film side of the business. He demonstrated the apparatus at various photographic societies and clubs (he was to donate a Cinématographe to the Royal Photographic Society), and also became an able cinematographer. It is probable that some of the English subjects in the Lumière catalogue were taken by him, including scenes of **Queen Victoria**'s Diamond Jubilee on 22 June 1897. He is also known to have photographed two of the main events at Henley regatta and five 'admirable' films at the Aldershot Jubilee Review, which took place on 1 July. At present nothing is known of his personal life, but he should be remembered as one of the first cinematographers in England to film news and topical events using the Lumière machine after its derestriction. (JB)

References

Barnes, *The Beginnings of the Cinema in England* (vol. 2).

FULLER, Loïe (1862–1928)

Influential American dancer who provided an inspiration for fellow performers, artists and film-makers. Marie Louise Fuller made her stage debut at the age of four, thereafter pursuing an acting career in stock companies, vaudeville and with **Buffalo Bill Cody**'s Wild West show. In 1889 she devised her famous 'Serpentine Dance' in which lengths of silk were skilfully manipulated under constantly changing coloured lighting. An appearance at the Folies Bergère in 1892 brought her to the attention of Toulouse-Lautrec, Jules Chéret and Auguste Rodin, all of whom produced works based on her act. Such was her fame that she became widely imitated, often under her own name, something she makes much complaint of in her autobiography. According to Terry Ramsaye, an 1896 Vitascope film claiming to show 'La Loïe' actually featured her sister. But French companies apparently proved more successful in capturing the dancer on film: a Lumière film of 1896 claimed to feature the Serpentine Dance, while Pathé productions included *La Loïe Fuller* (c.1900), a longer version *La Loïe Fuller* (1901) and a coloured film, *Loïe Fuller* (1905, 'Edition nouvelle avec transformations'). Her dancing won fresh critical acclaim during the Paris Exposition of 1900, and she continued to make appearances in Europe and the USA throughout the next twenty-five years. Whether it was ever her on film or not, the very name of Loïe Fuller made her one of the first stars of the cinema. (BA)

References
Gabrielle Brandstetter and Brygida Maria Ochaim, *Loïe Fuller: Tanz, Licht-Speil, Art Nouveau* (Freiberg: Rombach, 1989).
Loïe Fuller, *Fifteen Years of a Dancer's Life* (London: Herbert Jenkins, 1913).

G

GAMMON, Frank R
See **RAFF, Norman C.**

GAUMONT, Léon (1864–1946)

Producer. Léon Gaumont, modestly born but mechanically minded, was fascinated by photography. The seventeen-year-old's notebook contains advanced ideas on filming and on successive projection. In 1881 he entered the Paris workshops of **Jules Carpentier**, one of the best-known precision instrument manufacturers of the time and, years later, the constructor of the Lumière Cinématographe. In 1888 Gaumont married Camille Maillard, who brought as her dowry a piece of land on the rue des Alouettes, near the Buttes Chaumont, the eventual site of the Gaumont studios and of the 'cité Elgé'.

In 1893, Gaumont went to work for Félix Richard in his shop, the Comptoir Général de Photographie, at 57 rue Saint-Roch in Paris. Richard became embroiled in a legal battle with his brother Jules and, in June 1895, offered to sell out to Léon Gaumont. The latter bought the business and, on 10 August 1895, in partnership with the engineer Gustave Eiffel (the creator of the tower), the astronomer Joseph Vallot and the financier Alfred Besnier, formed a company, L. Gaumont and Co. He accepted a proposal from **Georges Demenÿ**, **E-J. Marey**'s old collaborator, that he should manufacture and market Demenÿ's chronophotographic camera and his projector/viewer, the Phonoscope. This last machine, rechristened the Bioscope, went on sale in November 1895, and the Biographe camera soon after. Both failed: the Phonoscope used glass discs and the camera used non-perforated film. Gaumont recovered from this setback by manufacturing, with engineer L-R. Decaux and Demenÿ, a camera/projector using 60mm perforated film (1896), followed by a model using 35mm perforated film (1897).

The first films in the Gaumont catalogue were bought from, among others, **Albert**

Londe, P. Gers and Deslandes. Soon after, Gaumont's young secretary, **Alice Guy**, was entrusted with the production of films. The company reached second place (after Pathé) in the market for French cinematographic equipment, producing the Chrono de Poche (1900) for amateurs, the Chronophone for sound projection (at the end of 1902) and the Chronochrome for projecting colour films (1912). In 1906, the Etablissements Gaumont was founded as a limited company. It flourished until 1914, thanks to an excellent group of film directors including Louis Feuillade, Jean Durand, Roméo Bosetti, Léonce Perret and Emile Cohl.

In the 1920s, the firm produced one avant-garde film-maker, Marcel L'Herbier, but otherwise stayed faithful to its conservative image, financing the films of Feuillade, Henri Fescourt and Léon Poirier. It also expanded its distribution and exhibition activities (the famous Gaumont-Palace survived right up to 1972, when the magnificent building, the company's emblem, was bulldozed). In 1929, Gaumont retired; the Gaumont-Franco-Film-Aubert (GFFA) was created the same year. In 1934 GFFA filed for bankruptcy, and four years later a new company appeared, La Société Nouvelle des Etablissements Gaumont (SNEG), which has continued to this day. Léon Gaumont, whose name was also commemorated in the Gaumont-British Picture Corporation, died on 10 August 1946. (LM)

References
Abel, *The Ciné Goes to Town* (1994).

GEE, Alfred James (1878–1966)

Exhibitor, cameraman. The career of A. J. Gee is typical of an adventuresome younger generation that became entranced with the cinema and remained dedicated to its charms throughout their lives.

Born in Staffordshire, England, by 1897 Gee was the operator of a **Robert Paul** Theatrograph, and was active in the Manchester area. He travelled to Denmark the next year as the operator for Mr Swanborough's 'Wargraph', opening in Copenhagen at Peter Rasmussen's Cirkus Variété on 23 September 1898 with films of the Spanish-American War. He returned the next year with films of the Boer War, and settled in Copenhagen in 1900, exhibiting films there and in provincial cities and towns, eventually in 1905 founding (with Soren Nielsen) the first permanent cinema in Alborg, the Biografteatret in Nytorv. This grew into a small chain of provincial theatres and a modest distribution company that was active between 1906 and 1910. Three years later Gee was also involved as a cameraman with such small Danish production companies as Det nye danske Films Kompagni Ltd. and Biorama, also founded by his early partner, Nielsen. Continuing as a theatre manager through the 1930s, he remained in Copenhagen after his retirement and died in 1966 at the age of eighty-eight. (DR)

References
Marguerite Engberg, *Dansk Stumfilm*, vols. 1 and 2 (Copenhagen: Rhodos Forlag, 1977).
Gunnar Sandfeld, *Den stumme Scene* (Copenhagen: NYT Nordisk Forlag/Arnold Busck, 1966).

GELABERT, Fructuoso (Fructuoso Gelabert Badiella) (1874-1955)

Catalan film-maker. Born in Barcelona, the son of a cabinet-maker from Majorca, Gelabert was a photographer and mechanic who paid an early visit to the first Lumière screenings in Spain in 1896 and in the following year eagerly constructed his own camera on lines similar to the Cinématographe. His first effort, written, directed and starring himself, was a fiction film, *Riña de café*, made in Barcelona in August 1897, followed up in 1898 by *Dorotea*. However, most of his output consisted of local actualities, such as *Salida del público de la iglesia parroquial de Sans* (1897) and *Salida de los trabajadores de 'La España Industrial'* (1897). His first news film, *Visita de Doña Maria Cristina y Don Alfonso XIII a Barcelona*, was shot in 1898 and subsequently sold to Pathé.

Gelabert, who now established his name as a producer of Spanish actuality and news film, continued as a jack-of-all-trades film-maker for the next twenty years. Among his rather humdrum efforts, typical of the early Spanish cinema before a revival in the 1920s, was a succession of literary and dramatic adaptations. He developed several film devices, established laboratories and small studios, and made his final film, *La puntaire*, in 1928. (LMcK)

References
Emilio C. Garcia Fernandez, *Historia iIustrada del cine español* (Madrid: Planeta, 1985).

GEORGIADES, George (Demetrius Anastas Georgiades) and TRAGIDES, George

Exhibitors. Typical of the enterprising individuals who seized on **Thomas Edison**'s latest wonder, the Kinetoscope, is the story of Georgiades and Tragides; like fast-disappearing quarks influencing the chain reaction in a laboratory and then vanishing for ever, they appear briefly in 1894–5, set tumultuous events in motion, and are immediately lost to history.

In New York in the spring of 1894, George Georgiades and his partner George Tragides (spelled Tragidis in some contemporary documents and in the *London Directory* for 1895, but which appears variously in the literature as Tragedis Papastakyotenipoulos or George Tragedis, Trajedis or Tragedes) purchased three Kinetoscopes from the Edison agents, the Holland brothers. In late July 1894, Georgiades demonstrated a Kinetoscope for Henri Flamans, the editor of *Le Magasin pittoresque*, its first appearance in Europe.

Forming the American Kinetoscope Company with offices at 95 Queen Street, London, and 20 boulevard Montmartre, Paris, Georgiades and Tragides opened Kinetoscopes at several locations in London, among them Old Broad Street. Seeking to expand their business they were introduced to the 25-year-old instrument maker **Robert Paul** by his friend and later collaborator **Henry Short**, and asked Paul to make copies of the machine. Finding that Edison had not taken out a British patent on the machine, Paul began making copies of the Kinetoscope both for Georgiades and Tragides and on his own account. By January 1895, the two Greeks had evidently mixed their genuine machines with Paul's copies, since Edison's legitimate agents **Maguire and Baucus** cabled Edison seeking to use his name in a suit against parties using 'one genuine with four spurious machines'. (In Paris the previous April, Edison's agents the **Werner** brothers had also possibly run into the wildcat Georgiades operation, advertising that 'our firm is the only one in France which sells the authentic apparatus made by M. Edison'.) On 6 March 1895, George Georgiades opened a Kinetoscope exhibition at the Tabacaria Neves in Lisbon, the machine's first showing in Portugal and his final documented appearance in the entertainment world. (DR)

References

Talbot, *Moving Pictures* (1912).
Hendricks, *The Kinetoscope* (1966).
Mannoni, *Le grand art de la lumière et de l'ombre* (1994).

GIBBONS, Sir Walter (1871–1933)

Film showman and music hall magnate. Gibbons abandoned his original employment with a Wolverhampton nail factory to join the Calder O'Berne Opera Company. Following a career as a music hall singer, he acquired an Urban Bioscope projector and, in 1898, launched the Anglo-American Bio-Tableaux, a variety film show that initially concentrated on news subjects. In 1900 he produced the Phono-Bio-Tableaux, a series of films synchronised to phonograph cylinders that presented famous music hall artists such as Vesta Tilley, Lil Hawthorne, Alec Hurley and **G. H. Chirgwin**. The Lil Hawthorne film survives. Gibbons experimented with artificial lighting and, in 1901, was reported to have a London studio and plant capable of processing and dispatching a film in sixty-five minutes. He is also reported to have sent cameramen out to film the later stages of the Boer War, including C. Rider Noble.

On the death of his father-in-law, G. Adney Payne, he succeeded to the directorship of the London Syndicate Halls, subsequently opening the Palladium as the flagship of his music hall empire in 1910. Gibbons severed his connection with the Palladium in 1912, but, in 1928, returned as managing director of the General Theatres Corporation, which initiated a programme of cine-variety at the theatre. Within a few months, however, a boardroom wrangle led to his resignation. His considerable fortune was dissipated on other theatrical projects, leading to bankruptcy shortly before his death. (BA)

References

Ian Bevan, *Top of the Bill: The Story of the London Palladium* (London: Frederick Muller, 1952).
S. Theodore Felstead, *Stars Who Made the Halls* (London: T. Werner Laurie, 1946).

GILMORE, William Edward

Business manager. William E. Gilmore was the *éminence grise* behind **Thomas Edison** and the Edison Manufacturing Company. A tough and frequently bullish character who had as great an influence as any on the nascent American film industry, Gilmore was appointed vice-president and general manager of the Edison Manufacturing Company on 1 April 1894, taking over from Alfred O. Tate. For his very first act, Terry Ramsaye surmises, Gilmore 'brought down a hard fist on a surprised desk and demanded action'. It became Gilmore's task to oversee the increasingly complex exploitation of Edison's business interests, which meant much else besides film, and indeed Gilmore had been employed in the first instance to tackle the problem of the financially unstable North American Phonograph Company, licensees for the Edison Phonograph. It was replaced by the National Phonograph Company, with Gilmore as its president.

On the film side Gilmore soon became suspicious of **W. K-L. Dickson**, who while still in Edison's employ was working in secret for the **Latham**s, and engineered Dickson's departure from the company in April 1895. By this act Gilmore did much to give birth to the many different cinematographic machines and subsequent patent litigation that was to keep himself and Edison fully occupied for years. Gilmore's attempts to stifle competition only encouraged the stubborn; it was his refusal to supply **Robert Paul** with films that led the rogue British Kinetoscope manufacturer to go into production with the first British films. Gilmore was also the key figure in the negotiations with **Thomas Armat** and **Raff and Gammon** that led to the acquisition of what became the Edison Vitascope and the start of projected Edison film in April 1896. And it was Gilmore who caught **Albert Smith** and **J. Stuart Blackton** red-handed pirating exclusive Spanish-American War films, and who then brought American Vitagraph, along with many others, in as Edison licensees. But it was also Gilmore who detected change as the film business began to establish roots, and who moved Edison away from the licensing system towards its own developing production schedule in 1900, which meant a new studio and more staff, most notably **Edwin S. Porter**.

Much of Gilmore's belligerence stemmed from the considerable battles he faced over the chaotic Phonograph business; with the film side it was just a question of cracking the whip. Of film production itself he knew little and cared less. That he had a softer side is perhaps shown by his predilection for nepotism – two of his brothers-in-law were awarded key managerial positions in the Edison organisation.

In June 1908 he left Edison to manage the Essex Press, a printing business, and was replaced by **Frank L. Dyer**, Thomas Edison's lawyer and biographer. (LMcK)

References

Musser, *Before the Nickelodeon* (1991).
Ramsaye, *A Million and One Nights* (1926).

GIREL, François-Constant
(1873–1952)

Lumière operator. Constant Girel was the son of a pharmacist and studied the subject in Lyon, at which time his brother-in-law was employed at the Lumière factory. He was taken on as a Lumière operator some time in 1896, filming for them in Germany in September of that year, when he made contact with **Ludwig Stollwerck** and filmed Tsar **Nikolas II**'s inspection of the German army at Breslau. It was undoubtedly the Stollwerck connection that led him to Switzerland, where he worked for another Lumière representative, **Henri Lavanchy-Clarke**, before filming the Tsar again towards the end of the year at Cherbourg and Chalons.

On 6 December he left for Japan, arriving at Kobe on 9 January 1897, where he met up with the Lumière representative for Japan, **Inahata Shotaro**. The pair then inaugurated the cinema in Japan with a programme at Osaka's Nanchi theatre on 15 February 1897. Girel's competence as a cameraman has been questioned, but he filmed a wide number of Japanese scenes, many of which ended up in the Lumière catalogue. He returned to France after a year, when he was replaced by **Gabriel Veyre**. He subsequently approached Pathé Frères, but failed to find further work in film, and went back to pharmacy. (LMcK)

References

Denise Boehm-Girel, paper delivered at 1995 Lyon/Lumière conference.
Peter B. High, 'The Dawn of Cinema in Japan', *Journal of Contemporary History*, vol. 19 no. 1, January 1984.

GLIEWE, Max

Inventor, engineer. Long hidden in the imposing shadow cast by **Oskar Messter**, Max Gliewe was a highly skilled and innovative engineer who made significant contributions to film technology from its beginnings through the turn of the century. When the operators of the small cinema theatre at 21 Unter den Linden in Berlin repeatedly turned to the engineering firm of Gliewe & Kügler in Spring 1896 for the repair of their Kinétographe of **Méliès** and Reulos (bought from the **Isola** brothers in Paris and widely advertised as an Isolatographe), it was Gliewe who recognised that the Maltese cross movement would be a decisive improvement on the badly-working machine's drunken-screw intermittent, and he began to manufacture his own film projectors including a five-sided Maltese cross. Apart from selling to individual showmen, Gliewe obtained an order for fifty machines from the firm of **Haydon** and **Urry**, Upper Street, Islington, London, and his apparatus is the likely origin of the British company's Eragraph projector. In Autumn 1896, Messter also turned to Gliewe, replacing his trial equipment based on **Robert Paul**'s Theatrograph intermittent with Gliewe's double-plate design with a five-sided Maltese cross (by late 1897 four-sided) that became a trademark of Messter equipment. Gliewe designed Messter's most popular Victorian machine, the Model X, in 1898–9 of which some 500 examples were sold, and in 1899 created a new machine which allowed frame adjustments while the film was running without shifting the picture on the screen. Messter's firm absorbed Gliewe & Kügler on 1 October 1900, and in 1902 Gliewe's partner Theodore Pätzold developed a three-bladed shutter for his own shows which Gliewe quickly added to the Messter projectors, just as John A. Pross was adding a similar shutter to Biograph apparatus in the United States: this was the final step towards fully modern equipment which eliminated flicker on the screen. In each of these developments Gliewe was the progenitor of sophisticated engineering innovations that were essential to the evolution of modern projection equipment. (DR)

References
Oskar Messter, *Mein Weg mit dem Film* (Berlin: Max Hesses Verlag, 1936).
Christian Ilgner and Dietmar Linke, 'Filmtechnik – Vom Malterserkreuz zum Panzerkino' in Martin Loiperdinger (ed.), *Oskar Messter: Filmpionier der Kaiserzeit* [KINtop Schriften 2] (Basel: Stroemfeld/Rotor Stern, 1994).

GORKY, Maxim (1868–1936)

One of the first Russian writers to comment on moving pictures, and later an important literary influence on Soviet cinema, Aleksei Maksimovich Peshkov (who took the penname of 'Maksim Gorky') was born in Nizhiny Novgorod, which was renamed in his honour after his death.

Gorky saw the Lumière presentation organised by **Charles Aumont** at the annual Nizhiny Novgorod All-Russian Exhibition on 30 June or 1 July 1896 (the show had opened on 22 June), and on 4 July published an evocative account (signed 'I. M. Pacatus') in a local newspaper which has become the most famous of all early literary responses to film ('Last night I was in the kingdom of the shadows'). After a second article for an Odessa paper, Gorky wrote a short story, *Revenge*, based on the death of one of Aumont's 'show girls', in which a prostitute kills herself after

seeing the 'normal family life' portrayed in the Lumière film, *Repas de bébé*.

After his return from voluntary exile in the 1920s, Gorky was proclaimed the model for all Soviet art, and his doctrine of 'socialist realism' became mandatory for writers and film-makers alike. His play, *The Lower Depths*, originally a Moscow Art Theatre success in 1902, was filmed by Renoir in 1936, and his autobiography inspired three widely circulated films by Mark Donskoi: *The Childhood of Gorky* (1938), *Among People* (1939) and *My Universities* (1940). In 1955, the Moscow studio which had been previously Ermoliev's and Mezhrabpom-Rus was renamed after Gorky. (IC)

References
Yuri Tsivian, *Early Cinema in Russia and its Cultural Reception* (London/New York: Routledge, 1994).
Richard Taylor and Ian Christie (eds.), *The Film Factory: Russian and Soviet Cinema in Documents, 1896–1939* (London: Routledge, 1988).
Leyda, *Kino* (1960).

GRACE, Dr William Gilbert (1848–1915)

Cricketer. The greatest and most famous of all cricket players and an emblem of the Victorian era. Playing for Gloucestershire and England (and captaining both), Grace was the dominant figure both as a batsman and bowler in cricket's 'golden age', scoring 54,896 runs (including 126 centuries, the 100th in 1895) and taking 2,876 wickets in a first-class career that lasted from 1865 to 1908.

As one of the most popular and recognisable figures of his day, it was natural that he should be of interest to the early film-makers, and three films survive. The remarkable *Dr Grace's Jubilee Procession*, taken by **Prestwich**, shows Grace and a line-up of cricketing greats (Arthur Shrewsbury, F. S. Jackson, A. C. MacLaren and many others) walking past the camera on the occasion of Grace's fiftieth birthday. The only film of Grace in action is **Williamson**'s 1901 *Cricket*, showing Grace and Prince Ranjitsinhji (the subject of the very first cricket film, taken by **Henry Walter Barnett** in Australia in December 1897) at batting practice. The third, showing Grace at his final test match in June 1899, and possibly shot by **Jasper Redfern**, has been re-created on film from a Filoscope flip book by the National Film and Television Archive, London. (LMcK)

References
Barry Anthony, 'Earliest Cricket on Film', *Wisden Cricket Monthly*, December 1993, pp. 32–3.

GREEN, George (1861–1915)

Exhibitor, producer. Glasgow-based fairground and cinema-theatre pioneer, who gave his first public cinema show during the Christmas season of 1896–7 at 'The Carnival', a venue he owned and ran in the city, using a machine obtained from **Robert Paul**. From Easter 1898 George Green travelled with a fairground Bioscope show throughout Scotland and the north-west of England. In 1902 he began to look for permanent venues and bought the Whitevale theatre, Glasgow, chiefly for film exhibition. Following the death of one of his sons, John, in 1914, George ceased travelling. He died a year later, leaving a chain of some ten or more cinemas in various parts of Scotland.

Just prior to his death, George Green and Sons had also established Green's Film Services in Glasgow, a Scottish renting and distribution network. A supplementary service, *Scottish Moving Picture News*, was added soon afterwards, providing cinemas with local newsreel subjects. In 1919 the firm expanded, establishing a second office in London, when the newsreel service was renamed *British Moving Picture News*. During the First World War the company also produced propaganda films for the War Office, including *Patriotic Porker* (1916). (MH)

References

Janet McBain, *Pictures Past* (Edinburgh: Moorfoot Publishing, 1985).
Vanessa Toulmin, 'Telling the Tale', *Film History*, vol. 6 no. 2 1994.

GREEN, John C. ('Belsaz') (1866–1951)

Magician, exhibitor. Using the stage name 'Belsaz', Green was a magician and touring showman who had travelled widely in Canada and the USA. Learning of the impending debut of the Edison Vitascope in Ottawa, and without having even seen moving pictures, Green offered his services as lecturer and entertainer to Ahearn and Soper's Electric Railway Company, owners of West End Park, where the Vitascope was due to appear under the auspices of the **Holland** brothers. Green was accepted, and on 21 July 1896, following the regular Belsaz magic show, the people of Ottawa witnessed a programme which included celebrated Canadian actress **May Irwin** in *The Kiss*. Long believed to be Canada's first projected film show, French-speaking Canada had already been visited by the Lumière operators **Louis Minier** and Louis

Pupier, who had presented their first show in Montreal on 28 June 1896. The first films to be seen in English-speaking Canada, and Green's presentation of them, were a huge success, playing to thousands for a number of weeks, and Green promptly acquired a projector of his own, touring Canada with a combined magic and moving pictures show. At the beginning of the new century, once it became clear that the days of travelling shows were over, Green settled down and turned to managing theatres in Canada and the USA. He remained devoted to magic, but abandoned his interest in films. (LMcK)

References

Morris, *Embattled Shadows* (1978).

GRIMOIN-SANSON, Raoul (1860–1940)

Inventor. Born at Elbeuf (Seine-Maritime), Raoul Sanson (the Grimoin was added later) was fascinated early on by conjuring and photography. At first he worked on photoengraving, and in 1892 made (in Belgium) some anthropometric plates. Returning to France, he came into contact with **E-J. Marey**, **Georges Demenÿ** and **Albert Londe**. In 1895, his interest aroused by moving pictures, Grimoin-Sanson bought a Kinetoscope manufactured by **Robert Paul**. He wanted, like many others, to project Edison films onto a screen. His camera/projector, the Phototachygraphe, was demonstrated in February 1896 to a journalist from *L'Intransigeant*, and he patented the fairly crude mechanism the following month, and later an improved model, the Multiplex. In 1897, he approached several retailers with a new machine that incorporated a four-arm Maltese cross.

He then conceived a panoramic projection process, Cinecosmorama or 'Cineorama', patented on 27 November 1897. A limited company was created, which financed the building of ten cameras and ten projectors. The cameras were arranged in a circle and filmed simultaneously, by means of a single central drive. When projected, the ten films created a gigantic panoramic moving scene. He produced several films around Europe, and in Paris placed his ten cameras in the basket of a balloon to take aerial views. Cineorama was installed at the 1900 Universal Exposition in Paris, the ten projectors arranged in a circle in a cabin so that the films all joined together on the circular screen. But the ten arc lamps created such a heat that this installation never functioned, despite the inventor's later claims.

The Cineorama company went bankrupt, and all its equipment was sold in 1901. Grimoin-Sanson gave up cinema and entered the cork industry. In 1920 he financed a film, *Le Comte de Griolet*, whose originality consisted of superimposing, at the bottom of the picture, a conductor's baton to guide the choir and musicians. Like the film itself, which was hurriedly produced and badly acted, this simplistic innovation met with no success. In 1926, he claimed to have been the first to use the Maltese cross in a film projector (**Jules Carpentier** and René Bunzli were in fact its true propagators). These pretensions to priority featured in a 1927 film, *L'Histoire du cinéma par le cinéma*, where he presented himself as an equal of Marey and **Lumière**, raising a controversy which led to unending arguments about the history of the invention of cinema. While the work of many pioneers demands further research, that of Grimoin-Sanson, glorified and exaggerated unceasingly by himself, requires relatively less. (LM)

References

Jean-Jacques Meusy, 'L'Enigme du Cinéorama de l'Exposition Universelle de 1900', *Archives* 37, January 1991.

GUY, Alice (1873–1968)

Director. The world's first woman director has been perhaps over romanticised in some quarters, but she nevertheless had a remarkable career by any standards. The youngest of four daughters of a Parisian businessman, she spent part of her early childhood in Chile, before being educated in Paris. Her father died when she was quite young, and she saw shorthand typing as a means to financial independence. She became secretary for Félix Richard, manufacturer of photographic products, and when **Léon** **Gaumont** bought out his business in 1895 she joined Gaumont as his secretary. By 1897 Gaumont was expanding from the construction and marketing of projectors to a full film service. This meant producing films, for which Gaumont turned to his enterprising secretary, who (working with cameraman Anatole Thiberville) was to become chief producer at Gaumont film from 1897 to 1906, with an output (still a matter of some confusion) numbering hundreds of titles. Among these are the much-cited *La Fée aux choux* (1900, remade in 1902), a copy of Lumière's *Arroseur arrosé* (1897), *La Vie du Christ* (1898–9) in eleven tableaux, a second *Vie du Christ* in 1906, and scores of short sound films made from 1902 using the Gaumont Chronophone process.

Initially, the greater part of Gaumont production was actuality film (including many dance films), but from 1903 there was an increasing emphasis on fiction. The films grew longer, and Guy produced such comparatively ambitious titles as *L'Assassinat du courrier de Lyon* (1904) and *Esmerelda* (1905), based on Victor Hugo's *The Hunchback of Notre Dame*. Towards the end of her time at Gaumont she saw in a strong team of new film-makers, notably Victorin Jasset (who designed her ambitious and distinctive *La Vie du Christ* of 1906) and Louis Feuillade. In 1906, however, she married Anglo-French Gaumont cameraman Herbert Blaché, accompanying him to New York when he was appointed to manage the Gaumont office in 1907.

In 1910, having given birth to a daughter and keen to return to film-making, Guy-Blaché (as she was now known) founded her own production company, Solax. A minor but lively enterprise, which remained on the American scene for three years, Guy-Blaché directed many of the films herself, notably *A Child's Sacrifice* (1910) and *Dick Whittington and his Cat* (1913). On being released from his Gaumont contract in October 1913, Herbert Blaché replaced Solax with Blaché Features, moving on to form the US Amusement Corporation in April 1914, and Guy-Blaché directed several films, now of feature length, for both companies. From 1914 to 1917 she also made features starring the Russian Olga Petrova for Popular Plays and Players, another Herbert Blaché company.

The Blachés were divorced in 1922, and Alice returned to France, but she failed to find further employment in the film industry. She wrote several children's books, but the remainder of her life was spent in obscurity until the French government bestowed on her the

Légion d'honneur in 1953. She returned to the USA in 1964 to live with one of her daughters, and died in a nursing home in Mahwah, New Jersey. As interest in early women film-makers continues to grow, Alice Guy has become a hugely important figure in an alternative history of the cinema. As more of her films come to light, her reputation can only grow. (LMcK)

References

Abel, *The Ciné Goes to Town* (1994).
Alice Guy, *Autobiographie d'une pionnière du cinéma (1873–1968)* (Paris: Denoel/Gonthier, 1976) [translated as Anthony Slide (ed.), *The Memoirs of Alice Guy Blaché* (Metuchen NJ/London: Scarecrow Press, 1986)].
Francis Lacassin, 'Out of Oblivion: Alice Guy Blaché', *Sight and Sound*, vol. 40 no. 3, Summer 1971.

H

HADDON, Alfred Cort (1855–1940)

British zoologist and ethnologist. Professor of zoology at the Royal College of Sciences and assistant naturalist to the Science and Art Museum of Dublin, in which capacity he visited the Torres Strait islands, north of Queensland, Australia in 1888 and 1889, to examine marine biology. Fascinated by the customs of the native islanders, Haddon put together a team of scientists for the Cambridge Torres Strait Expedition of 1898. Spending almost seven months on the islands and in New Guinea from April 1898, Haddon took along a **Newman** and Guardia 35mm camera and recorded a number of films on the Murray Islands in September 1898. Problems with the camera in the tropical heat meant that only a few films could be taken (by Haddon himself) of dances and fire-making. These still exist and are of high quality. In addition, Haddon made a number of phonographic recordings of islander speech, which have also survived. It is not known if the films, the first ever use of the medium as an ethnographic record, were ever screened, but scenes from them were used as illustrations in Haddon's official expedition reports. Haddon wrote many books, including *Magic and Fetishism* (1906) and *History of Anthropology* (1910), and can be properly said to have established the basic field techniques of modern anthropology. (CL/LMcK)

References

Alfred C. Haddon, *Head-Hunters: Black, White and Brown* (London: Methuen, 1901).
Chris Long and Pat Laughren, 'Surprising Survivals from Colonial Queensland', *Cinema Papers* 96, December 1993.
A. Hingston Quiggin, *Haddon, the Head Hunter: A Short Sketch of the Life of A. C. Haddon* (Cambridge: Cambridge University Press, 1942).

HANCOCK, Sophie (c. 1855–1926)

One of a number of prominent women Bioscope pioneers. Throughout the 90s and early 1900s the firm of W. C. and S. Hancock dominated Britain's West Country fairground scene. This was due in part to their enormous collection of rides and shows, but also because of the flamboyant characters who ran the firm – William, Charles and their older sister Sophie, who was particularly well remembered, long after her death, for her outrageous hats, booming voice and colourful use of the English language. Verbal accounts suggest that the firm was persuaded to enter the cinema-show business by one of their in-laws, Richard Dooner (1870–1951), who worked as the lion-tamer in their menagerie show. His father, James Dooner, an ex-shadowgraph artiste, had given brief demonstrations of a cinematograph apparatus in Bristol. (In the early 1900s the Dooners would move to South Wales and tour the 'Dooner's Electrograph' Bioscope show, prior to opening a small but prosperous chain of cinemas. And in 1934 Richard Dooner became president of the National Cinematograph Exhibitors Association.)

The first recorded sightings of a Hancock show incorporating film occurred during the 1898 season, when they travelled with a joint exhibition entitled 'Edison's Electric Biograph and Japanese Entertainment'. By 1900 the original combined show had been replaced by a more ornate, purpose-built 'walk-up' booth – the 'Bio-Tableau'. In 1906, the start of the golden age of the Bioscope show, the 'Bio-Tableau' was modified to form a double-entrance centre-organ show, 'Hancock's Electric Palace of Varieties'.

The Hancocks continued to reign supreme until 1913 when the firm's entire, uninsured, collection of rides and shows was inadvertently razed to the ground in Devonport, following an arson attack by local suffragettes on an adjacent woodyard. The fire was also recorded on film by a locally based Pathé cameraman, and brief footage still survives. Despite the setting up of a nationwide relief fund by the showman's paper, *The World's Fair*, the firm never recovered.

Charles died in 1916, William in 1918 – and Sophie in 1926, in a London park. (Other notable contemporaries of Sophie Hancock include the nonagenarian operator Elizabeth Crecraft ('Crecraft's Wild Beasts and Living Pictures') of the West Midlands and South Wales, and Annie Holland ('Holland's Palace of Light') of the north and west Midlands.) (MH)

References

Mervyn Heard, *Wild Beasts and Living Pictures* (1983).

HATCH, Sir Ernest Frederic George (1859–1927)

Member of Parliament, amateur film-maker. Hatch was a Conservative MP with a particular interest in foreign issues. He travelled widely, most notably on a world tour from 1899 to 1900 to the Far East and Canada, during which he was accompanied by 'a skilled operator' with a cinematograph camera. The identity of this operator is unknown, but he was apparently kept busy, as about fifty films seem to have been taken during the tour, including some twenty shot in China, such as *Street Scene in Pekin* and *An Old Chinese Woman Spinning*, and about the same again in Japan and the Rocky Mountains.

By May of 1900 the pair were back in Britain. Two months later Hatch gave an exhibition of his films at Lord Wimborne's house in Mayfair, London, in aid of charity. But by this time the Boxer Rebellion in China was hot news, and while Hatch's films showed only views of daily life, the hunger for any visual reference to the events in China was such that the films quickly found a distributor. Harrison and Co. advertised Hatch's films in the trade press in September under the heading, 'Genuine cinematograph films of China', and the following month they were being shown at several London music halls. As the Chinese news cooled, Harrison also released the other films Hatch had taken during the trip, including panoramas taken from trains in the Rockies, geisha dances and several school scenes shot in Japan.

Hatch himself clearly did not consider his filming activities of great importance, failing to mention them in his book about the trip, even though this was one of the earliest ventures with a film camera into the Far East and, indeed, Canada. Hatch did not continue his association with the cinematograph: leaving Parliament in 1906 he followed the well-trodden Tory career path, serving on numerous government committees and eventually receiving a knighthood. (SB)

References

Optical Magic Lantern Journal, September 1900 to February 1901.
Ernest Hatch, *Far Eastern Impressions* (London: Hutchinson, 1904).

HATOT, Georges

Director. Hatot worked at the Hippodrome theatre, Paris, where he directed crowd scenes. In 1896 he directed the first of several comic and dramatic films he would make for the Lumière firm until 1901, including the thirteen-scene Passion play, *La Vie et la Passion du Jésus-Christ* (1897), with the pantomime actor Bretteau playing Christ. His dramas included a succession of famous deaths: *Execution de Jeanne d'Arc*, *Assassinat du Duc de Guise*, *Mort de Marat* and *Mort de Robespierre* (all 1897); his comedies, or records of various comic stage acts, included the celebrated **Footit and Chocolat**. Hatot's early film output is a useful reminder that Lumière did not only produce actuality film.

He subsequently directed dramas for Pathé before, in 1906, joining the new company of Eclipse, a French offshoot of the Charles Urban Trading Company, where he formed a team with ex-Gaumont designer and director, Victorin Jasset. The pair moved to Eclair in 1908, where they specialised in film series with regular characters (for example, Nick Carter) and produced a number of films in North Africa. (LMcK)

References

Abel, *The Ciné Goes to Town* (1994).

HAYDON, Frank and URRY, George

Manufacturers. Haydon and Urry, a firm of scientific engineers headed by Frank Haydon and George Urry, ran a business from 34 Gray's Inn Road, London, moving in late 1896 to 353 Upper Street, Islington. They produced the Autocosmoscope, advertised as 'the most perfect penny-in-slot seeing machine ever produced' showing 'lifelike reproductions of living pictures', though this stereo viewer showed only still images. Soon they were advertising a film projector, the Eragraph, purportedly of their own design and manufacture, having applied for a patent on 10 February 1897 (it received provisional protection only). It is possible, however, that the Eragraph owed more than a little to the projector design of German engineer **Max Gliewe**. Originally advertised as 'the New

Kinematograph', legal pressure may have made them change it to the Eragraph, first advertised under that name on 24 April. Four months later Haydon and Urry could boast that their projector was established in twenty principal theatres and music halls around the country. Their chief associate and exhibitor was **Randall Williams**. The Eragraph was a strong and reliable machine, popular with many travelling showmen.

Haydon and Urry also produced a small number of films, employing the brothers Richard and James Monte as operators, including scenes of Henley regatta, **Queen Victoria**'s Diamond Jubilee procession and two popular comedies, *The Bride's First Night* and its sequel, *Twelve Months After*, both released in December 1898. Little is known of Haydon and Urry themselves, though George Urry appears to have been their technician and to have headed the partnership. (DG)

References

Barnes, *The Beginnings of the Cinema in England* (vol. 2).

HEISE, William

Engineer. William Heise was **W. K-L. Dickson**'s 'right-hand man' in the development of the Edison Kinetoscope. Listed in the account books for 1890 Kinetoscope work as 'machinist' (he made the first experimental film perforator for Dickson), Heise went on to take an important part in the development of the first successful motion picture system. He operated the Kinetograph camera for many filming sessions from the earliest days, and can be seen in several photographs relating to Kinetoscope production, and as a Black Maria studio cameraman in drawings in *The Century* magazine (June 1894) and *Frank Leslie's Popular Monthly* (February 1895). He also has the distinction of appearing in what researcher Hendricks has called, 'the first "modern" motion picture in America', as he shakes hands with Dickson in a brief test that was reproduced in *The Phonogram* in October 1892.

When Dickson left Edison's employment in April 1895, Heise continued to produce films for the Kinetoscope and later the Vitascope, including a number of artistes from Barnam and Bailey's Circus in May that year and the popular cameo, the **May Irwin** *Kiss* of 1896. From May 1896 Heise was able to use a newly constructed portable camera, and Edison film production was freed from the constraints of the Black Maria. Scenes of Herald Square, Central Park, and the elevated railway on 23rd Street, New York, were among the first subjects, followed by sequences taken on a trip to Niagara Falls, scenes at Coney Island, short comedies and military subjects.

Working with the new head of the filming department, **James White**, Heise continued as an Edison cameraman, filming many subjects (some of them imitations of popular Biograph and Lumière films) such as the train film, *The Black Diamond Express*, and embarking on a major expedition to record President **William McKinley**'s inauguration. With White off around the world for ten months in 1897–8, Heise produced twenty-five copyrighted subjects, including winter scenes, in February 1898. He left Edison's employ in October that year, though he was shortly to return in a non-film role. (SH)

References

Hendricks, *The Edison Motion Picture Myth* (1961).
Musser, *The Emergence of Cinema* (1990).
Musser, *Before the Nickelodeon* (1991).

HEPWORTH, Cecil Milton (1874–1953)

Producer, director, writer, inventor. Perhaps the leading creative figure in the British silent cinema, Cecil Hepworth was the son of the noted magic lanternist and scientific lecturer, T. C. Hepworth. He first encountered films when he saw **Robert Paul**'s Kinetoscope exhibit at Earl's Court in 1895. His inventiveness and knowledge of photographic and lantern techniques led to a varied career in the early film industry. On 21 July 1896 he was assistant to **Birt Acres** when the latter gave a royal command performance at Marlborough House. While writing for *Photographic News* and other journals, Hepworth operated as a travelling showman during 1897, also writing

The ABC of the Cinematograph, the first British book to be published on the new phenomenon. In 1898, with his cousin Monty Wicks, he joined **Charles Urban** at Maguire and Baucus in Warwick Court, a firm which shortly afterwards changed its name to the Warwick Trading Company. His first film for them was of that year's Oxford and Cambridge boat race, which he had developed at **Alfred Wrench**'s shop at 50 Gray's Inn Road.

Summarily sacked by Urban, Hepworth and Wicks set up their own film company, Hepworth and Co. (with their eponymous trademark Hepwix) in 1899 at Walton-on-Thames, where they were soon joined by H. V. Lawley. Hepworth acted as director, writer, producer and occasional actor, while gradually building up an impressive roster of popular stars that made the renamed Hepworth Manufacturing Company (registered 1904) pre-eminent in the British film business before the First World War. Among the stars were Gladys Sylvani, Alma Taylor, Chrissie White and Henry Edwards, and his directors included Percy Stow and Lewin Fitzhamon, the latter of whom made the immensely popular *Rescued by Rover* (1905). Many of the most celebrated early titles produced by Cecil Hepworth were in fact not directed by him.

In 1910 he experimented with synchronised sound with his own Vivaphone system. By 1915 the company had turned to feature-film production, with Hepworth now regularly directing, but their fortunes declined with those of British films as a whole, and after a failed attempt to regain former glories with *Comin' Thro' the Rye* (1923) the company went bankrupt in 1924. Hepworth clung on to the fringes of the film industry, ending up directing trailers for National Screen Services. He lectured on film history, and became chairman of the BFI's History Committee, assisting in the research behind the first volume of Rachael Low's *The History of the British Film*.

A major figure in the early years of British film-making and a source of inspiration and prestige for the industry at that time, he followed the typical pattern of an innovator unable to move with the times. His autobiography, *Came the Dawn*, though uncertain about the order of events for the early years, is a richly detailed and informative account of the period. (LMcK)

References

Cecil M. Hepworth, *The ABC of the Cinematograph* (London: Hazell, Watson & Viney, 1897).
Cecil M. Hepworth, *Came the Dawn: Memories of a Film Pioneer* (London: Phoenix House, 1951).

HERTZ, Carl (Louis Morgenstein) (1859–1924)

Magician. One of several famous magicians who were to add films to their repertoires during the early years of cinematography, Carl Hertz was born in San Francisco and, after becoming proficient in the art of magic, toured the USA and Europe appearing in various music halls. Like **David Devant**, the popular conjuror of the Egyptian Hall, Piccadilly, Hertz acquired one of the first Theatrograph projectors made by **Robert Paul**, and took it with him on his tour of South Africa and the Antipodes. He had sailed from England on 28 March 1896 aboard the Royal Mail steamer, *Norman*, and during the voyage had exhibited the Theatrograph to the passengers. He was thus probably the first person to have shown films at sea. On arrival in South Africa, Hertz gave a press show at the Empire Theatre of Varieties, Johannesburg on 9 May and two days later presented the first public screening of moving pictures ever to be held in that country. The films shown on that occasion included *Highland Dances*, *Street Scenes in London*, *Trilby Dance*, *Military Parade* and the famous *Soldier's Courtship*, which Paul had shot on the roof of the Alhambra theatre, Leicester Square, in April. This little comedy must have been sent out to him by Paul after Hertz had left England.

Hertz visited various towns in South Africa and then went on to Australia, which he had first visited in 1892. Here he showed the Theatrograph to a invited audience at the Melbourne Opera House on 17 August 1896, and four days later gave the first public performance to a paying audience at the same venue. This was the first time that films had been seen by the general public in Australia, if we discount the films previously exhibited by the

Edison peepshow Kinetoscope. After Australia he took his magic show and Theatrograph to Ceylon (Sri Lanka), India, China, Japan, the Fiji islands and Hawaii. In 1924 he published his autobiography. As far as is known, Hertz never appeared in any films, but he deserves to be remembered in the history of the cinema as an important figure who brought films to a wider audience throughout the world. (JB)

References

Barnes, *The Beginnings of the Cinema in England* (vol. 1).
Barnouw, *The Magician and the Cinema* (1981).
Carl Hertz, *A Modern Mystery Merchant* (London: Hutchinson, 1924).
Chris Long, 'Facts and Fables', *Cinema Papers* 92, April 1993.

HITCHCOCK, Mary Ellen

Author and explorer. Of all the unlikely pioneers of the cinema, Mary Hitchcock (née Higgins) might well win a prize in the category, 'strange but true'. Born in Virginia, she married a US navy commander, Roswell D. Hitchcock, with whom she travelled widely. When he died the urge to travel continued, and teaming up with Miss Edith Van Buren, a grand-niece of the former US President, these two prosperous women determined to visit Alaska. It was then the summer of 1898, and the height of the gold rush, but, rather than panning for gold, they hoped to make their names through showmanship, taking an 'animatoscope' and a bowling alley up north (along with a music box, a parrot, two cages of live pigeons, two Great Danes, stuffed olives, oysters, a zither, a mandolin, an ice-cream freezer and the largest tent ever brought into the Yukon). This unconventional scheme was suggested by a man named Von Millengen, who came along as technical manager.

When they arrived in the 'Golden North' it soon became apparent that there was little interest in the bowling alley, as it took up too much space in the boom town of Dawson City. But animatoscopes were in great demand, and the women found that they already had competition in the form of one 'Arizona Charlie', whose film of a train passing the camera had sent the entertainment-starved miners wild. But, run on cheap petrol, his machine blew up on the second night. That should have left the field clear for Von Millengen and the women, but unfortunately their animatoscope, films (and redundant bowling alley) were delayed in transit, and when the equipment finally arrived they found that their limelight retort and gas bags were full of holes.

However, by the middle of September everything was working, and the show opened to great acclaim. They had brought about a dozen films to Alaska, including 'the **Corbett** fight' and films relating to the Spanish-American War, such as the funeral of the Maine victims. 'Arizona Charlie' (surname Meadows) had none of these war views, and in any case he was now banned by the theatre as a fire hazard, so the triumph of the women was total. But they did not continue long in the animatoscope business, returning to the USA a month later, where Mary gave lectures and published her account of the trip. She soon returned to the Klondike, however, remaining there for five years, during which time she staked over a hundred claims. This adventurous life was strangely contrasted with her New York existence, where she presided over a salon at the Waldorf-Astoria. Interestingly, at about the same time that the two women were showing films in Alaska, **Robert Bonine** was also there filming the gold rush for Edison. Some of the films shown in Dawson at the turn of the century were rediscovered in the 1970s, preserved in good condition in the permafrost. (SB)

References

Mary E. Hitchcock, *Two Women in the Klondike: The Story of a Journey to the Gold-fields of Alaska* (New York/London: George Putnam's Sons, 1899).

HOLLAMAN, Richard G. (1854–1929)

President of the Eden Musée, an amusement house and musical theatre on New York's 23rd Street. The Eden Musée was founded in 1883 in imitation of London's Madame Tussaud's waxworks, and in the 90s was run by Englishman Richard G. Hollaman, who first introduced moving pictures as an attraction at the Musée by installing an **Anschütz** Electrical Schnellseher in 1892, followed by **Charles Chinnock**'s imitation Kinetoscopes in 1895.

Moving pictures on a screen came via the Lumière Cinématographe on 18 December 1896. Making a logical step from waxworks of the famous to moving images of the same, the Eden Musée became the pre-eminent showcase for the new art in the USA. The Musée turned for a short while to the Cinématographe Joly, a machine operated by **Eberhard Schneider**, but after a fire in June 1897 Hollaman booked the Lumière machine once more, while commissioning engineer Frank Cannock to construct a projector specifically for the Musée's use. This had been installed by August 1897, with the peripatetic **Edwin S. Porter** assisting in its operation.

Hollaman's most notable foray into film came after he failed to acquire the *Horitz Passion Play* (a mixture of film, slides, music and lectures based on a Passion play performed in an Austrian village) in late 1897, the rights being purchased by theatrical producers **Klaw and Erlanger**. Hollaman, having seen the Horitz film, and feeling that he could do better, decided to produce a film version of the Oberammergau Passion play. However, his text was based on an old play by Salmi Morse, and the resultant film, photographed on the roof of the Grand Central Palace, Lexington Avenue, by **William Paley**, bore little relation to its supposed source. The eventual film starred Frank Russell as Christ and was 'directed' by Henry C. Vincent. Stage director Vincent, however, had no conception of moving pictures, and was not about to be told his own business, so Paley and the company had to make the film in his unwitting absence. The finished film lasted twenty minutes (narration, musical interludes and possibly slides were added to extend the programme) and was given a press showing on 28 January 1898. *The Passion Play of Oberammergau* proved very popular (even when the Oberammergau claims were exposed) receiving praise from the clergy and running twice daily for three months. Versions of the production then toured the country.

Edwin S. Porter rejoined the staff of the Musée at this time as William Paley's films of the Spanish-American War supplanted the *Passion Play*. The Musée offered a kind of proto-news service, arranging its war films in chronological order, eventually adding a new film a day to the programme, and in October 1898, as interest in the war was waning, combining film, music and sound effects into a *Panorama of the War*. The Eden Musée's association with film diminished as the medium grew wings, but, as Charles Musser has demonstrated, its story shows the vital creative function of the exhibitor at this period in film history. (LMcK)

References
Musser, *Before the Nickelodeon* (1991).
Charles Musser, 'The Eden Musée in 1898: The Exhibitor as Creator', *Film and History*, vol. 11 no. 4, December 1981.

HOLLAND, Andrew M. and George C.

Canadian entrepreneurs. Motion picture films as a commercial business made their debut on 14 April 1894 at 1155 Broadway, New York, at the Holland brothers' Kinetoscope parlour. Ten machines were set up, with customers paying 25 cents to view a row of five machines, which offered such sights as **Eugen Sandow** and the two **Ena Bertoldi** films, *Blacksmith Scene* and *Highland Dance*. Shortly afterwards, on 17 May, a second parlour was opened by the Holland brothers in a Masonic temple in Chicago, with a further ten machines.

The men to whom **Thomas Edison** had entrusted the first commercial exploitation of his invention were Andrew and George Holland, Ottawa businessmen who had variously dealt before in publishing, bookselling, typewriters, steamship lines and, crucially, Edison Phonographs. With the formation by **Norman Raff** and **Frank Gammon** of the Kinetoscope Company to exploit the new machine, Andrew Holland (the prominent figure of the two and a founder member of the Company) was well placed and eager to take up the opportunity. Following the successful debut of the Kinetoscope, the Holland brothers further exploited the machine, including selling six to **George Georgiades**, who had taken the Kinetoscope to Paris by July 1894.

Then in 1896 came the launch of the Vitascope and projected Edison film, and the Hollands were granted exclusive rights to its exploitation in Canada. The Vitascope made its debut on 21 July 1896 in West End Park, Ottawa, a joint venture betwen the Hollands and the Ottawa Electric Railway Company, with magician **John C. Green** ('Belsaz') hosting. The Vitascope moved on to Toronto in September (where it was joined by the newly arrived Lumière Cinématographe). Having sold the various territorial rights to Canada, and earning what money they could from the seemingly passing phenomenon, the Holland brothers pass out of cinema history. (LMcK)

References
Hendricks, *The Kinetoscope* (1966).
Morris, *Embattled Shadows* (1978).

HOLMES, Elias Burton (1870–1958)

Lecturer. Born into a prosperous Chicago family, as a boy E. Burton Holmes gave magic shows to family and friends. As a young man, he toured the USA and overseas, making lantern slides from his photographs of the trips. Slides of an 1890 visit to Europe were shown at the Chicago Camera Club, of which he was secretary. After this success he gave a public performance, *Through Europe with a Kodak*, to aid club funds. The lectern lamp failing midway, his ad-lib performance proved more effective and he later worked without a script. Sophisticated and elegantly tailored, his stage appearance was striking and his delivery 'crisp'. Returning from a trip to Japan in 1893, he decided to become a professional lecturer, with Oscar B. Depue as lantern operator, but found that his local success with the Japan lecture – and a later lecture based on an 1895 cycle tour of England, France, Italy and Switzerland – was not repeated elsewhere, and he continued lecturing with only patchy success.

In the summer of 1897, Depue bought a Gaumont camera in Paris and began making moving pictures, first shown as a tailpiece to Holmes's slide lectures, with the camera modified as a projector. From 1899–1900, interspersed at relevant moments throughout the shows, the films (including the Grand Canyon and the Hopi Indians' snake dance, shot on a home-made successor to the Gaumont camera) became increasingly important. Depue constructed a new 60mm projector and another camera in 1899, using the latter on a 1901 world tour that took in Siberia, China and Japan, but in 1902 abandoned the bulky format for a more convenient 35mm Warwick Bioscope camera.

Holmes and Depue made many expeditions in the succeeding years: to Norway, Alaska, Egypt, Greece and elsewhere. In 1904 Holmes coined the term 'travelogue', and a contract with Paramount (1908–22) resulted in several years of weekly travelogue releases in Paramount theatres. Burton Holmes continued to lecture until shortly before his death in 1958. (SH)

References

X. Theodore Barber, 'The Roots of Travel Cinema: John L. Stoddard, E. Burton Holmes and the Nineteenth-Century Illustrated Travel Lecture', *Film History*, vol. 5 no. 1.
Oscar B. Depue, 'My First Fifty Years in Motion Pictures', *Journal of the SMPE*, vol. 49, December 1947 [reprinted in Fielding, *A Technological History of Motion Pictures and Television* (1967)].

HOPWOOD, Henry Vaux (1866–1919)

Author of the most important Victorian book on cinematography. Hopwood was custodian in the library of the Patent Office in Chancery Lane, London, when he started work on *Living Pictures*, a comprehensive history and handbook of the new science. He gathered material for the book throughout 1898 with appeals for information in *Optician and Photographic Trades Review*, who published it the following year. It is a thoroughly researched and lucid account of a difficult subject, detailing patents and giving advice on production and presentation. The complexities of the technology are tempered with occasional philosophical musings: 'The whole history, not of this world alone, but of every sphere that is or has been, is still in vibrating existence, and one universal perception extending through the infinity would embrace within the tremblings of the boundless ether an eternal and universal living picture of all past events.' In September 1899 *Optician* published an article by Hopwood on trick films entitled 'Kinematographic Pictures: Their Errors and Falsities', together with a supplement to bring his book up to date.

He stayed with the Patent Office throughout his career, rising to the post of assistant librarian. He retained an interest in cinematography but was unable to find the time to produce a revised edition of his book, which task eventually fell to a trusted colleague, R. B. Foster. Hopwood contributed a preface to the 1915 edition. He died on 5 December 1919. (SH)

References

Barnes, *The Beginnings of the Cinema in England* (vol. 4).
R. B. Foster, *Hopwood's Living Pictures* (London: Hatton Press, 1915).
Henry V. Hopwood, *Living Pictures: Their History, Photo-Production and Practical Working* (London: Optician and Photographic Trades Review, 1899).

HOWE, Lyman Hakes (1856–1923)

Travelling showman, exhibitor. Lyman Howe was a prominent travelling showman with a fixed circuit of middle-class film exhibitions that promoted, in Charles Musser's apt phrase, 'high-class moving pictures'. Born in Wilkes-Barre, Pennsylvania, Howe had received only brief schooling when he went on the road in the early 70s as a travelling salesman, later working for the Central Railroad of New Jersey after his father's early death. He went on the road again in 1883 exhibiting an intricate miniature working model of a coal mine, and between 1890 and 1896 travelled across eastern Pennsylvania and then upstate New York giving phonograph concerts with an Edison machine. In 1896, he tried to acquire a Vitascope from **Raff and Gammon**, but the territory he wanted, and already knew from his phonograph tours, went instead to a Philadelphia group. He built his own motion picture projector, the Animotiscope, which he premiered in his home town on 4 December 1896 using Edison films spliced together in a long programme. With this machine Howe added films to his concert presentations, featuring the phonograph and the Animotiscope through to the end of the 1899 lecture season.

Usually travelling a circuit of church halls and small towns, Howe gradually moved into opera houses, and by 1903 he had established a number of centrally booked travelling companies and had himself withdrawn from personal exhibition. As nickelodeons proliferated in small towns, Howe moved into larger cities, exhibiting in opera houses or legitimate theatres and meeting halls specially rented for the occasion. The emphasis was still on 'high-class' programmes, with films of the Olympic games, the wedding of King Alphonse of Spain and a variety of travel programmes and news-worthy events. His road companies developed a stable exhibition circuit for annual or twice-yearly appearances across the east and Mid-west. His activities are comparable to the lecture presentations of John L. Stoddard (1850–1910) and **Burton Holmes**, and represent an important alternative pattern of exhibition to either fixed theatres or fairground showmen. In addition to contracting for special films from a variety of European and American suppliers, Howe had been making his own films since 1901, experimenting at first with local views, then news scenes, and finally travel films. His business lasted, as something of an anachronism, until 1920, and after Howe's death continued as a commercial film laboratory and distributor of educational short subjects. (DR)

References
Charles Musser, with Carol Nelson, *High-Class Moving Pictures: Lyman H. Howe and the Forgotten Era of Traveling Exhibition, 1880–1920* (Princeton NJ: Princeton University, 1991).
X. Theodore Barber, 'The Roots of Travel Cinema: John L. Stoddard, E. Burton Holmes and the Nineteenth-Century Illustrated Travel Lecture', *Film History*, vol. 5 no. 1, 1993.

HUGHES, William Charles
(1844–1908)

Optician, lantern manufacturer. Concerned with supplying cinematograph equipment almost from the birth of the industry, Hughes was the successor of William Parberry Hughes, chemist and druggist, of 151 Hoxton Street, London. Before becoming a manufacturing optician W. C. Hughes had entertained on the stage, receiving high praise for his dramatic readings, humorous songs and performances of magic and mystery. From 1879 to 1882 Hughes traded in optical equipment and magic lanterns from Hoxton Street, but in 1883 moved to Brewster House, 82 Mortimer Road, off the Kingsland Road. The following year he patented an improved Choreutoscope, a special mechanical lantern slide (previously manufactured by Beale of Greenwich) for producing on the screen dancing skeletons and similar effects, and based on an intermittent mechanism related to the Maltese cross that would later be used in many film machines.

Early in 1897 he began to sell equipment designed by **Prestwich** (the Moto-Photo-scope projector and Moto-Photograph camera), and eventually designed and produced his own cameras, projectors and accessories. One novel projector used a piston mechanism. A huge 'Street Cinematograph' peepshow based on the Photo-Rotoscope projector, equipped with viewing apertures for sixteen spectators or more, was apparently popular. Hughes was responsible for two films of **Queen Victoria**'s 1897 Diamond Jubilee procession, and in 1898 penned a series of articles in the *Optical Magic Lantern Journal* entitled, 'A Little Information About the Cinematograph'. His business survived into the next century, by which time he had earned himself an honourable place among the pioneers of the British film industry. He died on 7 August 1908, aged sixty-four. (SH)

References
Barnes, *The Beginnings of the Cinema in England* (vols. 2–4).

HYMAN, Edgar M. (?–1936)

Theatrical manager, cameraman and showman. During the 90s Hyman was the manager of the Empire Theatre of Varieties, Johannesburg, where **Carl Hertz** gave South Africa's first film shows in May 1896. Greatly impressed by this novelty, Hyman acquired a camera from **Charles Urban** in 1897. Hyman was undoubtedly making films by the following year, among which were street scenes in Johannesburg, and he may also have filmed on the SS *Scot* during a voyage from Britain to South Africa. In September 1898 he claimed to have filmed President Kruger leaving his house in Pretoria en route to the Raadzaal, though in an interview **Joseph Rosenthal** stated that this film was his own work. What is certain is that in January 1899 Hyman, together with the Empire's musical director, Dave Foote, presented a show of this and other films to the President himself and his

69

guests in the Residency, Pretoria; Kruger was said to be most impressed, especially with the film of himself.

Later that year, with the Boer War about to flare up, Hyman was on his way back to South Africa after one of his periodic visits to London. Arriving in Johannesburg he found the Empire closing in preparation for the coming hostilities, and was forced to decamp with the company to Cape Town, where he found another hall in which to give his shows. Thus Hyman was in the right place to witness the first British and colonial troops arriving in South Africa. In November he filmed Sir Redvers Buller in Cape Town, and over the next couple of months recorded a variety of British and colonial regiments disembarking or marching through the city. Hyman himself followed the troops to the western front some time in December 1899, after which he apparently joined up with Joseph Rosenthal at the Orange River, and ended up filming the raising of the British flag over Pretoria in June 1900.

After the war Hyman continued in the music hall business, and in 1912 formed a company running a chain of theatres and distributing films in South Africa. Unfortunately, in the following year the company went into liquidation, a sad reverse for the man who had helped bring the cinema to South Africa. (SB)

References

Barnes, *The Beginnings of the Cinema in England* (vols. 3 and 4).

Thelma Gutsche, *The History and Social Significance of Motion Pictures in South Africa, 1895–1940* (Cape Town: Howard Timmins, 1972).

I

INAHATA Shotaro

Japanese Lumière representative. Hailing from Kyoto, as a young man Inahata was sent on a scholarship to La Martinière technical school in Lyon, where he studied muslin-weaving and spinning from 1877 to 1885, and made the acquaintance of **Auguste Lumière**, who was attending the same school. Establishing himself as a successful businessman in Japan, he went back to France in 1896, and on his return was followed by **François-Constant Girel**, a Lumière Cinématographe and fifty reels of film. On 15 February 1897, with Girel as operator, Inahata gave Japan its first projected film programme at the Nanchi theatre in Osaka. According to Japanese sources, Girel was not at ease with the machinery and nearly caused an explosion, but the show was a considerable success, and Inahata was soon giving performances in Kyoto and other cities. However, the Edison Vitascope had followed the Cinématographe exactly one week later at Osaka's Shinmachi theatre, and the fastidious Inahata found the ensuing competition wearying and distasteful. He handed over the business to **Yokota Einosuke** and returned to the weaving and spinning business. Among the films taken by Girel is one that is probably of the Inahata family taking a meal. (LMcK)

References

Peter B. High, 'The Dawn of Cinema in Japan', *Journal of Contemporary History*, vol. 19 no. 1, January 1984.

IRWIN, May (Ada Campbell)
(1862–1938)

Stage comedienne, music hall singer and star of America's first screen kiss. Born Ada Campbell in Canada, she made her vaudeville debut in 1875. After her double act with her sister broke up in 1883 she played comedy roles in the legitimate theatre, returning to variety in 1887 in a series of farcical sketches. From the mid-90s she starred in stage comedies, often introducing ragtime songs such as, 'A Hot Time in the Old Town Tonight'. In April 1896 she was persuaded by Edison's agents **Raff and Gammon** to appear with John C. Rice in a filmed scene from their Broadway success, *The Widow Jones*. Though *The May Irwin Kiss* lasted for only fifteen seconds, the close-up sequence caused immense enthusiasm (and an almost equal degree of disapproval) when shown by the Vitascope at music halls throughout the USA. May Irwin made her last stage appearance in 1922, having starred in at least one other film, *Mrs Black is Back* (1914). Her partner in what Terry Ramsaye described as a 'high vacuum kiss' also appeared on screen again, playing a lady dentist's patient in Biograph's *The Kleptomaniacs* (1900). (BA)

References

G. C. D. Odell, *Annals of the New York Stage* (New York: Columbia University Press, 1927–49).

Ramsaye, *A Million and One Nights* (1926).

ISOLA, Emile (1860–1945)
and **Vincent** (1862–1947)

Showmen, manufacturers, impresarios. Born in Blinda, Algeria, the Isola brothers were trained as mechanics, but their passion for magic brought them to Paris in 1880, where they worked in railway machine shops while developing their magic skills by giving performances in cafés in the evenings, ultimately becoming full-time itinerant performers. According to legend, they were backed in their purchase of the Théâtre des Capucines in 1892, on a boulevard near the Grand Café, by a wealthy woman whose dying son they had entertained. Renamed the Théâtre Isola, they featured their own magic shows, some with the aid of electricity, and were competitors to **Georges Méliès**.

Adding films to their theatre's presentations on 8 April 1896, their first projector was a Kinétographe **de Bedts**, which they renamed the Isolatographe; using the same name, they sold a Kinétographe of Méliès and Lucien Reulos just two weeks later to the new theatre at 34 Unter den Linden, Berlin, but the apparatus worked poorly. Within weeks they were manufacturing their own projectors, still called the Isolatographe, for use as far away as Vienna, Brussels and Moscow.

Fundamentally Parisian theatre managers, they directed a series of theatres: the Parisiana, the Olympia, and finally the nearly bankrupt Folies Bergère, which they rebuilt into a great music hall with first-class variety shows. (DR)

References

Paul Duval, *Folies Bergère* (Paris, 1954).
Barnouw, *The Magician and the Cinema* (1981).

J

JANSSEN, Pierre-Jules-César
(1824–1907)

Astronomer, chronophotographer. Jules Janssen was permanently lamed by an accident in early childhood. He studied at the University of Paris, and in 1865 became professor of general science in the school of architecture. He was an enthusiastic observer of eclipses. In 1870, when Paris was besieged during the Franco-Prussian War, he fled the surrounded city in a balloon so that he could reach the path of totality of a solar eclipse in Africa. And on 8 December 1874, equipped with his photographic revolver, Janssen travelled to Japan to record and observe the transit of the planet Venus across the face of the sun. The photograph most sought by astronomers was that showing the precise moment when the outline of the planet first encroached on the sun's disc. As that moment was unpredictable, a clockwork 'revolver' was devised to take a sequence that would include the required image. The revolver took forty-eight exposures in seventy-two seconds on a daguerreotype disc. This process was no longer in general use, but it proved ideal for the project, the metal plate ensuring an absence of halation (flare), which could have been a problem if a glass plate had been used (a wet plate would in any case have been inconvenient to use in such a camera). With the sun as the source there was no shortage of light, so the 'slow' daguerreotype process was ideal, and the images were of good quality. Two English expeditions also used apparatus as suggested by Janssen to record the transit of Venus.

Janssen presented the photographic revolver to the Société Française de Photographie in 1875, and to the Académie des Sciences in April 1876, where he suggested that it might be used for the study of animal movements, especially those of birds, when materials sensitive enough to permit the very brief exposures necessary became available. Janssen's experiments influenced **E-J. Marey**'s later chronophotographic work, and his camera used a modified version of the Maltese cross-type mechanism that would later be of such importance in cinematograph engineering design. For two three-year periods (1891–3 and 1900–2), he served as president of the Société Française de Photographie, a position also held by Marey and **Louis Lumière**.

Janssen appeared in two very early Lumière films, *Débarquement du Congrès de Photographie à Lyon* – where he is easily distinguishable by his particularly bushy white beard – and *M. Janssen causant avec M. Lagrange*, filmed on 11 June 1895 and shown to the Congress the next day. For the latter film, Janssen and Lagrange were secreted behind the screen and spoke the dialogue of their conversation as the film was projected. In 1904 he published his great *Atlas des photographies solaires*, containing more than 6,000 solar pictures. He died on 23 December 1907 at

Meudon, France, where he had been director of the Observatory. A crater on the moon is named after him. (SH)

References
Coe, *The History of Movie Photography* (1981).
Hecht, *Pre-Cinema History* (1993).

JEFFERSON, Joseph (1829–1905)

The first major actor to appear on screen. The filming by **W. K-L. Dickson** of eight scenes from Jefferson's long-standing stage success, *Rip Van Winkle*, in August 1896 provided the newly established Biograph company with considerable prestige and demonstrated the cinema's potential for preserving historic performances. Born into a family of actors, Jefferson made his debut in 1832. He became well known on the New York stage in the 50s, and, in 1865, appeared as 'Rip' in Dion Boucicault's adaptation of Washington Irving's tale at the Adelphi theatre, London. Thereafter the piece, described by Biograph as 'America's Greatest and Most Popular Play', remained at the centre of his repertoire. The play was also filmed by his son, Thomas Jefferson, in 1914. (BA)

References
G. C. D. Odell, *Annals of the New York Stage* (New York: Columbia University Press, 1927–49).

JEFFRIES, James J. (1875–1953)

Boxer. Born in Carroll, Ohio, Jim Jeffries moved to California in 1881 and remained there until the end of his life. Originally an ironworker, he took up boxing in 1896 with a success that owed more to brute force than sporting finesse. Having been **Jim Corbett**'s sparring partner for the 1897 world heavyweight contest, he won the championship himself by defeating **Bob Fitzsimmons** in 1899, an event filmed in part by Vitagraph before their arc lamps burned out. Jeffries defended the title up to 1903, retired the following year, then made a comeback in 1910, when he was heavily defeated by Jack Johnson.

His successful defence of the title on 3 November 1899 against Tom Sharkey at the Coney Island Sporting Club, organised by **William Brady**, was filmed in its 25-round entirety by the American Mutoscope and Biograph Company, the first fight to be filmed successfully by artificial light. Filming at night by the light of 350 miniature arc lamps (and pirated on the night by **Albert Smith** filming for Vitagraph), Biograph employed

four cameramen: **F. S. Armitage**, **Billy Bitzer**, **Arthur Marvin** and **Wallace McCutcheon**. A 'fake' re-enactment, as was becoming common, was also produced by Lubin. (LMcK)

References
Musser, *The Emergence of Cinema* (1990).

JENKINS, Charles Francis (1867–1934)

Inventor. C. Francis Jenkins and **Thomas Armat** together invented one of the most effective motion picture projectors of their day, presenting projected films for paid admission in September 1895.

Jenkins was raised on a farm near Richmond, Indiana, and by 1890 the amateur inventor was working as a civil service stenographer in Washington DC. His motion picture experiments began as early as 1891, and from 1893, funded by one James P. Freeman, he employed an engineer to work on an apparatus for 'the recording and reproduction of action', possibly a rotary-lens camera and/or cabinet peepshow device. By the summer of 1894, he had apparently had some success with projecting moving images of very limited size, and in 1895 he quit his job to pursue inventing full time.

In October 1894 Jenkins had met Thomas Armat at the Bliss School of Electricity, and on 25 March 1895 they made a formal agreement to work together. Armat wanted to use Jenkins's cameras to supply films for his projection experiments; Jenkins wanted Armat to fund the projection developments. Soon abandoning experiments with continuously moving film, they tried a mutilated-gear mechanism, but it was quickly damaged by the stresses involved. Armat sketched out an idea for a piston arrangement to move the film, spurring Jenkins to revive an arrangement that he had tinkered with previously – the eccentric gear, or 'beater', movement (similar to that patented in France in 1893 by **Georges Demenÿ**). This proved successful and in late September 1895, charging 25 cents admission, they projected Kinetoscope films to audiences at the Cotton States Exposition, Atlanta, in two small screening rooms served by a common projection booth.

'Borrowing' one of their three Phantascopes (a name he used for most of his motion picture devices, leading to confusion for modern researchers), Jenkins departed in mid-October to give a projection demonstration in his birthplace, Richmond, and did not return. He filed a patent as sole inventor, but this was ruled to be 'in interference' with a joint patent taken out previously, and eventually the case was decided in favour of the joint application. On 18 December 1895 Jenkins demonstrated 'his' projector to a distinguished audience at the Franklin Institute, Philadelphia, and was awarded a medal for progress in the field. After protestations by Armat, most of the developments were recognised as joint efforts. Embittered by the dispute, Jenkins later falsely claimed successful film projection at Richmond on 6 June 1894 – more than a year before his documented demonstrations in that town. In the spring of 1896, while Armat negotiated with **Raff and Gammon** to allow Edison to exploit their projector, Jenkins formed a short-lived agreement with the Columbia Phonograph Company, but eventually sold the Phantascope rights to Armat (though he continued to exhibit with a version of his machine, claiming its superiority over the Vitascope).

Jenkins went on to found the Society of Motion Picture Engineers (now SMPTE). In 1925, neck and neck with British pioneer John Logie Baird, he demonstrated mechanical television. By the late 1920s he had become a prominent figure in American television development, employing novel transmission equipment that involved prismatic glass scanning discs. Backed by the De Forest Radio Company, he operated experimental television stations in Washington DC and New York, and by 1931 was selling receivers for the home. Jenkins eventually held more than 400 patents in such diverse areas as paper containers, automobiles and radio aerials for aeroplanes. (SH)

References

C. Francis Jenkins, *Animated Pictures* (Washington, 1898; reprinted Arno 1970).

Bruce Cory (ed.), *Masterpieces of Moving Image Technology* [exhibition catalogue] (New York: American Museum of the Moving Image, 1988).
H. Mark Gosser, 'The Armat–Jenkins Dispute and the Museums', *Film History*, vol. 2. no. 1, 1988.
John V. L. Hogan, 'The Early Days of Television', *Journal of the SMPTE*, vol. 63, November 1954 [reprinted in Fielding, *A Technological History of Motion Pictures and Television*, 1967].
Gene G. Kelkres, 'A Forgotten First: The Armat-Jenkins Partnership and the Atlanta Projection', *Quarterly Review of Film Studies*, vol. 9 no.1, Winter 1984.
Musser, *The Emergence of Cinema* (1990).

JOLY, Henri (1866–1945)

Inventor. One of the early French researchers, who, along with **Lumière, de Bedts** and a few others, conceived perforated cinema film as early as 1895.

Born at Viomenil, Vosges, in 1866, Henri Joly started in 1889 as gymnastics instructor at the school of Joinville, where **Marey** and **Demenÿ** sometimes came to take chronophotographs. Attracted by all things mechanical, he discovered the Edison Kinetoscope at its presentation in Paris in September 1894. Early in 1895 he met **Charles Pathé**, a phonograph merchant with a shop in Vincennes. From May 1895, Pathé imported the Kinetoscopes manufactured in England by **Robert Paul**. The fairground clientele tired of always seeing the same films, and the copies were out rapidly, so Joly offered to make a camera for Pathé in order to renew the stock of films. Pathé advanced the necessary funds, and on 26 August 1895 Joly filed his patent for a camera capable of serving both the projector and Kinetoscope. His machine used a mechanical movement inspired by the Demenÿ system. With this camera, in September or October 1895, Joly made *Le Bain d'une mondaine*, a 'smoking-room' film for the Kinetoscope. On 8 November 1895 he filed another patent for the 'Photozootrope', a large Kinetoscope with four eyepieces. Some examples were manufactured, but it was not a great success.

In 1896, Pathé came to understand the importance of the camera/projector manufactured by Joly. He broke with the inventor but reserved for himself the rights in the precious camera and started to exploit the machine and its films, with the success that everyone knows. Joly deposited three other patents in 1896: one for a camera, another for a method of avoiding flicker, and a third for a process of film-in-depth. In association with the businessman and engineer Ernest Normandin, he exploited the 'Cinématographe Joly' (called the 'Royal Biograph' after the disaster at the Bazar de la Charité in 1897, when a Joly projector had been in use, even though the fire had been caused by a Molteni ether lamp). The Joly-Normandin Cinématographe was exhibited in Britain (where it followed Lumière at the Empire, Leicester Square) and Ireland as Professor Jolly's Cinematograph.

In 1900, with the brothers Ernest and Edgar Normandin, Joly created the Société du Biophonographe, energetically exploiting an electric system for synchronising the projection of film with the sound from a phonograph. Some sound films were made and projected, such as *Lolote*, a short talking playlet, but the company went bankrupt in 1902. Joly sold his patents to Georges Mendel, who in turn launched into the production of talking films.

In 1906, Joly created the Société des Phonographes et Cinématographes Lux, which produced a number of films, but he left two years later, following disagreements. He continued his researches, studying new systems for sound cinema. In 1905 he envisaged a system of recording sound film by means of a beam of light reflected from a mirror which vibrated in response to sound waves, but he was unable to translate his research into concrete form, and to earn a living he worked in an ironmonger's. Twenty years later, he was working as a nightwatchman. Joly, who had introduced Charles Pathé to the technique of cinematography, died in Paris in 1945, destitute and totally forgotten. (LM)

References
Mannoni, *Le grand art de la lumière et de l'ombre* (1994).

K

KAWAURA Ken'ichi

Producer. Kawaura Ken'ichi was a wealthy businessman who ran the Yoshizawa Company (a family firm that he had acquired through marriage) with numerous interests, including the selling of pictures and lantern slides and the organisation of widespread lantern shows. Through his contact with an Italian adviser to the Japanese army, Cipione Braccialini, Kawaura somehow acquired a Lumière Cinématographe in January 1897, and he was able to launch his first film show at Yokohama's Minato theatre on 9 March 1897. Kawaura's Yoshizawa Company was destined to become a major force in early Japanese exhibition, importing Lumière and then **Georges Méliès** titles, and opening a London office in 1902.

Kawaura went to the 1904 St Louis International Exposition, where he showed films of the Russo-Japanese War as well as scenes of everyday Japanese life. He then journeyed throughout the USA, visiting the Edison and Lubin studios, and on his return to Japan in 1907 ordered the construction of Japan's first film studio at Mejuro, on lines very similar to what he had seen at Edison. The Yoshizawa Company was one of the four major Japanese firms (another was that run by **Yokota Einosuke**) which, in imitation of the Motion Picture Patents Company in the USA, combined in 1909, when Kawaura sold out and retired from the business. The combine became Nikkatsu in 1912, Japan's most enduring film company. (LMcK)

References
Joseph L. Anderson and Donald Richie, *The Japanese Film: Art and Industry* (Princeton NJ: Princeton University Press, 1982, expanded ed.).
Peter B. High, 'The Dawn of Cinema in Japan', *Journal of Contemporary History*, vol. 19 no. 1, January 1984.

KEITH, Benjamin Franklin (1846–1914)

Theatre owner, manager. Benjamin Franklin Keith's unbroken commitment to the new medium of motion pictures from June 1896 onwards was a significant factor in making the vaudeville circuit the most important American venue for early film exhibition.

Born in Hillsboro Bridge, New Hampshire, Keith worked at Bunnell's Museum in New York in the early 60s, later joining P. T. Barnum and then the Forepaugh Circus. In 1883 he presented a show in Boston in partnership with Colonel William Austin, and then slowly began to open a series of vaudeville theatres across the country, all operating under his innovative idea of providing refined entertainment at popular prices. His reforms of the previously vulgar forms of vaudeville were immensely successful and he brought many theatrical stars into the variety theatre, as well as raising performers' salaries.

Keith's Union Square theatre in New York was the site of the first American exhibition of the Lumière Cinématographe, opening on 29 June 1896, and Keith obtained the exclusive American rights to the Lumière apparatus for its first few months of use in the USA, opening quickly in Philadelphia, Boston and other cities. Dominant in New England, New York City and the mid-Atlantic states, Keith's vaudeville theatres became a significant and stable early circuit for American film exhibition with his contract for Biograph exhibitions in late 1896; he remained loyal to that firm until July 1905 even in the face of declining business after 1902, finally replacing Biograph with the Edison Kinetograph service of Percival Walters. Keith merged his theatre circuit with the 'continuous vaudeville' houses of F. F. Proctor in June 1906, and from about that time converted many large but marginally profitable popular vaudeville theatres in smaller New England towns into nickelodeons, sometimes alternating popular vaudeville and film presentations. He withdrew from his business engagements in 1909 due to ill health, though he remained an active patron of art and musical organisations in Boston, and some 400 theatres bore his name at the time of his death in 1914. (DR)

References

The Green Book Album, March 1909.
Musser, *The Emergence of Cinema* (1990).

KENYON, James
See **MITCHELL, Sagar**

KLAW, Marc
See **ERLANGER, Abraham**

KLEINE, George (1864–1931)

Producer, distributor. A key figure in the establishment of the film industry in the USA, George Kleine's father, Charles, ran a small optical store in New York, manufacturing and selling stereopticons (magic lanterns) and other optical devices. On joining the family firm, George moved to Chicago and set up the Kleine Optical Company in 1893. The company sold stereopticons, lantern slides and, from September 1896 onwards, motion picture equipment. Initially dealing only in American products, this included **Edward Amet's** Magniscope and from 1899 an exclusive arrangement for Edison films and film equipment in the Chicago area. From 1903, to Edison's annoyance, he began dealing in Biograph and European films as well, and he was one of those who were instrumental in establishing the film rental system in the USA. He also moved into production with the formation of the Kalem

Company in 1907 (named from the initials of its founders: Kleine, Long and Marion). He became a key figure in the bitter patents fight that arose in 1908, instigated by Edison and solved (temporarily) by Kleine with the creation of the Motion Picture Patents Company.

Kleine continued to derive his greatest prestige from importing European films, notably the Italian epics, *Quo Vadis* (1913) and *Gli ultimi giorni di Pompei* (*The Last Days of Pompei*) (1913). The First World War severed many of his European contacts, and he largely withdrew from the film industry, by now a very wealthy man. In the 1920s he continued to distribute films and to maintain a position of prestige within the industry, while further developing his long-running interest in educational films, but had retired by 1928. (LMcK)

References

Rita Horwitz and Harriet Harrison, *The George Kleine Collection of Early Motion Pictures in the Library of Congress: A Catalog* (Washington: Library of Congress, 1980).

KOMADA Koyo

Japanese *benshi*, or lecturer. Komada Koyo was the first Japanese film star, not for his appearances on film but for the commentary he gave to accompany films. The *benshi*, a peculiarly Japanese form of lecturer, were the stars of the first years of Japanese cinema, greatly embellishing the simple plots being played out on the screen, adapting narratives to suit all occasions, and gaining huge popularity in their own right, so much so that they had a severely restricting effect on Japanese film form for many years.

Komada first appeared as a *benshi* for the Edison Vitascope of **Arai Saburo** in March 1897 at the Kikikan theatre, an important early venue for film in Japan and for Japanese film. By 1899 Komada had become an independent promoter with his Association of Japanese Motion Pictures (Nihon Sossen Katsudo Shashin Kai), by which he instigated several films taken by **Shibata Tsunekichi**, starting with films of geisha dances shown at the Kabuki theatre on 20 June 1899 and then the first Japanese fiction film, *Inazuma goto Hobaku no Ba* (*The Lightning Robber is Arrested*); Komada's commentary for this film could be adapted to fit any type of criminal known to the audience, and the film was immensely popular. Other films followed in 1899, all shot by Shibata, of which the most notable was a record of the Kabuki actors **Danjuro IX** and

Kikugoro V, *Momiji-gari (Maple Leaf Hunters)*. Komada went on to have a successful career as a *benshi*, later giving commentary to the Russo-Japanese War films that dominated Japanese screens in 1904–5. (LMcK)

References
Peter B. High, 'The Dawn of Cinema in Japan', *Journal of Contemporary History*, vol. 19 no. 1, January 1984. Komatsu Hiroshi, 'Some Characteristics of Japanese Cinema before World War I', in Arthur Nolletti Jr. and David Desser (eds.), *Reframing Japanese Cinema: Authorship, Genre, History* (Bloomington and Indianapolis: Indiana University Press, 1992).

KOOPMAN, Elias Bernard (1860–1929)

Businessman. One of the four men who founded the KMCD syndicate, which later became the American Mutoscope and Biograph Company. Elias Koopman, unlike his partners (**Dickson**, **Marvin** and **Casler**), had a commercial rather than a technical background, running the Magic Introduction Company which marketed magical toys and optical novelties, including the Photoret pocket watch detective camera invented by Casler and Dickson (**Billy Bitzer** was also a company employee).

After being involved in the establishment of the American operation during 1895 and 1896, Koopman came to England in January 1897. The 'American Biograph' opened at the Palace theatre in Shaftesbury Avenue in March, and ran continuously until the end of 1902. However, the agreement that Koopman negotiated with the Palace was unsatisfactory, and though he became managing director of the British Biograph Company, he was soon overshadowed by the dominating personality, and greater financial skill, of the chairman, **W. T. Smedley**. A combination of poor results and a suggestion that he was not spending as much time running the company as he ought forced his resignation in June 1903. Koopman continued to trade as a merchant in London until 1927. He then returned to the USA and in August 1929 committed suicide in a New York hotel. (RB)

References
Hendricks, *Beginnings of the Biograph* (1964). Brown and Anthony, *The History of the British Mutoscope and Biograph Company* (1996).

KRIZENECKY, Jan (1868–1921)

The first Czech film-maker. The cinema arrived in the Czech lands of the Austro-Hungarian Empire on 15 July 1896 when the Lumière Cinématographe was demonstrated by one Goldschmidt, working for the Lumière concessionaire **Eugène Dupont**, at the Casino, Karlovy Vary. Thereafter numerous travelling showmen visited Karlovy Vary and Prague throughout 1896 with film projectors in tow, but it was two years later that the first native Czech films were made.

Jan Krizenecky was an architectural student and a keen photographer who had visited Paris and, with colleague Josef Pokorny, purchased a Cinématographe. In June 1898 he first exhibited at the Architecture and Engineering Exhibition in Prague some short actualities and three short comic films under the banner of 'Cesky Kinematograf' (Czech Kinematograph), thus allying cinema to the growing demand for Czechs to be recognised as a nation. The films were *Dostavencicko Ve Mlynici (Appointment at the Mill)*, *Plac a Smich (Tears and Laughter)* and *Vystavni Parkar a Lepic Plakatu (The Billsticker and the Sausage Vendor)*, and all three starred popular comic café performer and postcard publisher, **Josef Svab-Malostransky**, who went on to have a very successful film career.

Following these first experiments, Krizenecky filmed various topical events with his modified Cinématographe, notably the Sokol sports festival in Prague in 1901. Taken from a high tower to capture the full effect of the spectacular gymnastic display, this was an event that he would return to annually. He continued to write and direct films over the next decade, eventually working for Kinofa, the first Czech film company. Leaving the world of film in 1910, he went on to work for the Prague city archive. (LMcK)

References
Zdenek Stabla, 'Beginnings of the Czech Cinema', in Holman, *Cinema 1900–1906* (1982). Zdenek Stabla, 'The First Cinema Shows in the Czech Lands', *Film History*, vol. 3 no. 3, 1989.

KUHN, Edmund
See **WEBSTER, Charles**

L

LATHAM, Woodville
(1837–1911), **Gray** (1867–1907) and **Otway** (1868–1906)

Woodville Latham

Producers, showmen. In the summer of 1894, two young brothers, Gray and Otway Latham, drug company salesmen operating out of New York, became concessionaires for the Edison Kinetoscope and formed the Kinetoscope Exhibition Company with an associate, Samuel J. Tilden, and former classmate, **Enoch J. Rector**. The firm's chief aim was to photograph and exhibit prizefight films. Rector, working at the Edison plant, enlarged the capacity of the Kinetoscope, and in June Michael Leonard fought Jack Cushing in the Black Maria studio. In August the Latham-Rector-Tilden Kinetoscope parlour opened at 83 Nassau St, New York, with six enlarged machines, each showing one round. The venture was a success, and a second fight was arranged between **James Corbett** and Peter Courtney (Corbett's royalties would eventually exceed $20,000). In September a second parlour opened in New York City, followed shortly after by others in Boston, Chicago, St Louis and San Francisco.

Determined to get life-size motion pictures on the screen, they called upon their father, Major Woodville Latham, for assistance. Major Latham had had a distinguished career as an ordnance officer of the Confederacy during the American Civil War. For a time he was professor of chemistry at the University of West Virginia. In December, the Lathams formed the Lambda Company (the Greek 'L' for Latham), and a start was made in their quest for a motion picture projector. **W. K. L-Dickson** was in on the deal, though he was still working for Edison, and **Eugène Lauste**, previously an Edison employee, was taken on as mechanic. Shortly after the first camera test in February, a film was made on the roof of the workshop at 35 Frankfort Street, New York: it showed Woodville Latham smoking a pipe, while the others in the team fooled around. A press demonstration of the Panoptikon projector was held on 21 April 1895 at Frankfort Street. Motion picture production started in earnest, however, on the roof of Madison Square Garden on 4 May with the Griffo–Barnett fight, when a 'top loop' mechanism was employed in the camera (to prevent the intermittent mechanism pulling on the unexposed stock), so enabling much longer lengths of film to be taken at one time. Other films included the Nicholas Sisters' 'split dance', Duncan C. Ross and Ernest Roeber wrestling, a picturisation of the hit song, 'The Sidewalks of New York', and – filmed in Atlantic City – *The Waves*.

On 20 May a public showing opened in a small store at 156 Broadway. Despite the use of 2-inch wide film to enable more light to be thrown on the screen, the projector, little more than a Kinetoscope with an arc lamp behind it, was inadequate. The *Photographic Times* commented: 'There is considerable room for improvement and many drawbacks have yet to be overcome.' But some encouragement was given: 'Even in the present state the results obtained are most interesting and even startling. Quite a crowd of people visit the store ... making their exit wondering "How it's done".'

Rector eventually left the company to pursue other motion picture possibilities, and a young nephew of the Lathams, LeRoy Latham, toured Virginia with the Panoptikon. The machine was renamed the Eidoloscope and in May 1896 gained an intermittent. The top loop, designed earlier to reduce the stress on the long lengths of film used in their camera, and known as the 'Latham Loop', was added to the projector, to reduce tension on the intermittently moving film. (A similar arrangement was being developed at about the same time by **Thomas Armat**.) Films produced by Gray Latham and Lauste included *Bullfight*, shot in Mexico and lasting for more than ten minutes.

Caught up in internal squabbling and complex legal and technical problems, by 1898 the Lathams were forced to abandon motion pictures, and by the early years of this century they had lost their patent interests to the photo firm of Anthony and Scoville. Otway and Gray were both dead by 1910, the latter fatally injured in a tram accident. Old Major Latham outlived them both, and shortly before he died in 1911 gave testimony regarding the 'Latham Loop' at a hearing of the Motion Picture Patents Company. (SH)

References
Hendricks, *The Kinetoscope* (1966).
Musser, *The Emergence of Cinema* (1990).
George C. Pratt, 'Firsting the Firsts', in Deutelbaum, *'Image' on the Art and Evolution of the Film* (1979).
Ramsaye, *A Million and One Nights* (1926).

LAUSTE, Eugène Augustin (1857–1935)

Pioneer mechanic in the earliest days of motion pictures, and inventor of early optical sound-film systems. Born in the Montmartre district of Paris on 17 January 1857, he 'early displayed inventive and mechanical talents of a high order', and before he was twenty-three had filed patents for numerous devices. In 1886–7 he became chief mechanical assistant to **W. K-L. Dickson** at Edison's establishment at West Orange, where he stayed until 1892, and was involved in the first Kinetoscope experiments. For a while he worked on developing a gasoline engine for possible motor car use, then in 1894 became associated with the **Latham**s and their Eidoloscope/Panoptikon projects, constructing projectors, cameras and printing equipment and shooting the first film for the machine: the Griffo–Barnett prizefight. Years later, Dickson credited him with the invention of the 'Latham Loop' and second sprocket that enabled much longer films to be taken. He subsequently worked with **Jean LeRoy**, and in 1896 Lauste joined Dickson at American

Biograph, shot a number of films for the company, and for some time was in charge of their laboratory and experimental plant near Paris. Historian Gordon Hendricks considered Lauste next to Dickson and **Muybridge** as the most significant contributors to motion picture invention in the USA.

Having long been fascinated by the possibilities of sound recording, particularly on celluloid film, in 1900 he started to construct some elements of a system. He left American Biograph in 1901, moving to Britain, and in 1904 built his complete apparatus for experimental purposes. It was very crude but he was encouraged, and applied (with backers R. T. Haines and J. St Vincent Pletts) for a British patent on 11 August 1906 for 'A new and improved method of and means for simultaneously recording and reproducing movements and sounds.' (This patent became a 'best seller' for the Patent Office when sound-film research reached its zenith in the late 1920s.) By now he was working at Dickson's experimental laboratory in England, but Dickson declined to get involved with his sound experiments. Aided by funding from the London Cinematograph Company, he made various experiments with light valves and oscillating mirrors to find a workable method of producing the necessary narrow beam of light, and by 1910 had achieved success with a vibrating wire acting between the poles of two magnets. At about this time he began an association with German experimenter Ernst Ruhmer, who had had some success with recording sound optically with the 'Photographone', and in 1910 Lauste took his first experimental sound films in the garden of his home in Brixton, London. During a 1911 (1913?) trip to the USA he demonstrated his camera/projector, and shot at least one short sound film, and in 1912 he began experiments to devise a pneumatic amplifier for his system.

Though lack of capital and the First World War meant that he was never to succeed in making his sound-film processes commercial, his researches and experiments were of lasting importance. Lauste's son Emile later became a film cameraman, and at seventy-two years of age, Eugène Lauste was still working, now for Bell Laboratories. (SH)

References
Merritt Crawford, 'Some Accomplishments of Eugène Augustin Lauste – Pioneer Sound-Film Inventor', *Journal of the SMPE*, vol. 16, January 1931; and Merritt Crawford, 'Pioneer Experiments of Eugène Lauste in Recording Sound', *SMPE Journal*, vol. 17, October 1931 [both reprinted in Fielding, *A*

Technological History of Motion Pictures and Television (1967)].

Harald Jossé, *Die Entstehung des Tonfilms* (Frieburg/ Munich: Verlag Karl Alber, 1984).

LAVANCHY-CLARKE, François-Henri (1848–1922)

Swiss businessman. From 1889 Henri Lavanchy-Clarke was the representative in Switzerland of the English firm of Lever brothers, manufacturers of Sunlight Soap. He had to face the competition of Marseilles soap and to combat custom duty, which was heavier on individually wrapped pieces of soap (an English innovation) than on consignments imported in bulk. The boldness of his publicity campaigns impressed his employers, pioneers in commercial advertising, and led to his interest in moving images, which he saw as a further means to promote Sunlight Soap. The Swiss National Exhibition held in Geneva from 1 May to 18 October 1896 was confined to native products. Lavanchy-Clarke therefore had the idea of building on a site next to the exhibition a vast Japanese pavilion called Le Palais des Fées. Despite the limitations imposed on publicity, the public readily associated it with Sunlight Soap. Among the attractions offered to sightseers, the Cinématographe Lumière had a prominent place. Seventy thousand spectators attended his film show during the six months of the exhibition, and it attracted considerable press attention. He then organised further screenings throughout the country, always linked to advertising (entry to the show cost less to housewives who had a coupon cut from the *Sunlight Almanac*).

Almost all the Swiss subjects in the Lumière catalogue were filmed under Lavanchy-Clarke's direction and date from 1896–7. Some specifically advertise Sunlight by 'product placement' (*Laveuses, Défilé de 8éme Bataillon*) or Le Palais des Fées (*Cortège arabe, Danse Eygptienne*). Many show the Swiss Village, which was the principal attraction of the Geneva exhibition. The traditional attribution of the 'Swiss' views in the Lumière catalogue to **Alexandre Promio** is not confirmed by any formal proof, and the date of the films makes it implausible. The frequency with which Lavanchy-Clarke appears in the films suggests that he was the producer not the cameraman, the latter function possibly being performed by his younger brother Emile Lavanchy (1857–1923).

It appears that Lavanchy-Clarke, the owner of one Cinématographe and possibly a second, was never subject to the three-party contract which in other cases in 1897 bound concessionaire, the Lumière factories and the operator, and which established a permanent control of receipts and performances. We do not know the reason for this independence, nor why Lavanchy-Clarke was involved as an intermediary in the negotiations which led to the contract on 26 March 1896 with **Ludwig Stollwerck**, a Cologne sweet manufacturer, for the exploitation of the Cinématographe in the German empire.

Stollwerck's company represented the Edison Kinetoscope and had since 1895 supported the researches of the Englishman **Birt Acres,** before negotiating indirectly with Lumière. **Georges Demenÿ** may provide the key. Lavanchy-Clarke, who in 1889 founded a company for the exploitation of coin-in-the-slot machines, had shown an interest in research into moving images well before the Cinématographe. With his stepfather, William Gibbs Clarke, he was one of the four founders of the Société Française du Phonoscope (1892–5), which aimed to develop the work being carried out by Demenÿ. Lavanchy-Clarke himself appears on a Phonoscope plate dating from 1893 or 1894 (he is sitting in a chair polishing one of his shoes). The two other founders of the company were Demenÿ and Ludwig Stollwerck. The German industrialist had had ties with William Hesketh Lever (1851–1925), probably since the end of the 80s. This link allows us to place, if not explain, the involvement of Lavanchy-Clarke in the network which, in this connection, also extended to England. It was probably Lavanchy-Clarke who took a Cinématographe to Port Sunlight (the model factory village built by Lever on the River Mersey near Liverpool), and he was one of the cameramen who filmed **Queen Victoria**'s Diamond Jubilee celebrations in London in June 1897.

Lavanchy-Clarke did not play a decisive role in the expanding Lumière English production, but he was certainly influential in his employers' large-scale use of Cinématographe shows for advertising. On at least two occasions, between November 1897 and February 1898, the soap and dairy product industries – Lever brothers and Nestlé – co-operated on intensive campaigns, using on the first occasion films of the Jubilee and on the second a cricket test match between England and Australia, taken by **Henry Walter Barnett** in Sydney in December 1897. In the publicity the 'famous Lumière Cinématographe' was explicitly mentioned as a supplementary attraction and a guarantee of quality.

In 1899, a year after the opening of the Helvetia soap factory, producing Sunlight Soap made under licence, Lavanchy-Clarke retired from the firm and apparently gave up his cinematographic equipment. A strange character, whose missionary calling found an outlet in philanthropic work for the blind, he was more an impresario than a businessman, a man for advertising and public relations rather than a manufacturer. His grandson deposited in the Archives du Film du Centre National de la Cinématographie 200 original Lumière films which had remained with the family. (RC)

References

Roland Cosandey, 'Le Catalogue Lumière 1896–1907 et la Suisse: éléments pour une filmographie nationale', *1895*, no. 14, December 1993.
Roland Cosandey and Jean-Marie Pastor, 'Lavanchy-Clarke: Sunlight & Lumiére, ou les débuts du cinématographe en Suisse', *Equinox* no. 7, June 1992.

LEAR (Albert Kirchner)

Producer of religious and pornographic films. In the autumn of 1896 the photographer and pioneer film-maker **Eugène Pirou** arranged for the filming of the striptease from Louise Willy's stage success, *Le Coucher de la mariée*. This pioneering risqué film was directed for Pirou by one Léar (real name Albert Kirchner), and it is just possible that this is the man behind a company called Lear and Co. in Cairo which was prosecuted in 1901 for exporting pornographic pictures to Europe. Pirou himself was well known for trading in risqué postcards at this time, and perhaps the two men met through this trade. In any case, the success of *Le Coucher de la mariée* led Léar to continue to work in the cinema, and in January 1897 he and two colleagues, Anthelme and Pacon, patented a film camera and formed a company to exploit it. Léar then teamed up with an educationalist, Father Bazile, and together they made a dozen short comedy films in the summer of 1897.

Such an association between a former pornographer and a priest is not quite as bizarre as it seems; the French Catholic Church was very interested in visual propaganda at this time, and, through its publication division *La Bonne Press*, was determined to use the new medium of cinema for its own purposes. In the summer of 1897 Léar, in collaboration with Michel Coissac (later a noted film historian), made a twelve-scene version of the *Passion du Christ*, shot in Paris using actors who had appeared in a *tableau vivant* version of the Passion. This was the first film version of the Bible story, and was shown widely (in February 1898 in the USA it formed part of an illustrated lecture given by the Revd Thomas Dixon, author of *The Clansman* on which D. W. Griffith's *The Birth of a Nation* would be based). Though the representation of Christ on film outraged some, the theme was to be tackled by many other film-makers during this period. In 1898 Léar opened a short-lived cinema in the basement of the Olympia theatre, but in the same year sold all his negatives to Gaumont. He died fairly soon after this. (SB)

References

Jacques Deslandes, *Le Boulevard du cinéma à 'époque de Georges Méliès* (Paris: Editions du Cerf, 1963).
Mannoni, *Le grand art de la lumière et de l'ombre* (1994).

LE BLOND, Elizabeth Alice F. (?–1934)

Mountain film-maker. A member of the British nobility, Mrs Aubrey Le Blond (she married her third husband Francis Bernard Aubrey Le Blond in 1900) lived mainly in Switzerland from the 1880s, becoming the first president of the Ladies' Alpine Club in 1907. She wrote several books on mountaineering and mountain photography, and was known as an expert Alpine camera artist (writer E. F. Benson describing her pictures as 'quite unrivalled'). What turned her towards animated photography we do not know, but certainly she had acquired a camera and had taken some films by early 1900, her 'interesting subjects … of snow sports in alpine regions' are praised in the 1900 edition of **Cecil Hepworth**'s *Animated Photography*. She probably managed to sell some of her films, since ten are listed in **James Williamson**'s 1902 film catalogue, all taken in the Engadine valley in Switzerland, including St Moritz. These were between 50 and 100 feet each, and included three films of bob-sleigh racing, three of tobogganing and two of skating on the Kulm rink. Few though they may be, these films make Le Blond the world's first mountain film-maker, ahead of such pioneers as Frank Ormiston Smith and Frederick Bullingham, and also one of the first women to make films.

Le Blond evidently did not think her film-making of any great significance as she fails to mention it in her autobiography, perhaps because her life encompassed so many other activities: as well as writing and photographing, she lectured, travelled widely, worked in the

Service de Santé Militaire in the First World War, and was made a Chevalier de la Légion d'Honneur in 1933. (SB)

References

Mrs Aubrey Le Blond, *Day in, Day Out* (London: Bodley Head, 1928).

LE COUTEUR, William John
(1858–1905)

Producer. Originally a surgeon, Le Couteur founded an exclusive 'Photographic Association' in 1894 at the suggestion of the Duke of Newcastle. He also became the agent for the Demenÿ/Gaumont film equipment, and a large selection of 60mm paper-print film clips taken by him in 1897 survive in the British film copyright records. At this time his film work must have been quite extensive, and he claimed to have spent over £200 filming **Queen Victoria**'s Diamond Jubilee with three cameras. Despite his social connections, Le Couteur was not a successful businessman, and in 1898 was replaced as head of the Gaumont agency in England by his one-time assistant, **A. C. Bromhead**. In May 1905, depressed by his lack of success and increasing financial worries, he and his wife Maud committed double suicide at the Photographic Association premises in Brook Street, Hanover Square, London. (RB)

References

Clive Holland, 'A Photographic Ghost – A Chat with Mr John Le Couteur', *The Idler* 1897, pp. 94–107.

LENO, Dan (George Wild Galvin)
(1860-1904)

British music hall, pantomime and film comedian. Billed on his 1897 American appearance as 'The Funniest Man on Earth', Dan Leno's humour was often based on the hardships he had endured as a young variety performer. Like Chaplin, both his parents were entertainers, his slum birthplace in London's Somers Town suggesting that they were far from successful. Economic necessity dictated his debut as an acrobat at the ramshackle Cosmotheca music hall, Paddington, in 1864. By 1866 his father had died and his mother's remarriage to the comedian Will Leno led to a migration to Liverpool, where Dan and his brother regularly appeared as 'The Brothers Leno – Champion Dancers'.

For the next fifteen years the family pursued engagements throughout the north of England, Scotland and Ireland. By his late teens Dan was appearing as a solo performer, winning a 'world' clog-dancing competition at Leeds in 1880. Following a triumphant London debut in 1885, a succession of pantomime engagements at the Surrey theatre and Drury Lane established him as the nation's favourite comedian. Leno's adroit use of mime gave emphasis to a stream of absurd, yet believable, patter that revolved around the uncertainties of everyday life. As a shop assistant, swimming instructor or housewife, he struggled to explain himself to an increasingly confused, but delighted, audience. When words failed, he would break into manic dances or take gigantic leaps across the stage: a form of expression that was to make him an ideal subject for film-makers.

As with Stan Laurel, who resembled him closely, the diminutive Leno had a Hardy-like foil in the massive form of Herbert Campbell (1846–1904). The two comedians became a theatrical institution as they entertained Drury Lane audiences in sixteen consecutive productions. Towards the end of their lives Leno and Campbell featured in several comedy films. Both appeared in *The Rats* (1900), *Burlesque Attack on a Settler's Cabin* (1900), *Burlesque Fox Hunt* (1900), all made for Warwick; and for Biograph, *Dan Leno and Herbert Campbell Edit 'The Sun'* (1902). Leno's solo films, made for Warwick, Biograph and **Birt Acres**, include *Dan Leno's Attempt to Master the Cycle* (1900), *Dan Leno's Cricket Match* (1900), *Dan Leno's Day Out* (1901), *Dan Leno, Musical Director* (1901), *Dan Leno's Record Score* (1901), *Bluebeard* (1902), *Dessert at Dan Leno's House* (1902) and *An Obstinate Cork* (1902). Sadly, all are lost, but a Kinora reel does survive. For Leno, the strain of continuous performance led to a series of breakdowns and an early death at the age of forty-three. (BA)

References

J. Hickory Wood, *Dan Leno, His Infinite Variety* (London: Methuen, 1905).

LEO XIII (1810–1903)

Pope. Perhaps the single most remarkable coup achieved by a film cameraman in the 90s was when **W. K-L. Dickson**, after months of trying, managed not only to film Pope Leo XIII but to get him to bless the camera as he did so. According to Dickson, the American Biograph Company was approached by a group of Roman Catholic prelates, among them Monsignor Martinelli and Cardinal

Gibbons, who had been impressed by the Biograph and especially by the popular reaction to the scenes of President **William McKinley**. They thought that it would make an excellent film if the Catholics of America could see similar picures of the Pontiff and 'receive the Pope's benediction'.

Armed with letters of recommendation and the encouragement of the Biograph Company, which had gained much prestige for its exclusive pictures of the famous, Dickson (by now working for Biograph's British division) went to Italy early in 1898. Four months of negotiation followed before Dickson obtained permission to film a man who had not even posed for a photographer for eight years. In April/May 1898 he took twelve scenes in five sittings of the Pope in the Vatican grounds, in his carriage, walking, being carried in a sedan chair and seated with attendant clerics. Crucially, Dickson secured film of Leo XIII raising his hand in blessing (both from his carriage and while seated): meant for the Biograph audience, it gave every impression of being bestowed on the camera itself. Pope Leo was not shy of the camera, performing for it with evident enthusiasm in what is a charming series of films that became justly famous. (LMcK)

References

H. L. Adam, 'Round the World for the Biograph', *Royal Magazine*, June 1901.

LE PRINCE, Louis Aimé Augustin
(1842–1890?)

Inventor. The son of a major in the French artillery, young Louis was given lessons in photography by family friend, L. J. M. Daguerre, and after college at Bourges and

Paris did postgraduate work in chemistry at Leipzig. He studied art, and specialised in the painting and firing of art pottery. Invited to Leeds by John R. Whitley, he stayed and joined the firm of Whitley Partners, brass founders, and in 1869 married Miss Lizzie Whitley, who had trained at the Sèvres pottery. During the Franco-Prussian War he survived the siege of Paris as an officer of volunteers, and on his return to England the Le Princes set up a school of applied art in Park Square, Leeds. Le Prince carried out photography on metal and pottery, and his portraits of **Queen Victoria** and Gladstone were placed in the foundation stone of Cleopatra's Needle in London.

In 1881 he went to the USA and became manager of a group of artists who made large circular panoramas in New York, Washington and Chicago. Soon afterwards he started experimental work on moving picture machines in the workshops of the New York Institute for the Deaf, where his wife taught, and in 1886 he applied for an American patent for a machine using one or more lenses (illustrating the most difficult proposition, incorporating sixteen lenses). The patent was granted in January 1888, but deleted claims for machines with one or two lenses as having been already covered by others. His patents in Britain, France and elsewhere, however, allowed a one-lens version. In Paris, sometime in 1887, he produced a sixteen-lens machine, which used two picture bands moving alternately, to demonstrate 'proof of working', and several sets of pictures were taken. Back in Leeds he rented a workshop at 160 Woodhouse Lane and engaged woodworker Frederick Mason and J. W. Longley, inventor of an automatic ticket machine, and by the summer of 1888 had constructed two 'receivers' (cameras), each with a single lens and intermittently moving take-up spool. Paper negatives were exposed in his father-in-law's garden apparently as early as October 1888, and scenes of traffic on Leeds Bridge were taken at about the same time, at between twelve and twenty pictures per second.

Projection was more of a problem, due to the unsuitability of the paper base and the registration difficulties with unperforated bands. Undeterred, Le Prince (who according to Frederick Mason was 'most generous and considerate and, although an inventor, of an extremely placid disposition which nothing seemed to ruffle') built a 'deliverer', or projector, having three lenses and three picture belts and apparently using the Maltese cross intermittent movement. This probably used belts of glass slides, the fibre belts moving alternately to ensure that an image was always on the screen, thereby reducing flicker. A single-lens projector featured a rather impractical spiral arrangement for delivering the slides to the lens in succession. These machines did not succeed to Le Prince's satisfaction, and he probably experimented with celluloid, which offered a more suitable image base, in 1889.

While Le Prince was experimenting in Leeds, his wife and family remained in New York, having rented and renovated a mansion in preparation for showing his apparatus and motion pictures. Apparently troubled by financial problems, in the summer of 1890 he packed up his equipment ready for the move to New York, and in August went to France with his friends, Mr and Mrs Wilson. He left them at Bourges to visit his brother at Dijon, where he was last seen boarding the train for Paris on 16 September. He subsequently disappeared, and despite intensive searches by French and English detectives, not a single clue as to his fate was ever discovered. (SH)

References

Christopher Rawlence, *The Missing Reel. The Untold Story of the Lost Inventor of Moving Pictures* (London: Collins, 1990).
E. Kilburn Scott, 'Career of L. A. A. Le Prince', *Photographic Journal*, May 1931 [reprinted *Journal of the SMPE*, vol.17, July 1931 and in Fielding, *A Technological History of Motion Pictures and Television* (1967)].

LEROY, Jean Aimé (1854–1932)

Showman. LeRoy claimed to have been the first in the world to project a film to an invited audience at the Riley brothers' optical shop, New York, in February 1894, a year before the generally accepted 'first screening' by the Lumières in Paris of their *La Sortie des usines Lumière*, showing workers leaving the Lumière factory at Lyon.

Born near Bedford, Kentucky, USA, LeRoy's father was (ironically) from Lyon. The young LeRoy was apprenticed to a New York photographer at sixteen, and some years later, hearing of Henry R. Heyl's motion projections of posed photographic sequences, made a crude motion picture viewing device for animating 200 posed shots of a waltz, taken on glass plates. He later claimed that in 1893 he had obtained film from **Wordsworth Donisthorpe** in England and built a projector, with gripper-roller movement, to show it;

that after a private preview of an Edison Kinetoscope in December 1893 he had adapted his machine to take perforated film and on 5 February 1894 had projected two Kinetoscope films – *Washing the Baby* and *The Execution of Mary Queen of Scots* – to an audience of about twenty-five at Riley's optical store, 16 Beekman Street, New York; and that he projected films to a paying public early in 1895, from which a handbill dated 22 February and advertising 'Le Roy's Marvelous Cinematographe' at the Opera House (Clinton, New Jersey) still exists. It has been pointed out that the two Kinetoscope films cited were produced after the 1894 date claimed for the show, and that there is no evidence of there having been an 'Opera House' in the small town of Clinton. (Some researchers have even suggested that the handbill is a fake, printed years later to support his claims.) LeRoy did not patent his projector, and there are no contemporary references to either of the latter two events. Supporters have suggested explanations for this, but taken together they cast significant doubts on the authenticity of LeRoy's claims. Though certainly present at the dawn of film projection, it seems he inflated and predated his own achievements. (SH)

References

Leo Sauvage, *L'Affaire Lumière* (Paris: Lherminier, 1985).
Macgowan, *Behind the Screen* (1965).

LI HUNG CHANG (Li Hong-jang) (1823–1901)

Chinese politician. A soldier turned politician, Li Hung Chang was the virtual head of government in China during Emperor Kuang Hsu's infancy, and was certainly the most prominent Chinese figure to western eyes. He strove to introduce western ideas to China, and it was while on a diplomatic visit to the USA in 1896 (having previously attended the coronation of Tsar **Nikolas II**) that he encountered, and found himself 'starring' in moving pictures. Docking in New York on 28 August 1896, his journey to the Waldorf was filmed by **W. K-L. Dickson** for Biograph and released as *Li Hung Chang – 4th Avenue and Broadway*. Edison also filmed his arrival. The following day he met President Grover Cleveland, Dickson again filming the journey (*Li Hung Chang – 5th Ave and 55th Street*). The next day he visited Grant's tomb and laid a wreath, once again filmed by Dickson. Later he was shown a Mutoscope record of one of

Dickson's films. He was delighted with the results, and **Harry Marvin** astutely promised to send him one of the machines.

Li returned to China, and Biograph followed after, **Fred Ackerman** filming in the country during the Boxer Rebellion and taking two further films of Li: one showing him being presented with the Mutoscope in Beijing; the other, in a fine early example of cinematic reflexivity, showing Li viewing himself through the same Mutoscope. An adroit and highly successful politician, Li died soon after the humiliation of the Boxer Rebellion. (LMcK)

References
Hendricks, *Beginnings of the Biograph* (1964).
Kemp Niver, *Early Motion Pictures: The Paper Print Collection of the Library of Congress* (Washington DC: Library of Congress, 1985).

LITTLE TICH (Harry Relph)
(1867–1926)

Diminutive music hall performer, equally popular in Britain and France. The sixteenth child of a 77-year-old Kent publican, Harry Relph was born with six digits on each hand. From his earliest professional performance, at a Gravesend pleasure garden in 1880, his deformity and lack of height (four feet six inches when fully grown) were emphasised for publicity reasons, though he always resented being promoted as a grotesque. Billed initially as Young Mackney (after the famous blackface performer G. W. Mackney) and later as Little Tichborne (an ironic reference to the grossly overweight claimant to the Tichborne fortune), Harry proved himself to be an inspired comedian and a dancer of genius. By the time of his London music hall debut in 1884 he had shortened his stage name and developed a speciality dance in which he appeared to defy gravity, either leaning forward at a precarious angle or balancing on the tips of 28-inch wooden boots. Three Drury Lane pantomimes (1891–4), established him as one of Britain's foremost comedians, and an engagement at the Folies Bergère in 1896 was the first of many appearances in the French capital.

Little Tich sang many comic songs and was a skilful instrumentalist, but his greatest successes were furiously energetic dances in which he often burlesqued artists such as **Loïe Fuller** and La Belle Otéro. The surviving film of the Big Boots dance, made by **Clément-Maurice** for the Phono-Cinéma-Théâtre in 1900, has been described by Jacques Tati as 'a foundation for everything that has been realised in comedy on the screen'. Despite his international fame it seems he only appeared in two further films: **Georges Méliès'** *Le Raid Paris – Monte-Carlo en deux heures* (1905) and four scenes made for Pathé in 1907 showing him as a horse guard, his La Belle Otéro and Loïe Fuller parodies, and the big boots dance once again. An imitator called Little Pich made three films for Gaumont in 1902, while the Big Boots dance was re-created by Sammy Curtis for a music hall scene in the Will Hay comedy, *Those Were the Days* (1934). (BA)

References
Mary Tich and Richard Findlater, *Little Tich: Giant of the Music Hall* (London: Elm Tree Books, 1979).

LONDE, Albert (1858–1917)

Medical researcher, chronophotographer. In 1878 a laboratory for medical photography had been set up at La Saltpêtrière hospital in Paris. To pursue his medical studies, in 1882 Londe constructed a camera fitted with nine lenses arranged in a circle. A series of electromagnets energised in sequence by a metronome device released the nine shutters in quick succession, taking nine pictures on a glass plate. He used the camera to study the movements of patients during epileptic fits. Londe's improved camera of 1891 used twelve lenses (in three rows of four) and was used for medical studies of muscle movement in subjects performing a variety of actions as diverse as those of a tightrope walker and a blacksmith. The sequence of twelve pictures could be made in anything from 1/10 of a second to several seconds.

The layout of Londe's laboratory at La Saltpêtrière in many ways resembled **Marey**'s Station Physiologique, and was similarly subsidised by the Parisian authorities. Though the apparatus was used primarily for medical research, Londe noted that it was portable, and he used it for a variety of subjects – for example, horses and other animals, and waves. General Sébert developed, in conjunction with Londe, a chronophotographic device to help in the study of ballistics. Londe's pictures were used as illustrations in several books, notably by Paul Richer, that were widely read by the medical and artistic fraternity. (BC)

References
Coe, *Muybridge and the Chronophotographers* (1992).
Albert Londe, *La Photographie moderne* (Paris: G. Masson, 1888): second expanded edition 1896.

LUBIN, Siegmund (1851–1923)

Film-maker, producer, exhibitor, manufacturer. Siegmund Lubin, with his Lubin Manufacturing Company of Philadelphia, was one of Edison's earliest rivals in the motion picture business, and remained a vigorous force in film-making, equipment manufacture and exhibition until the beginning of the First World War.

Siegmund Lubszynski emigrated to the USA from Germany in 1876, travelling the entire country as a salesman of jewellery, metal polish, spectacles and other goods. Settling in Philadelphia in 1882, he opened an optical manufacturing and retail business at 21 South 8th Street in 1885, particularly exploiting two patents for a novel form of eyeglasses. In late 1896 he developed the Cineograph projector with help from **C. Francis Jenkins**, and it was offered for sale in January 1897 at a price of $150. In February Lubin became an agent for Edison films; in March he founded the Cineograph Exhibition Service for vaudeville theatres; and on 15 May 1897 he began making films with *Unveiling of the Washington Monument*. He produced many short comedies and actualities, including local scenes of preparations for the Spanish-American War and battle re-creations, but the staple of his early film-making was re-created boxing films, using either 'counterparts' for the original fighters, or getting the boxers themselves to restage the fight.

Like other companies at the time, Lubin remade any appealing title from rival companies, producing among others versions of *The Great Train Robbery*, *Personal* and *Uncle Tom's Cabin*, and pirated for his own sale many films by Edison, Méliès, Pathé and others, advertising that his stock included any film made anywhere in the world. Through 1903 Lubin was constantly battling patent infringement suits brought by Edison, briefly fleeing the country in 1901 and temporarily ceasing production in 1903. By September 1907 Lubin was releasing three titles a week from new studios at 926 Market Street, and in 1908 he joined the Motion Picture Patents Company, ending his long legal battles. Throughout this period Lubin films were aggressively priced for the market, undercutting all his competitors' rates.

Lubin films were characteristically sensational in content: a film of the Thaw-White scandal, *The Unwritten Law*, was made in 1907 while the gripping murder trial was still in progress. Lubin bought a 1,000-seat movie house in Philadelphia in late 1906, and by 1908 he was operating a chain of nearly 100 theatres on the East Coast, the nucleus of the later Stanley-Warner circuit. In 1912 he abandoned his Lubinville studios at 20th Street and Indiana in Philadelphia to move to a 500-acre estate across the Schuylkill River from Valley Forge, which featured a spacious modern printing laboratory. Frank Borzage, Henry King and Oliver Hardy began their careers as Lubin actors, but the company developed no major stars who stayed with the firm. Not only price competitive, Lubin was also a vigorous promoter, installing luxurious fronts on his theatres and promoting his 1914 serial, *The Beloved Adventurer*, with a book-length novelisation illustrated with scenes from the film.

As he turned sixty-five, Lubin sold his company to the Vitagraph Corporation of America in August 1916 and retired from the motion picture business. He died at Ventnor, New Jersey, on 11 September 1923. Of the early American companies, including Edison, Biograph, Selig and Vitagraph, Lubin was the only one to attempt to create a vertically integrated firm that melded production, distribution, exhibition and manufacture into a single entity. But as films, audiences and business practices became more sophisticated, they left Lubin behind, a feisty and combative figure who exemplified the rough-and-tumble days of the beginnings of the film industry. (DR)

References

Joseph P. Eckardt and Linda Kowall, *Peddler of Dreams. Siegmund Lubin and the Creation of the Motion Picture Industry* (Philadelphia: National Museum of American Jewish History, 1984).
Linda Woal, 'When a Dime Could Buy a Dream: Siegmund Lubin and the Birth of Motion Picture Exhibition', *Film History*, vol. 6 no. 2, 1994.

LUMIERE, Claude Antoine (1840–1911)

Father of Louis and Auguste, inventors of the Cinématographe. Born on 13 March 1840 at Haute-Saône, Ormoy, France, Antoine was orphaned at fourteen. He took up carpentry and studied scientific books, before becoming apprenticed to painting teacher Auguste Constantin, and after military service studied under the photographer Nadar. He married in 1861 and set up a small photographic portrait studio at Besançon, where his sons Auguste and Louis were born. He later moved to Lyon, where a third son, Eduard, was born, along with three daughters. Antoine set up a small factory producing photographic plates, but even with Louis and a young sister working from 5 a.m. to 11 p.m., it was a struggle to make it a success. In 1882 it looked as if they would fail, but when Auguste returned from military service the boys designed the machines necessary to mechanise their father's plate production, together with a very successful new photo plate ('étiquettes bleue'), and by 1884 the factory was employing a dozen workers.

In the autumn of 1894 Antoine was inspired by an Edison peepshow Kinetoscope, and took a length of film to show his sons, encouraging them to produce a system that would produce similar living pictures, but project them onto a screen. He maintained an interest in the project's progress, organising with **Clément-Maurice** the first show to a paying public on 28 December 1895 at the Salon Indien in the basement of the Grand Café, boulevard des Capucines, Paris. The owner refused an offer of 20 per cent of the receipts and charged instead a flat rate of 30 francs a day. An afternoon preview was arranged for an invited audience, including **Georges Méliès**, with photographer Jacques Ducom in charge of the electric arc, engineer **Charles Moisson** (who made the first trial Cinématographe) turning the handle, and Antoine collecting the invitations. He also appeared in one of the films, *Partie d'écarté*. That evening, thirty-three members of the public paid 1 franc each to see the Cinématographe presentation. Within three weeks, takings amounted to 2,000 francs a day.

Though the **Skladanowsky**s had projected very short films at the Berlin Wintergarten theatre the previous month, and projections to a paying public had been given by the **Latham**s and **Jenkins/Armat** in the USA, that evening's show is often credited as the world's first cinema presentation to a paying public. It certainly heralded the beginnings of the French film industry, which was to become one of the most important in the world. By now, Antoine had become something of a financial embarrassment to the Lumière firm, incurring mounting debts with the purchase of various villas, and he was eventually bought out. During his retirement he took up painting, and exhibited in several Salons. He died on 16 April 1911. (SH)

References

Mannoni, *Le grand art de la lumière et de l'ombre* (1994).
Jacques Rittaud-Hutinet, *Antoine, Auguste et Louis Lumière* (Lyon: Editions Lyonnaises d'Art et d'Histoire, 1994).
'Les Lumières', *Prestige de la photographie* (Paris: e.p.a., 1980).

LUMIERE, Auguste Marie Nicolas (1862–1954)

Medical researcher and co-patentee of the Cinématographe. Born at Besançon, France, on 19 October 1862, as a young man Auguste worked with his brother Louis to establish the success of their father Antoine's photographic materials factory. He was later involved in the development of the Cinématographe: while Louis was chiefly responsible for the mechanism, Auguste arranged for Alfred Molteni (a leading manufacturer of projection lanterns) to make the necessary lamphouses. Auguste appeared in several of the early films himself, directing the activity in *Démolition d'un mur* and, with his wife Marguerite and daughter Andrée, enjoying the role of family man in the proto-home movie, *Repas de bébé*, and again with young Andrée in *Pêche aux poissons rouge*.

Even while he assisted Louis in the exploitation of the Cinématographe, Auguste's interests were focused on research in medical and related fields. He was the first in France to set up a working X-ray machine. In 1910 he established a laboratory in Lyon employing 150 workers, and housing departments of chemistry, physics, 'histologie', 'serologie' and analysis – and a research library of 30,000 volumes, where he worked on tuberculosis and cancer. Auguste Lumière died on 10 April 1954 aged ninety-two. Much fêted by a grateful France, the Lumière brothers appeared on several commemorative postage stamps and medallions. In 1995, however, plans to feature them on the 200 franc banknote were cancelled as the presses were rolling, following new sensitivity about their activity in the Vichy regime of the Second World War. (SH)

References

Mannoni, *Le grand art de la lumière et de l'ombre* (1994).
Jacques Rittaud-Hutinet, *Antoine, Auguste et Louis Lumière* (Lyon: Editions Lyonnaises d'Art et d'Histoire, 1994).
'Les Lumières', *Prestige de la photographie* (Paris: e.p.a., 1980).
Paul Vigre, *La Vie laborieuse et féconde d'Auguste Lumière* (Lyon: Durand-Girard, 1942).

LUMIERE, Louis Jean (1864–1948)

Inventor of the Cinématographe and the Autochrome colour photography process. Born on 5 October 1864, young Louis' education was interrupted by violent headaches, but at home he studied piano, drawing and sculpture. He later worked at his father Antoine's photographic plate factory, contributing significantly to its success. After seeing an Edison Kinetoscope, Antoine suggested that they work on developing a motion picture system. Louis' brother Auguste attempted to design a camera but with little success, until Louis suggested a mechanism similar to the one used in a sewing machine to advance the cloth step by step. Though Auguste gave credit to Louis, the successful machine was patented in France on 13 February 1895 in the name of both brothers, in common with their other inventions. The first model was made by their engineer **Charles Moisson**. The machine was a combined camera, projector and printer, the perforated film moved intermittently by a form of claw pulldown – a pair of pins which, inserted into the perforations on either side of the film then moved down, carrying the film with them. The cam motion mechanism (improved in a supplement to the patent dated 30 March 1895) formed the basis not only of the Lumières' instrument but of a large number of later mechanisms, some still in use today.

The Cinématographe (a name used earlier by experimenter **Bouly**) gave its first public presentation to the Société d'Encouragement de l'Industrie Nationale in Paris on 22 March 1895. Only one film was available, *La Sortie des usines Lumière* (*Workers Leaving the Lumière Factory*), shot by Louis. It followed a presentation of colour stills, with which the Lumières were experimenting at the time. Other film presentations soon followed: on 17 April at the Sorbonne, and on 10 June at the Congrès des Sociétés Françaises de Photographie, by which time there were seven more subjects, including *Pêche aux poissons rouge* and *Pompiers: Attaque du feu*. Two films were taken at the Lyon Congress, one of the Congress disembarking from a boat and another of a conversation between astronomer/photographer **Janssen** and the Consul-General of Rhône, M. Lagrange. Several more demonstrations preceded the first show to a paying audience in Paris in December.

Louis ordered twenty-five Cinématographes from engineer **Jules Carpentier**, followed by an order for a further 200, and within weeks agents took them throughout Europe and the USA, and within months all over the world, shooting scenes and giving film shows. Quite soon this policy of appointing official agents rather than selling the device outright was abandoned as other manufacturers made alternatives available. Within two or three years, however, the technical limitations of the Lumière perforated film meant that it was superseded by the 'Edison' standard.

The Lumières continued their photographic developments, including experiments with large film formats. At the Paris Exposition in 1900, they projected Cinématographe pictures onto a giant screen 20m wide. Shortly afterwards film production was wound down (some trick films were produced in 1905) and in 1902 **Charles Pathé** bought out the Lumière patents and Cinématographe interests. In 1902, Louis opened a Photorama exhibit in Paris: another of his inventions, this used a band of film and fast-revolving lenses to produce, by means of persistence of vision, a circular, static panorama. The brothers launched their successful Autochrome colour transparency system, the result of many years' experimentation, in 1907. Louis pursued an interest in stereoscopy, first with Photo–Stereo–Synthesis plates – 3-D portraits visually similar to holograms – and in the 1930s stereoscopic films. In 1935 he was fêted during the fortieth anniversary of cinema, and the following year flew to London for the celebrations of the anniversary of the the first Lumière film show in Britain. In 1948, shortly before he died, Louis Lumière was interviewed for French television by Georges Sadoul. Bemedalled and proud, the elderly inventor gave a formal account of the origins of the Cinématographe for the audiences of a new worldwide medium. (SH)

References

Mannoni, *Le grand art de la lumière et de l'ombre* (1994).
Jacques Rittaud-Hutinet, *Antoine, Auguste et Louis Lumière* (Lyon: Editions Lyonnaises d'Art et d'Histoire, 1994).
Georges Sadoul, 'Entretien avec Louis Lumière', *Cahiers du Cinéma*, vol. 27 no. 159, October 1964.
'Les Lumières', *Prestige de la photographie* (Paris: e.p.a., 1980).

M

McCUTCHEON, Wallace ('Old Man') (c.1858–?)

Producer, director. Wallace McCutcheon, previously a stage director, was taken on by American Biograph in the spring of 1897 following the departure of **W. K-L. Dickson** and **Elias Koopman** for England. As head of production he supervised the film-making of others, but also wrote, directed and on occasion filmed for himself. In this he found particular creative assistance from his friend Frank Marion, notably in the 1902–3 period when the company was making the switch from the 68mm large format to standard 35mm. Among his most noted productions were the *Foxy Grandpa* series (1902) and two proto-Westerns based on the life of the scout Kit Carson, *Kit Carson* and *The Pioneers*, both 1903, and both employing multi-shot narratives that give an indication of the coming changes to film production. Edison's *The Great Train Robbery*, also of 1903, showed a far greater fluidity of movement and owed far less to the stage, but McCutcheon and Marion's *The Escaped Lunatic*, made at the same time as the Edison production, is an embryonic chase film of some significance, an idea developed further in the highly popular *Personal* of the following year.

In May 1905 McCutcheon and his regular cameraman A. E. Weed were lured away from Biograph by Edison, and he now found himself working alongside **Edwin S. Porter**, the director of *The Great Train Robbery*. Biograph went through a low period creatively and financially that McCutcheon's return in late 1907 could not repair. McCutcheon had failed to find the same creative relationship with Porter that he had had with Marion (also now departed from Biograph and soon to form the Kalem Company with **George Kleine** and Samuel Long), but he was to play his part in reviving the fortunes of Biograph by employing in 1908, albeit as an actor, the greatest director of the silent era, D. W. Griffith (it was **Harry Marvin** who decided that Griffith should direct).

By this time McCutcheon was in poor health and many of his production duties were being undertaken by his eldest son, Wallace McCutcheon Jr., with whom he is sometimes confused ('Old Man' McCutcheon, named George in some sources, had eight children, all of whom he employed variously as actors). Wallace, the son, was a musical comedy performer and occasional film actor who was married for a short while to Pearl White (of the *Perils of Pauline* fame) and later shot himself dead in 1928. Both Wallaces had left Biograph by mid-1908, whereupon Griffith became the sole director for the Biograph company. In 1909 Wallace Snr. was directing at Gaston Méliès' new studio in Fort Lee, New York, apparently staying on in a supervisory role when Méliès moved to San Antonio, Texas, in 1910. (LMcK)

References

Musser, *The Emergence of Cinema* (1990).
Richard Schickel, *D.W. Griffith* (London: Pavilion, 1984).

MACINTYRE, Dr John

Scottish doctor. In April 1897 Macintyre became the first person to combine the two remarkable discoveries of 1895: **Röntgen** rays (X-rays) and the cinema. In that month he demonstrated X-ray cinematography to the Glasgow Philosophical Society. His subject was the motion of a frog's limbs, which he manipulated mechanically and illuminated with a Crookes tube. His camera was protected by lead foil, the lens removed and replaced with a lead diaphragm with a small aperture. He then filmed the X-rays directly as they passed through the frog's leg (a subject chosen for its flatness and thin skin, requiring only a low exposure), and showed the film to his audience in loop form. One of the screenings Macintyre gave was on the Society's Ladies' Night, with a lay as well as professional audience, an intriguing indication that he saw his film as being as much an entertainment as a scientific display.

There was much interest in Macintyre's work, illustrations of which were published in scientific journals. Similar experiments were also conducted by the Frenchmen Roux and Balthazard in the same year. His film survives, but Macintyre does not appear to have pursued the subject beyond 1897. (LMcK)

References
Lisa Cartwright, *Screening the Body: Tracing Medicine's Visual Culture* (Minneapolis/London: University of Minnesota Press, 1995).
Dr John Macintyre, 'X Ray Records for the Cinematograph', *Archives of Skiagraphy*, vol. 1 no. 4, 1897.

McKINLEY, William (1843–1901)

Twenty-fifth president of the USA. McKinley was born in Ohio, fought as a major in the Union army during the Civil War and afterwards became an attorney. Elected a Republican congressman and governor of Ohio in 1891 and 1893, he became president in 1896. His five years in office saw the rise of motion pictures in the USA, in which he frequently appeared as a subject. **W. K-L. Dickson**'s *McKinley at Home, Canton, O.* (1896) showed the then presidential candidate walking across his lawn with his son. One of the very first Biograph titles to be exhibited, and the star attraction of the official opening programme on 12 October 1896 at Hammerstein's Olympia music hall, the film caused great excitement, both by its topicality (the event was virtually a Republican party rally) and in the startling clarity of the Biograph image (McKinley also had a family connection with Biograph, as his brother Abner was one of the original investors in the American Mutoscope and Biograph Company). McKinley's inauguration on 4 March 1897 was also a major news event given extensive coverage by Biograph, Edison and Lumière, the latter firm coming towards the end of its time in the country.

McKinley's term in office was dominated by the Spanish-American War of 1898, which in turn became an important early news film story. McKinley won a second term in 1900, then on 5 September 1901, during a visit to the Pan-American Exposition in Buffalo, New York, he was assassinated by the anarchist Leon Czolgosz. **James White**'s Edison camera team were out in force and captured a remarkable series of news pictures recording the unfolding events, from McKinley reviewing the guard of honour and making a speech, to the puzzled and angry crowd captured in a panning shot as the news spread of the assassination. To add to their funeral films, Edison staged a re-creation of the electrocution of Czolgosz, hence making a complete documentary of the assassination. McKinley's successor, Vice-President Theodore Roosevelt (1858–1919) was to become the first media-friendly politician of the new century, actively supporting and encouraging the new art and proving extremely adept at adopting it for self-promotion. (LMcK)

References
Musser, *The Emergence of Cinema* (1990).
Ramsaye, *A Million and One Nights* (1926).

MAGUIRE, Franck Z. (c.1860–1910) and BAUCUS, Joseph D.

Businessmen. The commercial film industry in Britain began with the opening of the first Kinetoscope parlour in London at 70 Oxford Street on 17 October 1894. It was run by two Americans: Maguire and Baucus. Franck Z. Maguire had been an agent for the Edison Phonograph, working the territories of Japan and China in the late 80s. Joseph D. Baucus was a member of a Wall Street legal firm. They became Edison's official agents for exhibiting and marketing the Kinetoscope in Europe, Edison having granted them the world rights, excluding the USA and Canada. Shipping Orders numbers 53 and 128, which still survive at the Edison National Historic Site, West Orange, New Jersey, document the arrival of the first Kinetoscopes and Kinetoscope films in England for Maguire and Baucus. Seven of the films, the first to be commercially seen in Britain, were named in the London press on 18 October: *Carmencita, Bar Room, Cock Fight, Wrestling Match, Barber Shop, Annabelle Butterfly Dance* and *Blacksmith Shop*. Negotiations between Edison and Maguire and Baucus determined that films would be made in the Black Maria for exclusive use in Kinetoscopes sold by them. The letters 'MB' appeared on a film for the first time on *Buffalo Dance* (24 September 1894). The letter 'C' was later used, referring to the name of their company, the Continental Commerce Company.

Maguire and Baucus's success with the Kinetoscope was short-lived, however, as they could not control the Kinetoscope market. As

Edison had not patented his Kinetoscope for use outside of North America, **Robert Paul** began to make his version of it in late 1894, and by early 1895 Paul and **Birt Acres** were producing the first British films.

The Kinetoscope had a commercial life of about seventeen months, before it was replaced by film projectors from the start of 1896. Now Maguire and Baucus, with offices in New York and London, became agents for Edison films and projectors. In 1897 they also acquired the rights to distribute Lumière films in Britain and the USA. **Charles Urban** joined the company in the same year as the manager of their London office. His appointment transformed the company, which was renamed the Warwick Trading Company the following year after its London address, Warwick Court.

By 1902 the Warwick Trading Company had become one of the most important film producers and distributors in the country, with a high reputation for documentary and records of important current events. As well as Lumière, the company distributed **G. A. Smith**, **Williamson** and Star (**Méliès**) films, but its fortunes declined after Urban's departure in 1902, at which time Baucus was Warwick's chairman and Maguire one of its directors. Maguire would later suffer for a number of years with what he called 'nervous prostration'. In July 1910, from his home in Rhode Island, he wrote to **Thomas Edison** and asked for an 'opening'. Edison did not offer him a position. Franck Maguire died on 12 November 1910. Nothing further is known of Baucus. (FG)

References

Barnes, *The Beginnings of the Cinema in England* (vols. 1–5).

MAREY, Etienne-Jules (1830–1904)

Physiologist and chronophotographer. Born at Beaune, France in 1830, Marey went to Paris in 1849 to enrol at the faculty of medicine and to study surgery and physiology. He qualified as a doctor in 1859, and in 1864 set up in a small Parisian laboratory at 14 rue de l'Ancienne Comedie, where he studied the circulation of the blood, publishing *Le Mouvement dans les fonctions de la vie* in 1868. From 1863, Marey perfected the first elements of his 'methode graphique', which studied movement using recording instruments and graphs. Using polygraphs, sphygmographs, dromographs and other myographs, he succeeded in analysing diagrammatically the walk of man and of a horse, the flight of birds and insects. The results – published in *La Machine animale* in 1873 – aroused much interest and led Leland Stanford and **Eadweard Muybridge** to pursue their own photographic researches into horse movement. In turn, the influence of Muybridge and of those in Marey's circle, including Alphonse Penaud, led the physiologist to use photography for the study of movement.

Marey very much admired the results Muybridge had achieved at Palo Alto, but was dissatisfied with the lack of precision in the images of birds. In 1882, he perfected the 'photographic gun', inspired by the 1874 'photographic revolver' of the astronomer **Jules Janssen**, and capable of taking twelve exposures in one second. In 1882 Marey opened the Station Physiologique in the Bois de Boulogne, funded by the City of Paris, with **Georges Demenÿ** as his assistant. Marey quickly abandoned his gun and in 1882 invented a chronophotographic fixed-plate camera, equipped with a timed shutter. Using this, he succeeded in combining on one plate several successive images of a single movement. To facilitate shooting in different positions, the camera was placed inside a large wooden cabin which ran on rails. Numerous plates were made at the Station between 1882 and 1888, including the famous 'figures geometriques'.

In 1888 Marey again improved his invention by replacing the glass plate with a long strip of sensitised paper. The first 'film' on paper, taken at twenty images a second, was shown (but not projected) at the Académie des Sciences on 29 October 1888. The strip was moved intermittently in the camera by an electromagnet. Two years later, Marey replaced the paper strip with a transparent celluloid film 90mm wide and 1.20m or more long. A pressure plate immobilised the film and a spring restarted it when the pressure was released. All the cameras which followed were based on the principle first applied by Marey: the intermittent movement of a sensitive film behind an objective lens, the film's static moments corresponding with the opening of the shutter.

Between 1890 and 1900, Marey (assisted by Demenÿ up to 1894, then by **Lucien Bull** and Pierre Nogues) made a considerable number of motion analysis film-strips of high technical and aesthetic quality – the Cinémathèque Française alone possesses 400 original negatives - including the very beautiful self-portraits of Marey and Demenÿ, the recording of the movement of a hand and the famous falling cat filmed in 1894. That year, Marey accepted the resignation of Demenÿ, who wished to exploit commercially his master's methods. 1894 also marked the publication of Marey's *Le Mouvement*, an important work which covered all his researches. He exercised a considerable influence on all the pioneering inventors of the cinema in the 90s. His works, widely reported in the international press, were a strong inspiration for **Thomas Edison** and **Louis Lumière**, among others. Marey, the real founding father of cinematographic technique, died in 1904. His researches were followed up by Bull and Nogues at the Institut Marey, where they made microscopic, X-ray and high-speed analysis films. (LM)

References
Marta Braun, *Picturing Time: The Work of Etienne-Jules Marey (1830–1904)* (Chicago/London: University of Chicago Press, 1992).
Etienne-Jules Marey, *Le Mouvement* (Paris: Masson, 1894).

MARINESCU, Dr Gheorge (1863–1938)

Romanian neurologist. A specialist in the study and treatment of nervous diseases at the Pantelimon hospital in Bucharest, while working in Paris in 1898 Marinescu had the idea of making use of the cinematograph as a further tool in the investigation of his field. In mid-1898, having previously experimented with chronophotography in his studies under the influence of **E-J. Marey**, he purchased a Lumière Cinématographe from **Paul Menu**, and began to film the movements and gestures of those suffering from severe nervous ailments, his first film being *Walking Difficulties in Organic Hemiplegia* (1898). He would make his patients walk before the camera in four directions against a black background, and thereby analyse their movements before and after treatment.

He wrote a number of papers on his work for French medical journals, praising the cinematograph as a tool for medical investigation, and continued this work to 1901 with his assistants, C. Parhon and M. Goldstein, and a cameraman, Constantin Popescu, who shot for him such titles as *A Case of Hysterical Hemiplegia Cured Through Hypnotic Suggestion* (1899), *Walking Difficulties Due to Progressive Locomotory Ataxia* (1900) and *Pseudo-Hypertrophic or Myosclerotic Paralysis Among Myopathies* (1901). Other Romanian doctors of the period, A. I. Bolintineanu and Iaon Athanasiu (later a subdirector of the Institut Marey in Paris) were equally enthusiastic about the use of film in medical studies. Marinescu's films of those afflicted with nervous complaints show a procession of shuffling figures passing by the camera in a display that is curiously haunting. (LMcK)

References
Tosi, *Il cinema prima di Lumière* (1984).

MARVIN, Arthur (?–1911)

Cameraman. The brother of American Biograph founder **Harry Marvin**, Arthur was a mainstay of the company from its earliest years until his death in 1911. First recorded working for Biograph in 1898, he and **Billy Bitzer** were sent to Cuba to film the wreck of the *Maine* and other scenes relating to the Spanish-American War, and thereafter he worked as one of Biograph's main camera teams on both studio and outdoor subjects. A large, genial and easygoing character, according to Bitzer he described himself rather grandiloquently as 'the captain of the good ship Take-it-Easy with nine decks and no bottom, which sails on forever and forever sails on'.

Though 'seldom affected with the exuberance of ambition' (Bitzer), Marvin continued with the company to become cameraman for a number of D. W. Griffith's early films, including his very first, *The Adventures of Dollie* (1908), having pointed out Griffith (then an actor) as a man with potential. Griffith was soon to go to Harry Marvin, general manager of Biograph, and gently suggest that Billy Bitzer was more suitable than his brother for the artistic work that Griffith had in mind. Nevertheless, Marvin did some imaginative work for Griffith, notably the ingenious lighting effects for *Pippa Passes* (1909). Marvin died suddenly and prematurely after shooting his final film, *Priscilla's Engagement Ring* (1911). (LMcK)

References
Robert M. Henderson, *D. W. Griffith: The Years at Biograph* (London: Secker & Warburg, 1970).

MARVIN, Henry Norton ('Harry')
(c.1863–1940)

Engineer, executive. Harry Marvin, a college teacher, had met **W. K-L. Dickson** in the 80s, and in 1894 Dickson, then still working for **Thomas Edison** and also involved with the **Latham**s, proposed to Marvin a flip-card device that would compete with the Kinetoscope. **Elias Koopman**, **Herman Casler**, Marvin and Dickson set up the KMCD group to develop the idea, applying for a patent for the Mutoscope viewer in November. Soon Casler had constructed a large-format camera, and the first test in June 1895, probably shot at the Syracuse engineering workshop of Casler's employer C. E. Lipe, showed Marvin and Casler in a mock sparring match. In June 1895 Harry Marvin obtained sufficient finance to open the Marvin Electric Rock Drill Works in Canastota, New York, for the manufacture of rock drills based on his patent. Casler was superintendent, and worked on his motion picture experiments on the same site. On 22 September, the group met at Marvin's home in Canastota, where a group portrait was taken, and it may have been at that time, due to the drop-off in the peepshow motion picture business, that it was decided to develop a projector.

In December the group formed the American Mutoscope Company (later American Mutoscope and Biograph, usually referred to as Biograph), which would become one of the leading producers and exhibitors in the field, with a British associate company. In December 1896 Edison successfully appealed against the Patent Office rejection of his (Edison's) camera patent, offering a new set of specifications. Harry Marvin claimed that the new specifications were for an entirely different invention, but this claim was thrown out on a technicality. Later, Marvin suggested that fraud had been involved. Discouraged by low profits and Biograph's comparative success, Edison contemplated selling his motion picture business to Biograph for $500,000. On 12 April 1900, Harry Marvin paid Edison a $2,500 option, but the deal fell through. In July 1901 the Edison company was about to be granted an injunction against Biograph, over a claimed patent infringement, but following a deposition by Marvin that such an injunction would 'bankrupt and utterly ruin our company', a stay was granted. In March 1902

Edison's case was dismissed, and all Edison's key motion picture patents declared invalid.

Marvin stayed with Biograph throughout the Motion Picture Patents Company years, and was the man who as vice-president and general manager of the company decided that Biograph actor D. W. Griffith would make a useful director (on the suggestion of his brother **Arthur Marvin**, a longtime Biograph cameraman). It was the conservative production policies of Marvin and the Biograph board, frustrating Griffith's wishes to make longer films, that eventually sent him elsewhere to greater things. (SH)

References
Robert M. Henderson, *D. W. Griffith: The Years at Biograph* (London: Secker & Warburg, 1970).
Hendricks, *Beginnings of the Biograph* (1964).
Musser, *The Emergence of Cinema* (1990).

MASKELYNE, John Nevil (1839–1917)

Magician and illusionist who, with **David Devant**, presented films in London from the spring of 1896. Born in Cheltenham on 22 December 1839, he was a descendant of Nevil Maskelyne (1732–1811), the Astronomer Royal. Early in life he teamed up with George Alfred Cooke and they presented a unique entertainment of magic as 'Maskelyne and Cooke', which soon became a household name. In 1873 they presented their shows at the Egyptian Hall, Piccadilly, London, where they remained until 1904. Here, they completely transformed the art of conjuring into a dramatic performance of wizardry and an entirely new concept in the performing arts, which earned the Egyptian Hall the title of 'England's Home of Mystery'. A frequent visitor was the young **Georges Méliès**, who was greatly influenced by what he saw there. Some of the finest magicians of the day were among the performers, including David Devant, who was to incorporate the new 'Living Photographs' as a regular feature. He managed to obtain a Theatrograph, one of the very first film projectors made by **Robert Paul**, introducing it into the programme on 19 March 1896, two days before Paul himself gave his first commercial screenings at Olympia. Though Maskelyne was not at first enthusiastic about including films as an adjunct to magic acts, he nevertheless soon changed his mind and personally introduced each film from the stage. He also appeared in one of Paul's early films, *Maskelyne: Spinning Plates* (1896).

Maskelyne himself became involved in cinematographic invention. He was a clever mechanic and many of the illusions used in the performances were created by him and constructed in his own workshops. Ideas for a film projector designed on entirely new lines began to occupy him and his son, Nevil. They wondered if the irritating flicker produced by conventional machines could be overcome by employing a continuously running film rendered optically stationary. The invention was patented on 28 May 1896 and appeared at the Egyptian Hall as the Mutagraph, featuring in a striking early film poster. Devant and the Maskelynes made their own films, and as a result of experimenting with slow-motion cinematography Nevil (the son) was later enlisted by Britain's War Office to film artillery shells in flight for purposes of analysis. (JB)

References

Barnes, *The Beginnings of the Cinema in England* (vols. 1 and 2).

MATUSZEWSKI, Boleslaw (1856–?)

Film-maker, theoretician, cameraman, showman. Little is known of Boleslaw Matuszewski outside the period 1895–1901. He was born in 1856 in Pinczow, Poland, figured with his brother Zygmunt in the circle around the Warsaw photography studio, Paryska Fotografia Lux-Sigismond and Co. in 1895, and had his method of fixing photographs in enamel featured in the brochure, *Les Portraits sur maux vitrifés* (Paris, July 1901). But his activities in his six known years are an important legacy of early cinema. He may have been a Lumière operator and involved in filming the coronation of Tsar **Nikolas II** (he was certainly one of the Tsar's court cinematographers for a period), and he began making films for Lux-Sigismond by the middle of 1897, including *Operacje chirurgiczne w Warszawie*, the record of a surgical operation, and *Podrę ze, uroczysto sci I polowania w Spale I Bialowiezy*, scenes of folklore in north-eastern Poland. He arranged many screenings in both Warsaw and Paris; **E-J. Marey** spoke highly of his work in scientific film in 1899; and the year before he had presented the medical film of Dr **Eugène-Louis Doyen** in Warsaw.

His most significant achievement was an astonishing pamphlet published in Paris on 25 March 1898, *Une nouvelle source de l'histoire*, in which he not only affirmed his belief in the authenticity, exactitude and precision of the filmed image but also called for the establishment of a national archive to preserve motion pictures as important evidence of lives and activities, an archive that would have the same authority and standing as the Bibliothèque Nationale. His second booklet, *La Photographie animée*, of the same year discusses the applications of the cinema in the fine arts, industry, medicine, education, science and military life. Possessing remarkable foresight, to all reports indisputably energetic, Matuszewski made three further folklore films in Poland in late 1898 and then disappears from the historical record. (DR)

References

Boleslaw Matuszewski, *Une nouvelle source de l'histoire* (Paris, 1898) [reprinted in *Nove Zredlo Historii* (Warsaw: Filmowa Agencja Wydawnicza, 1955), with an essay by Wladyslaw Banaszkiewicz; translated in James Ballantyne (ed.), *Researcher's Guide to British Newsreels*, vol. III (London: BUFVC, 1993)].
Boleslaw Matuszewski, *La Photographie animée: Ce qu'elle doit être* (Paris, 1898).
Virgilio Tosi, 'Matuszewski e Marinescu: due pionieri del cinema', *Bianco e Nero* vol. 44 no. 1, January-March 1983.

MELIES, Georges (1861–1938)

Magician, film-maker. At once the cinema's first true artist and the most prolific technical innovator of the early years, Méliès was a pioneer in recognising the possibilities of the medium for narrative and spectacle. He created the basic vocabulary of special effects, and built the first studio of glasshouse form, the prototype of European studios of the silent era. The success of his films contributed to the development of an international market in films and did much to secure the ascendancy of French cinema in the pre-1914 years. Outside this historical contribution, Méliès' films are the earliest to survive as a total, coherent artistic creation with its own validity and personality. They had a visual style as distinctive as Douanier Rousseau or Chagall, and a sense of fantasy, fun and nonsense whose exuberance is still infectious after almost a century.

Méliès' parents had built up a prosperous footwear business, and at twenty-one, after military service, Georges joined his older brothers in the factory. Rescue from this mundane prospect came in 1884, when he was sent to London to learn English. He was enchanted by the London pantomimes, but much more by the magic shows of **Maskelyne** and Cooke at the Egyptian Hall, Piccadilly, which inspired him to study stage illusionism. In 1888 his share of the family business, which his father had handed over to his sons, and a rich marriage, enabled him to take over the small but famous Parisian home of stage magic, the Théâtre Robert-Houdin, at 8 boulevard des Italiens.

Over the next decade Méliès devised some twenty-five major stage illusions, many of which were later to inspire his films. Already a respected personality in the Parisian entertainment world, Méliès was naturally invited to the Lumière show at the Grand Café on 28 December 1895. Recognising in the Cinématographe a new attraction for his theatre, he attempted to buy it. When the Lumières refused him, he went to London to acquire one of **Robert Paul**'s earliest projectors. This, with the aid of an engineer, Lucien Reulos, he converted into his first film camera. Able only to buy a stock of unperforated Eastman film, he was obliged to commission a perforator from a local engineer. In May 1896, a month after he had begun showing Paul and Edison films at his theatre, Méliès was able to shoot his first film, *Une Partie de cartes*. By September, with Reulos and Lucien Korsten, he patented a new camera, which was subsequently advertised as the Kinétographe Robert-Houdin. In December he adopted the Star trademark.

By the end of 1896 Méliès had shot eighty films, each 20m in length, and had already explored the effects that could be obtained by accelerated motion (in *Dessinateur: Chamberlain*) and substitution. He claimed that this effect, which was to be so basic to his work, was discovered one day when his camera jammed briefly while filming in la place de l'Opera: when the film was printed and screened, Méliès was thrilled to find that a motor bus had changed into a hearse. At once he perceived that the trick was a more effective means of producing the disappearance of a lady (*L'Escamotage d'une dame chez Robert-Houdin*) than the elaborate machinery of his stage illusions.

Early in 1897 Méliès constructed a studio at Montreuil-sous-Bois, in which he was able to develop his productions and trick work. In the course of the next few years he widened his repertoire of trickery using elaborate double and multiple exposures and producing effects of growing or diminishing figures by techniques analogous to the Phantasmagoria magic lantern. His productions also became more lavish in their use of costumes and fantastic or rococo décors, all painted by Méliès himself. His proudest achievement was the role he claimed as the creator of *vues composées* – that is, *mise-en-scènes* rather than the actualities which were the regular subjects of the first film-makers. Méliès was also a pioneer in assembling a number of 'films' or shots to tell a continuous story. This technique was analogous to the tableau style of magic lantern narrative rather than to modern notions of film editing, but in the years 1898–1900 it represented a significant advance.

Méliès' sheer variety was staggering. Apart from the trick films based on his stage illusions, his 500 films included dramatised actualities such as *L'Affaire Dreyfus* or *Le Sacre d'Edouard VII (The Coronation of King Edward VII)*; fairy stories (*Cendrillon, Le petit chaperon rouge*); topical satires (*Le Tunnel sous la manche, Le Raid Paris–Monte Carlo en deux heures*); social tracts (*Les Incendiaires, La Civilisation à travers les ages*); historical subjects (*Jeanne d'Arc, La Tour de Londres et les derniers moments d'Anne de Boleyn*) and even adaptations of Shakespeare's *Julius Caesar* and *Hamlet*. Best-loved, though, are his comedy science fiction films in gentle parody of Jules Verne (*Voyage dans la lune, Voyage à travers l'impossible, A la Conquête du Pole*).

Méliès' films won a worldwide market – and attracted worldwide plagiarism. His celebrity is attested by his choice as president of the Congrès International des Fabricants de Films, held in Paris in 1909. The Congress, however, heralded a new era of the industry which would have no place for the pioneer, independent artist-artisan like Méliès. His trick work demanded a static camera; and this, combined with his distinctive – and so unchanging – graphic vision, seemed archaic in the era of D. W. Griffith. He signed a distribution contract with Pathé, ceding his independence; and soon his film activity would come to an end.

The war of 1914 brought other troubles. His wife had died in 1913. His brother Gaston, who had run an American branch of the firm which had eventually seceded, also died in 1915. The Théâtre Robert-Houdin was closed by the war and eventually swept away by urban development. Méliès turned his studio into a theatre, but by 1923 that too had failed and the property was sold, along with all the scenery, props and costumes from the films. About the same time, with nowhere to store them, he ordered the destruction of all his negatives. Now penniless, he married his former actress and longtime mistress, **Jehanne d'Alcy**. They lived from the proceeds of a tiny boutique, selling toys and novelties on the Gare Montparnasse. This period was, said Méliès later, 'a true martyrdom'.

Rediscovered by a new generation of film enthusiasts in the early 1930s, this great pioneer was belatedly fêted, and eventually he and his wife were given a place in the home for cinema veterans at the Chateau d'Orly, where he spent his final days, seemingly contented, still drawing, reminiscing and occasionally performing little conjuring tricks. (DRB)

References

David Robinson, *George Méliès: Father of Film Fantasy* (London: BFI/MOMI, 1993).

Paolo Cherchi Usai (ed.), *Lo schermo incantato: Georges Méliès (1861–1938)* (George Eastman House/Edizioni Biblioteca dell' Immagine/Le Giornate del Cinema Muto, 1991).

MENU, Paul (?–1973)

The first Romanian film-maker. Cinema arrived in Romania on 27 May 1896, when a Lumière programme sponsored by the local French-language newspaper, *L'Indépendence Roumaine* was presented in Bucharest. Titles featured were reported as *A Dinner, The Cycling Lesson, The Zoo, Coming Out of Church after Mass, A Picnic, The Paris Opera Square* and *Arrival of the Train*. The managers of *L'Indépendence Roumaine* subsequently acquired a Cinématogra phe and entrusted it to Paul Menu, a photographer and the son of a French optician living in Romania. Menu took his first films on 10 May 1897, recording the ceremonies surrounding the anniversary parade celebrating victory in the Independence War of 1877. He filmed the King and Queen, and one example, *HM the King Riding to the Palace, Escorted by his General Staff and by the Foreign Military Attachés* survives. The following day he filmed horse-racing scenes at the Baneasa racing field.

Menu's films were premiered on 8 June 1897 to an invited audience, many of whom were reported delighted to recognise themselves on the screen. Menu shot further films in Bucharest, recorded the Danube floods and filmed the Romanian navy. In 1898, however, he gave up cinematography for good, selling his camera to **Gheorge Marinescu**. (LMcK)

References

Manuela Cernat, *A Concise History of the Romanian Film* (Bucharest, 1982).

MERRY, Tom (William Mecham) (1853–1902)

Cartoonist, performer. William Mecham, a professional caricaturist who also gave 'Lightning Cartoon' presentations on the music hall stage, was the first celebrity of any kind to appear in a British film. **Birt Acres** filmed four separate performances of 'Tom Merry' (Mecham's pen-name) drawing personalities famous in his day. Catalogue and advertising titles vary a little, but the main title was probably *Tom Merry Lightning Artist Drawing Mr Gladstone* (that is, William Gladstone the former prime minister). The other three films featured Merry drawing (sometimes 'sketching') Lord Salisbury, the German Emperor

Kaiser **Wilhelm II** and the Prince Bismarck. The latter two films would have been made to show alongside Acrès' films of the opening of the Kiel Canal. That particular ceremony took place in June 1895, but the first reference to the films featuring Merry comes later. They were shown as part of **Robert Paul**'s first theatrical programme at the Alhambra on 25 March 1896, and mentioned in several reviews.

From this simple beginning sprang the art of the animated cartoon film of today. Less expert artists than Merry took longer to complete their films, and as reels could not at the time be extended, simple stop-frame was introduced to ensure completion within the required minute. Merry, whose main work was the large colour centre spread of *St Stephen's Review*, a weekly magazine of political comment, also illustrated *The History of Canvey Island* by Augustus Daly. Published posthumously, the dedication reads: 'In memoriam of William Mecham, artist, cartoonist, and caricaturist, better known to the British public by his professional soubriquet, Tom Merry, who died suddenly at Benfleet Station (adjoining Canvey Island), Essex, on Thursday, August 21st, 1902, aged 49 years.' By a stroke of good luck he remains immortal: a few frames of his Kaiser Wilhelm film are preserved in the National Film and Television Archive. (DG)

References
Denis Gifford, *British Animated Films: 1895–1985* (Jefferson/London: McFarland and Company, 1987).
Simon Houfe, *Dictionary of British Book Illustrators and Caricaturists 1800–1914* (London: Antique Collectors' Club [Suffolk], 1978).

MESGUICH, Félix (1871–1949)

Lumière operator in France, the USA, Canada and Russia. Born in Algeria, Mesguich served as a Zouave before moving to France and joining the Lumière brothers, where he was assistant to Perrigot at the first provincial screening of the Cinématographe, held in Lyon on 25 January 1896. He was then among the operators sent by the Lumières to launch the Cinématographe in the USA in June 1896. Exhibiting at the Eden Musée and Keith's Union Square theatre in New York, as well as other major cities, Lumière programmes were highly successful throughout the USA to the end of 1896, but the business failed to keep up with the strengthening competition, and ceased to be a major force on the American scene by 1897.

Mesguich returned to France, by way of Canada (where he filmed Niagara Falls), in the autumn of 1897, when he was next sent to Russia, working for Lumière concessionaire Arthur Grünewald and exhibiting Lumière films for Tsar **Nikolas II** at Yalta. Mesguich remained in Russia until September 1898, when he returned to France, left the Lumières, and went on to shoot experimental sound films for **Auguste Baron**, then producing some of the world's first advertising films, starting with an 'animated poster' for 'Ripolin' in October 1898, then 'phantom rides' sponsored by Compagnie des Wagons-Lits. He then embarked on a three-month jaunt through France, Germany, Austria and Switzerland, touring the films and cylinders of **Sarah Bernhardt**, Coquelin and others originally filmed by **Clément-Maurice** for the Phono-Cinéma-Théâtre at the Paris Exposition of 1900. He returned to Paris in 1901 to present the films at the Olympia for the **Isola** brothers.

Thereafter, Mesguich toured the world as a news cameraman, commissioned by a variety of companies, filming **Queen Victoria**'s funeral; the coronation of Edward VII in 1902; scenes shot in Europe and on a second visit to Russia; the unofficial Olympic games in Athens in 1906; views of Palestine, Algeria and Egypt; and (so he claimed) shots from a Wright biplane in flight in 1908. A world tour conducted in 1909–10 took him through Ceylon, India, Cambodia, Vietnam, Burma, Singapore, Japan and China. He served in the First World War in his Zouave regiment. His memoirs, published in 1933, are lively and readable, if somewhat cavalier with the facts. (LMcK)

References
Félix Mesguich, *Tours de manivelle: Souvenirs d'un chasseur d'images* (Paris: Bernard Grassett, 1933).
Rittaud-Hutinet, *Le Cinéma des origines* (1985).

MESSTER, Oskar (1866–1943)

Showman, manufacturer, producer, film-maker, executive, collector. Widely known as 'the Father of the German Film Industry', Oskar Messter, born in Berlin on 21 November 1866, grew up in a scientific and manufacturing household: his father Eduard had founded a company in Berlin in 1859 that manufactured and sold optical equipment, eyeglasses and medical apparatus. The firm also made optical devices for magicians and showmen, pioneered electrical lighting for theatres and organised magic lantern projections with its own equipment. Immersed in this atmosphere from childhood, Messter acquired business, mechanical and theatrical skills that he would fully apply to the new medium of cinema.

In early 1896, Messter began to design a film projector to project Kinetoscope films, but not until he was brought a **Robert Paul** Theatrograph for repair did he abandon continuously running film and find a solution in intermittent projection, using Paul's seven-sided Maltese cross gear. His first apparatus was ordered by a Russian showman, Rogulin, on 3 June, and completed on 15 June: Messter was now in the film business, and he would build sixty-four more projectors by the end of the year, forty-two sold in Germany, and twenty-two in the rest of Europe.

Contrary to most historical accounts, Messter was not the only manufacturer of cinema apparatus in Germany, or even Berlin, at this time. **Max Gliewe** of the Optical Works Gliewe and Kügler in Berlin, had independently begun making projectors with a five-sided Maltese cross in late spring 1896; **H. O. Foesterling** was producing equipment after the design of Frenchman Victor Continsouza by the summer; Georg Bartling of Leipzig showed a projector at the Berlin Industrial Exhibition that opened on 1 May 1896; and the established magic lantern firm of Eduard Liesegang of Stuttgart offered a machine designed by **Alfred Wrench** in England. Gliewe quickly came to work with Messter, and the engineer Georg Betz was also an important early collaborator. Messter's high quality of both design and manufacture was the foundation of his success, coupled with his continuous introduction of new and improved models: by October 1897 he published a 113-page catalogue offering a huge variety of equipment.

Messter began film production in late 1896 with *Am Brandenburger Tor zu Berlin*. He soon erected the first film studio in Germany, on the Friedrichstrasse in Berlin, and a year later his catalogue offered eighty-four films, a variety of comic scenes, sports films, street scenes, military subjects and cabaret acts. On 21 September he took over the direction of the twice-failed theatre at 21 Unter den Linden; on 1 November he gave his first projection at Berlin's famous Apollo variety theatre, and launched a projection service for theatres throughout the region. By 1901 his involvements had grown to the point that he divided his companies into specialised firms for production, distribution and manufacture.

His subsequent career in motion pictures illustrates an energetic and innovative mind, combined with an acute sense of business and history, as he explored the new medium for both commercial and non-commercial purposes: time-lapse photography of blooming flowers (from early 1897); experiments with microscopic cinematography (1900–10); the first German projection of sound films (Apollo theatre, Berlin, 1903); English-language sound films celebrated at the St Louis World's Fair (1904); establishment of the star system through his promotions for actress Henny Porten (1912); 500 theatres equipped with his Biophon synchronised sound system by 1913; introduction of his Thaumatograph Model XVII projector, an industry standard (1914); founding of a weekly newsreel (*Messter-Woche*, 1914); construction of high-speed military reconnaissance cameras (1915); and co-founder and first president of the German Film-Technical Association.

In April 1918, all of the Messter film companies were sold to the newly founded UFA monopoly for 5.3 million gold Marks, becoming one of the cornerstones of the gigantic concern that would dominate the German film industry until the end of 1945. But Messter, aged fifty-seven, was hardly in retirement. From 1922 he actively enlarged his collection of historical film equipment (subsequently donated to the Deutsches Museum in 1932). In August 1928, he was one of the founders of the Tobis sound-film company, and in 1936 published his autobiography, based in part on a decade of meticulous correspondence with all of the living film pioneers and inventors he could contact. He died at his retirement home on the Tegernsee on 6 December 1943. (DR)

References

Martin Loiperdinger (ed.), *Oskar Messter: Filmpionier der Kaiserzeit* [KINtop Schriften 2] (Basel: Stroemfeld/Roter Stern, 1994).
Martin Loiperdinger (ed.), *Oskar Messter: Erfinder und Geschäftsmann*, KINtop 3 [special issue] (Basel: Stroemfeld/Roter Stern, 1994).

Oskar Messter, *Mein Weg mit dem Film* (Berlin: Max Hesses Verlag, 1936).
Dr Albert Narath, 'Oskar Messter and His Work', in Fielding, *A Technological History of Motion Pictures and Television* (1967).

MINIER, Louis

Lumière operator. Two Frenchmen, Louis Minier and Louis Pupier – the former a naval officer, the latter his assistant – presented Canada's first public film show on 28 June 1896 in Montreal, using a Lumière Cinématographe. This was a full month before the screening usually documented as Canada's film premiere. Over the next two months Minier and Pupier played at the Palace theatre in Montreal, before performing at the Toronto Industrial Exposition and then at another exposition in Montreal, and finally touring the main towns of Quebec.

Minier returned to France in the winter of 1896, leaving Pupier to continue touring with an aide named Jackson, but the senior man returned in the spring of 1897 with a new assistant, Fauré. In mid-summer they were joined by **Félix Mesguich**, following his tour of the USA, who showed his Lumière films at the Palace theatre. Mesguich was followed by other Lumière agents: M. Prosper later that year, and by F. J. Blanchard in 1900. Meanwhile, in 1898, Minier had become a professor at Laval University in Montreal. (SB)

References
Germain Lacasse, 'Cultural Amnesia and the Birth of Film in Canada', *Cinema Canada*, vol. 3 no. 108, June 1984.

MITCHELL, Dr Robert A.

Amateur film-maker. The man now documented as the first Irish film-maker may be so only through the survival of his films, which he had the foresight to donate to the National Film Library (now the National Film and Television Archive) in the 1930s. There may well have been other people in Ireland who purchased cine cameras for personal use at this time, but Mitchell's films are the only ones that have survived. So far as is known they were never shown commercially, neither were they intended to be. Mitchell was a lawyer from County Down, working in Belfast, who took his films in 1898, the year in which he made a visit to South Africa. His surviving films, which are singularly uninteresting, mostly show scenes at sea and in South Africa,

and indicate a personal interest in yachting. (LMcK)

References
Brian McIlroy, *World Cinema 4: Ireland* (Trowbridge: Flicks Books, 1989).

MITCHELL, Sagar James (1866–1952) and KENYON, James (?–1925)

Producers Sagar Mitchell and James Kenyon formed one of the many provincial production and distribution companies situated in northern England. Their releases, known as Norden Films, were named after their trade address, the Norden Film Works, 22 Clayton Street, Blackburn, Lancashire. They also had premises at 21 King Street and 40 Northgate in the same town. They acquired their first projector in November 1897, and their local newspaper reported on their first production, *Blackburn Market on a Saturday Morning*, in their issue of 27 November. They had no studio, and virtually all Norden Films were staged in outdoor locations. By November 1901 they were able to advertise 'Hundreds of local pictures fifty to a thousand feet long'.

Mitchell and Kenyon are especially noted for their many 'fake' war films: rough but lively re-creations of the Boer War in the 1899–1900 period (*The Dispatch Bearer*, *Winning the VC*), and from July 1900 a string of Boxer Rebellion subjects, including titles such as *Attack on a Mission Station*, which preceded **James Williamson**'s successful film of a similar title and subject by three months. The Transvaal and China were clearly re-created in the Blackburn area, and the films aroused controversy even at the time for being passed off as the real thing. In June 1902, with the ending of the Boer War, their library of fifteen faked war films was assembled into a special show entitled *Hands Off the Flag*. (DG)

References
The Beginnings of the Cinema in England (vols. 4–5).

MOISSON, Charles

Mechanic, projectionist. Late in life, Charles Moisson recalled how **Antoine Lumière** had arrived at his office in 1894, where Moisson was working with **Louis Lumière**, bearing a piece of Edison Kinetoscope film, so initiating the Lumières' interest in motion pictures (other sources suggest that this discussion involved the Lumières and **Clément-Maurice**).

Moisson was the Lumières' chief mechanic, and worked with the brothers on the design of the prototype of the Cinématographe camera, helping to construct the first working example. For the trials, the machine used bands of perforated photographic paper. He was operator of the Cinématographe at several of the early Lumière projections in 1895, including the demonstration to the Belgian Photographic Association on 10 November 1895, and the first show to a paying public at the Grand Café on 28 December 1895. The famous engraving of a Lumière Cinématographe projectionist is said to represent Moisson. Five months later, on 14 May 1896, he was in Russia with **Francis Doublier** to photograph the coronation of Tsar **Nikolas II**. Later in the year he travelled to Italy for the Lumières, but does not seem to have pursued a further career as one of their travelling operators. Moisson's first model Cinématographe survives at the Conservatoire National des Arts et Métiers, Paris. (SH)

References

Sadoul, *Histoire générale du cinéma*, vol. 1 (1946).
Jacques Rittaud-Hutinet (ed.), *Auguste et Louis Lumière: Correspondences 1890–1953* (Paris: Cahiers du Cinéma, 1994).

MUYBRIDGE, Eadweard (1830–1904)

Photographer. Born Edward Muggeridge at Kingston upon Thames, England, on 9 April 1830, he later changed his name to Eadweard Muybridge. He emigrated to the USA in 1851, working in New York in bookbinding and selling. He acquired an interest in photography, which developed after his move to California in 1855. On a visit to England in 1860 he learned the wet-collodion process, acquiring the best photographic equipment available, and returned to the USA. In 1867, under the trade pseudonym 'Helios' he set out to record the scenery of the far West with his mobile darkroom, christened 'The Flying Studio'. He produced notable stereoscopic views and, later, panoramas, including an important series featuring San Francisco.

His reputation as a photographer of the first rank spread, and he was approached by the president of the Central Pacific Railroad, Leland Stanford, to attempt to photograph a horse trotting at speed, to settle a long-standing controversy among racing men as to whether a trotting horse had all four hooves off the ground at any point. In May 1872 Muybridge photographed the horse Occident, but without any great success, as the current wet-collodion process normally required many seconds for a good result. In April 1873 he managed to produce some better negatives, in which a recognisable silhouette of the horse showed all four feet above the ground at the same time.

Soon after, Muybridge left his young wife, Flora, to go on a photographic trip. While he was away, she had an affair with a Major Harry Larkyns and became pregnant. Muybridge – an imposing figure in broad-brimmed hat and long white beard – discovering that the child was not his, confronted Larkyns and shot him dead. Tried for murder in February 1875, Muybridge was acquitted by the jury on the grounds of justifiable homicide; he left soon after on a long trip to South America.

On his return, he took up the action photography project once more. Using a new shutter design he had developed, which operated in as little as 1/1000 of a second, he obtained more detailed pictures in July 1877. He then devised a new scheme, which Stanford sponsored at his farm in Palo Alto. A 50ft long shed was constructed, containing twelve cameras side by side, facing a white background marked off with vertical numbered lines. Each camera was fitted with Muybridge's high-speed shutter, released by an electromagnetic catch. Thin threads stretched across the track were broken by the horse as it moved along, closing spring electrical contacts which released each shutter in turn. Thus in about half a second, twelve photographs were obtained showing all the phases of the movement. Though the pictures were still little more than silhouettes, they were very sharp, and sequences published in scientific and photographic journals throughout the world excited considerable attention. By replacing the threads with an electrical commutator device, releasing the shutters at precise intervals, Muybridge was able to take series of actions by other animals and humans.

From 1880 he lectured in the USA and Europe, projecting his results in motion on the screen with his Zoöpraxiscope projector. This machine, described by the *Illustrated London News* as "'a magic lantern run mad" (with method in the madness)', was basically a projecting phenakistiscope, with a contra-rotating shutter. The silhouette images, derived from his sequence photographs, were painted around the edge of a large glass disc (later, translucent coloured paintings were used). In August 1883 he received a grant of $40,000 from the University of Pennsylvania to carry on his work there. During 1884 and 1885, using the vastly superior gelatine dry-plate process and new camera apparatus, he produced over 100,000 sequence photographs, of which 20,000 were reproduced in *Animal Locomotion* in 1887. The subjects included animals of all kinds, and human figures, mostly nude, in a wide range of activities. His motion sequences were projected in the Zoöpraxographic Hall at the Chicago Exhibition of 1893. The following year Muybridge returned to his birthplace in England; his last publications were *Animals in Motion*

(1899) and *The Human Figure in Motion* (1901).

His influence on the world of art was enormous, overturning the conventional representations of action hitherto used by artists. His work in pioneering the use of sequence photography led to the science of chrono-photography developed by Professor **E-J. Marey** and others, and stimulated many inventors, notably **Thomas Edison**, to work which led to the introduction of cinematography in the 90s. (BC)

References

Coe, *Muybridge and the Chronophotographers* (1992).
Eadweard Muybridge of Kingston upon Thames [exhibition guide] (Kingston: Museum and Heritage Centre, 1984).
Robert Bartlett Haas, *Muybridge: Man in Motion* (Berkeley and Los Angeles: University of California Press, 1976).
Eadweard Muybridge, *Animal Locomotion: An Electro-photographic Investigation of Consecutive Phases of Animal Movement* (Philadelphia: Lippincott, 1887).
Eadweard Muybridge, *The Human Figure in Motion: An Electro-photographic Investigation of Consecutive Phases of Muscular Actions* (London: Chapman & Hall, 1901, reprinted Dover 1955).
Eadweard Muybridge, *Animals in Motion* (London: Chapman & Hall, 1899, reprinted Dover 1957).
Eadweard Muybridge, *Descriptive Zoopraxography or the Science of Animal Locomotion Made Popular* (Pennsylvania: University of Pennsylvania, 1893).

N

NEWMAN, Arthur Samuel (1861–1943)

Camera manufacturer. In 1862 Arthur Newman was employed by a firm of electricians, but when the company began to manufacture hand cameras he transferred to this work. Newman developed a number of improvements in hand-camera design, and by 1889 had set himself up in partnership as a manufacturer of cameras, shutters and changing boxes. When this partnership was dissolved in 1890, Newman joined with a London businessman and keen photographer named Julio Guardia to form the camera manufacturer of Newman and Guardia. Guardia handled the marketing of the cameras which Newman designed. In 1896 Newman, having seen a Lumière show, also began to design a moving picture projector, but though he took out a patent at the end of the year it was not until the end of 1897 that Newman and Guardia had a machine ready for manufacture. At £30 the 'N and G' Kinematograph Camera was rather expensive, but one was immediately

bought for Sir **George Newnes**'s Antarctic expedition. By 1899 Newman and Guardia was also marketing a film perforator and a printing machine, and offering a developing and printing service.

Newman and Guardia gained a reputation for the quality of its camera equipment, but problems began in 1906 when Julio Guardia died. Newman was not a success running the company himself, and in 1908 resigned his directorship, agreeing also to relinquish his shares in the company if he could keep the rights to the film equipment he had designed. In 1909 Newman set up a new partnership with James A. Sinclair to form Newman and Sinclair Ltd., and opened a workshop to manufacture film equipment. Newman designed the New-man-Sinclair reflex camera, a lightweight design carrying 400ft of negative in film boxes placed side by side, and in 1910 Herbert Ponting took one on Captain Scott's ill-fated polar journey. Newman also assisted in the development of **Kasimierz Proszynski**'s Aeroscope camera, a lightweight film camera with a compressed-air engine that Newman and Sinclair began manufacturing in 1912, and which remained popular with explorers and war photographers. Newman's camera designs continued to have a reputation for robust reliability, and provided footage for such well-known documentaries as John Grierson's *Drifters* (1929), Robert Flaherty's *Man of Aran* (1934) and Basil Wright's *Song of Ceylon* (1934). (NH)

References

Kevin Desmond, 'ASN: Arthur S. Newman', *Eyepiece*, July/August 1985, pp. 148–52.

NEWNES, Sir George (1851–1910)

Publisher. George Newnes was the Manchester representative of a London firm which sold ornaments and home furnishings, when in 1881 he had an instant publishing success by launching a popular magazine of short items called *Tit-Bits*. In 1884 Newnes moved to London and in 1890 scored his second great success with the *Review of Reviews*, which carried a monthly digest of the principal magazines and journals.

Newnes had a passion for new inventions, which brought him into contact with the pioneers of moving pictures. In 1889 **Wordsworth Donisthorpe** used his prototype Kinesigraph to take a series of sequential images of Trafalgar Square, and he approached Newnes for the financial backing to develop a viable system of projection. Newnes commissioned two experts, one a magic lantern maker, to investigate the Kinesigraph, but, as Donisthorpe noted sadly, 'both these "experts" reported adversely. ... They agreed that the idea was wild, visionary, and ridiculous, and that the only result of attempting to photograph motion would be an indescribable blur.' Newnes's business continued to flourish with the creation of the *Strand Magazine* (1891), the Liberal evening paper, *Westminster Gazette* (1893) and *Country Life* (1897). He was made a baronet in 1895.

In 1898 he returned to his interest in moving pictures by investing £2,000 in the newly formed Mutoscope and Biograph Syndicate. With Arthur Pearson, a successful publisher whom Newnes had first employed on *Tit-Bits*, and Edward Hudson, the printer of *Country Life*, Newnes now became involved in plans to develop the Mutoscope peepshow viewer into a medium of news. The Mutoscope and Biograph Company hoped to flood the country with Mutoscopes, and in 1899 its chairman admitted that 'if there is any value in the shares it comes from the fact that we are going to be a part of the illustrated journalism of this country in the future'. In 1900 the company launched the 'Home Mutoscope', and its chairman confidently declared that 'the novelty of the illustrated newspaper has worn down a little, and what the public want just now is a mutoscopic or biographic newspaper, in which the reader may see the progress of current events'. However, the Home Mutoscope failed to catch on, and Newnes, who became a Liberal MP in 1900, quickly lost interest in the Mutoscope and Biograph Company, bringing his investment in moving pictures to an end. He appears on film himself in Biograph's *Antarctic Expedition – Sir George Newnes Farewell to Officers and Crew* (1898). (NH)

References

Coe, *Muybridge and the Chronophotographers* (1992). Brown and Anthony, *The History of the British Mutoscope and Biograph Company* (1995).

NIKOLAS II, Tsar of Russia (1868–1918)

The last Russian tsar seems to have had an equivocal attitude towards moving pictures, personally enthusiastic yet fearful of their social impact. Already an enthusiastic photographer, he was one of the first monarchs to see the Cinématographe, when **Alexandre Promio** gave a court presentation on 7 July 1896. Another Lumière operator, **Charles Moisson**, had filmed his coronation on 14 May of that year, contributing eight subjects to the Lumière catalogue (nos. 300–7); and Moisson's assistant on that occasion, **Francis Doublier**, told Jay Leyda that they had also been filming when the Tsar's distribution of alms two days later ended in a crowd disaster and many deaths. However, he claimed that the police had immediately confiscated both camera and film.

Nikolas created the post of 'court cinematographer', which appears to have been held by as many as five people, including **Boleslaw Matuszewski**, K. von Hahn, V. Bulla, Aleksandr Drankov and Aleksandr Khanzhonkov, the latter two of whom would become Russia's first important film producers. Yet another Lumière operator, **Félix Mesguich**, claimed to have shown a new Cinématographe programme to the Tsar in autumn 1897 at his southern palace in Livadia. In 1911 the Tsar encouraged Khanzhonkov, who had been an

101

army officer before entering the film business in 1906, to produce the commemorative *Oborona Sevastopolya (Defence of Sebastopol)*, at 2,000m one of the longest films made anywhere by that date. Closer co-operation followed, when in 1913 both Khanzhonkov and Drankov were allowed to breach normal censorship restrictions covering the portrayal of the imperial family for two films marking the tercentenary of the Romanovs, *Votsareniya doma Romanovikh (Accession of the Romanov Dynasty)* and *Tryokhsotletiye tsarstoivaniya doma Romanovikh (Tercentenary of the Romanov Dynasty's Accession to the Throne)*.

Despite the success of these ventures, police reports were reaching Nikolas of films which could be considered socially disruptive, and in 1913 he wrote in the margin of one such report: 'I consider cinematography to be an empty, useless and even pernicious diversion. Only an abnormal person could put this fairground business on the same level as art. It is all nonsense and no importance should be attributed to it.' No contemporary film record remains of the revolutions which deposed Nikolas and eventually led to his and his family's execution, but his homes movies were used by Esfir Shub in her third compilation film, *Rossiya Nikolaya II: Lev Tolstoy (The Russia of Nikolas II and Leo Tolstoy)* (1928); and when he was first portrayed in a Soviet historical fiction film, Elem Klimov showed him at work in his darkroom in *Agonia* (1975–81). (IC)

References

Peter Kenez, 'Russian Patriotic Films', in Karel Dibbers and Bert Hogenkamp (eds.), *Film and the First World War* (Amsterdam: Amsterdam University Press, 1995).
Leyda, *Kino* (1960).

NOGGERATH, Franz Anton
(1859–1908)

Producer, exhibitor. Nöggerath owned a music hall, Variété Flora, in Amstelstraat, Amsterdam, and after films were shown there from 1896 to 1897, he and his son Franz Anton Jr. (1880–1947) decided to take up cinematography themselves. By 1899 they had begun production, and in November of that year were said to be making Boer War fakes on the roof of the Flora. In 1907 they opened the first major cinema in Amsterdam, the Bioscope-Theater. At about this time another son, Theodor (1882–1961), became a film cameraman, and was active in the second decade of the new century. (SB)

References

Geoffrey Donaldson, 'De eerste Nederlandse speelfilms en de gebroeders Mullens', *Skrien*, no. 28.

NORTON, Charles Goodwin
(1856–1940)

Lanternist, film-maker, projectionist. C. Goodwin Norton was born 8 April 1856 in Shere, near Guildford, Surrey. He worked as a cabinet-maker but when his left hand was partially paralysed in an accident, he opened a stationery shop in St Pancras, London. He later recalled how he purchased a lantern and slides at a book sale, gave several private shows before buying a bi-unial and launching into public performances, while retaining his stationery business. He became well known for his spectacular lantern entertainments (eventually using a triple lantern and featuring dissolving views), introducing films into his programme during the latter half of 1896. He then acquired a Velograph camera and produced quite a number of films through to the end of the century, some or all of which were processed by **G. A. Smith** of Hove, and included such titles as *Street Panorama*, *Promenade* and *Circus*. Other subjects included variations of the familiar *Waves* and *The Gardener and the Hose*, featuring Norton himself as the gardener, and his son Charles Douglas Norton as the mischievous boy. Norton also took the lead in *The Postman and the Nursemaid*, in which the maid was played by his daughter, Alice. More original were *Shop*, an advertising film in which a boy sticks a bill on the Norton's shop window announcing 'Animated Photographs, C. Goodwin Norton', and *Good Night*, a scene outside the shop at closing time.

As well as producing films he continued as an exhibitor. He adapted an early projector to take a reel containing about twenty short films, and gave shows for the Empress Eugénie, wife of Napoleon III (10 September 1896), the royal family at Buckingham Palace (8 January 1897) and Cowes, Isle of Wight (3 January 1899), and for King Edward VII and family on 14 December 1901. He may also have been a projectionist for Harrods department store at this period. Thanks to a donation by his daughter Alice to the National Film Archive, many of the films from Norton's shows, both his own productions and others, have survived, and those featuring the activities of children have a rare charm and distinctive 'home-movie' style. An unpublished biographical note concentrates on his army experiences. He died at Osterley, Middlesex on 22 March 1940. (SH)

References

C. Goodwin Norton, *The Lantern and How to Use It* (London: Hazell, Watson and Viney, 1895).
Barnes, *The Beginnings of the Cinema in England* (vols. 3 and 4).

O

Madame OLINKA

Travelling show-woman. Her origins are obscure, but she is likely to have come from eastern Prussia or western Poland. She booked her appearances, mostly in variety theatres, through an agent in Breslau, who advertised her as 'The most sensational act of the day. A first-class box-office attraction.' Her trade advertisements appeared from early summer 1896, by which time she must have bought her projection apparatus, which came from **H. O. Foersterling** in Berlin; she used Foersterling's advertising campaign for his 'Edison's Ideal' presentations until at least 1898. Her trade advertisements soon carried glowing endorsements from theatre managers across northern Europe, and her schedule was intense. On 27 September 1896 she opened at the Centralhallen-Theater in Hamburg; a week later (October 4) at the Wilhelm theatre in Gorlitz; two weeks after that (October 25) she was at the Variété Flora in Amsterdam; and by the middle of November she was exhibiting in The Hague and Rotterdam.

Madame Olinka had the habit of presenting each film from the stage of the theatre as it was shown, describing the images in stentorian tones that one reporter found 'very original and strange'. In spring 1898 she was in Posnan, Poland, and in May 1900 in the north German city of Halle, now using an 'Edisongraph' projector, which may still have been her original Foersterling apparatus. But in Halle, she was no longer introducing her films from the stage and she disappears thereafter from the historical record, a pioneering and active exhibitor who remains an enigma. (DR)

References

Rossell, 'The New Thing with the Long Name', *Film History*, vol. 7 no. 2, Summer 1995.
Geoffrey Donaldson, 'Wie is Wie in de nederlandse film tot 1930: Madame Olinka', *Skrien*, no. 127, May/June 1983, pp. 26–7.

OLIVER, Félix

The first Uruguayan film-maker. The Lumière Cinématographe reached the Salon Rouge, Montevideo, on 23 July 1896. In 1898 Félix Oliver, a Uruguayan of Spanish descent, having brought back a camera, projector and some films from a trip to Europe, took the first films of Uruguayan scenes. His first known title is a cycling film, *Una carrera de ciclismo en el velodromo de Arroyo Seco*. In 1899 he established a film salon in Montevideo. Returning to Europe in 1900 Oliver met and befriended **Georges Méliès**, picking up a number of film techniques from him. Returning to Uruguay, Oliver continued to film local scenes and news stories for a number of years afterwards. His nephews Mariano and Juan Oliver also became filmmakers. (LMcK)

References

Hennebelle and Gumucio-Dagron, *Les cinémas de l'amérique latine* (1981).
Eugenio Hintz, *Historia y filmografía del cine uruguayo* (Montevideo: Ediciones de la Plaza, 1988).

OTT, Frederick P. (1860–1936).

Mechanic. Fred Ott was one of **Thomas Edison**'s laboratory team who worked on the Kinetoscope, as well as the Phonograph and other projects. Such men included **W. K-L. Dickson**, Charles Brown, Charles Batchelor and Fred's older brother John. The ebullient Fred Ott was the joker among them, and when Edison was approached by journalist Burton Phillips of *Harper's Weekly* requesting 'some nice looking person' to perform a sneeze for the Kinetograph that might be used to illustrate an article, the moustached Ott was the unlikely but willing choice. Dickson and William Heise took the film in the first week of January 1894 and had it copyrighted as a photograph at the Library of Congress on 9 January 1894 under the title, *Edison Kinetoscopic Record of a Sneeze*. At such a short length the film was not intended for the Kinetoscope but purely as a one-off for publicity purposes. The film, or rather the image of Fred Ott's sneeze, became famous, and in later years Ott was happy to claim that he was the first ever 'film star', which in a way was true. (LMcK)

References

Hendricks, *The Edison Motion Picture Myth* (1961).
Gordon Hendricks, 'A New Look at an "Old Sneeze"', *Film Culture* 22/23, Summer 1961.

P

PACCHIONI, Italo (1872–1940)

Pioneer Italian film-maker. Already established as a successful studio photographer, in 1896 Pacchioni, with the aid of his brother Enrico and a mechanic, built a motion picture camera and projector, after the Lumières had refused to sell them a Cinématographe. His first film was a direct riposte to the Lumières: *Arrivo del treno nella stazione di Milano*, which had the advantage of a considerably more spectacular location than La Ciotat offered the Lumières. Also in 1896, Pacchioni made three one-minute staged films: *La gabbia dei matti* (*The Madhouse*), *Battaglia di neve* (*Snow Fight*) and *Il finto storpio* (*The Fake Cripple*), all performed by himself and his family. During the succeeding years Pacchioni also filmed actualities: *La fiera di Porta Genova*, *Il vecchio verziere di Milano*, *Ginnasi della Mediolanum*, *I funerali di Umberto I* (1900), *I funerali di Giuseppe Verdi* (1901). Pacchioni also experimented with stereoscopic films, but seems to have taken little interest in cinema after the first years of the new century. (DRB)

References
Bernardini, *Cinema muto italiano 1896–1904* (1980).

PACHT, Lauritz Vilhelm (1843–1912)

Showman, painter, lithographer. Vilhelm Pacht introduced the cinema to Denmark, when he opened a show of living pictures at his Panorama on the square in front of the city hall in Copenhagen on 7 June 1896, just a few days before **Max Skladanowsky** exhibited his Bioskop in the pantomime theatre of the Tivoli Gardens (11 June). A well-known and modern-thinking member of Charlottenborg society, Pacht was a respected painter by the late 60s, and in 1874 opened Denmark's first printing studio for the production of heliotypes and colour lithographs. He opened his Panoptikon, a 'cabinett' of scientific and natural curiosities and entertainments, in 1885, and two years later set up a factory which manufactured paint and artists' materials, including the new ready-to-use paint in tubes. He presented gramophone concerts with an Edison Phonograph, and dabbled in a variety of electrical and panoramic attractions.

When word of the existence of 'living pictures' reached Denmark, he characteristically set out on a trip to Berlin, Paris and London to investigate the phenomenon and see if it could be added to his presentations in Copenhagen. The Lumières refused him a Cinématographe, and Pacht returned with either a **Birt Acres** Kineoptikon or a **Robert Paul** Theatrograph, together with a selection of films by Acres and Robert Paul. French sources until only recently had stated that Pacht opened a Lumière Cinématographe in Copenhagen, but the Lumières had already given the Danish concession to photographer Harald Limkilde, who suddenly decided to open his apparatus on 28 June in Malmö, Sweden, on the occasion of an industrial exhibition; the Cinématographe never appeared in Copenhagen.

The Danish royal family visited Pacht's screening on 10 June; but on 18 June Pacht's tent was burned to the ground in an arson fire started by an electrician Pacht had dismissed, with the loss of all his apparatus and films. The show was reopened with a new machine and new films on 30 June, and this remained an occasional attraction at Pacht's Panoptikon until 1900. Well established in Copenhagen, Pacht continued to run his various establishments, and to teach painting at the art school until his death in 1912. (DR)

References
Gunnar Sandfeld, *Den stumme Scene: Dansk biografteater indtil lydfilmes gennembrud* (Copenhagen: NYT Nordisk Forlag/Arnold Busk, 1966).
Marguerite Engberg, *Dansk Stumfilm I* (Copenhagen: Rhodos Forlag, 1977).

PALEY, William C. ('Daddy') (1857–1924)

Cameraman and showman. Born in Lincolnshire, England, Paley emigrated to the USA where he became an X-ray (**Röntgen** ray) exhibitor until his health started to suffer from the effects of this apparatus (the first of several bouts of illness which were to dog his life). But Paley was an inventive man, and abandoning X-rays, in 1897 he built a film projector which he named the Kalatechnoscope, and was soon taken on as a cameraman by **Richard Hollaman** for the Eden Musée, partly to film a version of the Passion play staged on a New York rooftop. But a more adventurous assignment was about to begin: war was brewing with Spain at this time, and in March 1898 Paley contracted with the Edison company to film incidents from it, and took his first war views in the same month, filming US troops ready for embarkation in Florida. In June he joined the dozens of journalists following the troops as they invaded Cuba.

Paley soon became known among the war correspondents as 'the Kinetoscope Man', distinctive both for his own bulk and for the novel camera he operated. But he found that filming warfare was not easy: expecting to see cavalry charges, instead it was a war of hidden snipers, and Paley sadly concluded, 'I don't think there is much in this campaign for the kinetoscope'. Then his camera malfunctioned, and living out in the open, constantly soaked by the rain, he went down with fever and almost died on the voyage back to the USA. But he returned to camerawork after his recovery, and the following year established a long-term arrangement with the showman F. F. Proctor, over the next few years filming various scenes around New York and wider afield in Quebec as an Edison licensee.

By mid-1904 Paley had formed a partnership with William F. Steiner, and they began releasing short comedies. But at this time the Edison company was cracking down on independents, and in November they sued several companies, including Paley-Steiner, and by the summer of 1905 the partnership was being dissolved. This was not the end of Paley's woes: in late 1906 or early 1907 he was forced out of business as an independent producer and renter and was looking for work as a freelance cameraman. He next surfaced in 1910, shooting Westerns at the Star Film Ranch in San Antonio, Texas, for Gaston Méliès (brother of **Georges**). The following year the company moved to California, and it is likely that Paley spent much of the rest of his life in the West.

In March 1912, employed by the Nestor Company to film the California mountains, he suffered a fall, and one leg had to be amputated. Ageing and almost destitute, his colleagues set up a fund to help him, and though only a few hundred dollars were raised this must have made life a little easier during his final years, which were spent at Forest Lawn, Hollywood. (SB)

References

'Bill Paley, the Kinetoscope Man', *The Phonoscope*, August 1898, pp. 7–8.
Musser, *The Emergence of Cinema* (1990).
Ramsaye, *A Million and One Nights* (1926).

PARNALAND, Ambroise-François
(1854–1913)

Cameraman, inventor. Born at Tournus, Saône-et-Loire in 1854, Ambroise-François

Parnaland arrived in Paris in 1890 as a chartered accountant. Like his brother Louis, he was fascinated by things mechanical, and they both filed several patents for various mechanisms. On 24 April 1895, Ambroise-François decided to found the firm Parnaland Frères to exploit his patent inventions. The logo 'P. F.' would later cause confusion with that of Pathé Frères.

Parnaland was soon attracted by chronophotography. On 26 February 1896 he filed his first patent for a camera, the Phototheagraphe, in which the unperforated film was moved along by means of a piston. After other clumsy attempts, Parnaland reached near-perfection with a patent of 9 June, having designed an efficient movement mechanism. The Parnaland camera, the Cinepar, was marketed in 1896. The following year, Parnaland made his first films, constructed and sold his cameras, and opened a shop at 5 rue Saint-Denis. In 1898, he filmed the surgical operations of Dr **Eugène-Louis Doyen**, with the cameraman **Clément-Maurice**. But Parnaland marketed the films, without Doyen's permission, and Doyen took him to court. Meanwhile, the Parnaland camera was used by Clément-Maurice to make the Phono-Cinéma-Théâtre sound films.

In 1904, Parnaland collaborated with Emmanuel Ventujol, a former colleague of the Lumières. Several dozen films, intended for fairground use, were produced up to 1907. But Ventujol left the firm soon after, and Charles Jourjon, a lawyer, offered to provide financial backing. On 22 April 1907, the limited company, 'films l'Eclair, anciens établissements Parnaland', was created by Jourjon and Parnaland, and a catalogue listing all the Parnaland films made between 1897 and 1907 was published. But the beginnings of the Eclair company were difficult and costly (a chateau at Epinay was bought to serve as studio and office). Parnaland, a somewhat naive partner, was soon removed from management. Between 1910 and 1911, he was again making and marketing cameras, but business went badly. In 1912, Parnaland returned to accountancy. He died a year later on 23 May 1913, while the Eclair company, the third most significant French firm after Pathé and Gaumont, triumphed on the screens with the adventures of Zigomar. (LM)

References

Laurent Mannoni, 'Ambroise-François Parnaland, Cinema Pioneer, Co-founder of the Eclair Company', *Griffithiana*, vol. 16 no. 47, 1993.

PATHE, Charles Morand (1863–1957)

Producer, manufacturer. Charles Pathé, the third son of Jacques and Emilie Pathé, established pork butchers, was born at Chevry-Cossigny, a market town in the Seine et Marne *départmente*, on 26 December 1863. After what he later described as a difficult childhood and youth, lengthy military service and a hazardous journey in South America, Charles returned to France and, in October 1893, he married. While working in a firm of lawyers for a meagre salary, he chanced on the novelty of the moment, the Edison Phonograph, which was a sensation at the Vincennes Fair on the east of Paris, and with partly borrowed money, he bought one. On 9 September 1894 he returned with his wife to one of the best-known fairs of the period, Monthéty to the east of Paris, and in the one day, at a charge of 20 centimes per listener, made 200 francs. Quick to recognise the advantages of selling rather than using the Phonograph, he bought three examples in London, and successfully resold them. Shortly after, another curiosity appeared – the Edison Kinetoscope. Charles, who had opened a shop at 72 cours de Vincennes in Paris, revisited London in 1895, bought Kinetoscopes manufactured by **Robert Paul** and resold them to fairgrounds. Later in 1895, he was associated for a while with **Henri Joly**, who manufactured for him a camera to take films for the Kinetoscope.

But the future of Charles Pathé was decided by the arrival of the Lumière Cinématographe. On 28 September 1896, with his brother Emile, he formed the Société Pathé Frères, with offices at 98 rue de Richelieu in Paris. A year later, the company became, thanks to a certain Claude Grivolas, the Compagnie Générale de Cinématographes, Phonographes et Pellicules

(Anciens Etablissements Pathé Frères), with the two brothers as directors. From then on, the company, under the direction of Emile (phonograph) and of Charles (cinematograph), flourished, expanded and sold all over the world. 'I did not invent the cinema, but I industrialised it', wrote Charles Pathé later. A modest first factory had been functioning since 1896 at Vincennes. Charles Pathé himself probably made the first films of the Société Pathé Frères, including *Le Passage à niveau à Joinville le Pont* and *L'Arrivée d'un train en gare de Bel-Air*.

For several years the phonograph underwrote the success of the company. In 1898, a phonograph cylinder factory was built at Chatou, west of Paris and, in 1903, enlarged. In August 1900 the company amalgamated with the Manufacture Française d'Appareils de Précision (Anciens Etablissements René Bünzli et Victor Continsouza) to form the Compagnie Générale de Phonographes, Cinématographes et Appareils de Précision. From then on Charles Pathé developed both the manufacture of negative and positive film, the creation of factories and studios, and the making of cameras and projectors for sale worldwide. From 1902, new film studios and new factories for the manufacture and development of film were constructed at Vincennes, at Montreuil sous Bois and at Joinville le Pont. The company then extended, creating branches all over the world: February 1904, Moscow; July 1904, New York, and so on. At the beginning of 1908 Charles Pathé decided to create centres of film production abroad that would be more or less independent of the French parent company: in 1909 at Rome and Moscow, in 1910 in the USA at Jersey City, and later in Holland, Belgium and elsewhere. The number of films produced continued to increase, growing from seventy in 1901 to nearly 800 in 1912.

In 1907, Pathé, following British and American practice, started to rent his films instead of selling them. A little earlier he had undertaken, in collaboration with exhibitors, the construction of permanent halls, the first of which, the Omnia-Pathé in Paris, opened on 15 December 1906. By now many Pathé films were hand-coloured, but very soon mechanical colouring processes were perfected in the company's laboratories and, by 1912, the Pathé-Color stencil process was used in at least one film in five. In 1912, Charles Pathé, reviving an idea he had first proposed in 1909, created the famous Pathé Kok, the 28mm-format 'home cinema' (to be supplanted by the Pathé-Baby in 1922).

As the company had expanded, Charles had surrounded himself with numerous devoted collaborators: commercial travellers and branch managers, such as Sigmund Popert, J. A. Berst, Hache; directors or producers such as Ferdinand Zecca, Albert Capellani, Pierre Decourcelle, Paul Gugenheim or Louis J. Gasnier; chemists and engineers, such as Jacques Marette, Henri Garrel; experts like Dr J. Comandon and a whole galaxy of valued performers to whom Charles Pathé paid tribute in his memoirs.

Charles Pathé, in addition to having the obstinacy and drive needed to create and lead the company that carries his name, was a shrewd and pragmatic businessman with an exceptional commercial talent. However, as co-director in 1912 with his brother Emile, Pathé was obliged from early 1914 to attempt to restructure this huge empire. But four years of war provoked the breakup of the firm. In 1927, with the creation of Kodak-Pathé, Charles Pathé retired. He died at Monaco on his ninety-fourth birthday. (HB)

References

Jacques Kermabon (ed.), *Pathé: Premier empire du cinéma* (Paris: Centre Pompidou, 1994).
Charles Pathé, *Souvenirs et conseils d'un parvenu* (Paris, 1926).
Charles Pathé, *De Pathé-Frères à Pathé Cinéma* (Nice, 1940).

PAUL, Robert William (1869–1943)

Foremost pioneer of the British film industry in its formative years. Robert Paul was born on 3 October 1869 at 3 Albion Place, off Liverpool Road, Highbury, north London. He was educated at the City and Guilds Technical College, Finsbury. Before starting business on his own account in 1891, he worked in the

electrical instrument shop of Elliott brothers in the Strand, where he obtained a practical knowledge of instrument making. His own business was conducted from 44 Hatton Garden. His main concern was producing instruments to meet the ever-growing demands of the electrical industry, and in this he was very successful. In addition to his achievements in the electrical field, Paul holds a unique position in the history of the early cinema. His talents were such that he combined not only the roles of inventor and manufacturer but also those of producer, exhibitor and cinematographer. No other film pioneer ever matched his extraordinary versatility, yet Paul himself regarded his film work as just a sideline to his electrical interests.

Paul's involvement with cinematography came about by chance, when he was asked to make replicas of Edison's Kinetoscope, a peepshow device for viewing 35mm films by transmitted light, which had not yet been patented in England. Having agreed to manufacture the machines for his clients, Greek entrepreneurs **Georgiades** and **Tragides**, he then decided to make others for himself. The only films available were controlled by the Edison company, and so in order for Paul's Kinetoscope business to succeed, it was essential that he make his own films. With only the Kinetoscope machine and its films to go on, Paul, with the assistance of a professional photographer, **Birt Acres**, designed and manufactured a cinematograph camera, now known as the Paul-Acres camera.

By 29 March 1895, the first successful English film had been shot, featuring Paul's friend **Henry Short** outside Clovelly Cottage, Barnet, the home of Birt Acres. Between February and June 1895 Acres went on to film other subjects for Paul, including *Oxford and Cambridge University Boat Race*; *Arrest of a Pickpocket* (the first dramatic photoplay made in England); *The Derby*; *Comic Shoe Black*; *Boxing Kangaroo*; *Performing Bears*; *Boxing Match*; *Carpenter's Shop*; *Dancing Girls*; *Rough Sea at Dover*; and *Tom Merry, Lightning Cartoonist*. These are the very first films made in England, and were seen for the first time from 27 May to October at the Empire of India Exhibition, Earl's Court, where Paul had installed a number of his Kinetoscopes. At that time, of course, the projection of films upon a screen was still largely unknown. After the last of these films were taken, the incompatible Paul and Acres parted company. Thereafter, each went his own independent way, Paul to ever greater success and Acres to eventual oblivion and bankruptcy.

On 24 October 1895, Paul filed a patent application for a moving picture journey through time, inspired by the H. G. Wells novella, *The Time Machine*, in which the audience would experience the physical sensation of being transported through time and space. Among the methods suggested for achieving this illusion was screen projection of Kinetoscope films. Though the idea never materialised, something of the sort eventually appeared as Hale's Tours of the World, which simulated a railway journey by means of films shot from the front of a locomotive.

Paul achieved screen projection at the beginning of 1896, when he published details of his first projector, the Theatrograph, in the *English Mechanic* (21 February). This was the first commercially produced 35mm film projector to be produced in Britain. The previous day, Paul had given a demonstration of his Theatrograph at his old technical college in Finsbury on the very same day that the Lumière Cinématographe was shown at the Polytechnic, Regent Street. A further demonstration of the Theatrograph was given at the Royal Institution on the 28th. Its public debut occurred on 19 March at the Egyptian Hall, Piccadilly (presented by **David Devant**) and two days later Paul exhibited it at Olympia. The first model of the Theatrograph had some defects, but despite its imperfections it nevertheless proved to be the prototype for the modern projector. Within a few days of the launch of the first Theatrograph, Paul produced a second improved model, which he patented on 2 March 1896. In all, Paul was to design and manufacture no fewer than five different models before quitting the film business in 1910. Among the innovations he introduced were an intermittent mechanism based on the Maltese cross, modern-type sprockets that prevented wear on the film, and a number of features that rendered the machine fireproof. He also envisaged the mobile electric generator for fairground showmen.

After his breakup with Birt Acres, Paul did not resume film production until April 1896, when he constructed a new camera based on the design of his second Theatrograph projector. By this time screen projection was becoming the recognised way of presenting films, rendering the Kinetoscope peepshow obsolete. In addition to the various actualities shot in the streets, a little comedy called *A Soldier's Courtship* was staged on the roof of the Alhambra theatre, Leicester Square, where he was then exhibiting. This starred **Fred Storey**, Julie Seale and Paul's wife Ellen as the interloper. It

became so popular that he made a second version the following year. Paul also recorded the topical events of the day, and his film of the Derby of 3 June 1896 was shown at two major London theatres within twenty-four hours of the event taking place, thus marking the true beginning of the news film.

Paul was one of the first English producers to realise the possibilities of cinema as a means of presenting short comic and dramatic stories, and to this end he built the first studio in England, with an adjacent laboratory capable of processing up to 8,000ft of film per day. He employed a staff of very able technicians, some of whom – **G. H. Cricks**, J. H. Martin, **Jack Smith**, **Walter Booth** – went on to achieve success in their own right. Paul's films were some of the most technically advanced for the times, his trick films being extremely ingenious. His choice of subject matter was more varied than that of any of his contemporaries, and his coverage of topical events, including the war in South Africa, was matched only by that of the Warwick Trading Company and the Mutoscope and Biograph Syndicate.

By the turn of the century his film projectors were being exported to the Continent, as well as to Australia and other British dependencies. He entirely dominated the home market and it is no wonder that he earned his title, 'Father of the British Film Industry'. In 1920 his business was amalgamated with Cambridge Scientific Instruments Ltd. When he died on 28 March 1943, at the age of seventy-four, he left industrial shares valued at over £100,000 to form a trust - the R. W. Paul Instrument Fund – administered by the Institution of Electrical Engineers, of which he had been a continuous member since 1887. The income was to be used primarily for the provision of instruments of a novel or unusual character to assist physical research. (JB)

References

Barnes, *The Beginnings of the Cinema in England* (vols. 1–5).
Robert W. Paul, 'Before 1910: Kinematograph Experiences', *Proceedings of the British Kinematograph Society*, no. 38 (London: BKS, 1936) [reprinted in Fielding, *A Technological History of Motion Pictures and Television* (1967)].

PAULUS (Paul Habans) (1845–1908)

One of the earliest stars of the French music hall, and the first to earn a huge salary, fame initially came to Paulus as a result of a verse he sang about General Boulanger in 1886. He then worked almost continuously in Paris and

Marseilles, and was well known for his powerful voice and delivery, presenting the character of a fashionably dressed boulevardier who sings of the joys of good living and the importance of patriotism. Paulus toured to London and the USA in 1891-2, and managed the Ba-ta-clan and the Marseilles Alhambra theatres, rather unsuccessfully, before retiring in 1903.

His brief meeting with the cinematograph occurred in early 1897, when he was filmed by **Georges Méliès**. This took place in the magician's *laboratoire* near the Paris Opera, just before his studio was completed. In order to film at all, some thirty arc and mercury lamps were rigged up, one of the first times artificial light was used for cinematography. Paulus was filmed singing five of his songs, including 'Derrière l'omnibus' and 'Coquin de printemps', and these were then projected at his Ba-ta-clan theatre. The reasons for this project are somewhat unclear: by this time Paulus was aged and infirm, and it is suggested that the films would spare him performing live; but it is implied elsewhere that Paulus was planning to sing along with the films from behind the screen. In any case, according to Méliès, his appearance on the screen was greeted every night in the theatre by enthusiastic applause. He died in poverty, having lost the remainder of his savings in a failed wine business. (BA/SB)

References

Chantal Brunschweig, Louis-Jean Calvert and John-Claude Klein, *100 Ans de chanson française* (Paris: Editions du Seuil, 1972).
Madeleine Malthète-Méliès, *Méliès l'enchanteur* (Paris: Opera Mundi, 1973).

PERRY, Joseph Henry (1864–1943)

Magic lanternist and film-maker for the Salvation Army. Perry was born in Birmingham, England, and emigrated with his family to New Zealand at the age of ten. At the age of nineteen he joined the Salvation Army, and in 1885 was posted by the Army to Australia. Following the early death of his wife, Perry turned to his hobby of photography to help support his three young children, setting up a commercial studio in Ballarat. Perry's abilities as a photographer, along with his imaginative use of advertising lantern slides projected in the streets of Ballarat, led to his appointment by the Army as their official equipment operator and to the creation in 1892 of the Limelight department, of which Perry took full control in 1893. Originally using projected lantern slides as both advertisements and illustrations to lectures, the arrival in 1896 of the new Salvation Army commandant for Australasia, **Herbert Booth**, saw the introduction of projected film, stimulated by the appearance of a number of projectors in Australia. Perry purchased a Motorgraph, produced by the London firm of W. Watson and Sons, in February 1897. After a private exhibition to Army members in March, Perry undertook his first public screening at Albany on 4 April 1897, attracting large crowds. He toured Australia for the next two months before turning to the production of his own films, beginning with a Melbourne street scene in October 1897. Serious production began in February 1898 following the construction of a glass-walled studio at the Army's Melbourne headquarters. Used for the production of photographic slides as well as films, the studio was to remain Australia's main film production centre until 1907.

The purpose of the Army's film production was chiefly to raise funds, with touring lectures accompanied by a mixture of films, slides and wax cylinders, but they also eventually took commissions and offered a film-processing service. Under Herbert Booth's direction Perry shot many actualities and Australia's first narrative films, including the 'multimedia' presentations, *Social Salvation* (1898–9) and the famous *Soldiers of the Cross* (1900) (for details of these films, see Booth entry). In Chris Long's phrase, the Limelight department 'shot film for propaganda, patronage and profit', and did so on all three counts with great success. While they retained a single camera (a Lumière Cinématographe), which restricted the films of their narrative works to minute-long sections, Perry shot everything.

Late in 1900 Booth fell ill and Perry formed his own touring company, the First Biorama Company. Booth was becoming increasingly distanced from the Army, departing Australia in 1902, though the Army's interest in film continued to flourish without him. Perry produced a two-hour show, *Under Southern Skies*, in 1902, a documentary on the history of Australia, but he thereafter turned increasingly to secular commissions, including many news stories. In 1908 a new studio was constructed by the Limelight department, and in 1909 Perry produced *Heroes of the Cross* (a remake of *Soldiers*) and *The Scottish Covenanters*. However, they found that film competition in Australia had become too great, and in any case the then regime felt that the image of the cinema was not suitable for the Army, so the

Limelight department was disbanded. Perry took up work in the commercial film industry, joining Co-operative Films and distributing in the Dutch East Indies throughout the 1920s. His sons, Orizaba, Reginald and Stanley, all pursued long careers in the Australian film industry. (CL/LMcK)

References
Chris Long, 'Screening the Salvation Army', *Cinema Papers* 97/98, April 1994.

PERSIMMON (1893–1908)

Racehorse. Sired by St Simon out of Perdita II, bred at the Sandringham stud, owned by the Prince of Wales (the future Edward VII) and trained by Richard Marsh, Persimmon was one of the most celebrated racehorses of the late-Victorian era. Described as having 'a bold head, perfect shoulder and wonderful power behind the saddle', his greatest win was the 1896 Derby when, ridden by Jack Watts, he set a course record of 2 minutes 42 seconds, beating his great rival St Frusquin by a neck. The close finish and the royal connection made it a hugely popular victory, and consequently **Robert Paul**'s short film of the finish of the race became a triumph. **Birt Acres** had filmed the unremarkable 1895 Derby for Paul, but Paul's feat of getting his film of 3 June onto the screen at London's Alhambra and Canterbury music halls within twenty-four hours of the race's finish caused amazement and was a tremendous advertisement for the new medium. People stood and cheered the film, demanding that it be shown again and again, and calling out 'God bless the Prince of Wales'.

Though film of news events had already been taken, notably the coronation of Tsar **Nikolas II** the previous month, Paul's Derby film qualifies as the first true news film for the speed of its screening, initiating a tradition for speedy newsreel work that was to flourish in Britain in particular. Paul proceeded to film the Derby from the same, rather poor camera position (just after the finishing post) for the next few years, leading to much confusion later on between the 1896 film and other, similar, records. The Prince of Wales was to win the Derby again in 1900 with Persimmon's true brother, Diamond Jubilee, but nothing could match the extraordinary scenes of enthusiasm and delight that followed the most famous Derby of them all. (LMcK)

References
Barnes, *The Beginnings of the Cinema in England* (vol. 1).

'The Prince's Derby, Shown by Lightning Photography', *Strand Magazine*, August 1896.

PETERSON, Numa Wilhelm (1837–1902)

Photographic manufacturer, producer. Owner of the large and successful photographic suppliers Numa Petersons Handels & Fabriks AB, in addition to his photographic display at the 1897 Jubilee Exhibition in Stockholm, Peterson built a cinema building in the style of Renaissance Stockholm, inaugurated by **Alexandre Promio** and managed by **C. V. Roikjer**. During July and August 1897, Peterson produced the short films of **Ernest Florman**, and at the closing of the Exhibition moved his Cinématographe to the Gamla Panoptikon at 12 Kungsträdgårdsgatan, where it ran from 27 October 1897 until 30 August 1898. In mid-1897 he sent his assistant Adolf Berggren with a Lumière programme on a tour of the small towns in the north.

After his death in 1902, the company was taken over by his son, Mortimer Peterson (1867–1920), and in 1904 produced a group of sound films synchronised with gramophone records and directed by Otto Bökman, including a scene from the popular musical play, *The Värmlanders*. (DR)

References
Bengt Idestam-Almquist, *När Filmen kom till Sverige* (Stockholm, 1959).
Rune Waldekranz, *Levende Bilder: De första biograferna* (Stockholm, 1955) [reprinted as 'La nascita del cinema in Scandanavia' in Paolo Cherchi Usai (ed.), *Schiave bianche allo specchio* (Pordenone: Edizioni Studio Tesi, 1986)].

PFEFFER, Wilhelm Friedrich Philipp (1845–1920)

German botanist. Wilhelm Pfeffer, working at the University of Leipzig, in 1900 published a paper on the use of the cinematograph in studying plant growth. Pfeffer's innovation was to extend the chronophotographic experiments of **E-J. Marey** into the true film world by time-lapse cinematography, producing a minute-long film over a period of weeks by exposing one frame at a time at regular spaced intervals. Thus, by condensing time, the film could make the stages of plant growth visible. Now a commonplace technique in television documentaries, time-lapse cinematography was brought to general and popular notice by the work of Percy Smith for **Charles Urban**, with such titles as the famous and archetypal, *The Birth of a Flower* (LMcK).

References
Tosi, *Il cinema prima di Lumière* (1984).

PIASECKI (or PYASSETSKY), Dr Pawel Yakovlevich (1843–1919)

Military doctor, geographer, artist. After conducting some experimental work in medicine, Piasecki set off on an expedition to Mongolia and China in 1874–5. He published a long, engagingly written account of the trip, which must have been well received as it was translated into both French and English. The expedition was accompanied by a photographer, and Piasecki himself made many drawings. Perhaps this experience of travel illustration gave him the idea for a more sophisticated approach to visual travelogues, which consisted of drawing pictures of places or events on long, slowly unwinding panoramas of paper. Piasecki demonstrated one such strip to the Russian Imperial court in December 1895, and though they apparently rejected his offer to make another of Tsar **Nikolas II**'s coronation in 1896, he went ahead anyway, and his 58m panorama still survives in the Hermitage Museum.

But a bigger challenge was ahead. The five years up to 1900 saw the fastest ever rate of rail construction in Russia, notably on the trans-Siberian railway. Piasecki, with the advantages of his Far Eastern experience, was involved in making a panorama of the view along the line, both on film and on his paper-roll system, though there is some confusion as to what his precise role was in this project. On 3 May 1898 the *Morning Post* reported that Piasecki had been commissioned some time before to make a cinematograph of the whole line as far as Krasnoyarsk, and that a special carriage had been constructed for 'preparing the films'. The report added that the task had already been accomplished and that the Tsar 'seated in his study, was enabled by the aid of Dr Piasecki's pictures to obtain precisely the same views of the Siberian country traversed by the line as he would have had if he had made the journey by train'.

According to **Alice Guy**, the film had been commissioned by the Compagnie des Wagons-Lits, and filmed by a Gaumont operator. She recalls it being shown in the Paris studio of the set designers Jambon and Bailly, and Jambon is credited as the painter, though Piasecki won the gold medal for it at the Paris Exposition.

What seems most likely is that he acted as the 'producer' of both the film and the paper-roll, Gaumont and Jambon respectively carrying out the detailed work, with the whole project possibly financed by the French rail company. The panorama alone was a major undertaking, consisting of four huge rolls (one of which was over 900m long, and survives today) unspooling at different distances from a mock carriage in which the 'passenger' sat, served by eastern attendants. The 'trip' lasted nearly an hour, and was a big success both at the Paris Exposition in 1900 and the St Louis World's Fair in 1904. (SB)

References
Sehnsucht: das Panorama als Massenunterhaltung des 19 Jahrhunderts (Frankfurt: Stroemfeld/Roter Stern, 1993).
Anthony Slide (ed.), *The Memoirs of Alice Guy Blaché* (Metuchen NJ/London: Scarecrow Press, 1986).

PIROU, Eugène

Photographer, pornographer. Though Eugène Pirou has long been recognised as one of the pioneering film-makers in France, his work as a stills photographer is less well known. He was working as a portrait photographer from at least the time of the Paris Commune in 1871, where he took pictures of the slain communards. In 1888 he photographed General Boulanger in full uniform, and the following year was present at the Paris Exposition, where **E-J. Marey**'s chronophotography was on display, and perhaps this is where his interest in moving photography began. In 1896 he wrote to the Eastman Kodak Company asking for information about the Edison Vitascope, but nothing seems to have come of this and instead he teamed up with **Henri Joly**, who had developed a projector. This allowed Pirou to be one of the first rivals to the Lumières in France, presenting films at the Café de la Paix in Paris in April 1896. By this time he had dubbed himself as the *photographe des rois*, and appropriately the first films he made were of the visit of Tsar **Nikolas II** to France in October 1896, depicting various official activities.

But Pirou's real importance is in pioneering another type of production, the risqué film. In the autumn of 1896 he produced *Le Coucher de la mariée*, in which Mlle. Louise Willy re-created the most sensational part of her eponymous stage hit, and performed a striptease. The resulting film was unusually long at 60m (around three minutes), and was such a sensation when shown in Paris (along with the films of the Tsar's visit) that Pirou opened at two other venues in the city, and even exhibited at the Casino in Nice. Anxious to cash in, other film-makers, including **Georges Méliès** and **Charles Pathé,** also made striptease films, and so was launched an entire genre of risqué films, known in France as *scènes grivoises d'un caractère piquant.* Such films were not always welcomed, and one of them (probably the Pirou title) had to be withdrawn from a London music hall in January 1897 after protests from the more respectable clientele. **Léar,** the director of *Le Coucher de la mariée,* may have been a trader in pornographic pictures, another of Pirou's business interests, though Léar went on to make the first film of the life of Christ.

It is not clear what happened to Pirou after the turn of the century, but his place in film history was assured; in the brief period 1896–7 he had made over fifty films (frames of which are preserved in the Bibliothèque Nationale). Other achievements in these years include pioneering the amateur film business, and also (probably for the first time) enticing a theatrical star, Cécile Sorel, before the camera. (SB)

References

Jacques Deslandes, *Le Boulevard du cinéma à l'époque de Georges Méliès* (Paris: Editions du Cerf, 1963).
Donald E. English, *Political Uses of Photography in the Third French Republic* (Ann Arbor, Mich.: UMI Research Press, 1984).
Mannoni, *Le grand art de la lumière et de l'ombre* (1994).
Sadoul, *Histoire générale du cinéma,* vol. 1 (1946).

PORTER, Edwin Stanton (1870–1941)

Director, cameraman. The most significant creative figure in the earliest years of American film-making, Edwin S. Porter was born on 21 April 1870 in Connellsville, Philadelphia.

He left school at fourteen, working at a variety of occupations, chiefly as a telegraph operator but with a spell in the theatre, and also picking up a considerable knowledge of electricity that was to prove his passport into the world of film. Between 1893 and 1896 he served in the US navy. On his discharge he teamed up with Charles H. Balsey and Richard S. Paine, two friends who had acquired territorial rights for the Edison Vitascope from **Raff and Gammon** for California. Porter, however, soon set off again, teaming up with showman Harry J. Daniels, and equipped with the International Film Company's Projectograph projector to travel the Caribbean. He was back in New York by the summer of 1897, assisting for a while at **Richard Hollaman**'s Eden Musée theatre, moving on with Daniels once more to tour Canada, then returning in the autumn to work as an operator at the Eden Musée. Here he was instrumental in the exhibition of the *Passion Play* extravaganza and the Eden Musée's imaginative display of Spanish-American War films throughout 1898.

Porter left in 1900 to resume his career as a travelling showman, but when a fire destroyed his small projector business, he joined the Edison Manufacturing Company full time. Initially employed as a mechanic, Porter gradually turned to the production of films, working in partnership with George S. Fleming, and in a short time becoming responsible as cameraman and director for the greater amount of Edison product.

From basic beginnings, Porter absorbed much from his contemporaries, adopting trick work and narrative innovations, and in 1903 he directed two seminal American films, *The Life of an American Fireman* and *The Great Train Robbery.* The former film employed a simple but effective multi-scene narrative, in which a dramatised rescue was intercut with actuality film of a real fire brigade. The latter film, lasting twelve minutes, was the classic Hollywood film in embryo: an exciting story that built up its suspense by linked scenes, owed nothing to the theatre, was wholly comprehensible, offered the thrill of enacted crime, and ended with a revolutionary shock tactic as one of the gunmen points his gun at the camera and fires. The film caused a sensation, was a huge financial success, and its mythic power has yet to dim.

Porter continued to work for Edison until 1909, though his work seemed increasingly journeyman as the cinema started to progress beyond him. In November 1909 he left Edison to form his own production company, Defender, followed by the Rex Film Company, before selling his interest in 1912 and joining Famous Players, run by Adolph Zukor. Pursuing the prestigious and seemingly profitable strategy of 'famous players in famous plays', Zukor made Porter his chief director, but the features he made from such literary sources as *The Prisoner of Zenda* and *The Count of Monte Cristo* (both 1913) showed little cinematic virtuosity.

Porter was always more of a technician than an artist, enjoying best those films that involved camera trickery (such as *The Dream of a Rarebit Fiend* of 1906) and finding most contentment experimenting with projectors and other film equipment. Porter sold his share in Famous Players in 1915 and invested in the Precision Machine Corporation, producers of the Simplex projector. Made president of the company, he lost his fortune in the 1929 stock market crash, and spent the remainder of his life in obscurity, experimenting with film devices that were destined to be used by no one. (LMcK)

References
Musser, *Before the Nickelodeon* (1991).

POWER, Nicholas (1854–1921)

Projector manufacturer. Power's projectors were, along with Edison's machines, the first American projectors produced on a commercial scale. They were extremely popular, and a large number were exported to Britain and around the world. A dabbler in real estate before becoming involved with film presentation, Power was acting as projectionist at Koster and Bial's Music Hall, New York, in the autumn of 1896 or spring of 1897, and later at a vaudeville theatre in Brooklyn. Dismantling the intermittent movement of an Edison projector, he was unable to reassemble it in time for the evening show, and quit, either voluntarily or 'by request'.

Soon afterwards he set up a repair shop for Edison projectors, and in 1897 or 1898 developed his own machine, the Power's Peerless Projector. Few were sold, but shortly afterwards came the Power's No. 1 and several subsequent models, with the No. 4 of 1905 selling in its thousands, and the No. 5 proving equally popular. Power's 'Cameragraph' projectors incorporated a novel variation of the Maltese cross, designed to speed up the pulldown of the film and thereby reduce flicker on the screen. In a 1925 presentation to the Society of Motion Picture Engineers, F. H. Richardson regretted

that Power 'has passed to that bourne whence no traveler ever returns, into the shadows of which so many of the pioneers of the industry have already entered'. (SH)

References
F. H. Richardson, 'What Happened in the Beginning', *Transactions of the SMPTE*, September 1925 [reprinted in Fielding, *A Technological History of Motion Pictures and Television* (1967)].

PRESTWICH, John Alfred (1874–1952)

Engineer. Founder member of the Prestwich Manufacturing Company, established in 1895, Prestwich was an engineer of outstanding ability, who constructed some of the finest cinematographic apparatus of cinema's first decade. He is best remembered today, outside of film circles, for the 'JAP' motorcycle engine, so named from his initials.

John Alfred Prestwich was born in Kensington, London, and was educated at the City and Guilds School and the City of London School. Aged sixteen, he was employed by S. Z. de Ferranti, maker of electrical apparatus and scientific instruments. After two years he was articled to a firm of engineers and left, aged twenty, to start his own business, making electrical fittings and scientific instruments in a glasshouse in his father's garden. He was associated with the photographic firm of W. H. Prestwich, London (possibly W. H. was his father).

In 1896 John Alfred Prestwich teamed up with **William Friese Greene** to patent and construct a projector with twin lenses (arranged vertically) to provide projection from one lens while the film was being pulled down ready for the other. It was one of many early film devices intended to ensure that there was always an image on the screen, thereby eliminating flicker. It was promoted in 1898, but as with all machines requiring specially printed films, it had no influence on the development of cine technology; the solution to the flicker problem was resolved in other ways.

In November 1897 Prestwich was selling the Moto-Photograph apparatus, which **W. C. Hughes** had previously sold as the Moto Bijou Living Picture Camera, but which had been designed by one of the Prestwich family (probably John Alfred, since it shares the same mechanism as the Duplex machine he produced with Friese Greene). It was awarded a silver medal at the Glasgow International Photographic Exhibition.

Another member of the company was E. P. Prestwich, who seems to have undertaken most of the firm's limited motion picture production, including **Queen Victoria**'s Diamond Jubilee procession (1897); views of the launch of the *Albion* (1898), shot on both 35mm and 60mm for the Duplex machine; **W. G. Grace**'s Jubilee Procession at Lord's cricket ground in July 1898; and one of their few fiction films, *The Artist's Model* (1898). From 1897 the firm also sold three models of projector, with a superior fast-pulldown mechanism, and in 1898–1900 produced the 'Junior' amateur outfit for 17.5mm film, also sold by Hughes as 'La Petite', together with a reversing projector for showing films backwards for comic effect.

Under J. A. Prestwich's guidance the firm rapidly expanded and was soon engaged in a wide range of engineering products, most notably connected with the motorcycle industry. For nearly two decades he invented, designed and manufactured cinematographic equipment: cameras, printers, mutoscopes, cutting and perforating machines and projectors, including the Bioscope projectors for the Warwick Trading Company and **Charles Urban**. The firm later became known as J. A. Prestwich Industries Ltd., and was absorbed in 1964 by the Villiers Engineering Company. (SH)

References

Barnes, *The Beginnings of the Cinema in England* (vols. 1–4).

PROMIO, Jean Alexandre Louis
(1868–1926)

Lumière operator. Alexandre Promio, from a Lyon family of Italian descent, was assistant to a Lyon optician named Boulade when he (supposedly) witnessed the first presentation

of the Cinématographe in the city in June 1895. The new phenomenon greatly excited him, and on 1 March 1896 he left his job and was taken on by the Lumière firm, by then seeking to expand its business worldwide. With M. Perrigot he became responsible for the training of the Cinématographe operators who were to exhibit the machine the world over.

Promio was not to spend much time in Lyon, however, as he was also destined to become one of the most widely travelled of the Lumière team over the next two years. First journeying to Spain in April 1896, he introduced moving pictures to that country on 13 May at a private screening organised for the French ambassador and other dignitaries at the Hotel Rusia, 36 Carrera de San Jeronimo, Madrid, followed by a public screening at the same location on 15 May. He further exhibited in Spain, photographing local scenes and thus swelling the Lumière catalogue, as he was to continue doing throughout his journeys. Following a private screening for the Queen of Spain on 12 June in Madrid, Promio is next recorded in Russia on 7 July, when he gave a film demonstration for Tsar **Nikolas II** and the Tsarina in St Petersburg. At this same period he also seems to have visited England, Italy, Germany and Hungary. He was a member of the Lumière team that set out to conquer the USA, arriving early in September 1896 and filming several scenes along the East Coast, in response to a demand for American Lumière scenes. He left on 25 September (the negatives were developed in France), then moved on to Italy when he probably took the famous travelling shot from a Venice gondola, often cited as the first time that anyone had moved the camera.

Between December 1896 and January 1897 Promio was in Egypt, followed by Palestine (then part of the Ottoman empire), where he filmed scenes in Jaffa and Jerusalem. Between February and March 1897 he was in Turkey. Presumably returning to Lyon for a period, he next turns up in Sweden on 15 May 1897 for the filming of the arrival of King Oscar at the Stockholm exhibition in honour of his Silver Jubilee, during which time he also trained local operator **Ernest Florman**. Returning to Russia and St Petersburg he then covered the visit of President Fauré of France on 23–25 August. He returned once more to Lyon (possibly visiting Belgium), but was filming in England (and probably Ireland) in late September, presenting the results on the new Lumière Triograph projector at Gatti's music hall, London, in October, together with **George Francis**. By 1898 Promio's travels were largely over, and he settled in Lyon, still in the employ of the Lumière firm. He claimed to have filmed at **Queen Victoria**'s funeral on 1 February 1901, but soon after had left Lyon and the Lumières entirely.

Information on Promio's later career is sketchy. In 1907 he was making films for Pathé; in 1914–15 he saw military service. After the war he became photographer and cinematographer to the Algerian government. He died on Christmas Eve 1926. Promio was, in Rittaud-Hutinet's words, 'une sorte de dandy globe-trotter', always staying in the best hotels, tipping (or bribing) lavishly and revelling in the high society that was briefly attracted to the new phenomenon of moving pictures. Though such a well-known figure, there is little actual biographical information on him, and confusion abounds in existing sources. Even his correct forename has long been a puzzle. Jean-Claude Seguin-Vergara has shown persuasively that his full name was Jean Alexandre Louis, that he was known as Alexandre, and that all other names under which he is reported, such as Eugène, Georges and Albert, are a fantasy. (LMcK)

References
Coissac, *Histoire du Cinématographe* (1925).
Rittaud-Hutinet, *Le Cinéma des origines* (1985).
Jean-Claude Seguin-Vergara, 'La Légende Promio (1868–1926)', *1895*, no. 11, December 1991.

PROSZYNSKI, Kazimierz (1875–1945)

Polish inventor. Proszynski was a member of the Warsaw Photographic Society from a young age, no doubt influenced by his family: his grandfather managed a photographic business in Minsk from 1839, and his father was an enthusiastic amateur photographer. Shortly after commencing his studies at Liège Polytechnic in 1893, he started experimenting with cinematography. There are claims that by the end of 1894 he had made his own apparatus, the Pleograf. By 1898, he had developed and demonstrated the Bio-pleograf. This apparatus (like **Max Skladanowsky**'s first projector) used two films moving alternately, so that an image was always being projected, with no period of darkness between; an arrangement that was very successful in reducing flicker, but proved too cumbersome to be widely adopted. Demonstrations in 1899 included some of his own films, made from a single negative. In 1902–3 the Pleograf Company was formed in Warsaw to promote his invention, and within a year or two a single-film model had been devised.

In 1906 or 1907 he returned to complete his studies in Liège, taking his engineering degree in 1908. He continued working on the problem of reducing flicker, and was instrumental in promoting the three-blade shutter, which was a simple but important improvement in projection design. Shortly after he demonstrated this in Paris, it was adopted by the Gaumont Company and other equipment manufacturers. By 1910 he had developed the Aeroscope (originally Autopleograf) camera, which used compressed air as a power source, enabling it to be hand-held. This went into production in England in 1912, first by **Newman** and Sinclair, later by F. Van Neck. It became very popular, particularly for aerial photography, and was used by film-makers for many years, including the nature and travel photographer, Cherry Kearton, and newsreel and War Office 'kinematographer', Geoffrey Malins.

Between 1911–12 and 1915 Proszynski worked in London with the Warwick Trading Company, and experimented with the pneumatic synchronisation of films and sound disc. The Oko (Polish for 'eye'), an amateur camera/projector of novel design, used a 12cm-wide film with the miniature images in rows of fifteen, which were scanned from left to right, providing twenty minutes of projection from only 3ft of film. It was patented in 1912, but the war disrupted progress; in 1923 limited production started in Poland, but had ceased by 1925, by which time only about 100 examples had been made. The inventor stayed on in Warsaw; his later projects included the 'auto-lektor', a device for recording the text of books on sound film for the blind. In August 1944, Proszynski was arrested by the Germans and sent to Gross-Rosen concentration camp and from there to Malthausen, where he died in March 1945. (SH)

References
Bernard and Elizabeth Orna, 'Kazimierz Proszynski, A Forgotten Pioneer', *British Kinematography*, vol. 28 no. 6, June 1956.

PY, Eugène

Cameraman. Working for Lumière concessionaire Max Glücksmann, Eugène Py put on the first programme of Lumière films in Argentina, in Buenos Aires on 28 July 1896 at the Teatro Odéon. Those responsible for the first films in Argentina were all European emigrés: Py (known as Eugenio in Latin America) was French, Glücksmann Austrian, and both were associated with Belgian Henri Lepage, who imported the first French cinematographic equipment into the country and ran the Casa Lepage in Buenos Aires. In 1897, using a Gaumont camera, Py subsequently shot the first Argentinian film, *La Bandera Argentina* (*The Argentine Flag*).

Py continued to produce films for exhibition at the Casa Lepage for several years, chiefly simple actualities, working as part of the cross-national film production, distribution and exhibition system developed by Glücksmann in Argentina, Uruguay and Chile. Py's most notable assignment was to film the operations of Dr Posadas, conducted in the noon daylight, and taken with a Pathé camera from two angles: one showing the overall view, the other the detail of the operation. (LMcK)

References
Hennebelle and Gumucio-Dagron, *Les Cinémas de l'Amérique Latine* (1981).
Tosi, *Il cinema prima di Lumière* (1984).

R

RAFF, Norman C.
and GAMMON, Frank R.

Businessmen. The Kinetoscope Company (Norman Raff, Frank Gammon, Alfred O. Tate, Thomas Lombard, Erastus Benson and **Andrew Holland**) was one of three outside groups that marketed Edison's Kinetoscope and its films. The other two groups were the similarly named Kinetoscope Exhibition Company, run by the **Lathams**, and **Maguire and Baucus'** Continental Commerce Company. In August 1894 the Kinetoscope Company, headed by Raff and Gammon, was granted exclusive rights for selling regular Kinetoscopes within the USA and Canada, which they sold with territorial restrictions. In August/September 1894 Raff and Gammon employee Alfred Clark produced several films at the Black Maria studio in West Orange, including *Joan of Arc* and *The Execution of Mary, Queen of Scots*, the latter filmed outdoors and featuring a significant stop-motion substitution shot as the Queen (played by Robert Thomae, secretary and treasurer of the Kinetoscope Company) was beheaded. Black Maria subjects arranged (and paid for) by Raff and Gammon were identified by a letter 'R' to the right of the stage.

By the summer of 1895, the novelty had faded and business had declined, due in part to imitation machines by **Charles Chinnock**. Exhibiting the Kinetoscope at the Cotton States Exposition, Raff and Gammon representative Frank Harrison saw the **Jenkins/Armat** Phantascope projections, and expressed interest in securing a machine. In December 1895, Gammon went to Thomas Armat's office and was given a demonstration. Impressed, Raff and Gammon approached Edison who, aware of the falling-off in the Kinetoscope business, agreed that the Armat machine should be launched as the Edison Vitascope, the projectors and films being produced by the Edison Manufacturing Company. Concerned about Jenkins's activities and news of public screenings in Europe, they pressed ahead and in March arranged with Albert Bial of Koster and Bial's Music Hall, New York, to book the Vitascope, opening on 23 April to great success. Raff and Gammon set up the Vitascope Company to sell the state rights across the USA, and even sent **Charles Webster** to Europe with a machine. But problems abounded, including varying electrical supplies across the USA, poor films and film stock and a lack of trained operators. The rapid pace of local openings severely strained Raff and Gammon's resources, and Norman Raff suffered a nervous breakdown.

To improve the films a portable camera was constructed freeing the producers from the constraints of the Black Maria studio, and under Raff and Gammon's control many Edison Vitascope films of American life were made 'on location', with **James White** as producer. Some were shot on a rooftop studio above the Vitascope Company's office at 43 West 28th Street, New York. By October 1896, however, the Vitascope company was failing. The Edison Manufacturing Company was dissatisfied with Raff and Gammon: only seventy-three Vitascopes had been manufactured, and with other machines coming onto the market without restrictions, additional demand was unlikely. Also, limiting film sales to Vitascope entrepreneurs reduced profits. The Edison Manufacturing Company therefore started selling films to all potential customers, and the Vitascope was soon superseded by the

Edison Projecting Kinetoscope, sold without restrictions. (SH)

References
Hendricks, *The Kinetoscope* (1966).
Musser, *The Emergence of Cinema* (1990).
Ramsaye, *A Million and One Nights* (1926).

Don RAMIREZ

Showman. It was probably some time in 1899 that this Spanish showman opened a circus in Constantinople, and imported a projector to show films. However, at this time there was a ban on electricity in most of the city, the Sultan Abdul Hamid II (reigned 1876–1909) believing it could somehow be used for terrorism. The Spanish ambassador interceded with the Sultan on Don Ramirez's behalf, extolling the wonders of cinema pictures so effectively that an exhibition was commanded in the palace. *The Electrical Review* described the show: 'Moving scenes from the leading capitals of Europe were thrown on the screen for the delectation of the Sultan, who no doubt enjoyed them all the more, since he is not, like his friend the German Kaiser, a great traveller.' As a result of this, the Spaniard was permitted to install electricity in his circus.

In fact, the Sultan was not such a conservative when it came to modern technology: still photographs were extensively employed as a means of gaining information on events and progress in his empire and for gathering intelligence. And only a few months after his meeting with Ramirez it seems that the Sultan became convinced of the utility of film: he commissioned 'a cinematograph specialist' – perhaps it was the Spaniard himself – to prepare, 'regardless of cost', a series of films showing the working of the newly built Anatolian railway. It is unclear whether these films were actually made, but Abdul Hamid's interest in the cinema continued, and by 1906 he was employing an English 'bioscope attaché' to screen travel films for himself and his harem in the palace.

Ramirez was not the first man to bring films to Constantinople: the Lumières received a letter enquiring about their camera from a Constantinople photographer, Thodori Vafiadis, and a Lumière operator, Louis Janin, and three young colleagues from Lyon arrived in the city in May 1896. They started negotiations with the Sultan's officials to show their 'scientific marvel', but they too ran up against the electricity ban, and it was only after five months' delay that they were finally permitted to use an electric lamp for projection: but by that time Janin had left Turkey in frustration. Some time later, a certain Sigmund Weinberg, a Polish Jew whose brother was a photographer in Constantinople, arranged the public showing of a film in the well-known beer hall, Sponeck, near Galatasaray. Owing to the electricity prohibition, the film was projected by gas lamp. (SB)

References
'Electricity in Turkey', *The Electrical Review*, 26 May 1899, p. 842.
P. Mansel, *Sultans in Splendour* (London: André Deutsch, 1988).
Bulletin du Congrès Lumière, no. 4, 1995.

RAMOS, Antonio

Exhibitor who introduced film to the Philippines and subsequently established the film exhibition industry in China. Ramos, a Spaniard, on concluding his military service in the Philippines (then governed by Spain) purchased a Lumière Cinématographe, and with a collection of twenty films toured the Philippines, introducing the first films to that country in 1897. Following the introduction of American rule (a result of the Spanish-American War of 1898), Ramos moved to China, where a fellow Spaniard, recorded by Jay Leyda as being Galen Bocca (?), had had little success in exhibiting films in Shanghai since his arrival in 1899. Ramos, beginning at the Ching-Lin-Ko tea house in 1903, was a more forceful businessman, and his Ramos Amusement Corporation became China's first well-established film enterprise and the dominant force in Shanghai film exhibition for the next twenty years. Having expanded his exhibition business successfully throughout Shanghai, Ramos made a brief and ill-judged move into production in 1924, before the threat of revolution in 1927 forced him to sell up and return to Spain. (LMcK)

References
Leyda, *Dianying* (1972).

RASTUS, Joe, TOLLIVER, Denny and WILKINS, Walter

The first Afro-Americans to appear on film. Rastus, Tolliver and Wilkins were three of the dancers in a troupe entitled Lucy Daly's Pickaninnies then touring in *The Passing Show*, having run at the Casino theatre, New York, from 12 May to August 1894. Though the Pickaninnies came from fairly low down the bill, *The Passing Show*, produced by George Lederer, was an important milestone in American musical theatre, being the very first revue (as opposed to the usual vaudeville fare) and billed as 'a topical extravaganza'. They performed an energetic if somewhat untidy 'breakdown dance' routine for Edison's Kinetograph camera on 6 October 1894, with **W. K-L. Dickson** producing and **William Heise** on camera. It was a busy day at the Black Maria: those filmed included Walton and Slavin, comic boxers; Cleveland's minstrel show; and a number of performers from **Buffalo Bill Cody**'s Wild West show. *The Pickaninnies* film is described in an 1898 **F. Z. Maguire** and Co. catalogue as 'A scene representing Southern plantation life before the war. A jig and a breakdown by three colored boys.' (SH/LMcK)

References
Musser, *Before the Rapid Firing Kinetograph* (1996).
Hendricks, *The Kinetoscope* (1966).

RAYMOND, Matt (1874–1941)

Electrician, projectionist, cameraman. At twenty-one years old, Matt Raymond was employed as the electrician at the Royal Polytechnic Institute in Regent Street, London, with responsibility for installing the electric arc lamp for **Félicien Trewey**'s first Cinématographe performances. There were serious problems with the arrangement, and Raymond saved the day by quickly arranging the replacement of the arcs and lamphouse condenser. Trewey realised the value of the young electrician, and arranged for him to install the equipment at Cardiff in May 1896 and at the Free Trade Hall, Manchester. Returning to London in June, Raymond installed projection rooms for the Cinématographe at the Crystal Palace, at the Empire theatre, Leicester Square (in July), and in Sheffield, Dublin, Belfast and many other towns. Raymond probably acted as

Trewey's cameraman, taking the first English Lumière films including, *Cyclistes et cavaliers arrivant au cottage* (featuring Trewey), *Entrée du Cinématographe* (showing the frontage of the Empire theatre), *Pont de la Tour* and *Pont de Westminster* (all 1896).

Late in the year, after splitting with Trewey, Raymond joined Chard and Co. of Great Portland Street, who had their own projector. He acted as installer and operator at the Shakespeare theatre, Liverpool, that Christmas, when a selection of films was shown during the pantomime, *Babes in the Wood*. Soon afterwards he joined **Maguire and Baucus**, selling Edison projectors. In 1898 he bought a Warwick Bioscope and toured with it, eventually buying about twenty machines to install in various music halls around the provinces, subsequently expanding his operation to Belgium, Holland, Germany and France. On returning to England he founded the Raymond Animated Picture Co. (1905–25) and set up a chain of permanent cinemas. He served as treasurer of the Cinema Trade Protection Society between 1907 and 1920, and later the Cinematograph Exhibitors' Association. In November 1921, he became master of the 'Anima' masonic lodge, then composed entirely of members of the film industry. (SH)

References
Barnes, *The Beginnings of the Cinema in England* (vols. 1 and 4).
Rittaud-Hutinet, *Le Cinéma des origines* (1985).

RECTOR, Enoch J. (1862–1957)

Boxing film promoter, cine technician. Meeting up with ex-classmates **Otway** and **Gray Latham** and their associate Samuel Tilden (the wealthy son of a former governor of New York, who supplied much of the financing), the four formed the Kinetoscope Exhibition Company to make boxing films for the Kinetoscope, using Edison's studio. Rector was possibly involved in extending the capacity of the Kinetoscope viewer to take longer films. Later the company, renamed Lambda, made their own cameras and projectors, and Rector claimed credit for the 'Latham Loop' (introduced in their camera to reduce strain in the film and enable longer sequences to be taken, essential for fight films), but **W. K-L. Dickson** or **Eugène Lauste** may have been the true inventors.

Rector managed the Leonard–Cushing fight, but then he and Tilden left the Lathams'

Lambda company to set up on their own. They arranged to have four Edison cameras at the ringside when **Bob Fitzsimmons** and **Jim Corbett** were scheduled to fight in Texas in late 1895, but shortly before the bout was due to take place, prizefighting was outlawed in Texas and the fight could not be restaged elsewhere. Rector was involved in arranging for Fitzsimmons to fight Peter Maher in Mexico, and the match went ahead, but bad weather made photography impossible (in any case, the contest was over in seconds as Fitzsimmons knocked out Maher in the first round). Salvaging what he could from the expedition, Rector photographed a bullfight at Juarez.

Unhappy with the limitations of the Edison machine, he was soon working on his own camera, shooting various subjects in and around New York. In March 1897 Corbett and Fitzsimmons went into the ring at Carson City, filmed by Rector with three cameras using a 63mm format (so that the resultant film could be exploited exclusively) and taking 11,000ft of film. Rector installed a projector, the Veriscope, at the Academy of Music, 14th Street, New York, where he ran the film through the early summer of 1897, moving in July to the Park theatre, Brooklyn, and then elsewhere in the USA. Eventual profits on the film were reputed to have been more than $120,000. (SH)

References

Hendricks, *The Kinetoscope* (1966).
Musser, *The Emergence of Cinema* (1990).
Ramsaye, *A Million and One Nights* (1926).

REDFERN, Henry Jasper (1872–1928)

Optician, exhibitor, film-maker, radiographer. Redfern was a Sheffield-based optician who in 1898 was also offering photographic supplies and instruction, **Röntgen** rays (X-rays) and exhibitions of the Lumière Cinématographe, for which he was one of a number of agents in Britain at this time. Redfern operated from two addresses in Sheffield: 55–7 Surrey Street for his showrooms and 104–6 Norfolk Street for his 'Works and Studios'. Specialising in 'locals' (films of interest in his area), Redfern travelled around with his local football team during 1899, photographing at least four major matches and climaxing with the Cup Final at Crystal Palace, when Sheffield United played Derby (15 April 1899). He entitled the series *Football Events*. He also filmed local cricket matches. The following year he seems to have made a tour of Africa (Morocco, Tunisia, Algeria),

making travelogues, and eventually went wholeheartedly into the moving picture business with his 'World Renowned Animated Pictures and Refined Vaudeville Entertainments'. This package show ultimately led to his owning and operating a seaside summer show at Westcliffe: 'Jasper Redfern's Palace by the Sea'.

He remained in the local film business for another ten years, before devoting himself wholly to optical and medical work. He engaged in research into X-rays and the treatment of cancers at the Christie Hospital, Manchester, where x-ray burns ultimately caused him to lose the use of most of his fingers. His collection of motion picture memorabilia was presented to the Science Museum. (DG)

References

Barnes, *The Beginnngs of the Cinema in England* (vols. 4–5).
G. J. Mellor, *Picture Pioneers: The Story of the Northern Cinema 1896–1971* (Newcastle: Frank Graham, 1971).

REICH, Theodor (1861–1939)

Painter, printer, chronophotographer, inventor. Theodor Reich shared with many in his generation an inventive turn of mind, a momentary flirtation with the cinema and an ability to forsee its possibilities. Born in Vienna and educated as a painter and printmaker, he worked in photography in the 80s, and for the sports journalist Habnit sketched a chronophotographic camera for taking three or four pictures per second to analyse the motions of flight, but neither of the two friends could afford to make the apparatus. Moving to London, he worked as a photographic technician and printer, inventing and improving a method of photogravure printing widely used in Europe and the USA.

Inspired again by the analysis of flight, in 1895 he commissioned the London mechanic Keppel to make a new chronophotographic apparatus using 42mm-wide film and a claw intermittent, capable of making about ten exposures per second, with which he photographed pigeons in flight. He later claimed many private projections with the apparatus (unaware of other work in the field), beginning in May 1895, but an improved version was not patented until June 1896. The following year, a further patent was issued to Reich and John Henry Hill Duncan for a self-perforating combination projector and camera. In mid-1896, a company was formed to exploit Reich's machine, but all plans were abandoned after two consecutive fires were caused by the lamphouse igniting the film. Reich remained in London until 1904 working as a printer and a photographic technician, then returned to Vienna to end his career as the head of the photogravure department of an illustrated magazine. (DR)

References
Wilhelm Formann, *Österreichische Pioniere der Kinematographie* (Vienna: Bergland Verlag, 1963).
Agnes Bleier-Brody, 'Daten zur Urgeschichte des österreichischen Films', *Film-Kunst*, Jahrbuch 1960, Vienna, 1960, pp. 27–34.

REIS, Aurélio da Paz dos (1862–1931)

The first native Portuguese film-maker. Reis was a horticulturalist and owner of a successful florist shop in Porto, but also an amateur photographer who, after witnessing **Edwin Rousby**'s film shows in June 1896, decided to take up cinematography. Purchasing a **de Bedts** Kinématographe, he began that year to show a large number of actuality subjects taken by himself in the Lumière manner: *Saida do Pessoal Operario da Fabrica Confianca* (*Workers Leaving the Confianca Shirt Factory*), *Feira da Gado na Corujeira* (*Cattle Market at Corujeira*), *Rua Augusta, Lisboa* (*Augusta Street, Lisbon*), as well as exhibiting imported films. His first film programme took place at the Teatro Principe Real in Porto on 10 November 1896. Further screenings in Portugal followed, but after a disastrous show in Brazil on 15 January 1897, when technical problems ruined everything, the traumatised Reis abandoned cinematography and returned to his flowers and simple photography. (LMcK)

References
Ferreira, *A fotografa animada em Portugal* (1986).

REYNAUD, Emile (1844–1918)

Inventor, artist and showman. Reynaud's father was an horologer and medal engraver, and the Reynaud home was full of mysterious objects to fascinate the young Emile. His mother was a cultivated idealist, with progressive ideas where education was concerned, and an accomplished watercolourist. At fourteen, already knowledgeable in literary and scientific matters, Emile was apprenticed to a precision engineer in Paris, and later studied with the sculptor-photographer, Adam Salomon. Soon he was preparing lantern slides, photographic and hand-drawn, for the audiovisual lectures arranged by the Abbé Moigno. After the death of his father in 1865, Emile and his mother stayed at his uncle's chateau at Puy-en-Velay, where he continued his studies in his uncle's library.

Back with Moigno in Paris he gained extensive experience in all matters relating to projection. In 1876 he decided to make an optical toy to amuse a young child. Improving on the Phenakistiscope and Zoetrope, Reynaud devised the Praxinoscope (patented on 21 December 1877). Consisting of a cylinder with a band of coloured images set inside, Reynaud employed a central drum of mirrors, which were equidistant between the axis and the picture strip, so that as the toy revolved, the reflection of each picture seen in the mirror drum appeared stationary. The images blended to give a clear, bright, undistorted moving picture without flicker.

With his mother he took an apartment at the rue Rodier in Paris, using the adjacent apartment as a workshop to produce the Praxinoscope commercially, and receiving an Honourable Mention in the Paris Exposition of 1878. The following year he added a patent supplement for an improvement – the Praxinoscope Théâtre. The mirror drum and cylinder were set in a wooden box with a glass-covered viewing aperture, reflecting a card printed with a background. The moving subjects – a juggler, clowns, a steeple-chase – were printed on a black band, and thus appeared superimposed on a suitable scene. A further development was the Projection Praxinoscope, which used a series of transparent pictures on glass: an oil lamp illuminated the images, and the mirror reflections passed through a lens onto a screen. The same lamp projected a static background, and once again the moving pictures were seen in an appropriate setting. All three models were demonstrated to the Société Française de Photographie in 1880.

In December 1888 Reynaud patented his Théâtre Optique, a large-scale Praxinoscope intended for public projection. By using spools to feed and take up the extended picture band, sequences were no longer limited to short cyclic movements. The images were painted on gelatine squares and fastened between leather bands, with holes in metal strips between the pictures engaging in pins on the revolving wheel, so that each picture was aligned with a facet of the mirror drum. This was the first commercial use of the perforations that were to be so important for successful cinematography. In 1892 Reynaud signed an agreement with the Musée Grevin in Paris to present the 'Pantomimes Lumineuses' – the first animated pictures shown publicly on a screen by means of long transparent bands of images – and on 28 October gave the first show. Setting up the apparatus behind a translucent screen, Reynaud apparently gave most of the presentations himself, deftly manipulating the picture bands to and fro to extend the sequences, creating a twelve– or fifteen-minute performance from the 500 frames of *Pauvre Pierrot*. Two other early subjects were *Clown et ses chiens* (300 frames) and *Un bon boc* (700 frames). With special music compiled by Gaston Paulin, and magnificent poster artwork by Jules Chéret, the show was a success. It was closed from 1 March 1894 until 1 January 1895, reopening with new subjects, *Un Rêve au coin de feu* and *Autour d'une cabine*. Early in 1896 the clowns **Footit and Chocolat** performed a sketch, *Guillaume Tell*, for the Photoscenographe cine camera devised or acquired by Reynaud, and the resulting images were retouched, hand-coloured and mounted as horizontal bands for the Théâtre Optique. This was completed by August, and in November Reynaud filmed actor Galipaux in *Le première cigare* on an improved camera. This was ready for projection by early summer 1897. The following year conventional films, shown on a Demenÿ Chronophotographe, were mixed with the 'Pantomimes Lumineuses'.

Reynaud experimented unsuccessfully with an oscillating-mirror projector in an attempt to update his presentation technique, but the battle with the competition of the Cinématographe and its imitators, with their constantly changing programmes, was finally lost, and the last show took place on 28 February 1900. From 1903 to 1907 Reynaud worked on a device for viewing short stereoscopic sequences of movement, the Stereo-cinema, which resembled a double praxinoscope arranged vertically, but it was not financially viable. Before his death in January 1918, in a fit of depression, he smashed the Théâtre Optique mechanism and threw all but two of his picture bands into the Seine. Reproductions of the two bands – *Pauvre Pierrot* and *Autour d'une cabine* – are today still being shown, and represent the only surviving examples of his public screen motion picture work. (SH)

References

Dominique Auzel, *Emile Reynaud et l'image s'anima* (Paris: Du May, 1992).
Mannoni, *Le grand art de la lumière et de l'ombre* (1994).

RICALTON, James (1844–1929)

American photographer who brought some of the first films to China. The first film show in China took place in Shanghai on 11 August 1896 at the Hsu Gardens, but details are lacking. In July 1897 James Ricalton, a schoolteacher turned professional photographer hailing from Maplewood, New Jersey, presented a programme of Edison films at the Tien Hua Tea Garden, Shanghai, including Tsar **Nikolas II** visiting Paris and the dancers **Annabelle** and Little Egypt. Ricalton had first worked for Edison in 1888, and in 1891 joined the renowned photographic firm of Underwood and Underwood. He took several films of local scenes in Hong Kong, Shanghai and Canton, some of which appear in the 1898 Edison catalogue. He may have undertaken further film shows in 1898, before continuing as a photographer in China for Underwood and Underwood to record the Boxer Rebellion of 1900. He then journeyed around the world as a photographer, covering the Delhi Durbar of 1902–3 and the Russo-Japanese War of 1904–5, and wrote two illustrated books on his experiences: *China through the Stereoscope* (1902) and *India through the Stereoscope* (1907). He kept up some association with the motion picture world, however, as there are records of him working for Edison once again in 1912. (LMcK)

References

Leyda, *Dianying* (1972).

RIGG, John Henry

Engineer. John Henry Rigg, of 43 Skinner Lane, Leeds, was an electrical engineer and manufacturer of telephones, phonographs and other scientific instruments. He possessed his own recording studios and made phonographs of variety artists appearing at Leeds theatres. He was also manufacturer and co-patentee, with Ernest Othon Kumberg, a French engineer resident in London, of an early projector, the Kinematograph. This was the third English film projector to be publicly exhibited in Britain, opening at the Royal Aquarium, Westminster, London, on 6 April 1896. Kumberg was an associate with the Anglo-Continental Phonograph Company, who exploited the machine. It had a worm-gear intermittent mechanism – the subject of a patent dispute, settled in Rigg's favour – and, unusually, was driven by an electric motor. It seems to have had some success as it was used in many of the largest halls in the provinces. Rigg subsequently converted the projector for use as a camera.

Little is known about his film production, but one example, taken during a severe frost during the winter of 1896–7, depicted a group of skaters. Another, *Switchback in Operation at Shipley Glen*, was made in about September 1897. He made other films especially for use in his 'kinetophone', the Kinematograph projector synchronised with a loud-speaking phonograph which supplied suitable words or music to the accompanying films. Towards the end of 1896 he opened an agency at 186 Chestnut Street, Philadelphia. (SH)

References

Barnes, *The Beginnings of the Cinema in England* (vols. 1–4).

RILEY, Joseph (1838–1926), William (1866–1961), Herbert (1863–?), Arnold (?–?) and Bernard (?–?)

Lantern-slide dealers who entered the cinema business in its first months. Bradford 'stuff' dealer Joseph Riley bought a magic lantern for his two eldest sons Herbert and William, and the three gave shows for charity before setting up in the lantern-slide business. By the turn of the century the Riley catalogue listed 1,500 slide sets for sale or hire, and numerous lanterns. William, who ran the business – advertised as 'The Largest Lantern Outfitters in the World' – was later joined by brothers Arnold and Bernard. In 1894 Herbert emigrated to New York, where he managed the Riley brothers' US office. Family legend later related that William was invited to Paris to see the Lumière Cinématographe, and shortly afterwards the Rileys, enthused by living pictures, acquired the rights to **Cecil Wray**'s

1896 Kineoptoscope projector. They manufactured the machine and advertised it in the *Era* as 'Steady as Lumière's. No breakdowns. Most portable and the most perfect known'. There were two basic versions: one designed to fit into the slide-stage of a standard magic lantern ('an advantage possessed by no other apparatus'); the other, with its own lens unit, which fitted in front of the lantern.

In June 1897 the Rileys introduced their Kineoptoscope camera, again from the original designs of Cecil Wray, which basically comprised an adapted projector mechanism. They also began to produce their own 75ft films. The first may have been *The Three Macs* (May 1898), a comedy routine described as 'cigar business'. Four months later came a number of slapstick films including *Wearie Willy in the Park; or The Overfull Seat*, *The Nursemaid's Surprise* and, later, others produced in conjunction with **Bamforth** of Holmfirth. On 24 October 1898 the Rileys gave a royal command cinema show at Balmoral Castle, Scotland, which included a number of their own productions: *Highland Dances*, *March Past of the Black Watch* and others made specially for the occasion. That same year they were offering to sell or rent (a significant early example of this practice) films to purchasers of their projectors.

In 1902 Joseph Riley's stuff business went bankrupt. The lantern-slide business continued, but was wound up soon after the start of the First World War. Bernard was killed on active service; Arnold carried on for a while as 'Riley Brothers (1914) Limited', but eventually left the trade. With the publication in 1912 of *Windyridge*, William Riley became a best-selling novelist, and survived another half a century. (RB/DG/SH)

References

Barnes, *The Beginnings of the Cinema in England* (vols. 1–4).
Colin Gordon, *By Gaslight in Winter* (London: Elm Tree/Hamish Hamilton, 1980).

ROCK, William T. ('Pop') (1853–1916)

Exhibitor, business executive. While in recent years film-makers **J. Stuart Blackton** and **Albert Smith** have been given most of the credit for making the Vitagraph Company into the USA's most successful and important early film producer, a very strong case can be made that this firm's achievements are largely the consequence of the vigorous and innovative leadership provided by the company's president, the

English-born William T. Rock, universally known as 'Pop' Rock. His nickname comes not only from his membership of the oldest generation represented in the dynamic young medium of the cinema but also from his seniority as a pioneering film exhibitor.

The manager of a billiard parlour in Harlem, Rock bought the rights to exploit the Edison/**Armat** Vitascope in Louisiana on 16 June 1896, in partnership with the carnival showman and tightrope performer Walter J. Wainwright. Twelve days later they opened at the West End amusement centre in New Orleans. A vigorous advertising programme used slogans ('After Breakfast Visit the Vitascope'), coupons ("This coupon admits on the day of its date any child under age of ten years accompanied by an adult') and controversy (over the morality of the **May Irwin** *Kiss*) to keep their shows in the public eye. By August there were different programmes for morning and evening shows; in March 1897 the partners offered a two-hour programme of over fifty films at the Grand Opera House for the substantial admission of 25 cents.

When the Lumière Cinématographe arrived in New Orleans on 21 June 1897, Rock and Wainwright immediately made arrangements to order some hundreds of Lumière films for the Vitascope: by 11 July, they were advertising Lumière films at their 8.45p.m. showing and Vitascope films at 10.30p.m. The competing apparatus left the city in mid-August. Through these and many other active promotions (famously including a charge to the public for looking at the marvels of the projection apparatus itself), Rock and Wainwright became the only Vitascope concessionaires in the USA to make a profit.

In 1898 Rock moved to New York and began a partnership with the successful young film-makers Blackton and Smith, while keeping the previous exhibitions running in New Orleans and elsewhere. As president of the Vitagraph Company, Rock sent his original partner Wainwright to London as an agent to acquire foreign films, and by 1900 Vitagraph had nearly 250 foreign titles in their stock, mostly English and French, and including the **Georges Méliès'** trick films. Rock's aggressive yet gregarious style (even fighting when settling with Edison over royalties) brought Vitagraph to the forefront of the American film companies, but with the formation of the Motion Picture Patents Company (MPPC) in 1908, his rough-and-tumble experience was out of step with the corporatisation of the motion picture businessmen who now rose to prominence. He became the manager of Vitagraph's New York exchange, and when it was sold to the General Film Company in 1910, the next MPPC monopoly organisation, Rock went into semi-retirement. Negotiating the rights to the **Jim Jeffries**–Jack Johnson championship fight of 4 July 1910 on behalf of the MPPC, subsequently becoming a promoter of special projects for Vitagraph, until his sudden death on 27 July 1916, he will be remembered as a colourful and legendary figure of the earliest days of the movies. (DR)

References
Albert E. Smith (in collaboration with Phil A. Koury), *Two Reels and a Crank* (New York: Doubleday, 1952).
Eileen Bowser, *The Transformation of Cinema, 1907–1915* (New York: Charles Scribner's Sons, 1990).

ROIKJER, C. V.

Photographer, showman. When the Copenhagen theatre impresario Harald Limkilde heard of the forthcoming industrial exhibition in Malmö, Sweden, he cancelled his plans to open the Lumière Cinématographe in Denmark and converted Pilstorp's Summer-Theatre into a cinema, giving sixteen performances a day under the management of Swedish photographer, C. V. Roikjer. The showings (the first film screenings in Sweden) ran from 28 June 1896 through to 27 September, and Roikjer became one of the several Swedish photographers (**Numa Peterson**, **Ernest Florman**) to have a significant involvement in early Swedish film. From summer through to October 1897, Roikjer organised the film showings for Numa Peterson at King Oscar II's Silver Jubilee Exhibition. (DR)

References
Rune Waldekranz, *Levende Bilder: De första biograferna* (Stockholm, 1955) [reprinted as 'La nascita del cinema in Scandanavia', in Paolo Cherchi Usai (ed.), *Schiave bianche allo specchio* (Pordenone: Edizioni Studio Tesi, 1986)].

RONTGEN, Wilhelm Conrad
(1945–1923)

Physicist. Born in Lennep, Prussia (now Remscheid, Germany) Röntgen (or Roentgen), a professor at the University of Würzburg, was awarded the first Nobel Prize for physics in 1901 for his discovery of X-rays on 8 November 1895.

His discovery of the electromagnetic rays of a short wavelength that are produced when cathode rays impinge on matter was one of the key events in modern physics and had a profound effect on medicine, but it also proved of immense interest to the showmen who were starting to exhibit motion pictures. 'Röntgen rays' became a common feature alongside magic lantern shows and film screenings from such exhibitors worldwide as **Mark Blow** in Australia, **Yokota Einosuke** in Japan, **William Paley** (who suffered from the aftereffects of radiation) in the USA and **Jasper Redfern** (who became a noted radiologist and endured x-ray burns) in Britain. **James Williamson** used Röntgen rays as part of his pharmaceutical business, Dr **John Macintyre** demonstrated X-ray cinematography for scientific purposes as early as 1897, and a number of comic films employed the theme, for instance **G. A. Smith**'s *X-Rays* (also called *The X-Ray Fiend*, 1897) ('the Professor turns his apparatus upon the lovers and makes a startling revelation'). Both **Thomas Edison** and **Auguste Lumière**, in their very different ways, experimented with the uses of the X-ray. In a way not dissimilar to **Muybridge**'s analyses of motion, Röntgen's X-rays caused a revolution in human perception, anatomising life on the screen in a way profoundly analogous with the cinema. (LMcK)

References

Lisa Cartwright, *Screening the Body: Tracing Medicine's Visual Culture* (Minneapolis/London: University of Minnesota Press, 1995).
Richard Crangle, 'Saturday Night at the X-rays: The Moving Picture and the New Photography in Britain, 1896', paper given at 'Celebrating 1895' conference, Bradford 1995.

ROSENTHAL, Joseph ('Joe')
(1864–1946)

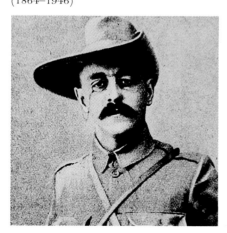

War and travel cameraman, director. Joseph Rosenthal came from a humble Jewish background in east London, and worked as a pharmaceutical chemist before joining the **Maguire and Baucus** company in 1896, for whom his sister, Alice, already worked as a film stock keeper. When **Charles Urban** formed the Warwick Trading Company out of Maguire and Baucus two years later, Rosenthal was sent on filming assignments, first in Europe and then as far afield as South Africa. The following year he was sent to South Africa on two more occasions, first to record the voyage of the ship en route, and then to cover the Boer War, which broke out in October. It was to be this particular assignment which made Rosenthal's reputation.

Arriving in January 1900, he initially went to the Natal front, before joining the rising star of General Roberts's column pushing north from the Cape. Travelling with two mules and a Cape cart, he could move relatively fast, sometimes even going ahead of the troops. He filmed several scenes around Bloemfontein, including *Hoisting the Union Jack* and *The Balloon Contingent*, though these and other films were lost when the ship carrying them back to England went down. However, other films arrived safely and showed such scenes as British troops on the march and fording rivers, and even included *Boer Prisoners Under Escort*. Camerawork could be a risky business: in filming one river crossing, Rosenthal records that 'a shell exploded right in front of me, and it was very lucky indeed that I was not hit'. He was present at the various British victories which came in the second quarter of 1900, managing to film the surrender at Kroonstad in May, and the raising of the British flag over Pretoria the following month. For most people this marked the end of the war (it was actually to continue until May 1902), and Rosenthal departed, leaving cameraman Sydney Goldman as Warwick's representative in South Africa.

Rosenthal's next assignment took him to the Far East: leaving London in August, he arrived too late to film any action in the Boxer Rebellion, but managed to record several battle incidents in the American colonial conflict then taking place in the Philippines. From 1901 he was in safer environs: firstly filming the opening of the Australian parliament by the Duke and Duchess of Cornwall and York in May, and then in 1902 making a variety of films for the Canadian Pacific Railway, including what may have been his first venture into drama with a version of *Hiawatha* enacted by the Ojibwa people. But a return to danger followed in 1904, when Rosenthal was sent to cover the Russo-Japanese War, some of which he had to film from behind the protection of a special camera shield (his films of the gruelling siege of Port Arthur were subsequently shown throughout the world).

At the end of the war, Rosenthal stayed in the Far East and Borneo for some time, before travelling to India to film the Prince and Princess of Wales's tour at the end of 1905. But at this point in his career he was dismissed by Charles Urban, and in 1908 set up his own company, Rosie Films, based in Croydon. He tried his hand at comedy directing, but it was no great success, and he concentrated on shooting documentary films for the rest of his career, which continued through the First World War. Rosenthal enjoyed an adventurous life, and pioneered the kind of professionalism which would be much valued in the film industry in the years ahead. (SB)

References
Stephen Bottomore, 'Joseph Rosenthal: The Most Glorious Profession', *Sight and Sound*, vol. 52 no. 4, Autumn 1983.

ROUSBY, Edwin

Exhibitor. The travelling exhibitor Edwin Rousby was one of many early purchasers of **Robert Paul**'s Theatrograph projector to take to the road in 1896 and make that apparatus the most widely used motion picture machine in the world next to the Lumière Cinématographe. By the end of August 1896, the English machine had opened in France, Portugal, South Africa, Sweden, Italy, Spain and Australia, as well as throughout the UK; by the same date the Edison/**Armat** Vitagraph had begun to be used widely in the USA and had just reached neighbouring Canada.

Rousby, who is usually described as a Hungarian electrician, but who may have been an American, opened his Theatrograph at the Circus Parish in Madrid on 7 April, and began a tour of the Iberian peninsula that would take him to Lisbon (18 June), Porto (17 July), Espinho (12 August), Figuera da Foz (15 August) and various other cities and towns. Returning to Lisbon on 27 August 1896, Rousby presented a special programme of 'Portuguese Views' photographed by **Henry Short** for Paul, which would be exhibited in London from 22 October as *A Tour in Spain and Portugal*. Throughout this Iberian odyssey, Rousby continued to obtain new films from Paul in

London, repeating the pattern so familiar from various Lumière operators, and on his last appearance in Lisbon gave 143 performances of 67 different films through to 15 January 1897. (DR)

References
Ferreira, *A fotografa animada em Portugal* (1986).
Rossell, 'The New Thing with the Long Name', *Film History*, Summer 1995.

RUDGE, John Arthur Roebuck
(1837–1903)

Inventor. Born in Bath, the son of a wood-turner and antique dealer, Rudge was a scientific instrument-maker by profession, as well as an entertainer who put on countless shows, earning the nickname 'Wizard of the Magic Lantern'. He started out using something similar to the Ross 'Wheel of Life', and later created a new type of apparatus, the Phantascope or Biophantic lantern. This carried seven slides in a rotating gallery moved by a cross-type mechanism, with a scissor-like shutter of two pieces of ground glass. The picture was held still for a moment, the shutter then obscuring the view (but not entirely shutting off the light) as the slide changed. He experimented with another similar device, but employing a slide gallery several feet long.

Rudge met **William Friese Greene** about 1880, the latter having a photographic shop nearby in Bath, and they formed a close association. Rudge did most of the technical work, while Friese Greene helped with the photography and put on some public demonstrations. This undoubtedly ignited Friese Greene's interest in moving pictures.

In the mid-80s, Rudge produced a lantern front with four converging lenses to project a slide with a sequence of four photographs on it. A rotating shutter directed the light to each one in turn, creating a 'moving' picture. Friese Greene's face was among a number photographed to record changing expressions, and he displayed one in the window of his Piccadilly shop. 1887 saw Rudge screening a series of twelve photographs of 'A Boy in an Eton Collar'. These were taken on a single plate, and some accounts say they were projected from a glass rotating disc. In 1890, Rudge demonstrated 'a new instrument' to the Bath Photographic Society, which worked on the 'dissolving view' principle. It had twin lenses which projected photographs alternately from two rotating discs, each one carrying seven pictures. His first demonstration was not completely successful, but he later sold one to a Birmingham showman. Rudge took out a provisional patent on 12 November 1884 for 'producing life-like effects with the optical or magic lantern', but he never completed it. Rudge's seven-slide lantern with slides, and his later double-disc mechanism, were acquired by **Will Day** and are preserved in the Cinémathèque Française. Aside from his projection work, Rudge claimed to be the first person to bring both electric light and X-rays to Bath. He also invented a coin-operated weighing machine, a miniature electric train, a quick-firing gun and a self-inflating lifebelt. (PC)

References
'Remarkable Novelties in Photographic Instruments', *Photographic News*, 30 May 1890.
Coe, *The History of Movie Photography* (1981).

S

ST DENIS, Ruth (Ruth Dennis)
(1878–1968)

Dancer. A major figure in the development of modern dance and one of the earliest performers for Edison's Kinetoscope. Ruth Dennis was born in Newark, New Jersey, and studied dancing as a child, making her professional debut at the age of sixteen. It was at this early stage of her career that she was filmed by Edison, billed in the December 1894 *Kinetograph Company Bulletin* as the 'Champion High Kicker of the World'. Less known is the fact that at about the same time she was also filmed for **Charles Chinnock**'s imitation Kinetoscope. She continued to make a haphazard living as a dancer in vaudeville and in musical comedies until 1905, when she choreographed and produced her first ballet, *Radha*. Though, according to Agnes de Mille, she 'dressed up as an Egyptian cigarette ad ... and gave Oriental mysticism a new lease of life by undulating in a roof garden restaurant', she was intensely interested in Eastern culture and dance forms. With her husband Ted Shawn she founded the Denishawn School of Dancing in 1915, developing such leading modern dancers as Martha Graham and Charles Weidman. Ruth St Denis and the Denishawn Dancers also appeared in D. W. Griffith's *Intolerance* (1916). (BA)

References
Ruth St Denis, *An Unfinished Life* (New York/London: Harper & Brothers, 1939).
Musser, *Before the Rapid Firing Kinetograph*, (1996).

SAMAMA, Albert ('Chikly')

Tunisian film pioneer. In 1897 Albert Samama (also known by the single name Chikly), together with a photographer named Soler, organised the first screenings of Lumière films in a Tunis shop. The original twelve-minute programme of films, bolstered by some magic lantern views, included such familiar titles as *La Sortie de l'usine* and *L'Arrivée d'un train*. In common with the introduction of film in many non-western countries, Tunisia was offered its first films from a businessman who also introduced other modern novelties: in Samama's case, the bicycle, radio and still photography. Unusually, Samama was to persevere in his film interests, returning to make the first Tunisian fiction film, a short entitled *Zohra* made in 1922, and then the first Tunisian feature film, *Ain al-Gheza* (*The Girl from Carthage*), in 1924, a remarkable achievement when African film-making in general was almost non-existent. Both films starred his daughter Haydée Chikly. (LMcK)

References
Roy Armes, *Third World Film-Making and the West* (Berkeley and Los Angeles: University of California Press, 1987).
Omar Khlifi, *Historie du cinéma en Tunisie* (Société Tunisienne de Diffusion, 1970).

SAMARSKY, Aleksei Dominikovich
(1855–?)

Photographer, merchant, travelling film projectionist. Samarsky was trained as a professional still photographer and owned a studio, but in 1896 was kicked out of his Moscow merchant guild, apparently because he went bankrupt. Coincidentally or not, Samarsky's interest in moving pictures grew up simultaneously with the Lumière Cinématographe shows held by **Charles Aumont**'s Théâtre-Concert Parisienne, which was located close to Samarsky's store in Kamergersky Lane, in the very centre of Moscow. That year, 1896, he applied for a patent for his Chronomotograph (registered 5 August 1896). Taking images at a rate of 15fps, the

Chronomotograph comprised a set of three huge wooden boxes, one of which housed the mechanism made from clock parts, while the other two were used for storing raw and exposed film. No films have survived, and not even titles or screening dates are known, but Samarsky mentioned ballet shows as the best subject for the use of his apparatus. He was also at this time experimenting with stereoscopic effects, producing films by using two simultaneous film recordings.

The Chronomotograph was not licensed in Russia until late in 1898, long after the Lumière Cinématographe had become well established, and Samarsky spent the following years touring throughout the country as a travelling film projectionist, with a show that included some unidentified films of his own production. (RY)

References
Sokolov, *Istoriya Izobreteniya Kinematografia* (1960).

SANDOW, Eugen (Frederick Muller)
(1867–1925)

Body-builder. Born Frederick Muller in Königsberg, Germany, 'The Modern Hercules', as he was known, was already an established entertainer when he travelled out to West Orange to be filmed in Edison's Black Maria studio on 6 March 1894. Like many others at the time, Sandow was greatly impressed by the legend of the 'Wizard', and it was said that he waived his $250 fee on this occasion for a chance to meet the great man and have his photograph taken with him. The film taken of Sandow was one of a number featuring athletes, gymnasts and acrobats taken by **W. K-L. Dickson** for use in the Edison Kinetoscope, and was featured in the first public exhibition of the Kinetoscope on 14 April 1894. Sandow was next filmed by **Max Skladanowsky** in 1895, wrestling with Grainer, a film which featured in the Skladanowskys' first programme on 1 November 1895 in Berlin. Further films of Sandow's 'Muscular Exhibition' were taken in early 1896 by the American Mutoscope and Biograph Company, whose Biograph projector made its first public appearance on a variety programme starring Sandow at the Alfin Theatre in Pittsburgh on 14 September 1896. One of the Biograph films of Sandow was included in the opening-night programme at the Palace theatre in London in March 1897.

Sandow married the daughter of an English photographer and settled in London, where he opened an 'Institute of Health' in St James Street. He was the author of several books on physical fitness, regimen and diet. He died as the result of a stroke after single-handedly lifting an automobile out of a ditch. (RB)

References
W. K-L. Dickson and Antonia Dickson, *History of the Kinetograph, Kinetoscope and Kinetophonograph* (New York: Albert Bunn, 1895; reprinted Arno 1970).
Charles T. Trevor, *Sandow the Magnificent* (London: The Mitre Press, 1946).
Hendricks, *The Kinetoscope* (1966).

SASHIN-FYODOROV, Vladimir Aleksandrovich ('Dobrotvorsky')
(1856–1918)

Comic actor, cameraman, producer. Fyodorov began his acting career in provincial Russian theatres, moving eventually to Moscow, where he also developed an interest in photography. In the summer of 1896 he acquired a Vitagraphe, a combined camera, projector and printer constructed by the French firm Clément et Gilmer, and on 1 September 1896 his first films were announced. These all depicted scenes of actors at Moscow's Fyodor Korsh theatre in the course of rehearsals, in their dressing rooms, during intervals, eating and leaving the theatre. Fyodorov produced similar 'behind the scenes' films for the suburban theatre of Pushkino in the summer of 1897, and again at the Korsh theatre on 1 September 1897. At the same time he also produced several films of general interest: *Free Fire Brigade of Bogorodsk in Moscow*, *Horse-drawn Railway in Moscow* and the fiction pieces *Playing the Ball* and an imitation of Lumière's *Arroseur arrosé*, in which Fyodorov played the gardener.

Though his films received much acclaim in Moscow, by 1898 his name disappears completely from the press reports of film activities. He continued his career as a theatre actor, but returned to films in the 1910s, acting in five films for Aleksandr Drankov and the Moscow branch of Pathé Frères. In 1915 he established the First Sign film company, with the intention of reproducing famous theatre performances on film, but whose debut production of Gogol's *The Inspector General*, though boasting an outstanding cast, was filmed in a wholly archaic manner. Illness overtook Fyodorov after 1916, his film business failed and he left the stage. None of his films appears to have survived. (RY)

References
S. Ginsburg, *Cinematography of Pre-Revolutionary Russia* (Moscow, 1963).

SCHNEIDER, Eberhard

Showman, engineer. A German of reportedly uncouth manner, Schneider patented a self-contained, automated stereoscopic viewer in Germany in 1888 and later claimed to have worked on motion picture equipment at the Krupp works in Oberhausen in the early 1890s. He then crossed the Atlantic and appears variously in the records of early film exhibition in the USA, most significantly as showing his American Cinematograph at the Eden Musée, where he caused a serious fire on 14 June 1897. Offering a complete film service that included advertising and other slides interspersed throughout his programmes, he found greatest success through a reframing device (as did **Albert Smith** at roughly the same time), leading to an extended residency at Proctor's Pleasure Palace, New York. Schneider's personal reputation was low, but he had a high reputation for quality motion picture apparatus. Edison lawsuits curtailed his exhibition activities, but he remained a successful equipment manufacturer for a number of years, marketing his Miror-Vitae projector in 1906, and was an early film renter on the New York scene in the same year. (LMcK)

References
Musser, *Before the Nickelodeon* (1991).
Musser, *The Emergence of Cinema* (1990).

SCHUBERG, John Albert ('Johnny Nash') (1875–1958)

Magician, cinema owner. Schuberg, whose professional name was Johnny Nash, came from a Swedish family living in Minneapolis, and was already an accomplished magician by his teens. In 1894 he moved to Canada, touring the country's fairs and variety halls. In 1898 he acquired an Edison projector and added films to his act. His first film show, on 15 December 1898, introduced Vancouver to scenes of the Spanish-American War, and he thereafter toured throughout Canada, along with a growing number of similar itinerant fairground entertainers. Wishing to end his family's travelling life, Schuberg converted an empty shop at 38 Cordova Street, Vancouver, into Canada's first cinema in October 1902. He opened further theatres in Winnipeg and elsewhere, eventually owning eight in Canada

and the USA, and by 1919 had become western Canada's leading cinema exhibitor, before selling out to another theatre chain. He eventually left the film industry and settled in Vancouver. (LMcK)

References
Morris, *Embattled Shadows* (1978).

SEALY, Lewis (William Armiger Sealy Lewis) (1850–1931)

Actor, exhibitor. Born in Bandon, Ireland, on 24 February 1850 and educated at the Cork College, while still in his teens Sealy joined a theatrical company in Liverpool. After various jobs in the theatre as an actor and stage manager, he became one of the first film exhibitors in England, showing films as early as August 1896. Sealy's main venue was the Metropolitan theatre in Edgware Road, but he also exhibited in other theatres in London. He then produced, with **Esmé Collings** as cinematographer, two films illustrating popular Victorian songs accompanied by live singers: *Simon the Cellarer* in three scenes, which was issued by **Philipp Wolff** in January 1899, and *Tomorrow will be Friday*. After this brief excursion into film-making, Sealy emigrated to the USA, where he again took up a theatrical career and became associated with George Arliss, Lillie Langtry and Olga Nethersole. He died in New York on 22 March 1931, aged eighty. (JB)

References
Barnes, *The Beginnings of the Cinema in England* (vols. 1–5).

SEGRETO, Affonso

Brazilian pioneer film-maker. One of four Italian immigrant brothers, the others being Gaetano, Luiz and Paschoal (the latter was a showman who opened Brazil's first film house in Rio de Janeiro on 31 July 1897; he died in 1920). In 1898 Affonso Segreto became the first native Brazilian to produce films in that country, following the introduction of the Lumière Cinématographe in Rio on 8 July 1896. (Advertised as the 'Omnigrapho', this is a rare example of the machine being billed under a name other than its own, if it was indeed the Cinématographe.) Segreto returned from Europe in June 1898 with a Cinématographe, and over the next few years filmed a wide number of actuality and news events, from local scenes to presidential activities; however, it was some years before the cinema became established in Brazil, owing to the lack of a fully developed electrical system. The Segretos remained key figures in the Brazilian film industry in the first decade of the century, when native production dominated the market, and Affonso had particular success with the popular genre of filmed re-creations of notorious local crimes. (LMcK)

References

Hennebelle and Gumucio-Dagron, *Les Cinémas de l'Amérique Latine* (1981).

SELIG, William N. ('Colonel')
(1864–1948)

Magician, photographer, actor, film-maker, producer. The longevity, prominence and varied activity of the Selig Polyscope Company of Chicago is a vivid example of the geographical diversity of film activity in the USA in the first decade of motion pictures, when production companies, manufacturers and exhibition services were widely dispersed along the eastern seaboard and throughout the Midwest.

William N. Selig was a magician and later a minstrel-show operator, who left Chicago in poor health to travel around the far western and southern states. In 1896 he saw a Kinetoscope in Texas and returned to his home town to open a commercial photographic printing studio, while trying to make a motion picture projector. A mechanic to whom Selig turned for help had unknowingly made a duplicate Cinématographe for a travelling Lumière operator, and Selig's camera and Polyscope projector were based on the drawings of the Lumière machine. He opened an exhibition service and had begun making local scenes by 1898, together with popular Spanish-American War scenes photographed at Camp Tanner in Springfield, Illinois. Selig continued to make local scenes and supply projection equipment for use in several Midwestern vaudeville chains and for sale through the Sears Roebuck mail-order catalogue. In 1901 he filmed extensively at the Armour and Co. meat-packing factories in Chicago, producing some sixty films, and many of his pictures featured prominent leaders of the day, among them Theodore Roosevelt, William Jennings Bryan, Admiral George Dewey and President **William McKinley**.

Like other pioneer companies, Selig also pirated the productions of others for sale through his own catalogues. His activity attracted the attention of Edison's lawyers, but Selig continued making films across the south-west. By 1904 he was specialising in slapstick comedies and minstrel-themed comic scenes, in addition to producing the first Westerns of G. M. 'Broncho Billy' Anderson, the later co-founder of the Essanay Company. Settling with Edison, Selig joined the Motion Picture Patents Company and in 1913 teamed up with Vitagraph, Lubin and Essanay to form the V-S-L-E distribution company; prominent among his later productions were the 1909 *Hunting Big Game in Africa*, a popular studio-made film celebrating Theodore Roosevelt's exploits on safari; the 1912 *The Coming of Columbus*, an elaborate three-reel production which gained him a medal from Pope Pius X; and the 1913 *The Adventures of Kathlyn*, the first genuine movie serial starring Kathlyn Williams. Selig maintained studios in Chicago and the Edendale district of Los Angeles, and produced many animal pictures, with the Selig Jungle Zoo near Eastlake Park becoming the largest collection of wild animals in the world with over 700 residents.

Selig retired and ceased active film production in 1918, the victim again of the poor health that had sent him on the road to California twenty-five years before, and though he continued to dabble on the fringes of the film world, he devoted much of his later life to sponsoring the expeditions of mountain climbers and explorers. In 1947 he was one of a small group of American pioneers (**Thomas Armat**, **George K. Spoor**, **Albert Smith**) given a special Academy Award for their contributions to the development of motion pictures. (DR)

References

Kalton C. Lahue, *Motion Picture Pioneer: The Selig Polyscope Company* (New York: A. S. Barnes, 1973). Anthony Slide, *The American Film Industry: A Historical Dictionary* (Wesport, Conn.: Greenwood Press, 1986).

SEN, Hiralal (1866–1917)

Bengali film-maker. The son of a lawyer, Sen was running a successful photography business when in 1898 he saw a film presentation by one Professor Stevenson that featured alongside the stage show, *The Flower of Persia*, at Calcutta's Star theatre. With Stevenson's encouragement and camera Sen made his first film, of scenes from *The Flower of Persia*, which was subsequently featured in the Star theatre programme. After Stevenson had moved on,

Sen purchased an **Urban** Bioscope from the Warwick Trading Company in London, and in 1899 with his brother Motilal Sen formed the Royal Bioscope Company.

Sen was initially dependent on imported film, generally exhibited at the Classic theatre, Calcutta, where the films featured in the intervals in the stage shows. When he began producing his own films regularly, they again primarily featured scenes from theatrical productions, this time staged at the Classic, such as *Bhramar*, *Hariraj* and *Buddhadev*, all between 1901 and 1904. This phase of his career culminated with his longest film, *Alibaba and the Forty Thieves* (1903), again based on an original Classic theatre staging. He also produced many local views and news films, took commissions, made advertising films and put on private shows for members of high society. As newer film ventures entered the marketplace, Royal Bioscope's fortunes declined, and production ceased in 1913. Shortly afterwards, all of Sen's films were accidentally destroyed by fire. (LMcK)

References
Ashish Rajadhyaksha and Paul Willemen, *Encyclopaedia of Indian Cinema* (New Delhi/London: Oxford University Press/BFI, 1994).

SESTIER, Marius (1865–1926)

Lumière operator in India and Australia. A chemist before joining the Lumière firm, Sestier was sent to India with a Cinématographe in June 1896. His first film show in India was held at the Bombay Novelty theatre on 7 July 1896, and ran until August, when he boarded a steamer for Australia, making the acquaintance of Sydney photographer **Henry Walter Barnett** during the voyage. Arriving in Sydney on 16 September 1896, two days later Sestier gave a private screening at Goodman's Lyceum theatre, and soon afterwards opened a Salon Lumière at 237 Pitt Street, Sydney. In October Barnett and Sestier began filming, starting with *Passengers Alighting from Ferry 'Brighton' at Manly*, the first Australian film, which was premiered at the Salon on 27 October. Encouraged by the success of this test film, the pair set out to film the Melbourne racing season. On 31 October they filmed the VRC Derby, and on 3 November the Melbourne Cup, a famous and highly popular set of films that concentrated on the social event rather than the race, and most of which ended up in the Lumière catalogue of films for international exhibition.

While in Melbourne Sestier presented a programme of Lumière films at the Princess theatre alongside the pantomime *Djin-Djin*. With further views taken on their return to Sydney, Sestier and Barnett were ready, on 24 November, to present an all-Australian film programme at the Criterion theatre. Further screenings continued to the end of the year, after which the pair broke up and Sestier moved on to Adelaide.

During the partnership, it was Sestier who took all the films and presented them, Barnett who stage-managed and made good use of his social contacts. In Adelaide Sestier teamed up with showman Wybert Reeve, first presenting the Cinématographe and a programme that included several of his Australian scenes from 26 December 1896. He further toured Australia up to May 1897, when his exclusive presentations of the Cinématographe ended and the machine became available for purchase to individual exhibitors. Sestier then returned to France, having left behind both the machinery and others trained by him to establish a native Australian film industry. On his return journey he may have passed through Indo-China and Japan. He then became director of the Lumière Patents Company. His first name is wrongly given as Maurice in several sources. (CL/LMcK)

References
Chris Long, 'Local Production Begins', *Cinema Papers* 93, May 1993.
Jean-Claude Seguin, 'Marius Sestier, opérateur Lumière. Inde-Australie: Juillet 1896–Mai 1897', *1895*, no. 16, June 1994.

SHIBATA Tsunekichi

Japanese film-maker. In June 1897 the Konishi camera store in Tokyo acquired a Gaumont camera. The chief clerk at the store, Asano Shiro, took the camera out and shot a few test scenes of the Nihonbashi, Asakusa and Ginza regions of the city. Some sources attribute these films to Shibata Tsunekichi, who otherwise first appears as a film-maker in 1899 filming three geisha dances, at the behest of **Komada Koyo**, *benshi* and proto-film producer. The dancers had trouble staying within the sight-lines laid down for them, but geisha films went on to become a very popular native product in the earliest years of Japanese film-making.

The geisha films were first shown on 20 June 1899. In September of the same year Shibata shot Japan's first fiction film, *Inazuma goto Hobaku no Ba* (*The Lightning Robber is*

Arrested), with Yokoyama Umpei playing the detective and Sakamato Keijiro the burglar. The following day Shibata shot *Shosei no Sumie (The Schoolboy's Ink Painting)*, with Yokoyama as a man painted with ink by two boys while he is asleep on a bench. In November 1899 he shot the most prestigious Japanese film so far, *Momiji-gari (Maple Leaf Hunters)*, intended as a historic record of the Kabuki theatre actors **Danjuro IX** and Kikugoro V. *Ninin dojoji (Two People at Dojo Temple)* was made in December. Shibata, by now Japan's most experienced camera operator, is last heard of accompanying Fukaya Komakichi to film the Boxer Rebellion in China, travelling with a contingent of the Japanese army throughout August 1900. (LMcK)

References

Peter B. High, 'The Dawn of Cinema in Japan', *Journal of Contemporary History*, vol. 19 no. 1, January 1984.
Komatsu Hiroshi, 'Some Characteristics of Japanese Cinema before World War I', in Arthur Nolletti Jr. and David Desser (eds.), *Reframing Japanese Cinema: Authorship, Genre, History* (Bloomington and Indianapolis: Indiana University Press, 1992).

SHORT, Henry William ('Harry')

Camera operator, mechanic. Harry Short, a friend of British pioneer **Robert Paul**, appeared in the first successful film taken in England, shot outside the home of **Birt Acres** in February or March 1895. We first hear of Short arranging for two Greek entrepreneurs, **Georgiades** and **Tragides**, to meet Robert Paul. They wanted Paul to make copies of the Edison Kinetoscope, which he subsequently agreed to do, so initiating the start of the film manufacturing industry in Britain. Short was at that time assistant to Birt Acres at Elliott's photographic works. Paul needed a photographer to help develop a camera and shoot the films for his Kinetoscopes, and Short introduced Acres to Paul. Henry Short – dressed in cricket whites, presumably to show up better on the film – himself appeared in their first test film. Reproductions of two fragments of this film, now known individually as *Incident at Clovelly Cottage* and *Cricketer Jumping Over Garden Gate*, were subsequently published.

Short was also involved in the design of film equipment: in February 1896 he patented an intermittent mechanism, but does not seem to have pursued its development. That summer he went to Spain and Portugal, and filmed fourteen subjects for Paul, including a bullfight, *Portuguese Railway Train* and *A Sea Cave*

near Lisbon, the latter proving one of the most successful early British films, and still in the Paul catalogue in 1903. In 1897 Short toured Egypt, where he photographed thirteen subjects, including *A Cairo Scene: Selling Water from a Goat Skin* and *A Scene of the Pyramids*. **Cecil Hepworth** commented sarcastically in the *Amateur Photographer*: 'animated Pyramids might be worth seeing. The Psalmist says something about mountains skipping like young rams'. That same year Short formed a company, the Anglo-French Filoscope Syndicate, to market the Filoscope, a flip book in a metal holder, equipped with a short lever to facilitate the action. It showed Robert Paul films, including the speciality dancers May and Flora Hengler, music hall artist **Chirgwin** and *A Soldier's Courtship*, filmed on the roof of the Alhambra theatre in April 1896. (SH)

References

Barnes, *The Beginnings of the Cinema in England* (vols. 1 and 2).

SIVAN, Casimir (1850–1916)

Inventor. Casimir Sivan, whose career reflects several aspects of early cinema in Switzerland, has only recently emerged from obscurity. Though primarily a master clockmaker and inventor of watch movements, a collector of watches and automatons and a promoter of professional training for clockmakers, he was also interested in the reproduction of sound (Le Bijou phonograph). After training at the Ecole Impériale d'Horlogerie in Cluses (1867–70), he settled in Geneva in 1888, taking Swiss nationality twelve years later.

Between 1893 and 1898 he was involved in various ways with the new 'moving pictures'. From March 1895, he held the Swiss concession for the Edison Kinetoscope and Kinetophone. On 23 May 1896 he filed a patent, co-signed by E. Dalphin, for a 35mm camera/projector. This camera may not have progressed beyond the prototype stage (Eastman House, Rochester, New York, holds two fragments of positive film, a camera and a Sivan-Dalphin projector). However in mid-1896 he arranged for some films to be made (a smoker, a man drinking from a bottle, men bathing) at the same time that **Lavanchy-Clarke** was producing (also in Geneva) Lumière's first Swiss films. One of Sivan's short films (showing the main façade of the Exposition Nationale Suisse, Geneva, 1896) is preserved at the Cinémathèque Suisse. During the same period, Sivan collaborated with the inventor **François Dussaud**, developing a micro-phonograph and a method of synchronising image and sound (1897), which deserves further study, particularly as Dussaud became consulting engineer at Pathé Frères at the turn of the century. (RC)

References

Roland Cosandey, 'Casimir Sivan: Redécouverte d'un inventeur', *Ciné-Bulletin* no. 197, February 1992.

SKLADANOWSKY, Max (1863–1939)

Inventor, film-maker, lanternist, showman. Born 30 April 1863 in Berlin, the son of a glazier who later became a small manufacturer, Max Skladanowsky is one of the genuine inventors of motion pictures whose extravagant claims in the 1920s and 1930s obscured his real accomplishments.

He was first apprenticed in photography, then glass painting, and finally in optics at the Hagedorn workshops, manufacturers of theatrical lighting and apparatus, including magic lanterns. In 1879 he went on tour with his father, Carl, and older brother Emil (b.1859), presenting dissolving magic lantern shows; and from 1881 to 1890 the family presented magic lantern, water fountain and mechanical theatre shows throughout Germany and central Europe. In 1890 Max and Emil constructed a mobile mechanical theatre, touring Germany during 1891 and Vienna, Budapest and Scandinavia in 1892. That same year they also constructed a chronophotographic camera designed for unperforated Kodak roll film and using a worm-gear intermittent movement, with which he shot his first film footage (forty-eight frames of Emil) on 20 August. By mid-summer 1895 Max had developed the Bioskop projector, a device derived from

dissolving magic lantern practice using two loops of 54mm-wide film, and comprising two lenses and electrical arc lamps and a worm-gear intermittent that projected alternate frames from each band so that it achieved the 16fps needed to reconstitute full motion.

The Bioskop was seen in a demonstration at the Gasthaus Sello in the Pankow suburb of Berlin in July 1895 by Julius Baron and Franz Dorn, directors of the Wintergarten theatre in Berlin, and they immediately contracted for a public exhibition at their theatre beginning on 1 November 1895 (also the date of the Skladanowskys' patent for his intermittent movement). Then located in the Martin Luther Strasse, the Wintergarten performances marked the first projections of film in Europe to a paying audience. Rear projection was used, with stagehands keeping the screen wet to increase its transparency, and original scores were composed for the nine films by Hermann Kruger. Film titles were projected by a magic lantern and each film, which lasted about six seconds, was repeated several times. The film titles for the initial programme were: *Italienischer Bauerntanz, Komisches Reck, Serpentine Tanz, Der Jongleur Paul Petras, Das boxende Kanguruh, Akrobatisches Potpourri, Kamarinskaja, Ringkampf* (a wrestling bout featuring **Eugen Sandow**) and *Apotheose*.

Following this month-long exhibition, the Bioskop opened in Hamburg (from 21 December 1895) and was contracted to open at the Folies Bergère in Paris in January 1896, but after the Lumière screening at the Grand Café in late December 1895, the Skladanowsky engagement was cancelled, though their fee was paid in full. Recent research suggests that a similar arrangement may have been made for the show to appear at the Empire theatre, Leicester Square, London, in January, but this booking was also cancelled.

The brothers then embarked on a tour of central Germany in March 1896, taking in Kothen, Halle and Magdeburg. This was followed by Oslo (then Kristiana), Norway (6 April–5 May); Groningen (14–24 May) and Amsterdam (from 21 May), the Netherlands; Copenhagen, Denmark (11 June–30 July); Stockholm, Sweden (from 3 August), returning to the Wintergarten, Berlin, in February 1897. A second film camera had been constructed in late autumn 1895, using a Maltese cross movement, and some films were taken with it in Berlin, Stettin and notably in Stockholm in August 1896, using professional actors from the Victoria theatre company.

Their last film show took place in Stettin, Germany, on 30 March 1897, with an improved single film band projector, the day that Max Skladanowsky's trade licence as an exhibitor expired (the Berlin authorities refused him a new licence since 'too many film licences were already in circulation'). From 1897 onwards, Skladanowsky concentrated on the production of flip books which mostly derived from his film footage. He began the Projektion für Alle (Projection For All) company to distribute 3-D anaglyphic lantern slides, published several albums of 3-D photographs, returned to giving magic lantern shows, and sold amateur film cameras, projectors and printing equipment. The Projektion für Alle company made a half-dozen films in 1913–14, some directed by his younger brother Eugen, but with no significant success.

In the mid-1930s, Skladanowsky's claims about his accomplishments led to deeply partisan arguments in the press, where the attacks were led by the historian and cameraman Guido Seeber. At that time, Skladanowsky was also touring with his original Bioskop machine, now in the film museum at Potsdam, for the fortieth anniversary of the birth of cinema. He died at Berlin-Niederschönhausen on 30 November 1939. While his solution to the problem of reconstituting motion on the screen proved to be a technological dead end, of the many inventors who tried to adapt the double-projection system of dissolving magic lanterns, only Skladanowsky produced a commercially used and widely seen apparatus. (DR)

References
Albert Narath, *Max Skladanowsky* (Berlin: Deutsche Kinemathek Berlin, 1970).
Manfred Lichtenstein, 'The Brothers Skladanowsky', in Paolo Cherchi Usai and Lorenzo Codelli (eds.), *Prima di Caligari: Cinema tedesco 1895–1920* (Pordenone: Giovanni del Cinema Muto, 1990).
Von Zglinicki, *Der Weg des Films* (1956).

SLIEKER, Christiaan (1861–1945)

Exhibitor. Christiaan Slieker grew up in a Friesian family of travelling fairground showpeople, and married the daughter of a renowned carousel owner. A prosperous firm, the family business was also always on the look out for a new attraction, from panoramas and a discus-throwing apparatus to an 'electrical fishery', which provided the family with a brisk trade at the 1895 Amsterdam World's Fair. In spring 1896, Slieker travelled to the Industrial Exhibition in Berlin to investigate the latest showman's apparatus, and returned with an **H. O. Foersterling** and Co. Kinematograf, an apparatus pirated from the design of Victor Continsouza in Paris. When Slieker gave his first film show at the fair on the Wilhelminaplein in Leeuwarden on 15 July 1896, he opened the first travelling movie show in the Netherlands, advertised as 'Edison's Ideal, Living Pictures … Discovered by the Messrs A. and L. Lumière'. Slieker's travelling show was called the Grand Théâtre Edison, and held 116 people, usually charging an admission of 50 cents for the twenty seats at the front, and 25 cents for the ninety-six remaining places.

Quickly moving on from Leeuwarden to the fairs and markets in Alkmar, Nijmegen, Utrecht and literally scores of other Dutch cities and towns, Slieker's Grand Théâtre Edison became a familiar and successful attraction across the country. He was soon imitated by other fairground entrepreneurs, especially Herman Fey, Frits van Haarlem, Carmine Riozzi and H. Grunkorn, and later Albert and Willy Mullens. And by the turn of the century many elaborately decorated shows were travelling a circuit that regularly included Belgium and parts of rural France and Germany, such as those of Antoon Wegkamp, Alex Benner, W. Lohoff and others. In 1906 Slieker advised his colleague showman Jean Desmet to convert his Toboggan Slide attraction into a film palace, thus launching one of the most elaborate of the travelling shows, Desmet's splendid Imperial Bioscope. The next year, Slieker gave up travelling the circuit and opened a business in Drachten, living on into a ripe old age and giving interviews about the birth of the movies. His original Foersterling projector is now in the collection of the Museum Smallingerland, Friesland. (DR)

References
Adriaan Briels, *Komst en plaats van de Levende Photographie op de kermis: Een filmhistoriche verkenning* (Assen: Van Gorcum & Comp. B.V., 1973).
Karel Dibbets and Frank van der Maden, *Geschiedenis van de nederlandse Film en Bioscoop tot 1940* (Weesp: Het Wereldvenster, 1986).

SMEDLEY, William Thomas (1851–1934)

Businessman. A chartered accountant from Birmingham, W. T. Smedley became chairman of British Mutoscope and Biograph, the largest film company in England during the Victorian period. Part of an international group and quoted on the London Stock Exchange, British Biograph used a special 68mm wide-gauge film, and the quality of their presentation was acknowledged by contemporaries to be outstanding. Smedley's association with the company is a reminder of the importance of professional management in the early English film business. His particular interest was the study of Shakespeare, and both he and his daughter were closely associated with the theatrical world of the time. It was no doubt due to this connection that British Biograph became the first film company in the world to produce extracts from a Shakespearean play, **Herbert Beerbohm Tree**'s *King John.*

Lower than expected results from the Mutoscope side of the business caused severe financial problems for British Biograph from 1900 onwards, and the company's survival was largely due to Smedley's policy of diversifying away from total reliance on the film business. The profitable parts were later incorporated in the 'Bio-Trust', and Smedley remained as chairman of this company until it was voluntarily wound up in 1919. (RB)

References

Constance Smedley, *Crusaders: The Reminiscences of Constance Smedley* (London: Duckworth, 1929).
Brown and Anthony, *The History of the British Mutoscope and Biograph Company* (1996).

SMITH, Albert Edward (1875–1958)

Producer, cameraman, magician. Smith was born on 4 June 1875 in Faversham, Kent, the son of a market gardener. While Albert was still a boy, the Smith family emigrated to the USA. The young Smith had a natural aptitude for mechanics, which led to his perfecting

and patenting a loose-leaf ledger system, developing early automobile parts, and also to a gift for magic and sleight of hand. It was this latter talent that led him in 1894 to team up with a talented cartoonist from England, **J. Stuart Blackton**, and another Englishman Ronald Reader to form a touring trio, presenting magic, magic lanterns, drawings, ventriloquism and recitations. Blackton found brief fame when he was filmed for Edison as a cartoonist in August 1896. Early in 1897 they acquired an Edison projector and began exhibiting films as part of their act. Their partnership of March 1897 was initially called Edison Vitagraph, a title deliberately close to the Edison Vitascope. Still performing their magic show (as they would do until July 1898), Smith and Blackton started producing advertising slides and the occasional advertising film under the title of the Commercial Advertising Bureau. Smith converted the projector into a camera and the American Vitagraph began film production in late 1897, initially shooting simple actualities, followed by their first fiction film, *The Burglar on the Roof*, in which Blackton acted and Smith operated the camera. The company also found great success with *Tearing Down the Spanish Flag*, a simple symbolic drama capitalising on the Spanish-American War.

The partnership was founded on Blackton's dramatic flair and Smith's technical know-how, which included a vital reframing device for the Vitagraph projector. They also soon found themselves battling against the Edison company over patent infringement and violation of copyright (they had been duplicating some of **William Paley**'s Spanish-American War films), then with exhibitor **William Rock**. This latter dispute, however, resulted in alliance, with Rock joining Blackton and Smith as the third member of Vitagraph in August/September 1898. 'Pop' Rock brought experience and stability to the company, though his presence did not prevent Smith getting into scrapes, such as the occasion of the **Jeffries** v. Sharkey boxing match on 3 November 1899, when Smith pirated film of the fight using the bright lights set up by **William Brady** and the Biograph camera team. Following the Edison law suit, Vitagraph had been operating under licence, passing on their negatives to Edison after so many months, and when this agreement was terminated in 1900, from 1901 to 1902 Vitagraph did not produce a single film.

After such rocky beginnings, with 1905 and the arrival of the nickelodeon period

Vitagraph began to flourish, becoming incorporated as the Vitagraph Company of America. It rapidly turned into a major producer and, along with Biograph, soon became the pre-eminent American film company in the pre-First World War period. A studio was opened in California in 1911, and a stock company developed that included such internationally popular actors as Florence Turner, Maurice Costello, John Bunny, Flora Finch and Clara Kimball Young. From being the technical genius of the partnership Smith became the financial brains behind Vitagraph, running the company with a somewhat cold-hearted efficiency, during which time Rock died and Blackton departed. Vitagraph ceased to be the power it had once been after the war, and the company was purchased by Warner Bros. in 1925.

On his retirement Smith indulged in his favourite occupation, yachting, and wrote a singularly inaccurate autobiography, which includes an entirely imaginary visit to the Boer War. In 1947 he was one of a small group of American pioneers (**George K. Spoor**, **William Selig** and **Thomas Armat**) given a special Academy Award for their contributions to the development of motion pictures. (LMcK)

References

Charles Musser, 'The American Vitagraph, 1897–1901: Survival and Success in a Competitive Industry', in Fell, *Film Before Griffith* (1983).
Anthony Slide, *The Big V: A History of the Vitagraph Company* (Metuchen NJ/London: Scarecrow Press, 1987 rev. ed.).
Albert E. Smith (in collaboration with Phil A. Koury), *Two Reels and a Crank* (New York: Doubleday, 1952).

SMITH, George Albert (1864–1959)

Film-maker, inventor. George Albert Smith is one of the most important figures in Victorian cinema. He was born on 4 January 1864 in London. After the death of his father, his mother moved the family to Brighton, where she would run a boarding house on Grand Parade. In the early 80s Smith began to perform in small Brighton halls as a hypnotist. From 1882 Smith and his new partner, Douglas Blackburn, developed a 'second sight act' (the assistant hides an object in the theatre and then the performer, blindfolded, leads him to it) and feats of 'muscle-reading' (the performer transmits to the blindfolded 'medium' on the stage the identity of objects selected by the audience). Successful shows were staged at the Brighton Aquarium. Smith claimed that genuine telepathy was practised, but Blackburn would later admit that the act was a hoax. However, representatives of the Society for Psychical Research (SPR) did believe that Smith and Blackburn had the gift of true 'Thought Reading'. Smith became closely involved with the Society's activities, and was appointed private secretary to its honorary secretary, Edmund Gurney, a post he held from 1883 to 1888. In 1887, Gurney carried out a number of 'hypnotic experiments' in Brighton, with Smith as the 'hypnotiser'. Gurney died in 1888 and his successors at the SPR, F. W. H. Myers and F. Podmore, continued to employ Smith as their private secretary. Smith would co-author the paper, *Experiments in Thought Transference* for the Society's journal in the next year.

In 1892, by which time Smith had left the SPR, he acquired the lease to St Ann's Well Garden in Hove. This was only a short distance from Brighton and the seafront. He developed the site into a popular pleasure garden, and a Hove newspaper described it in the following glowing terms: 'This delightful retreat ... presided over by the genial Mr G. Albert Smith, is now open. ... In the hot weather the refreshing foliage of the wooded retreat is simply perfect, while one can enjoy a cup of Pekoe in the shade.' Lawn tennis, 'ferns, flowers, grapes and cucumbers for sale in the glass houses', a gypsy fortune-teller, a monkey house, lantern exhibitions given by Smith of 'dissolving views' and the occasional 'thrilling parachute descent' provided it with a distinctive character. The garden would also become the location for his 'film factory'.

Smith saw and appreciated the Lumière programme in Leicester Square in March 1896, and would have been aware of **Robert Paul**'s great success with the new medium in the same year (Paul's films played in Brighton for that summer season). Either at the end of that year or in early 1897, he acquired his first camera, and John Barnes lists thirty-one films made by Smith in 1897. The few which have survived display a remarkable charm and fascination, and show how quickly he had learned to work within the confines of 75ft of film. By 1898, with *Santa Claus*, he was using superimposition to effect the arrival of Santa. As a magic lanternist, he understood the cutting techniques perfected with bi-unial and tri-unial (two-lensed and three-lensed) lanterns and brought this experience to his filmmaking. For example, Smith made only the studio shot of the train carriage in *The Kiss in the Tunnel* (1899), but when he inserted it into Hepworth's phantom ride, *View From an Engine Front – Train Leaving Tunnel*, he created an edited film which demonstrated a new sense of continuity and simultaneity across three shots. This filmic imagination was radical for the time, and it continued to develop in the next year. *As Seen Through a Telescope, Grandma's Reading Glass, The House that Jack Built* and *Let Me Dream Again*, all of 1900, were remarkable for the interpolative use of close-ups, subjective and objective point-of-view shots, the creation of dreamtime and the use of reversing. Smith was also instrumental in the development of continuity editing, teaching his contemporaries how to create a filmed sequence. Smith knew and corresponded with **Georges Méliès** at this time.

In 1897 he turned the pump house at St Ann's Well into a space for developing and printing and, probably in 1899, built a 'glasshouse' film studio in the grounds. Regarding his use of apparatus, great assistance was provided by the Brighton engineer **Alfred Darling** who was a gifted manufacturer of cameras, projectors, printers and perforators. Smith's wife, Laura Eugenia Bayley, acted in many of his films, as did the local Brighton comedian, Tom Green.

In the late 90s, Smith developed into a successful commercial film processor, with clients such as **Charles Goodwin Norton** and **John Benett-Stanford**. Chemicals were purchased from the Hove chemist and fellow film 'pioneer' **James Williamson**. His largest customer, however, was the Warwick Trading Company, and it was through this relationship that Smith became part of the company, developing a long partnership with its then managing director, **Charles Urban**. By 1902 Smith was referred to by Warwick as the manager of its 'Brighton Studio and Film Works'. The distribution of the G. A. S. Films was first handled by Warwick, and then transferred to the new Charles Urban Trading Company in 1903. Smith's films attracted international interest: the Vitagraph Company of New York alone had acquired twenty-nine Smith films by 1900.

The two-colour additive process known as Kinemacolor would dominate the rest of Smith's career in film. Urban acquired the Lee and Turner process in 1902, and financed Smith to develop it. This probably explains why he would produce no significant films after *Dorothy's Dream* and *Mary Jane's Mishap* in 1903. In either 1904 or 1905 he gave up the lease on St Ann's Well; by this time he had purchased a new home at Southwick, Sussex, and built what he called 'Laboratory Lodge'. It was here that Kinemacolor was developed. The initial demonstration of the process took place on 1 May 1908, with the first public demonstration following in early 1909. Special presentations of this new colour system also took place in Paris and New York. For this work Smith was awarded a Silver Medal by the Royal Society of Arts. Urban turned Kinemacolor into a new enterprise, the Natural Colour Kinematograph Company. It enjoyed a successful period from 1910 to 1913, producing over 100 short features at its studios in Hove and Nice. However, a patent suit brought against Kinemacolor by **William Friese Greene** in 1914 would lead to its collapse and effectively end Smith's life in the film business.

In his later years, Smith became a Fellow of the Royal Astronomical Society, and would spend time peering through his telescope in his Brighton seafront arch. In the late 1940s he was 'discovered' by the film community: interviewed by Ernest Lindgren, Rachael Low and Georges Sadoul, he was venerated by Michael Balcon as 'the father of the British Film Industry'. In 1955 he was made a Fellow of the British Film Academy. Several audio recordings of Smith have survived from the late 1950s. He died in Brighton on 17 May 1959. In Hove today, all that remains of Smith's film career is the park, St Ann's Well, and a one-storey shed which stands on the south side of the Brighton–Hove railway line, near to Hove Station. This was part of the original Williamson studio, but was acquired by Smith and Urban in 1910. On it one can still read the word 'KINEMACOLOR'. Hove Museum houses a permanent display on Smith, as well as Williamson. (FG)

References

Barnes, *The Beginnings of the Cinema in England* (vols. 2–5).

Trevor H. Hall, *The Strange Case of Edmund Gurney* (London: Duckworth, 1964).

D. B. Thomas, *The First Colour Motion Pictures* (London: HMSO, 1969).

SMITH, John William ('Jack')
(1878–1948)

Cameraman, business manager. Jack Smith began his career as a magic lantern operator, working a tri-unial lantern for the lecturer Horace Chester, subsequently leaving to join the magician **David Devant**, who in 1896 bought a Theatrograph film projector from **Robert Paul**. Smith next became a lantern operator for **Walter Gibbons**, who in 1898 bought an Urban Bioscope projector and began to tour the music halls as the Anglo-American Bio-Tableaux. Gibbons charged £20 a week for his Bioscope show, but conditions in the music halls were rather primitive and Smith later recalled that when projecting films from the circle, 'we used to get some boxes from the bar keeper, build them up between the seats, rope them down and show our pictures, all in amongst the audience'. In 1899 Walter Gibbons began to add his own films to the programme, and Smith starred with him in a short comedy film entitled *A Morning Wash*.

In 1900 Robert Paul recruited Smith as sales manager for his new equipment showroom in London, selling both cameras and projectors. Smith also made a number of fiction films at Paul's open-air studio, and was responsible for the company's news filming, personally covering many events including the arrival of the Boer leaders at Southampton in 1902. Smith also visited the USA, South Africa, Holland, Denmark and Norway on filming assignments for Robert Paul. In 1907 he left to become manager of the Warwick Trading Company, which was then being run by Will Barker. At Warwick, Smith took charge of fiction filming, but he still continued to take news film, providing much of the footage for the *London Day by Day* feature which Barker was running at the Empire theatre. In 1908 Robert Paul managed to persuade Smith to rejoin him as general manager, with responsibility for the manufacture of film cameras and projectors, but by the beginning of the following year he had returned to his old job as manager of Warwick.

In 1909 Will Barker left Warwick to establish his own company, Barker Motion

Photography, and in 1911 Smith joined him as general manager. On the outbreak of war in 1914 the two men became closely involved with the scheme for official filming at the front, and Barker Motion Photography was one of the seven firms which, in 1915, signed an agreement with the War Office and formed themselves into the British Topical Committee for War Films. In 1916 the Topical Committee had its greatest success with *Battle of the Somme*, and Jack Smith was recruited by Max Aitken (soon to be Lord Beaverbrook) to head the film section of the Canadian War Records Office in London. Smith used the darkrooms at Barker Motion Photography to develop footage from Canadian cameramen at the front, and arranged for its appearance in the official newsreel. At the end of the war, Smith resumed his work as general manager of Barker Motion Photography, but when Barker ceased film production in 1921 Smith became general manager of the Williamson Film Printing Company. (NH)

References

'Mr R. W. Paul's New Manager', *Kinematograph and Lantern Weekly*, 16 July 1908, p. 211.

'Mr Robt. W. Paul', *British Journal of Photography*, 31 July 1908, p. 582.

Jack Smith, 'One-Reel Production in One Day', *Kinematograph Weekly*, 17 June 1926, p. 58.

SMITH, Dr John Henry

Designer of a novel cinematograph apparatus, with which he filmed **Queen Victoria**'s Diamond Jubilee. Dr J. H. Smith was an Englishman who in 1889, with his partner Jakob Heusi, had established himself in Zurich as a manufacturer of chemical and photographic specialities. Smith was excited by the Lumière Cinématographe, and saw a glittering future for the movies. In his factory in Zurich-Wollishofen, near the city border, he began to construct a cine apparatus, which like the Lumière machine could serve as both camera and projector. The construction was both progressive and original. The mechanism was enclosed in a large barrel shutter, in which could be inserted wide blades for short exposure times, and small blades for longer exposure times; and when it came to projection, the blades could be set to provide an opening which reduced flicker. Smith obtained a Swiss patent for his device. For projection, he used a Pinascop lantern of his customer Rudolf Ganz, whose son Emil (b.1879), was taken on as his assistant. Smith also made his own film material, which for its quality – it was particularly light-sensitive, sharp and transparent – became noted in England.

To film the Jubilee, a world event that no one interested in this new development of photography wanted to miss, Smith travelled to London with his seventeen-year-old assistant. He had rented a viewpoint in the courtyard of Charing Cross Station, close by the Strand, and from there shot the entire procession with coaches and broughams, hundreds of riders and marchers from all the colonies. Two cameras were used. While one was turned, the other was reloaded with the help of a light-tight closed metal cassette. Smith and his assistant exposed sixteen rolls of film, each 60m long. The resulting production was shown in fairs and markets for years.

Dr Smith died a few years after his initial venture into cinematography, and the firm was taken over by his widow, but went bankrupt in 1907. Emil Ganz and his company remained closely tied to the cinema for decades. After the takeover of the Ganz firm, he busied himself with the sale of projectors, from 1907 as the general director of Ernemann, and later the Zeiss-Ikon projector divisions. (SH)

References

Barnes, *The Beginnings of the Cinema in England* (vol. 2).
Thomas Ganz, *Die Welt im Kasten* (Zurich: Verlag Neue Zurcher Zeitung, 1994).
Information kindly supplied by Thomas Ganz.

SPOOR, George K. (1872–1953)

Exhibitor, producer. George K. Spoor opened an early and successful exhibition service, ultimately named Kinodrome, in Chicago in 1897. Primarily servicing vaudeville accounts throughout the Midwest and down the Mississippi Valley, Spoor was energetically in competition with 'Colonel' **William Selig** and his Polyscope service, but instead of making his own films he relied on supplies of pictures from others: before 1900 those produced by **Edward Amet**, and later a variety of sources including **Georges Méliès**. He opened his distribution service, the National Film Renting Bureau, in 1904, and the increased demands of the nickelodeon era finally pushed him into film production in early 1907, when he founded the Essanay Company with Gilbert Maxwell 'Broncho Billy' Anderson, an important firm that made popular Westerns (starring Anderson), launched the careers of J. Walter Kerrigan and Francis X. Bushman, and briefly employed Charles Chaplin.

Essanay ceased production in 1918, and during the 1920s Spoor spent much of his time developing the Natural Vision system for widescreen 3-D films, producing the feature, *Danger Lights*, with that process in 1930. In 1947 he was one of a small group of American pioneers (**Thomas Armat**, **William Selig**, **Albert Smith**) given a special Academy Award for their contributions to the development of motion pictures. (DR)

References

Anthony Slide, *The American Film Industry: A Historical Dictionary* (Wesport, Conn.: Greenwood Press, 1986).
Martin Quigley Jr., *New Screen Techniques* (New York: Quigley Publishing Co., 1953).

STEWART, F. B. or F. D.

Photographer. Based in the British garrison town of Poona in western India from the 90s, Stewart took a number of photographs depicting British colonial and military life, including Poona race stand and the School of Signalling in the town. Somehow the Warwick Trading Company made contact with him, and by 1900 he had made a series of scenic films for them, mainly in Poona and nearby Bombay, including *The Indian Dhobie* and *Fire Brigade Turnout in Bombay*. He also made a couple of films showing Boer prisoners being brought to Fort Ahmadnagar, north-east of Poona, during the Boer War.

His next cinematographic activity seems to have been during the 1902–3 Coronation Durbar in Delhi, a vast ceremonial planned by Lord Curzon, at which Stewart's role was (later) described as 'Official cinematographer'. Such official recognition from the Durbar authorities seems quite plausible given Stewart's experience in photographing for the military in Poona. We do not know which film company he represented at the Durbar, nor who he worked for afterwards, though it seems he continued with camerawork, as R. Nataraja Mudaliar, a pioneer of the south Indian cinema later claimed that he had received his first training in operating a film camera from Stewart at his Poona residence sometime after 1912. (SB)

References

Stephen Bottomore, 'Filming the 1902–3 Delhi Durbar', *Historical Journal of Film, Radio and Television*, 15/3, 1995.

STOLLWERCK, Ludwig (1857–1922)

Exhibitor, investor. The long-established and still active German chocolate and sweets manufacturer Schokoladen-und Susswarenfab-rik Stollwerck and Co. of Cologne played a unique and curious role in the invention and early days of the cinema. Probably as a result of their interest in automated vending machines for their candy, they actively pursued an inter-est in the new technical entertainments of the late 19th century, including mechanical music boxes, panorama machines, automat restaur-ants and other devices, primarily through the passions of Ludwig Stollwerck, one of the five sons of the company's founder.

Ludwig Stollwerck was one of the three as-sociates in the Société Française du Phono-scope, founded on 20 December 1892, along with inventor **Georges Demenÿ** and William Gibbs Clarke of Lausanne (Stollwerck and Clarke together provided the 20,000FF capi-tal for the company). Through their subsidi-ary, Deutsche Automaten-Gesellschaft Stollwerck and Co. (DAG), Stollwerck became part of the Deutsche-Osterreichische-Edison-Kinetoscop-Gesellschaft created on 18 April 1895, which held exclusive rights to the Kinetoscope in German-speaking lands. They later tried unsuccessfully to gain the exclusive rights to the Edison Phonograph, and carried out negotiations with British pioneer **Birt Acres** to acquire rights to his Kineoptikon cinema apparatus (leading Acres to patent his device in Germany and to take his famous early films of the opening of the Kiel Canal), before deciding instead to acquire rights to the Lumière Cinématographe.

The first appearance of the Cinémato-graphe in Germany took place in the canteen of the Stollwerck factory in Cologne on 16 April 1896, opening to the public in Cologne four days later. Stollwerck quickly presented the Cinématographe in Berlin (28 April), Stuttgart, Dresden, Hamburg, Hanover and other German cities, frequently in conjunc-tion with industrial or trade exhibitions or as part of their own automat showrooms, as in Kiel (1 November). They also followed the example of the Lumière organisation, using their own representatives, such as Paul Beh-rens, who spent three months in Bremen (from 15 August) and ten days in Wilhelm-shaven (from 7 December), before moving to Jever on the 19th for a week. (DR)

References

Martin Loiperdinger and Roland Cosandey (eds.), *Des sous comme s'il en pleuvait: Quatre documents pour servir à l'histoire du Cinématographe* (Lausanne, 1992). Hauke Lange-Fuchs, *Birt Acres: Der erste Schleswig-Holsteinische Film Pionier* (Kiel: Walter G. Muhlau, 1987).

STOREY, Fred (1861–1917)

Dancer, comedian, stage director, scenic artist and British cinema's first leading man. Storey's dancing and artistic talents ensured that he was in demand throughout a long career in the theatre. After some years as a singer and dancer he made a major success in the pantomime *Mother Goose* at the Theatre Royal, Drury Lane, in 1880. During the ensuing decade he appeared in burlesques at the Gaiety theatre, while the 90s saw him alternating between musical comedies and ballets presented at the Alhambra theatre, Leicester Square. It was while appearing there in April 1896 that he participated in **Robert Paul**'s first fiction film, *The Soldier's Courtship*. His partner in the 80ft comedy, Julie Seale, was a popular dancer during the 90s and 1900s, and the interloper was played by Paul's wife Ellen. Storey made at least two subsequent screen appearances, *Speciality Dance by Fred Storey* (1899), filmed at Crystal Palace, and the title role in a 3,000ft version of his own play, *Rip Van Winkle* (1914). (BA)

References

W. Macqueen-Pope, *Gaiety: Theatre of Enchantment* (London: W. H. Allen, 1949).

SVAB-MALOSTRANSKY, Josef (1860–1932)

Czech actor, writer, director and publisher. Chiefly known as a highly popular comic ac-tor, Svab-Malostransky was a man of many talents whose film career unusually lasted from the pioneering days of 1898 until 1932. First working in a Prague bookshop after leaving school, he subsequently set up his own business publishing postcards and songs. He also developed a career as a café performer, and in June 1898 starred in three comic shorts made by the first Czech film-maker **Jan Kri-zenecky**: *Dostavencicko Ve Mlynici* (*Appoint-ment at the Mill*), *Plac a Smich* (*Tears and Laughter*) and *Vystavni Parkar a Lepic Plakatu* (*The Billsticker and the Sausage Vendor*).

Sustaining a career on both stage and film that included work with Antonin Pech, foun-der of the first Czech film company Kinofa (1908), he went on to become actor-manager of Prague's Svanda theatre in 1915, while con-tinuing his publishing career. As well as act-ing, he wrote film scenarios and on occasion directed, combining all three talents in such films as *The Five Senses of Man* (1912) and *Live Corpses* (1921). (LMcK)

References
Langdon Dewey, *Outline of Czechoslovakian Cinema* (Informatics, 1971).

SZIKLAY, Arnold

The first Hungarian film-maker, Sziklay was a businessman who is known to have taken film of Emperor Franz Joseph opening the Millennial Exhibition (oddly held in 1896) in Budapest, meeting the artist Mihaly Munkacsy and seeing his painting *Ecce Homo*. Sziklay used a camera reputedly of his own construction, but the results, though exhibited, were deemed to be a failure. The Edison Kinetoscope was a featured exhibit at the Millennial Exhibition as well. It does not appear that Sziklay, more of an opportunistic businessman than a keen film-maker, followed up this first experiment. (LMcK)

References
Istvan Nemeskurty, *Word and Image: History of the Hungarian Cinema* (Budapest: Corvina Press, 1974, 2nd enlarged ed.).

T

TESTER, John Frederick (1844–1916)

Businessman, film-maker. Born in Brighton, at one time Tester had been a travelling salesman with a wide interest in contemporary mechanical devices, such as sewing machines, phonographs and metal toys produced in Germany. In 1895 he formed the Electric-magnetic Toy Company, 29 Ludgate Hill, London, for the express purpose of exploiting a new magnetic toy called the 'Patent Magic Box', the invention of his eldest son, in which small fancy figures were made to perform lifelike motions. In 1896 the business was reconstituted as the British Toy and Novelty Company, trading from the same address.

An association was formed with **Birt Acres** to exploit Acres' Kineoptikon and films. The twenty or so films acquired from Acres were augmented by further titles supplied by **Esmé Collings**. Though successful performances are recorded at the People's Palace, Mile End Road, and the Regent Street Polytechnic, the enterprise soon ceased, and early in 1897 we find Tester running the 'Arcade' at 445 the Strand. Here were exhibited **Röntgen** X-rays and Edison's 'New Motor Phonograph', along with animated photographs projected by Heinze's Pholimeograph. Among the films shown were those of Acres and Collings, though the programmes also included films from other sources.

The Testers, father and son, also made their own films, among which was one of the Prince of Wales (the future Edward VII) on the deck of his yacht *Britannia* at Nice, which was subsequently exhibited at the Imperial Institute of Yachting and Fisheries Exhibition in 1897. It would be true to say that the Testers gave the films of Birt Acres and Esmé Collings a wider public than would otherwise have been the case. John Frederick Tester died in Fulham, London, in 1916. (JB)

References
Barnes, *The Beginnings of the Cinema in England* (vol. 5). Documents in the possession of the Tester family.

THOMAS, Arthur Duncan

Showman. The film business has always attracted its fair share of larger-than-life characters, and A. D. Thomas is a prime example. Thomas was a Devonshire farmer until 1893, when he became an (illegal) touring exhibitor of the Phonograph. After the Edison-Bell company had obtained a permanent injunction against him in 1897, he turned his considerable energies to the less restricted field of early cinematography (one source suggests that he had bought a projector from **Robert Paul** as early as April 1896). Brash, quick-witted and hardly ever truthful, Thomas was an archetypal example of an early peripatetic film exhibitor. **Cecil Hepworth** remembered him with some affection: 'He was an utter scamp, a very lovable fellow, and one of the greatest showmen who ever lived. His name ... soon changed to Edison-Thomas, and then, later on, to Thomas-Edison, and if people got it into their heads that he was the Edison, the great 'inventor' of moving pictures and many other things, well, that was their look-out. He didn't do anything to disillusion them. He plastered the whole town wherever he went – and he went nearly everywhere – with tremendous posters in brilliant colours describing his wonderful shows and his still more wonderful self'.

Despite (or perhaps because of) his flexible business ethics, Thomas expanded his enterprises rapidly, and by October 1898 claimed to be running twenty-one English shows in addition to having an interest in several continental ones. But by October 1901 he had overreached himself (he blamed it on falling interest in the Boer War), and he sold his business to **Walter Gibbons** and went to work for the Warwick Trading Company. The scale of the exhibiting business he had built up was revealed at his bankruptcy hearings in November 1902, when it was estimated that he had run up debts of over £9,000 and had been planning, in 1901, to turn his business into a limited company with a capital of £100,000. Perhaps surprisingly, Thomas and those like him, left an enduring legacy behind them: as late as the 1960s and early 70s cinema managers in circuit houses still engaged in 'stunts' and relied heavily on their 'showmanship' abilities for promotion, even though the social environment in England had changed so much that such an approach was totally archaic. (RB)

References

Barnes, *The Beginnings of the Cinema in England* (vol. 3).
Cecil M. Hepworth, *Came the Dawn: Memories of a Film Pioneer* (London: Phoenix House, 1951).

THWAITES, Ernest Jardine (1873–1933)

The first Australian film-maker. An engineer and inventor based in Melbourne, Thwaites constructed a movie camera in 1897, and with the assistance of Robert William Harvie started taking and processing films of local scenes from about March 1897 onwards. Finding a commercial outlet in the Melbourne Opera House, Thwaites and Harvie specialised in speedy news reporting, notably the screening in the evening of horse races, such as the Caulfield Cup, VRC Derby and Melbourne Cup of 1897, that had taken place earlier the same day. Thwaites continued

filming sports events in 1898, including cricket and Australian Rules football, and devised a flip book with scenes printed from his films, but he left film production in mid-1898 to market Edison Phonographs. (CL/LMcK)

References

Chris Long, 'Indigenous Production Begins', *Cinema Papers 95*, October 1993.

TOSCANO BARRAGAN, Salvador (1872–1947)

Mexico's first film-maker. Following the debut of the Lumière Cinématographe in Mexico in 1896 by **Gabriel Veyre**, engineering student Toscano Barragan acquired a Cinématographe, and early in 1897 opened a film salon at 17 Jesus Maria Street, Mexico City, moving later in the year to larger premises. The enterprising Toscano filmed local scenes, news events and in 1898 produced *Don Juan Tenorio*, Mexico's first fiction film, starring popular actor Paco Gavilanes. Remaining a force in Mexican film production into the new century, as local production and exhibition began to flourish, Toscano continued to produce local news film while exhibiting such landmark titles as **Edwin S. Porter**'s *The Great Train Robbery* (1903) and **Georges Méliès**' *Le Voyage dans la lune* (1902), often in rivalry with fellow pioneer, Enrique Rosas. *Memorias de un mexicano*, a documentary on Toscano's work based on his surviving films, was compiled by his daughter Carmen in 1950. (LMcK)

References

De los Reyes, *Los origenes del cine en México* (1983).

TRAGIDES, George
See **GEORGIADES, George**

TREE, Sir Herbert Beerbohm (1853–1917)

Actor and theatre manager. Tree was one of the major theatrical figures of the late Victorian and Edwardian periods, whose lavish productions, with their strong emphasis on the visual, to a certain extent prefigure the cinema. Tree himself was one of the first major actors to be filmed, and remained remarkably and commendably positive about the cinema when many of his peers sneered at the phenomenon. *King John*, four one-minute scenes from Tree's Her Majesty's theatre production, was filmed by **W. K-L. Dickson** and Walter Pfeffer Dando for the British Mutoscope and Biograph Company in September 1899. The first film of a Shakespeare play, only one sequence survives, showing Tree as the king enacting his death scene. In 1904 the storm scene from Tree's production of *The Tempest* was filmed for **Charles Urban**, and in 1911 his production of *Henry VIII* was shot at great expense by Will Barker.

Tree went to the USA in 1916, where he wrote enthusiastically about the creativity he found in Hollywood, and his *Macbeth* was filmed as a feature, with D. W. Griffith producing. His championing of the cinema in its earliest years contrasted markedly with that of his younger half-brother Max Beerbohm (1872–1956) the humourist and theatre critic, who made several disparaging comments on moving pictures in the 90s. (LMcK)

References
Luke McKernan and Olwen Terris (eds.), *Walking Shadows: Shakespeare in the National Film and Television Archive* (London: BFI, 1994).

TREWEY, Félicien (1845–1920)

Entertainer. Trewey is chiefly remembered today for having introduced the Lumière Cinématographe into Britain in 1896. Before that, he had enjoyed an international reputation in the music hall for his brilliant acts of ombromanie (hand shadows), balancing feats and clever manipulations of inanimate objects. His 'chapeaugraphy' involved transforming a simple piece of felt into any number of shapes to represent the headgear worn by particular characters, which he reinforced with the appropriate facial expressions.

Trewey was born at Angoulême and became one of the most popular entertainers in Paris during the latter half of the 19th century. He also travelled extensively in Europe and the USA. He was no stranger to English audiences when he arrived in London with the Cinématographe, for he had made several previous appearances at the music halls. In 1888, he played the old Alhambra (the future venue for **Robert Paul**'s Animatographe), where he was billed as 'Mons. Trewey, the Fantasiste, Humoristique, in his Shadowgraph Entertainment'. Trewey was a friend of the Lumières and had appeared in several of their early films, including *Assiettes tournantes* (*Spinning Plates*), *Chapeaux à transformation* (*Hat Transformation Tricks*) and *Partie d'écarté* (*A Game of Cards*). It is not surprising, therefore, that he should have received the exclusive concession for exhibiting the Lumière Cinématographe in Britain. He gave his first performance at the Marlborough Hall, Regent Street, on Thursday afternoon, 20 February 1896; a press show, with Britain's first cinema performance to a paying public taking place the next day, 21 February. Shortly afterwards, he was engaged by the Stoll theatre group to give shows at the Empire theatre, Leicester Square, previewing on 7 March and opening on the 9th. One of the acts sharing the bill with the Cinématographe was a minstrel troupe, and Trewey arranged to have them filmed performing in a nearby street. The busy frontage of the Empire was the subject of one of several 'actualities' directed by Trewey in England; another depicted the traffic in Piccadilly Circus. Presumably, he arranged for **Matt Raymond**, electrician/operator at the Polytechnic, to operate the camera. Trewey appears in one film himself, *Cyclistes et cavaliers arrivant au cottage*. There is one story about Trewey concerning a street scene that came out very badly: making a virtue of necessity, he billed it as 'London in the Fog'. Trewey subsequently appeared in other towns in England, Scotland and Wales where Stoll theatres were located. (JB/SH)

References
Barnes, *The Beginnings of the Cinema in England* (vol. 1).
Hopkins, *Magic* (1898).
Rittaud-Hutinet, *Le Cinéma des origines* (1985).

TRUJILLO DURAN, Manuel (1871–1933)

Journalist, astronomer, businessman, painter, photographer and the first Latin American film-maker. Film arrived in Venezuela in the form of the Edison Vitascope on 28 January 1897 at the Teatro Baralt, Maracaibo, following a performance of the Donizetti opera, *La Favorita*. The event was organised by Manuel Trujillo Durán, a dealer in American photographic supplies who had conducted business dealings with the Edison company in the past. Trujillo Durán was a keen photographer, and he soon introduced two films of his own into the film programme, *Muchachas bañandose en la laguna de Maracaibo* (*Young Women Bathing in Maracaibo Lagoon*) and *Un celebre especialista sacando muelas en el gran hotel Europa* (*A Famous Puller of Teeth at the Grand Hotel Europa*). Thus the first Venezuelan film show and the first Venezuelan films (which were also the first native Latin American films) ran close together, introduced by the same man, an entrepreneur and enthusiast of wide interests and abilities. The Lumière Cinématographe was brought into the country by **Gabriel Veyre**, when he arrived in Caracas in August 1897. (LMcK)

References
Hennebelle and Gumucio-Dagron, *Les Cinémas de l'Amérique Latine* (1981).

TURNER, Edward George (1872–1962)

Film distributor. E. G. Turner and J. D. Walker, founders of the first film company in Britain to rent films, formed their partnership in 1896 when (based in London) they toured the country with Edison Kinetoscopes and Phonographs. In August 1896 they acquired a **Wrench** cinematograph and introduced projected film into their touring shows, billing themselves as the North American Entertainment Company. The redoubtable Mrs Walker was their projectionist. Reforming as Walker and Turner in January 1897, they had found less success than they might have hoped when going for a better class of audience and emphasising the educational aspects, so (as Turner recalled) they 'went for the working classes'. This was a sound change of policy, and after a successful year's business they started to rent out the large collection of films that they had amassed, which ranged from the Edison and Lumière titles with which they had started out, to **Robert Paul**, **Birt Acres**, **G. A. Smith**, **James Williamson** and **Mitchell** and **Kenyon**'s popular Boer War fakes. Acquiring up to a dozen prints of any one title, they hired out anything from single films to half-hour programmes. Around 1900 Walker and Turner teamed up with G. H. Dawson (a school teacher who had hired films from them), the three names eventually blending to form Walturdaw in 1904, thereafter a leading film renter. In 1905 Walturdaw began film production for itself; in 1907 the company introduced its own synchronised sound film system, the Cinematophone. It continued a steady if unambitious path in film distribution until being wound up in 1924, though the name Walturdaw continued for some years after as a film equipment suppliers. Turner himself enjoyed a long period as a senior representative of the pioneering days, becoming chairman of the Kinematograph Renter's Society and the Kinematograph Manufacturer's Association, as well as a president of the Cinema Veterans Society. The series of articles he wrote for the *Kinematograph Weekly* in 1926 provide a detailed and valuable account of the British film business in the 1890s. (LMcK)

References
Low and Manvell, *The History of the British Film 1896–1906* (1948).
E. G. Turner, 'From 1896 to 1926', *Kinematograph Weekly*, 17 & 24 June, 1 & 15 July 1926.

U

UNGERLEIDER, Mór

Hungarian café owner and showman. Though film was first shot in Hungary in 1896 by **Arnold Sziklay**, the film programmes put on by Mór Ungerleider at his Velence Café in Budapest laid the true foundations of film-making in the country. Having originally simply projected film, Ungerleider adapted his projector to shoot film, and in 1898 formed the Projectograph firm with former stage performer, Jozsef Neumann. Projectograph showed films shot by Jozsef Becsi, as well as imported film, and rented and sold cinema equipment. Ungerleider continued to be a major force in Hungarian film exhibition into the 1910s, operating the Apollo cinema in Budapest, for many years the largest in Hungary. (LMcK)

References
Istvan Nemeskurty, *Word and Image: History of the Hungarian Cinema* (Budapest: Corvina Press, 1974, 2nd enlarged ed.).

URBAN, Charles (1867–1942)

Producer. The most significant figure in the early British film industry was an American of German parentage (von Urban) who was born in Ohio and raised in Cincinnati. Moving to Detroit in the 90s, he ran a stationery shop before becoming a phonograph salesman. It was through this activity that he came into contact with the inventions of **Thomas Edison**, and by 1894 was managing a Kinetoscope and Phonograph parlour in Detroit. In 1896 he obtained the agency rights for the Edison Vitascope projector for Michigan, and in 1897 became manager of the English branch of the firm of **Maguire and Baucus**, agents for Edison films in Europe. Establishing the business in London's Warwick Court, at which time the young **Cecil Hepworth** worked with him for a while, by 1898 he had re-formed the company as the Warwick Trading Company, and began to produce English films as well as marketing his own Bioscope projector. Urban's powerful, ebullient personality and drive lay at the heart of what was soon to become the most prominent British film company of the period, with its reputation firmly based on documentary and news film. Warwick became particularly noted for its travel and war films. **John Benett-Stanford** and **Joe Rosenthal** covered the Boer War, and other noted cameramen working for Warwick at the turn of the century included John Avery, F. Ormiston-Smith (who filmed an ascent of Mont Blanc) and **F. B. Stewart**.

The Warwick Trading Company were also agents for a number of British and French firms, including Frank Mottershaw, **James Williamson**, Lumière and **Georges Méliès**. The latter was commissioned by Urban to produce a celebrated record of the coronation of Edward VII, filmed at Méliès' studio in

Montreuil. Meticulous in its attention to detail, the film was completed before the event took place, but its release had to be postponed when the King fell ill with appendicitis. Warwick also sold cinematographic equipment manufactured largely by **Alfred Darling**. Urban's most notable professional association was, however, with **G. A. Smith**, the Hove pioneer. Urban first handled Smith's films, then employed him as an agent and engineer, and in 1902 commissioned Smith to work on an improvement to the Lee and Turner colour process. Kinemacolor, a two-colour additive system employing red and green filters and patented by Smith in 1906, was the most successful colour process of the early cinema period and added considerable lustre to Urban's name.

In 1903 Urban broke away from Warwick to form the Charles Urban Trading Company (trademark Urbanora), reinforcing his reputation as a supplier of quality documentary film, but also diversifying to form the Natural Colour Kinematograph Company (exploiting Kinemacolor), the Kineto company and the French firm Eclipse. He had a particular interest in encouraging the scientific film, producing such series as the *Unseen World*, which showcased the microcinematography of F. Martin Duncan and the zoological studies of Percy Smith.

Urban remained a figurehead for the industry up to the First World War. Employed by British propaganda outfits to produce the prestigious documentary feature film, *Britain Prepared* (1915), and later editing the greatest battle film of the time, *The Battle of the Somme* (1916), he then went on to promote the British war effort on American cinema screens. In 1917 he established and edited the American propaganda newsreel, *Official War Review*, and after the war attempted to re-establish himself in the USA. He founded the Kineto Company of America, whose chief product was the cinemagazine series, *Urban Movie Chats* (largely composed of pre-war Urban library film), and co-founded the newsreel, *Kinograms* (edited by Terry Ramsaye).

Urban had always been interested in developing the home and educational market for his films, beginning with his early involvement in the 17.5mm Biokam home camera/projector and, briefly, with the Kinora flip-book device. In about 1907 he bought the rights to the Spirograph projector, which showed motion pictures on a celluloid disc, from Theodore Brown (optical experimenter and editor of the *Kinematograph and Lantern Weekly*). Urban's engineer, Henry W. Joy, developed the machine, which was about to go into major production in 1923, along with Kinekrom (an improved version of Kinemacolor), but at this point Urban's business empire appears to have collapsed. He returned to Britain in 1923, but failed to find any footing in the changed British film industry, and his later years were spent in obscurity. When he died in Brighton in 1942, his great contribution to British filmmaking, and in particular his nurturing of a native talent for the filming of actuality, was largely forgotten. (LMcK)

References

Kevin Brownlow, *The War, the West and the Wilderness* (London: Secker & Warburg, 1979).
Ramsaye, *A Million and One Nights* (1926).
D. B. Thomas, *The First Colour Motion Pictures* (London: HMSO, 1969).
Urban Papers in the Science Museum, London.

URRY, George *See* **HAYDON, Frank**

V

VEYRE, Gabriel (1871–1936)

Lumière operator working in Central and Latin America, the Caribbean, Japan and China. Veyre was a chemist from Saint-Alban-du-Rhône, a small village in Isère, France, who joined the Lumière firm in the hope of adventure and to help out his financially straitened family. One of the team of Lumière cameramen who took the Cinématographe around the world, he arrived in New York on 19 July 1896 and made his way down to Mexico, where in August he and Lumière concessionaire C. F. von Bernard exhibited the Lumière Cinématographe in Mexico City, starting on 6 August 1896 with a private demonstration for an invited audience that included President Porfirio Diaz and members of his Cabinet at Chapultepec castle, Mexico City (Diaz's own residence). The first public screening, organised by Veyre and Bernard, took place at 9 Plateros Street, on 16 August 1896 (a press screening took place two days earlier), where public reaction was characteristically enthusiastic.

Veyre moved on to Guadeloupe in November 1896, and thence to Cuba, where the Cinématographe debuted in Havana on 24 January 1897, the Spanish authorities only allowing Veyre into the country on condition that he take propagandist pictures of military manoeuvres. By August 1897 he was in Caracas, Venezuela, moving then to Martinique and Colombia. He returned to France in October 1897, only to set out once again for Japan, travelling via Canada. He arrived in Japan in October 1898, where he replaced **François-Constant Girel**, subsequently visiting China between February and April 1899. By April 1899 he was in Hanoi, returning to France in February 1900 in time for the Paris Exposition. Some time in 1900–1, having left the Lumière firm, he journeyed as a solo operator to Morocco, where he demonstrated photography and cinematography for Sultan **Abd al-Aziz**, who possessed an insatiable desire for western inventions, well documented in Veyre's own published account. (LMcK)

References

Philippe Jacquier, 'Un opérateur de la Maison Lumière, Gabriel Veyre', in FIAF, *Le Cinéma Français muet dans le monde, influences réciproques* (Paris: Cinémathèque de Toulouse/ Institut Jean Vigo, 1988), pp. 57–60.
Rittaud-Hutinet, *Le Cinéma des origines* (1985).
Gabriel Veyre, *Au Maroc: Dans l'intimité du Sultan* (Paris: Librarie Universelle, 1905).

VICTOR, Alexander F. (1878–1961)

Magician, inventor. Victor was born in Bollnas, Sweden, on 20 June 1878; his father was a Swedish army officer. He studied for a period under the physicist Solemon Andree, who developed his interest in physics and mechanics. Victor was sixteen in 1894 when he attended a performance of Stephanio, a renowned magician. He joined the act and added several illusions while on tour in Europe. While Stephanio was performing in Paris in 1896, Victor saw a Lumière Cinématographe presentation. He later claimed that after much persuasion, the Lumières sold him a Cinématographe, 'Number 17', and some 15m films. Thus moving pictures were added to Stephanio's magic show. Late in 1896 Stephanio died in Cairo. Victor (so the story goes) successfully carried on the show, as 'The Boy Wonder of Magic and Illusion' (and later as 'Alexander the Great'), through the Near East and India until travelling to the USA.

In the summer of 1897 Victor rented a vacant shop store in Newark, New Jersey, and showed films on an Edison Projecting Kinetoscope, accompanied by live music from Bowman's Military Band. Until 1908, he operated two melodrama companies, and when these folded he worked at the Edison laboratories at West Orange, New Jersey, and also developed a motorised washing machine for the White Lily Washing Machine Company of Davenport, Iowa. He worked on various ideas for amateur motion picture equipment using images on discs, and in 1910 obtained funding from the directors of White Lily to form the New Victor Animato-Graph Co. (later the Victor Animatograph Co.), over the next few years producing and marketing several novel motion picture and slide projectors. In 1917 he designed and built the portable Victor Safety Cinema, using a variation of the French Pathé 28mm safety film, and urged the Society of Motion Picture Engineers to adopt this as a new standard for projection in schools and churches, but its success was limited. In 1923 Kodak announced the 16mm film standard, and Victor immediately designed and marketed a camera and projector, helping create the mass market for educational, industrial and religious film-users. Victor 16mm equipment remained highly successful into the sound-film era and postwar years. His final projects were a new 8mm camera and a 'Multicolor Televisor'. (SH)

References
Barnouw, *The Magician and the Cinema* (1981).
David H. Shepard, 'The Victor Animatograph Company and the Genesis of Non-theatrical Film', *Classic Film Collector*, no. 50, Spring 1976.
Samuel G. Rose, 'Alexander F. Victor: Motion Picture Pioneer', *Journal of the SMPTE*, vol. 72, August 1963.

VICTORIA, Queen of Great Britain
(1819–1901)

British monarch. Victoria ascended the throne in 1837, marrying Prince Albert of Saxe-Coburg-Gotha, the dominant influence on her life, in 1840. Following his death in 1861 the Queen became an increasingly secluded and remote figure, not held in any special regard by the British people. As her reign lengthened, however, her image changed to that of a venerable and respected figure worldwide (she became Empress of India in 1876), the figurehead of an age that began with the revolutionising effects of the railway and ended with an equally radical and transforming invention, moving pictures. Her first encounter with the latter occurred on 3 October 1896 at Balmoral, an event she recorded in her journal: 'At twelve went down to below the terrace, near the ballroom, and we were all photographed by Downey by the new cinematograph process, which makes moving pictures by winding off a reel of films. We were walking up and down, and the children jumping about.' The subjects of this film, which survives, included the Queen herself, seen in the pony cart that she often used, Tsar **Nikolas II** and the Tsarina, the Duke and Duchess of Connaught and several royal children (though not the two-year-old future Edward VIII). The photographer was the son of W. Downey of the photographic firm W. and D. Downey, which had a long association with the royal family. He used a camera employing 60mm film with four round perforations on either side constructed by T. J. Harrison of the Downey firm. The film was premiered on 23 November 1896 at Windsor Castle before the Queen in a mixed film programme for which Downey, father and son, employed both a **Robert Paul** Theatrograph and Harrison's own projector. The Queen recorded: 'After tea went to the Red drawing room, where so-called "animated pictures" were shown off, including the groups taken in September [sic] at Balmoral. It is a very wonderful process, representing people, their movements and actions, as if they were alive.'

However, Victoria's most substantial contribution to Victorian cinema was as the star of the Diamond Jubilee celebrations. The procession through London to St Paul's Cathedral on 22 June 1897 saw almost every British cinematograph firm and several from abroad represented along the route. The list included **Birt Acres, R. J. Appleton, Jules Fuerst** of Fuerst brothers (representing Lumière), **Henri Lavanchy-Clarke** (also with a Lumière Cinématographe), **Haydon and Urry, John Le Couteur** (with the 60mm Gaumont/Demenÿ camera), the Mutoscope and Biograph Syndicate, Robert Paul, **Prestwich**, Dr **J. H. Smith**, Adolphe Langfier for the Velograph Syndicate and **Alfred Wrench**, among many others. Several of these records survive of what was a major testing ground for the new industry. The films were soon on screens throughout the land, greeted everywhere with loyal enthusiasm, and the Queen herself saw some of them at a presentation held by **William Walker** at Balmoral on 25 October 1897.

The Queen was filmed on a number of subsequent occasions, including her review of the troops prior to their departure for the Boer War and a visit to Dublin in 1900, but after the Diamond Jubilee her next most notable role as a star attraction was at her funeral on 1 February 1901. Extensively covered by the film industry once again, by this time, however, a number of the pioneering firms of 1897 had already bowed out. With Queen Victoria's passing, films were now to make the stratospheric leap from 'animated photographs' to the motion picture industry that would dominate the new century. (LMcK)

References

Barnes, *The Beginnings of the Cinema in England* (vols. 1–5).

VILLIERS, Frederic (1852–1922)

War correspondent and artist. Villiers was one of the most flamboyant of those Victorian gentlemen who reported on the numerous small wars which took place in various parts of the world in the late 19th century. Amateur rather than professional when it came to the cinema, Villiers' main claim to fame in this regard is that he was the first person, as far as we know, who took a film camera to a battlefield. This occurred in the spring of 1897, during the brief war between Greece and Turkey.

Villiers claims in his autobiography to have filmed various scenes with the Greek forces during their engagement in Velestino, also noting, however, that these films were rendered unsaleable by the dramatic and action-packed fakes which **Georges Méliès** released at this time.

The following year Villiers made another attempt at filming a war, this time while following the British forces pitted against the dervishes in the Sudan, but again he was to face disappointment. Setting his camera up on one of the gunboats in the Nile, Villiers prepared to film the battle of Omdurman on the morning of 2 September, but as the gunboat opened fire, his camera was knocked over and the films exposed, leaving the artist to rely on his sketchbook as of old. For the next few campaigns he covered, Villiers abandoned the film camera, reporting on the Boer and Russo-Japanese wars as a correspondent and artist only. His next involvement with cinema was in the first Balkan War in 1912, to where he was sent by **Charles Urban** to film in the colour process, Kinemacolor, though little of the footage that he and other operators took included front-line action. Frederic Villiers, though very much the amateur and scarcely very successful, showed that the film camera had a place in warfare, and helped pave the way for a new generation of professional war cameramen. (SB)

References

Stephen Bottomore, 'Frederic Villiers – War Correspondent', *Sight and Sound*, vol. 49 no. 4, Autumn 1980.
Peter Johnson, *Front Line Artists* (London: Cassell, 1978).
Frederic Villiers, *Villiers, His Five Decades of Adventure* (London: Hutchinson, 1921).

W

WALKER, William (?– c.1937)

Showman, bookseller, film-maker. The first Scottish film-maker was an Aberdeen bookseller and stationery supplier, who as Walker and Co. owned several shops and pursued a sideline interest in lantern shows, which he gave all over Scotland, including programmes before royalty at Balmoral. In September 1896, keen to acquire a projector so that he could add moving pictures to his entertainments, but learning that the Lumière Cinématographe was unavailable, he purchased a

Wrench Cinematograph and gave his first show at 183 Union Street, Aberdeen, on 30 September 1896. Walker soon began to produce his own films, taken for him by his technical associate Paul Robello, who would remain a film-maker for many years, running the Scottish firm Robello and Mann into the 1920s. Walker and Robello took local views and advertisements for local shops by filming the shop frontage, and toured widely with shows that combined film, slides and music on such themes as Charles Dickens and Robert Burns.

In 1897 the Wrench machine was replaced by a **Paul** Theatrograph, and in that year Robello may have filmed the Diamond Jubilee procession of **Queen Victoria**. Certainly it was Walker who, on 25 October 1897, showed Jubilee films to the Queen at Balmoral, along with several of his other productions and a number of films supplied by **Maguire and Baucus**. He was to give another 'command' performance on 28 October 1898 at Balmoral.

Walker remained in the itinerant film exhibition business until 1910, when he established the Coliseum cinema in Aberdeen. He succumbed to some sort of financial crisis in the following year, however, and was forced to sell all his film, bookselling and stationery businesses, moving first to Glasgow, then to Newcastle, where he ran a cinema and was involved in film renting. He returned to Aberdeen in 1922, but played no further part in the film business. (LMcK)

References
Michael Thomson, *Silver Screen in the Silver City: A History of Cinema in Aberdeen* (Aberdeen: Aberdeen University Press, 1988).

WATKINS, Dr Robert Lincoln

New York doctor. There were a number of medical men from around the world who were quick to employ moving pictures in their studies: **Gheorge Marinescu** filmed the motions of his patients suffering from severe nervous ailments; **Eugène-Louis Doyen** filmed his surgical operations; **John Macintyre** combined X-rays with cinematography; and Watkins pioneered microcinematography. In September 1897 there are the initial reports of Watkins's first successful attempts to combine the moving picture camera with the microscope, a troublesome process as the powerful lighting required for the procedure was apt to burn up the subject before filming could take place.

Watkins was able to film minute animal life (rotifers), blood corpuscles in a frog's foot, a bird's webbed foot and the tails of fishes. Calling his combined mechanism the Micromotoscope, Watkins presented his films in loop form (as did Macintyre), giving a semblance of life to what were, of course, dead blood cells. He was clearly excited by his invention and keen to see it exploited, as he made approaches to the American Mutoscope and Biograph Company, but nothing came of this. Microcinematography was soon to make its appearance as a commercial attraction with F. Martin Duncan's *Unseen World* series made for **Charles Urban** in 1903. (LMcK)

References
Lisa Cartwright, *Screening the Body: Tracing Medicine's Visual Culture* (Minneapolis/London: University of Minnesota Press, 1995).
Hopkins, *Magic* (1898).
Robert Lincoln Watkins, *Diagnosis by Means of the Blood* (New York: The Physician Book Publishing Co., 1902).

WEBSTER, Charles H.

Projectionist, cameraman, producer. Charles Webster was an employee of the **Holland** brothers, who subsequently toured with Kinetoscopes in the company of **James White**. When the Kinetoscope business began to tail off in late 1895, White and Webster sold their machines and the latter entered Edison's employ. There he met his future business partner, Edmund Kuhn, whose wife was employed at West Orange hand-colouring **Annabelle**'s dances and similar films. With the arrival of the Vitascope and projected Edison film, Edison agents **Raff and Gammon** were keen to try out the European market and sent Webster with a Vitascope to London on 22 April. In London Webster met magician Paul Cinquevalli who had been interested in acquiring the English and French rights to the Vitascope before he saw the competition offered by Lumière. Webster reported on what he saw, that there were machines already in operation, and praising in particular the Lumière Cinématographe, then on show at the Empire ('they have no colors, prizefights or dancers, yet are received with cheers nightly'). He began touring Europe, but with only moderate success.

Webster left the Vitascope Company in late 1896 and formed the Cinographoscope Company, marketing an eponymous projector, and almost simultaneously formed the International Film Company with Edmund Kuhn. The company immediately began production of its own, as well as selling pirated Edison titles. It also marketed its Projectograph projector, a cheap and popular machine (**Edwin S. Porter** took one with him to Jamaica in 1897). Minor players in the burgeoning film production scene, the International Film Company's best-known work was the *Horitz Passion Play*, exhibited by **Klaw and Erlanger** in late 1897. A cheerful advertising film, *Dewars Scotch Whisky* (1897), is a surviving example of the company's output. Many of their films were simple actualities or copies of other companies' hits, and the company went out of business in 1898. (LMcK)

References
Musser, *The Emergence of Cinema* (1990).
Ramsaye, *A Million and One Nights* (1926).

WERNER, Alexis, Michel and Eugène

Entrepreneurs in audiovisual technology. On 22 August 1893 the brothers Michel and Eugène founded Werner Frères et Cie to sell typewriters, duplicators and similar machines. By August 1894 they were selling Edison Phonographs from their shop at 85 rue de Richelieu, Paris, and claiming to be the only French agents. They saw a Kinetoscope in September, and in October opened the first French Kinetoscope parlour at 20 boulevard Poissonnière, showing an **Annabelle** dance, *The Cockfight*, *A Bar Room Scene*, *Blacksmith's Shop* and *The Barbershop*. That same month they dissolved their original company, and Michel and the brothers' father Alexis, backed by a financier named Adrienne Charbonnel, formed a new company – Le Kinetoscope Edison, Michel et Alexis Werner – to concentrate on the new machine. Later, Michel and banker Henry Iselin formed another company to exploit the Kinetoscope throughout France. It was probably at 6–8 place de l'Opera (where the Werners had a shop) that **Antoine Lumière** saw the Kinetoscope, and set his sons the task of making a moving picture machine.

The Werners were also involved with a Kinetoscope company based in Brussels, and in June 1895 set up a fictitious company to exploit the Edison Kinetophone. There is considerable evidence that they were soon attempting to break away from the Edison product. On 18 June 1895, Eugène patented a 'kinetoscope' – basically the Edison machine but replacing the disc shutter with one of a cylindrical design. It is also possible that they obtained a camera from **Charles Chinnock** in the USA.

The Kinetoscope/Kinetophone ventures were not financially successful, and soon failed. The following year, the Werners patented a number of film devices, and produced several different camera/projectors. In 1899, the Werners left the film business and set up a factory to produce cycles and motor cars. (SH)

References
Laurent Mannoni, '1894: Les années parisiennes du Kinetoscope Edison', *Cinémathèque*, no. 3, Summer 1993.

WEST, Alfred John (1857–1937)

Naval photographer and showman. One of England's pioneers in cinematography, Alfred J. West is less well known than his contemporaries, largely because so few of his films have survived. He was a marine photographer with the Southsea firm West and Sons, which he ran with his brother George. While George concentrated on studio portraiture, Alfred built up a fine reputation for yacht photography and other marine subjects, inventing the first automatic shutter to allow him to capture moving objects without blurring. He began experimenting with cine film in 1897, using his links with the Royal Navy to film torpedo firings at Portsmouth. From these experiments grew the famous *West's Our Navy*, based for fourteen years at the Polytechnic in London, while also touring Britain and its empire. As a highly effective recruiting agent for the Royal Navy, West's film shows had official blessing, and very soon included British army subjects for the same reason.

He now had privileged access to film Britain's armed forces, but really came to prominence in 1898 when he received a royal request to film the cruise of HMS *Crescent*, commanded by HRH the Duke of York (later to become King George V). The resulting film was shown to officers and crew, and then to **Queen Victoria** on 27 August at Osborne House, Isle of Wight. Her Majesty was most impressed, and West's future in cinematography was assured. He went on to give his first public performance of cine film at Portland Hall, Southsea, in October that year, and thereafter built on his popularity with regular shows in London and elsewhere. A new company was formed to deal with this new business, Our Navy Ltd., and West subsequently left West and Sons.

Our Navy and Our Army, as West's film shows came to be known, contained a mixture of film, magic lantern slides, sound effects, musical accompaniment, narration and jingoistic songs sung with great patriotic fervour. He advertised performances in a number of ways, including the use of a large model naval ship, which was towed around the vicinity of the halls where the shows were to be performed. This model appears in one of the films which survive, where it is shown posing as a full-size ship being destroyed by naval gunfire (actually duck shot and explosives) during the Russo-Japanese War of 1905 (the real location was Portsmouth harbour).

Undoubtedly influenced by other cinematographers of the time, West also used dramatic photoplay with some of his documentary subjects, in order to grab the emotional interest of his audiences. This is well illustrated throughout his catalogue *A Synopsis of the Life-Work of Alfred West*, which includes the story of a village boy who joins the Royal Navy and undergoes various drills, voyages and escapades to become a seaman torpedoman; on returning home, he finds that his mother has died, but tears turn to joy when he later becomes engaged to his childhood sweetheart. Such touching additions added to the popularity of his shows, which required up to fifty people to stage, including a concert manager, lecturing assistants, publicity agents and projectionists. The cinematograph he used was built by James Adams, a Southsea photographer. Filming of marine subjects was achieved from on board his own steam launch, which afforded good close-up shots of all kinds of vessels.

West's extraordinary access to the navy and army makes one speculate whether military subjects claimed by topical companies of the time were actually commissioned from West. Such unusual access may be attributed mainly to his patriotic film programmes, which helped recruitment, and perhaps also because he was probably a freemason. The handful of West's surviving films are held by Wessex Film and Sound Archive. All of the original negatives were lost, it seems, when the business became too much for him and he was forced to sell his entire stock shortly before the First World War.

West, a Fellow of the Royal Geographic Society, retired to the Isle of Wight after the war, but returned to Southsea in 1928 and died there in lodgings in 1937. His obituary in the *Portsmouth Times* for 22 January 1937 was subheaded 'Godfather of the Films', in tribute to his work and the impact of *Our Navy and Our Army* on audiences throughout the British Empire. (DL)

Note: Alfred West is not to be confused with another British showman of the period, T. J. West, though the latter often encouraged this.

References

Barnes, *The Beginnings of the Cinema in England* (vol. 2).
Alfred J. West, *A Synopsis of the Life-Work of Alfred West* (Portsmouth: Wessex Press, 1912).
Alfred J. West, *Sea Salts and Celluloid* (1936, unpublished autobiography).

WHITE, C. L. ('Valley') (?-1898)

Travelling showman. C. L. 'Valley' White arrived as a teenager in Globe, Arizona, with his parents and younger sister in 1880, and worked for Charles McCoy Clark as a telegraph messenger boy. The family soon moved to San Francisco, and about fifteen years later – from July 1897 – White and a partner toured Arizona and New Mexico with a moving picture show. In some locations the Buckman Farce Comedy Company had preceded them, giving moving picture shows with an **Amet** Magniscope projector. Nevertheless, White's show went down well: 'Better than the Magniscope' was how Reid's Opera House, Tucson, billed it. Their programme of more than thirty films included *The Burning Stable*, *Shooting the Chutes* and *Spanish Bullfight*. Their itinerary took in Silver City, New Mexico and Tombstone, Arizona. Close to Christmas 1897, White and his partner (who had gambled away his share of the business) came to Jerome with the show. There White met and teamed up with his old boss C. M. Clark and they set off on a tour which took in Ash Fork; Kingman; Needles, California; Williams; and Holbrook, showing for a week in most towns. From Holbrook they hired a team of four horses and a wagon and set off for Fort Apache with a foot of snow on the ground, stopping to give a show at a ranch-house in Snowflake. Their Edison Projectoscope was fitted with a 'spoolbank', enabling continuous projection of a film (until the audience was 'fed up on it'). According to a later account by Clark, the films were presented from 7.30p.m. until midnight that night, with only an occasional change of pictures. Having only three rounds of the **Corbett**–Courtney fight, Clark and White showed rounds one and four, then reversed the films and showed them again, before showing the fifth round knockout. The motion pictures were followed by a country

150

dance until dawn, when chicken and biscuits were served for breakfast. At Fort Apache, they gave a show for the American Indians, who Clark said took fright when a New York fire department engine came at the camera.

The partners returned to Holbrook on 5 February 1898, and made arrangements to show in Gallup, New Mexico. White started for Gallup on Monday to advertise their arrival, but never made it out of town. He fell off the train as it was leaving the station, suffering head and horrible leg injuries. The doctor informed him of the worst, and he said goodbye to his partner and left messages for his family. He was given chloroform and never regained consciousness after having his legs amputated. C. L. 'Valley' White was buried in Holbrook cemetery, where his grave marker is today. (SH)

References
George C. Hall, 'The First Moving Picture in Arizona - or Was It? The Tragic Tale of C. L. White's Marvelous Projectoscope Show in Arizona and New Mexico Territories, 1897–1898', *Film History*, vol. 3 no. 1, 1989.

WHITE, James H.

Business manager, cameraman. In August 1894 James White, previously a Phonograph salesman, was taken on by the **Holland** brothers to work at their Boston Kinetoscope parlour, later visiting several American cities with the Kinetoscope in the company of **Charles Webster**. As the Kinetoscope business began to wane White returned to Phonographs, but when Webster was sent by **Raff and Gammon** to Europe with the Vitascope, White filled his post at Edison and rapidly came to play an important part in the Vitascope enterprise. In effect producer for Edison Vitascope titles made under Raff and Gammon's auspices, White was responsible for such noted titles of 1896 as the **May Irwin Kiss**, **J. Stuart Blackton**'s film debut in *Edison Drawn by World Artist* and films of **Li Hung Chang**'s arrival in New York, as well as undertaking some projection duties.

When the business relationship between Edison and Raff and Gammon began to crumble in late 1896, White returned to Edison and was put in charge of the Kinetograph department, overseeing a busy production schedule with cameraman **William Heise**. In mid-1897 White embarked on an extensive filming trip abroad with English cameraman Frederick Blechynden. First journeying across the USA (taking advantage of the railroad companies' desire for publicity to film many 'phantom rides' with all expenses paid), the pair travelled to Japan and China in early 1898, returning via Hawaii in May, by which time White had fallen gravely ill. On his recovery White resumed his post (having unfortunately been absent during the flaring up of the Spanish-American War), enthusiastically involving himself in every stage of production, even on occasion acting, though he always had a greater interest in actuality (for example the scenes he took of the Paris Exposition in the summer of 1900). In November 1900 he hired **Edwin S. Porter**, who soon took responsibility for fiction films while White concentrated on actuality and news films. He was thus in charge when the Edison camera team, out in force to film **William McKinley**'s arrival at the Pan-American Exposition on 5 September 1901, recorded the unfolding events surrounding the President's assassination.

In February 1903 White left to become manager of Edison's European business, supervising both film and phonograph interests, with his headquarters in London. In 1904 he became managing director of the National Phonograph Company, official Edison phonograph agents in Britain, and thereafter devoted most of his energies to the tumultuous phonograph business. In 1906 he retired, 'for personal reasons', only to emerge shortly afterwards as managing director of the General Phonograph Company. A zestful and enthusiastic character who thoroughly enjoyed every aspect of film production, he inspired much that was creative about early Edison films and left a gap in 1903 that was not to be filled. (LMcK)

References
Frank Andrews, *Edison Phonograph: The British Connection* (Rugby: City of London Phonograph and Gramophone Society, 1986).
'Chats with Trade Leaders: no. 2 – Mr James H. White', *The Optical Lantern and Cinematograph Journal*, December 1904, pp. 37–39.
Musser, *The Emergence of Cinema* (1990).

WHITEHOUSE, Alfred Henry

Showman and the first New Zealand filmmaker. Whitehouse was a travelling showman from Auckland who introduced film to New Zealand in the form of the Edison Kinetoscope in Auckland on 29 November 1895. He added the primitive version of the Kinetoscope with sound, the Kinetophone, to his repertoire in January 1896. Having acquired his own camera by 1898, Whitehouse began to shoot local topicals, such as *Uhlan Winning the Auckland Cup*. He was not an ambitious producer, but he took a group of his films to the Paris Exposition in 1900, returning to take up film exhibition for a while, but himself filming no more. (LMcK)

References

Jonathan Dennis and Jan Bieringa (ed.), *Film in Aotearoa, New Zealand* (Wellington: Victoria University Press, 1992).

WILHELM II, Kaiser, Emperor of Germany (1859–1941)

Emperor of Germany and the first European monarch to appear on film. As the embodiment of Teutonic martial values, Wilhelm was frequently filmed in a military setting. **Birt Acres**' *The German Emperor Reviewing His Troops*, taken at Kiel in 1895, was followed by many similar films showing Wilhelm with his army and navy. That he recognised the propaganda value of the cinema is demonstrated by a contemporary account of *The Kaiser's Manoeuvres* (1910): 'the Kaiser's interest in Kinematography is well known, and when facing the camera he gives a salute, doubtless intended for the audience who will see the picture'.

As with a number of other monarchs, Wilhelm acquired his own personal cinematographer, and prior to that **Ottomar Anschütz** had been appointed photographer to the Kaiser's family and had accompanied him on his trip to Palestine in 1899. The growing might of the German fleet was illustrated by a series of Biograph films taken with Wilhelm's permission at Kiel in 1900, the most powerful image being the celebrated *Battleship Odin With All Her Guns in Action*. (BA)

References

Hauke Lange-Fuchs, *Birt Acres: Der erste Schleswig-Holsteinische Film Pionier* (Kiel: Walter G. Muhlau, 1987).

WILLIAMS, Randall (1846–1898)

'King of Showmen', and generally accepted as the first to present a cinema exhibition at a British fairground. The venue was the King's Lynn Valentine's Day fair, where he opened his show on 15 February 1897.

Born in Liverpool, the son of a hawker, Randall Williams ran away from home at an early age to travel the fairs with his own conjuring show. Subsequently, in the 60s and early 70s, he was among a number of famous booth operators who sought to adapt the popular Pepper's Ghost illusion (a stage trick using live actors and giant mirrors) for fairground exhibition. His earliest rivals included George Walls, George Biddall, Alfred Walbrook, 'Colonel' William Clarke and George Mackey – all of whom followed Williams into the Bioscope business. From 1873, Williams was a regular exhibitor at the 'World's Fair', which took place at the Agricultural Hall, Islington, London, for a six-week season, commencing on Christmas Eve. For the 1896–7 season, Williams took the bold step of turning over his familiar 'Grand Phantascopical Exhibition' entirely to the presentation of moving pictures.

The supplier of Randall Williams's first projector is not recorded, but about this time he developed a strong association with the firm of **Haydon and Urry** of Upper Street, Islington. Frank Haydon, George Urry and their partner George Summerville were primarily makers and suppliers of coin-operated slot machines to pubs, penny-arcade owners, shop-showmen and fairground travellers. Possibly influenced by their neighbouring competitor, George Barron of the Interchangeable Syndicate Co., Upper Street, who had been advertising 'Edison' projectors for sale since September 1896, they set about developing their own patent device. Their first machine, the New Cinematograph, was offered for sale to the general public in late February 1897. In April it was superseded by the Eragraph, taking its name from the national showbusiness paper, the *Era*. Randall Williams both used and championed this machine up to the time of his death.

To ensure a supply of film for the Eragraph, Haydon and Urry established their own film production unit based in an adjacent photographer's shop in Church Street, which also functioned as a showroom and public cinema. To assist in the film-making process they employed two brothers, photographers Richard and James Monte. Home-produced subjects offered for sale by the company during the summer of 1897 included *The King on his Yacht at Cowes*, the 1897 Derby and footage of **Queen Victoria**'s Jubilee procession. Haydon and Urry's machine was strong and reliable, and they were soon to equip a large number of travelling showmen. Through his links as the firm's main film supplier and demonstrator, Richard Monte soon began to develop a fascination not only for the lifestyle of Randall Williams but also for Randall's seventeen-year-old daughter, Carrie, whom he married while she was still a minor.

On 14 November 1898, Randall Williams's career as a cinema pioneer was cut tragically short when he contracted typhoid fever in Grimsby and died. Very soon after this, Richard Monte – one of the trustees of Randall's estate – assumed ownership of Randall's show and also, more significantly, changed his name to Randall Williams. This has led to a great deal of confusion among cinema historians, further compounded by the fact that Monte also offered varying accounts of his own achievements during his lifetime, consistently, some would say pathologically, failing even to mention the existence of the real Randall Williams. Richard Monte died in the 1950s, after running a cinema for some years at Canvey Island. (MH)

References

The Era (1896–8).
Stephen Warfolk, *The Cinemas of Lynn* (1992).
Barnes, *The Beginnings of the Cinema in England* (vol. 2).

WILLIAMSON, James (1855–1933)

Producer, director, showman, inventor, manufacturer. Born Pathhead, near Kirkaldy, Fifeshire, Scotland, on 8 November 1855, Williamson was raised in Edinburgh until 1868, then in London where he became apprenticed to a chemist. From 1877 he lived in Eastry (Kent), where he married and practised pharmacy till 1886, relocating then to Brighton's twin town of Hove. Here he resumed the chemist's trade and sold photographer's supplies. He took up lantern photography as a hobby and, as an avocation, showmanship at local functions. His first exposure to cinematography was through a circle of friends and neighbours which included photographer and inventor **William Friese Greene**, pioneering cinematographers

G. A. Smith and **Esmé Collings**, and machinist and engineer **Alfred Darling**. These associations would prove decisive for him. His first experiments in cinematography date from 1894; his first viable films from 1897. But it was only in 1898 that he went seriously into the film business, with a camera he invented with Darling's help. In October 1898 he issued a brief catalogue of films, followed a year later by a longer catalogue, in which he encouraged other exhibitors to show films in groups with a unifying theme, a fairly novel idea at the time for film exhibitors, though not for lanternists.

His views on the proper use of the new medium were emphatic, personal and prophetic. He was one of the chief pioneers of the film narrative, beginning with faked news items, such as *Attack on a China Mission* (January 1901), in which he cut from one shot to another for dramatic effect introducing a primitive form of the race against time. In *Stop Thief!* (1901) he introduced the movie chase of more than one shot (this one, a comic sequence, had three); and *Fire!* (1901), in which a family is saved by an efficient crew of firemen, is the earliest film in which narrative action is moved along by a logical sequence of cutting from shot to shot. He recruited his actors from his family and friends, and acted in many of his own films.

In 1902 and 1903 he laid the foundations for movie realism with a trio of brief narratives about the hardships war creates for the dependants of soldiers: *The Soldier's Return* (1902), *A Reservist Before and After the War* (1902) and *Wait till Jack Comes Home* (1903), stories of Dickensian pathos and social awareness. With *The Deserter* (1903) he moved in the direction of melodrama with a tale about a soldier forced to desert his unit in order to be at his father's deathbed.

His output as a film-maker was never large by the standards of his time. Usually involved in several activities at once, he devoted much of his energies to an exhibition service which gave shows in institutions and private houses throughout Sussex. No doubt because of this, he was one of the earliest film-makers to give serious attention to the problems of exhibiting movies, first as a lecturer in the magic lantern mode and then in 1902 with a highly successful experiment in intertitling, *A Reservist Before and After the War*, which however seems to have met with opposition from conservative exhibitors and was never repeated. In December 1908, he invented and promoted a device with which exhibitors could make their own intertitles, and in 1910, the year in which he began to concentrate on the manufacture of film equipment, he patented a projector which could intersperse slide titles into the films it showed.

Williamson continued to make films until 1908, when he transferred his production duties first to Jack Chart and then to Dave Aylott, but in September 1909 he shut down commercial film production altogether and, shortly after that, his exhibition service. Always attracted to documentary, he now announced a series of informational films on scientific and nature subjects, an undertaking which failed in the early months of 1910. After this his activities were centred in and around London. In 1913 he revived production of a newsreel service, which, however, failed in the early months of the First World War. Already in operation by this date were a film processing plant at Barnet and a film equipment works at Willesden, where the famous Williamson camera was made, along with multi-lens turrets, printers, rewinders, developing apparatus and footage gauges which were widely used in the British film industry, and a variety of speciality cameras, notably a pioneering photogrammetry camera for scientific and military use, a photo-finish camera for horse-racing and a gun camera which photographed the air battles of two world wars. Twenty-five years after directing his last film, Williamson died of a heart attack at his home in Richmond on 18 August 1933. (MS)

References
Talbot, *Moving Pictures* (1912).
Low and Manvell, *The History of the British Film 1896–1906* (1948).
Sadoul, *Les Pionniers du cinéma 1897–1909* (1947).
Holman, *Cinema 1900–1906* (1982).

WILLS, Frederick Charles

Photographer for the Queensland Department of Agriculture, Australia. Assisted by Henry Mobsby (1861–1933), Wills shot what were the first ever governmental films as accompaniments to lectures promoting immigration to Queensland delivered by British touring lecturer George Randall. Having joined the Department of Agriculture as official artist and photographer in 1897, Wills enthusiastically put forward new ideas and suggested the use of the Lumière Cinématographe in October 1898. The scheme was given a year's approval, and Wills shot his first films of local Sydney scenes in early 1899. With Mobsby, Wills produced some thirty films in 1899, many illustrating agricultural processes with the intention of

attracting British farmers to the colony. However, Randall did not welcome the arrival of the films in Britain, feeling that they would appeal to the wrong sort of person, and the scheme was abandoned. Wills left the department in 1903, but Mobsby continued to produce occasional government films until his retirement in about 1930. Given only one private screening at the time, Wills's films still survive. (CL/LMcK)

References
Chris Long and Pat Laughren, 'Surprising Survivals from Colonial Queensland', *Cinema Papers 96*, December 1993.

WOLFF, Philipp

Supplier. Entering the film business late in 1896, the firm of Philipp Wolff soon became one of the largest suppliers of films in Europe, with offices in Berlin, Paris and London. Since its commencement, the business in England had been under the management of a man named Hessberg, who was known to a great number in the trade as 'Mr Wolff'. He specialised in foreign films, particularly French, but he also sold English subjects, and among the producers whose work he handled were **Robert Paul**, **G. A. Smith**, **John Benett-Stanford**, **Georges Méliès** and Lumière. Many of the most notable films of the day appeared in his lists and he had few, if any, rivals, in the choice of titles on offer.

As well as films, he also supplied projectors, cameras and accessories. The particular projector associated with the firm was called the Wolff Vitaphotoscope, which first appeared on the market under this name in 1897. It employed a Maltese cross movement and may well have been of French design. A developing and printing service was also provided, and the firm undertook the manufacture of special film to customers' orders. Philipp Wolff occupied premises at 9–10 Southampton Street, but after the death of Mr Hessberg in Barcelona in May 1899 from pulmonary tuberculosis, the firm seems to have undergone some reorganisation, and in December of that year removed to new premises at 46 the Strand. Though it did not survive long after the turn of the century, during its brief existence the firm of Philipp Wolff had become one of the most important dealers in the industry. (JB)

References
Barnes, *The Beginnings of the Cinema in England* (vols. 1–5).

WOOD, Robert Williams (1868–1955)

Experimenter in physical optics and an unsung pioneer of film animation. Born in Massachusetts, Wood studied at Harvard and Berlin before teaching at the University of Wisconsin from 1897 to 1901. He spent the remainder of a distinguished career as professor of experimental physics at John Hopkins University, also working on the Manhattan Project in 1940. It was while at Wisconsin that Wood's name became temporarily linked to the history of cinema. At the time, he was studying the propagation of sound waves and their reflections from surfaces, and he wanted some way to demonstrate the results. 'It occurred to me', he told the Royal Society in February 1900, 'that a very vivid idea of how these curious wave-fronts are derived from one another could be obtained if a complete series could be prepared on the film of a cinematograph, and projected in motion on a screen.'

Wood had previously taken still photographs of wave-fronts using spark illumination, but, finding it impossible to control the precise timing of the sparks, he was forced to abandon direct cinematography of the waves. Instead, a series of about 100 drawings were made, based on the stills, showing the various stages of a wave's progress, and these were then photographed separately on a film, 'by means of the animatograph, which Mr Paul has most kindly placed at our disposal'. (It is unclear to what extent **Robert Paul** was personally involved in this project.) The results could then be projected, so that 'we can actually see the wave going through its gymnastics'. In this way Wood was using a kind of cartoon animation, and, as the work must have been done some time in 1899 this makes him one of the earliest animators in film history. His method, which involved using a pin frame to line up three or four sheets of paper on which successive drawings were made, has something in common with later cel animation techniques. Wood's colleagues in this work were Max Mason (1877–1961), later physics professor at Wisconsin, and Professor Albert Brown Porter (1864–1909) of the University of Chicago. Porter seems to have been responsible for at least one of the three series of drawings which were made.

As well as being an ingenious experimenter, Wood was also a talented artist, musician and writer, who published a volume of illustrated nonsense verse in 1907, and perhaps it was this fusion of artistic and scientific talents which gave rise to his pioneering work in film. (SB)

References
Nature, 9 August 1900.
Philosophical Magazine, July 1900.
W. Seabrook, *Doctor Wood: Modern Wizard of the Laboratory* (1946).

WRAY, Cecil

Electrical engineer. Cecil Wray, of 2 Southbrook Terrace, Bradford, showed an interest in cinematography very early on, patenting on 3 January 1895 a lantern/prism device for projecting Kinetoscope peepshow pictures onto a screen. He later invented the more practical Kineoptoscope projection device – commercialised in 1896 by **Riley** brothers, also of Bradford, who acquired the patent rights – which was a mechanism designed to fit into the slide-stage of a standard optical lantern.

On 9 March 1896 Wray lectured to the Bradford Photographic Society on 'Phonographs, Kinetoscopes, and the Kinetograph', outlining advances in cinematography, and promoting the use of the Edison-Bell Phonograph in lieu of a shorthand secretary. Wray showed films in Bradford, using the Cinetograph (almost certainly his recently invented Kineoptoscope), on 11 June 1896. With Cecil William Baxter he set up premises at Borough Mills, Manchester Road, where they designed and manufactured a cine camera/projector of robust construction – known simply as the 'B & W cinematograph' – claimed to be the first to be used in Japan. Baxter and Wray patented a second apparatus on 6 May 1897, in association with Bradford clockmaker Joseph Oulton: the 'Perfection' cinematograph; markedly different from the previous machine, it shared similarities with the 'Riley' Kineoptoscope. An 1899 advertisement claimed, 'Never gets out of order ... will take Films of any length, from 50 feet to ½ a mile. ... Any of our Machines will photograph as easily as project.' They also offered films for sale, including those of **Georges Méliès**, but their partnership was short-lived, and by 1899 Cecil Wray was trading on his own from the same address, his advertisements proclaiming, 'In this Business we have led, others have followed'. (SH)

References
Barnes, *The Beginnings of the Cinema in England* (vols. 1–4).

WRENCH, Alfred

Optician, cinematograph manufacturer. The firm of Messrs John Wrench and Son, wholesale opticians of 50 Gray's Inn Road, London, was established in 1816 and was already well known as a manufacturer of optical lanterns and accessories when cinematography was invented. They entered the field in August 1896, when Alfred Wrench patented a cinematograph projector with novel sprocket intermittent, based on a ratchet and pawl. Appearing on the market very soon afterwards, and at £36 much cheaper than the few other machines available, it proved an immediate success, being perhaps the only serious British rival to **Robert Paul**'s Theatrograph. It was compact, quiet and gave a steady picture, and *Optician* considered it 'in every way the best such mechanism'.

In 1897 Alfred Wrench himself filmed **Queen Victoria**'s Diamond Jubilee procession, issued as seven films (total 800ft) with a camera/projector/printer of similar construction to the Lumière Cinématographe but incorporating improvements, including a movement with two triple-pin pulldown arms. The machine was designed with, and manufactured for, Alfred Wrench by **Alfred Darling**, and was marketed the following year. Late in 1897 Wrench also introduced a 'Cheap Form Cinematograph' at 9 guineas, based on the 'dog' or beater movement. The firm also set up a film developing and printing department in the basement of its premises that was used by **Cecil Hepworth**, among others. Alfred Wrench continued his association with

Darling, and together they devised the Biokam amateur apparatus for filming and projecting using 17.5mm centre-perforated film, and marketed with some success by the Warwick Trading Company in 1899.

The manufacturing business flourished until well into the next century, producing conventional Maltese cross projectors (they were perhaps the first to suggest the enclosure of the cross in an oil bath to reduce wear), while extending the film production side with the creation of the Wrench Film Company, a major British firm of the 1900–10 period, now largely forgotten because no films have survived. 50 Gray's Inn Road itself became a noteworthy focus for early British filmmaking, not only for the Wrench film services and equipment, but because it was the home of Will Barker's Autoscope Company (founded in 1900), briefly housed Walker and **Turner**, then the Wrench Film Company and finally in 1911 the Topical Film Company, founded by Herbert Wrench and William Jeapes, which produced the *Topical Budget* newsreel. The Edison Phonograph company was next door at no. 52. The Wrench firm was absorbed in about 1925 by Cinema Traders Ltd., Scientific and Illuminating Engineers. (SH/LMcK)

References

Barnes, *The Beginnings of the Cinema in England* (vols. 1–4).
Colin Bennett, *The Guide to Cinematography* (London: E. T. Heron & Co., 1917).
R. B. Foster, *Hopwood's Living Pictures* (London: Hatton Press, 1915).
Luke McKernan, *Topical Budget: The Great British News Film* (London: BFI, 1992).

Y

YOKOTA Einosuke (c.1870–?)

Showman, producer. When **Inahata Shotaro**, the Japanese businessman who introduced cinema to Japan with the Lumière Cinématographe on 15 February 1897, grew disenchanted with the work, he turned to Yokota Einosuke, the owner of a Kobe export-import business. The very opposite of the meticulous and restrained Inahata, Yokota was a flamboyant showman: in Peter B. High's phrase, 'part swashbuckler and part autocrat'. Having gained business experience in the USA, where he had done everything from washing dishes to selling door-to-door, Yokota returned to Japan with an X-ray machine with which he

toured the country, putting on shows in a hut he called 'The Hall of Mysteries'. On acquiring his Cinématographe from Inahata, Yokota journeyed to Tokyo, where **Arai Saburo** was already exhibiting the Edison Vitascope. The two became great rivals during 1897, Yokota opening two days after Arai on 8 March 1897 at the Kawakami theatre. Yokota made sure to stress the European credentials of his machine, as opposed to his American rival, and would come on stage sporting a black bow-tie and silver-topped cane.

Unlike Arai, who saw film as an upper-class novelty, Yokota chose to take films to the people, touring provincial Japan with a large tent he called 'Cinématographe Hall'. This laid the foundations of what was to be one of the major careers in early Japanese film. Expanding widely into film exhibition, by 1915 he was controlling 177 out of Japan's 339 cinemas. In 1907 he moved into production, approaching Makino Shozo to make films for him, initially haphazardly, but by 1910 with considerable success following the discovery of actor Onoue Matsunosuke and the establishment of the *ninja* tradition of action film. His firm was one of the four Japanese majors (the others were **Kawaura Ken'ichi**'s Yoshizawa Company, the Fukuhodo theatre chain and the cheekily named M. Pathé, which had no connection with the French firm) which formed a self-protecting trust in 1909, becoming the Nikkatsu company (abbreviated from Nippon Katsudo Shashin) in 1912. Yokota became the director and eventually the president of the trust for many years, until he was forced to resign in 1933. (LMcK)

References

Joseph L. Anderson and Donald Richie, *The Japanese Film: Art and Industry* (Princeton NJ: Princeton University Press, 1982, expanded ed.).
Peter B. High, 'The Dawn of Cinema in Japan', *Journal of Contemporary History*, vol. 19 no. 1, January 1984.

CONTRIBUTORS

BA Barry Anthony is an authority on Victorian stage entertainment and is co-author with Richard Brown of *The History of the British Mutoscope and Biograph Company.*

JB John Barnes is the author of the standard work on British Victorian cinema, the five-volume *The Beginnings of the Cinema in England 1894–1901.*

DB Dave Berry is the author of *Wales and Cinema: The First Hundred Years.*

HB Henri Bousquet is producing a multi-volume catalogue of early Pathé production.

SB Stephen Bottomore is a film-maker and writer, researching into many aspects of early cinema.

RB Richard Brown is a freelance historian and co-author with Barry Anthony of *The History of the British Mutoscope and Biograph Company.*

PC Peter Carpenter is a film-maker with a particular interest in William Friese Greene and his associates.

IC Ian Christie is an authority on Russian and Soviet cinema, and wrote and co-produced the BBC television series on early cinema, *The Last Machine.*

BC Brian Coe is a former curator of the Kodak Museum, now lecturing at the Museum of the Moving Image, London, and is the author of *The History of Movie Photography.*

RC Roland Cosandey teaches in Lausanne, Switzerland. He has published works on the Swiss cinema, animation and various aspects of early film.

DG Denis Gifford is the author of the *British Film Catalogue* (fiction and non-fiction volumes) and numerous works on film, radio and comics.

FG Frank Gray is curator of the South-east Film and Video Archive, England, and a senior lecturer in media studies and art history at the University of Brighton.

MH Mervyn Heard is an authority on magic lanterns, fairground bioscopes and other forms of Victorian entertainment.

SH Stephen Herbert is head of technical services at the National Film Theatre and Museum of the Moving Image, London.

NH Nicholas Hiley is head of information at the British Universities Film and Video Council, and has researched widely into the British media at the turn of the century.

DL David Lee is archivist at the Wessex Film and Sound Archive, Winchester, England.

CL Chris Long has written a series of articles entitled *Australia's First Films: Facts and Fables* for the journal, *Cinema Papers.*

LM Laurent Mannoni is the author of *Le grand art de la lumière et de l'ombre.* He is responsible for historical apparatus at the Cinémathèque Française.

LMcK Luke McKernan is a cataloguer at the National Film and Television Archive, London.

DR Deac Rossell is a former head of programming at the National Film Theatre and the author of 'The New Thing with the Long Name and the Old Thing with the Name That Isn't Much Shorter', *Film History* (Summer 1995), a major chronology of the cinema to the end of 1896.

DRB David Robinson is the author of works on Charlie Chaplin, Georges Méliès and a history of the cinema, and compiled *The Chronicle of the Cinema: 1895–1995* for *Sight and Sound* magazine.

MS Martin Sopocy is completing a book-length study of James Williamson.

RY Rashit Yangorov is a film scholar working on the history of early Russian and Soviet cinema.

SELECT BIBLIOGRAPHY

This bibliography lists some of the many works on Victorian cinema, with a short account of their content and current standing as works of reference in the constantly changing field of research into this period. Works on individual film-makers or companies are not included, except where the work also gives a broad picture of the period. The emphasis is on those works that have been of greatest use to the editors, and which give a good overview of their subject. One or two were not yet published at the time of writing, but were seen in draft form. Some key works that are unavailable in Britain are listed for their known importance. Much of the key work in Victorian cinema, however, is to be found in journals, such as *1895*, *Griffithiana*, *Film History* and *KINtop*.

Abel, Richard, *The Ciné Goes to Town: French Cinema 1896–1914* (Berkeley and Los Angeles: University of California Press, 1994).
Dry but impressively detailed account of the rise of French cinema, with an emphasis on business strategies, genres, filmic style (including analyses of individual films) and the key contributions of Gaumont, Lumière, Méliès and Pathé.

Barnes, John, *The Beginnings of the Cinema in England*, vol. 1 (Newton Abbot: David & Charles, 1976).
The story of how the Edison Kinetoscope and Lumière Cinématographe came to Britain, the first English films made by Birt Acres and Robert Paul, and Britain's first film shows to the end of 1896. Detailed descriptions of the equipment used and the films produced. Further volumes in the series are as follows: (vol. 2) *The Rise of the Cinema in Great Britain* (London: Bishopsgate, 1983), continues the story, covering 1897, the year of Queen Victoria's Diamond Jubilee; (vol. 3) *Pioneers of the British Film* (London: Bishopsgate, 1988), examines the producers, exhibitors, films and equipment of 1898; (vol. 4) *Filming the Boer War* (London: Bishopsgate, 1992), takes us through 1899, with the onset of the war being just one of the events covered. Together, these volumes (and one so far unpublished) form a five-volume set, *The Beginnings of the Cinema in England 1894–1901*. An essential reference for anyone interested in the origins of film in Britain and the personalities involved, and due to be republished in a new edition with a new publisher.

Barnouw, Erik, *The Magician and the Cinema* (New York and Oxford: Oxford University Press, 1981).
An engaging account of an under-researched area, namely the enthusiasm with which so many magicians embraced the arrival of film. Includes useful biographical accounts of Georges Méliès, Albert Smith, Billy Bitzer, David Devant and others, but does not do full justice to a large subject.

Bernardini, Aldo, *Cinema muto italiano*. Vol. 1: *Ambiente, spettacoli e spettatori, 1896–1904* (Rome: Editori Laterza, 1980).
A finely researched, beautifully illustrated and thorough treatment of the history of film exhibition and production in Italy up to 1904, this is the standard history of the period for Italy, and is the first volume of three which cover the period to 1914.

Brown, Richard and Barry Anthony, *The History of the British Mutoscope and Biograph Company: A Victorian Film Enterprise* (Trowbridge: Flicks Books, 1996).
Innovatory and detailed account of the economics underpinning the Victorian cinema industry, using the example of the British Mutoscope and Biograph Company. A considerable corrective to much prior writing on British films of this period, and writing on the early film industry in general, it stresses the economic imperatives that always drove the Victorian film-makers. With illustrations and a detailed filmography, itself a painstaking work of ingenious reconstruction from many sources.

Brunetta, Gian Piero, *Storia del cinema italiano: il cinema muto 1895–1929* (Rome: Riuniti, 1993).
Comprehensive and very sound history of film-making in Italy in the silent era, with clear accounts of the still little-known activities of the earliest Italian film-makers.

Ceram, C. W., *Archaeology of the Cinema* (London: Thames and Hudson, 1965).
Widely available in several languages, this book by German archaeologist Kurt Moreck (published pseudonymously) was a very useful addition to the literature of pre-cinema and early film at a time when little was in print. Covering magic lanterns, optical toys and chronophotography as well as the first films. An accessible, if factually inaccurate account, with many useful notes and references. The use of the illustrations (a wealth of material, mostly from the Barnes Collection, collected by Olive Cook, author of *Movement in Two Dimensions*, an important work on pre-cinema) is limited somewhat by the lack of page numbers in the illustrated sections.

Chanan, Michael, *The Dream that Kicks: The Prehistory and Early Years of Cinema in Britain* (London: Routledge & Kegan Paul, 1980).
Chanan's orientation to Marxist economics does not detract from this illuminating and sometimes provocative presentation of the invention of the cinema in Britain in a fully elaborated context of music hall, popular and middle-class culture. One of the few sources to discuss the origins of celluloid, the politics of the patent system and the business practices of early cinema.

Chiti, Roberto, José Pantieri and Paolo Popeschich, *Almanacco del cinema muto italiano* (Forlì: Centro Studi Cinetelevisivi, 1988).
Useful basic guide to silent Italian cinema, with a short biographical dictionary (every entry illustrated), basic histories of individual companies and essays on individual themes.

Christie, Ian, *The Last Machine: Early Cinema and the Birth of the Modern World* (London: BBC/BFI, 1995).
Published to accompany the BBC television series, *The Last Machine*, this follows the same pattern in offering an imaginative entry into the world of early cinema through such broad themes as Time, The City and The Body. Places the phenomenon of cinema in the world of Victorian and Edwardian ideas, and in the short space available is meant more to intrigue than to offer complete answers.

Coe, Brian, *The History of Movie Photography* (London: Ash & Grant, 1981).
The clearest and most reliable work on its subject. The author, then curator of the Kodak Museum, outlines in three chapters the beginnings of the cinema with accuracy, clarity and economy; the best popular introduction to the technology of early film.

Coe, Brian, *Muybridge and the Chronophotographers* (London: MOMI/BFI, 1992).
Prepared to accompany an exhibition at the Museum of the Moving Image, London. Author Brian Coe, familiar with the subject for forty years, packs a great deal of informative text and a wide range of illustrations into sixty pages.

Coissac, G.-Michel, *Histoire du Cinématographe de ses origines à nos jours* (Paris: Cinéopse/ Gauthier-Villars, 1925).
Though now being superseded by recent research, this detailed account of the birth and development of the industry (mainly in France) through its first thirty years retains an authority from having been written when many of the pioneers were still alive. Technical but accessible, with much on Marey, Demenÿ and in particular the Lumières.

De los Reyes, Aurelio, *Los origenes del cine en México (1896–1900)* (Mexico City: Fondo de Cultura Economica/Cultura Sept, 1983).
A detailed and accurately researched account of the Victorian cinema in Mexico, with an integrated view of the cinema's appearance in the culture of the period.

Deslandes, Jacques, *Histoire comparée du cinéma*. Vol. 1: *De la cinématique au cinématographe (1826–1896)* (Tournai: Casterman, 1966); and Deslandes, Jacques and Jacques Richard, *Histoire comparée du cinéma*. Vol. 2: *Du cinématographe au cinéma (1896–1906)* (Tournai: Casterman, 1968).
Thorough and richly detailed work covering in two volumes the emergence of moving pictures in the 19th century, with an emphasis in the second volume on the various national scenes.

Deutelbaum, Marshall A. (ed.), *'Image' on the Art and Evolution of the Film* (New York: Dover, 1979).
A useful collection of articles on silent film, sumptuously illustrated, from the magazine of the International Museum of Photography, Rochester, New York. Includes reminiscences

of Lumière operator Francis Doublier, the first films in Rochester, the Lathams' early Eidoloscope shows and one of the few published articles on Mutoscope reels.

Enciclopedia dello spettacolo (Rome: Le Maschere, 1954).
Massive eleven-volume encyclopaedia of the performing arts, with an impressive worldwide scope, fine illustrations and thorough coverage of film (under the general editorship of Francesco Savio), including both early filmmakers and many of the theatre and variety stars who featured in the first years of cinema.

Fell, John L. (ed.), *Film Before Griffith* (Berkeley and Los Angeles: University of California Press, 1983).
A very useful selection of essays on international aspects of early cinema gathered from such writers as Charles Musser, Gordon Hendricks, Eileen Bowser, Barry Salt and Raymond Fielding.

Ferreira, Antonio, *A fotografa animada em Portugal 1894–1895–1896–1897* (Lisbon: Cinemateca Portuguesa, 1986).
An exemplary work of research into the first film-makers and film shows in Portugal, showing what a rich history lies in the less frequented areas of early cinema research.

Fielding, Raymond (ed.), *A Technological History of Motion Pictures and Television* (Berkeley and Los Angeles: University of California Press, 1967).
A collection of historical papers from the *Journal of the Society of Motion Picture* (and *Television*) *Engineers*, including technical reminiscences by Dickson, Lumière, Armat, Jenkins and Paul; and articles on Le Prince, Messter and others. Illustrated with many photographs of early projector mechanisms.

Foiret, Jacques and Philippe Brochard, *Les Frères Lumière et le cinéma* (Paris: Musée National des Techniques/Nathan, 1992).
A rare example of a publication for children about the origins of cinema, this pocketbook is a delightful and accurate account covering the 'whole story' of pre-cinema, including how films were invented and details of the first shows in France. With charming watercolour illustrations by Loïc Derrien.

Forch, Carl, *Der Kinematograph und das sich bewegende Bild* (Vienna and Leipzig: A. Hartleben's Verlag, 1913).

This is the German equivalent of Hopwood's *Living Pictures*, a massively complete history of the technical development of cinema apparatus, worldwide, written by a knowledgeable engineer and division head of the German patent office. If anything, it is more thorough and detailed than Hopwood, and has yet to be surpassed as a source for European technical developments from the beginnings to 1912.

Gosser, H. Mark, *Selected Attempts at Stereoscopic Moving Pictures and their Relationship to the Development of Motion Picture Technology, 1852–1903* (New York: Arno, 1977).
This thesis examines the proliferation of suggested methods for reproducing life, not only in motion but in three dimensions, during the second half of the 19th century. A bonus is its clear account of the development of the first successful film systems.

Hecht, Hermann (ed. by Ann Hecht), *Pre-Cinema History: An Encyclopaedia and Annotated Bibliography of the Moving Image Before 1896* (London: Bowker–Saur/BFI, 1993).
A monumental collection of references relating to projection, moving images, panoramas and dioramas, etc. Patents are described, books abstracted and newspaper and journal extracts given. Many of the entries amount to short papers on their subjects. Despite its title, the work includes many references to the end of the century and beyond, including much information relating to Victorian cinema.

Hendricks, Gordon, *Origins of the American Film* (New York: Arno reprint, 1972), containing: *The Edison Motion Picture Myth* (University of California, 1961); *Beginnings of the Biograph* (Hendricks, 1964); *The Kinetoscope* (Hendricks, 1966).
Meticulously detailed accounts of the development of the Kinetograph, Kinetoscope and Biograph, based on extensive research of original records at the Edison Historical Site, New Jersey. Edison's technical knowledge is questioned, and Dickson's contributions highlighted. An essential reference for anyone interested in the subjects, but sometimes difficult to follow as the complexity of detail swamps the overall picture.

Hennebelle, Guy and Alfonso Gumucio-Dagron, *Les Cinémas de l'Amérique Latine: Pays par pays, l'historie, l'economie, les structures, les auteurs, les oeuvres* (Paris: Lherminier, 1981).
A survey of film production in Latin America, this is the only work of any substance to ack-

nowledge early film-making in the region in any sort of depth. It is divided into individual national histories, with generous space given to the arrival of film in each, together with basic but generally reliable facts.

Herbert, Stephen, *When the Movies Began ...* (London: The Projection Box, 1994).
This 26-page booklet is a chronology of film shows (and sources of production) throughout the world before May 1896. Includes a brief introduction of the chronophotographic experiments that led to the first successful films.

Hoffmann, Katrin (ed.), *Magische Schatten: Ein Kinderbuch zur Entehung des Kinos* (Frankfurt: Deutsches Filmmuseum, Frankfurt-am-Main, 1988).
A full overview of all pre-cinema and cinema apparatus and themes, this is hardly a children's book, except that from the Filmmuseum's point of view it absolved them from the technical necessity of fully annotating the illustrations. The text is lucid and direct, the design and choice of illustrations are energetic and clear, and the book is appealing. A good introduction to the field for readers of all ages.

Holman, Roger (ed.), *Cinema 1900–1906: An Analytical Study* (Brussels: FIAF, 1982).
A two-volume account of the seminal 1978 FIAF Brighton congress on early cinema, which broadly covered film production between 1900 and 1906, and is generally accepted to have established the modern school of early cinema studies. Volume one contains transcripts of symposium proceedings and papers presented at the symposium; volume two (edited by André Gaudreault) is a detailed filmography of all titles shown at the congress.

Hopkins, Albert A., *Magic: Stage Illusions and Scientific Diversions* (London: Sampson, Low, Marston and Company, 1898; Dover reprint 1976).
This large work on all aspects of magic has sections on the shadowgraphy of Félicien Trewey, chronophotography and early cinematography (including the scientific micro-cinematography of Dr R. L. Watkins). Illustrated with numerous *Scientific American* engravings.

Hopwood, Henry V., *Living Pictures* (London: Optician and Photographic Trades Review, 1899; Arno reprint, 1970).
The first comprehensive review of cinema technology, by a writer with a sophisticated understanding of the requirements of film production and presentation mechanisms, and a clarity of expression in explaining them to the general reader. Includes patent details and useful explanatory line drawings. Still used extensively as a standard reference work by researchers today. The 1915 revision by R. B. Foster is also useful: R. B. Foster, *Hopwood's Living Pictures* (London: Hatton Press, 1915).

Leyda, Jay, *Kino: A History of the Russian and Soviet Film* (London: George Allen and Unwin, 1960).
Still a very useful account in English of the Russian and Soviet cinema, with generous coverage of the arrival of film into Russia. Leyda's *Dianying: An Account of Films and the Film Audience in China* (Cambridge, Mass.: The MIT Press, 1972) is equally informative for the earliest years of film in China.

Liesegang, Franz Paul (trans. and ed. by Hermann Hecht), *Dates and Sources: A Contribution to the History of the Art of Projection and to Cinematography* (London: The Magic Lantern Society of Great Britain, 1986).
History of magic lantern projection, the Phenakistiscope; photography; chronophotography; the development of cinematography; colour cinematography; panoramic projection; sound-film projection; covering 1646–1926. Originally published as *Zahlen und Quellen: Zur Geschichte der Projektionkunst und Kinematographie* in Berlin in 1926, this is a translation – a heavily annotated and corrected edition of the original volume. Liesegang was extremely accurate, and Hecht has extended and clarified his work with respect. It is largely a technical history of projection apparatus (Liesegang came from a family of magic lantern and cinematograph manufacturers) presented chronologically and clearly and this remains a good basic outline of the mechanical and optical development of projection, not really replicated elsewhere in English.

Low, Rachael and Roger Manvell, *The History of the British Film 1896–1906* (London: George Allen and Unwin, 1948).
Of Rachael Low's celebrated multi-volume history of the British film, this first book is the weakest, covering only lightly an area of immense richness, though with very little in the way of serious error. It provides basic information, plus a number of interesting accounts

of such key figures of the period as Smith, Williamson, Paul and Urban.

Macgowan, Kenneth, *Behind the Screen: The History and Techniques of the Motion Picture* (New York: Delacorte Press, 1965).
This general film history has very good chapters on pre-cinema, chronophotography and the invention of moving pictures. An accessible, concise and generally accurate account, still useful as a general introduction to complex subjects.

Mannoni, Laurent, *Le grand art de la lumière et de l'ombre* (Paris: Nathan, 1994).
The most important recent account of pre-cinema and the birth of film production and exhibition (before 1897), particularly in France; clarifying and expanding on earlier accounts, with much new material based on original research, an extensive bibliography and list of patents.

Martinez, Josefina, *Los primeros veinticinco años de cine en Madrid: 1896–1920* (Madrid: Filmoteca Española, 1922).
Handsomely illustrated and thoroughly detailed account of early film production and exhibition in Madrid, while sketching in the broader picture of early film activity worldwide; a model of its kind.

Morris, Peter, *Embattled Shadows: A History of Canadian Cinema 1895–1939* (Montreal: McGill-Queen's University Press, 1978).
Very readable account of the beginnings of Canadian cinema, though parts have been superseded by more recent research.

Musser, Charles, *The Emergence of Cinema: The American Screen to 1907* (Berkeley and Los Angeles: Charles Scribner's Sons, 1990).
This is volume one of the *History of the American Cinema*, and the standard reference work. A meticulously researched, well-illustrated and highly perceptive account of the complex story of America's first films. Covers the economic, social and even psychoanalytical aspects of the subject as well as the technical.

Musser, Charles, *Before the Nickelodeon: Edwin S. Porter and the Edison Manufacturing Company* (Berkeley and Los Angeles: University of California Press, 1991).
Examines in detail Porter's role within the general context of cinema production and exhibition, and the wider context of turn-of-the-century popular culture. Much information

on the 19th century, based on extensive original research. An expansive, indispensable, well-illustrated reference.

Musser, Charles, *Before the Rapid Firing Kinetograph: Edison Motion Pictures, a Filmography with Documentation, 1890–1900* (Cineteca del Friuli/Giornate del cinema muto, 1996).
Seen only in limited proof form by the editors of this work, this volume will certainly prove to be the definitive work on its subject, listing every known Edison title for the period chronologically, with credits, supporting documentation and location of existing prints.

Quigley, Martin, *Magic Shadows: The Story of the Origins of Motion Pictures* (Washington: Georgetown University, 1948).
Motion Picture Herald journalist Quigley traces pre-cinema history in fourteen chapters, with the final thirty pages of the book detailing the introduction of film. A very readable account with many references given.

Ramsaye, Terry, *A Million and One Nights* (New York: Simon & Schuster, 1926).
A legendary history of pre-1925 cinema in the USA, told in a romantic style. To quote Thomas Edison's foreword note: 'A high degree of detailed accuracy has been attained. Ramsaye's theories, opinions and deductions are his own.' Though many of those deductions are questionable, the book is still useful as a guide to the lives of the early film pioneers.

Rittaud-Hutinet, Jacques, *Le Cinéma des origines: Les Frères Lumière et leurs opérateurs* (Seyssel: Champ Vallon, 1985).
An account of the first Lumière films and the operators Promio, Doublier, Mesguich and others who travelled the world shooting and showing motion pictures in 1896–7. Enthusiastic in its championing of some remarkable figures, it is unfortunately historically suspect on a number of occasions. Contains many frame enlargements from the films.

Rossell, Deac, '"The New Thing with the Long Name and the Old Thing with the Name That Isn't Much Shorter": A Cinema Chronology, 1889–1896', *Film History*, vol. 7 no. 2, special issue, Summer 1995.
Instantly the standard chronological reference to the earliest years of motion picture experimentation. A triumph in unravelling the names, dates and other complex facts of early patents, demonstrations, productions and shows worldwide.

Sadoul, Georges, *Histoire generale du cinéma, Part 1: L'Invention du cinéma 1832–1897* (Paris: Denoël, 1946).
Originally published in 1946, the second edition of 1948, and subsequent editions (incorporating corrections by Louis Lumière himself), still represent a useful account of cinema's origins. *Part 2: Les Pionniers du cinéma 1897-1909* continues the story with much valuable information.

Salt, Barry, *Film Style and Technology: History and Analysis* (London: Starword, 1983).
An unusual and valuable approach to film analysis; an examination of the extent to which technology has determined film style, including a short but illuminating section on the very early years, analysing the work of such film-makers as Georges Méliès and G. A. Smith. The author offers a lively counterblast to much modern film theory, and the work is handsomely illustrated. An expanded second edition was published in 1992.

Sokolov, Ippolit, *Istoriya izobreteniya kinematografia* (Moscow, 1960).
The major source on the still scarcely known area of early Russian film-making, invention and exhibition.

Spehr, Paul C., *The Movies Begin: Making Movies in New Jersey 1887–1920* (New Jersey: The Newark Museum, 1977).
Produced as an exhibition catalogue, this work gives a very clear account of the origins of American film (much of which was located in New Jersey), specifically the contributions of Thomas Edison and W. K-L. Dickson. The work covers film-making in the area until 1920, and has very useful backgound detail, studio information and a simple but very helpful who's who.

Talbot, Frederick A., *Moving Pictures: How They Are Made and Worked* (London: William Heinemann, 1912).
A review of the art and (especially) the technology of moving pictures just before the First World War. Talbot's popular account of the introduction of film in the USA, France and Britain must be treated with caution, but is still often quoted. An updated edition was published in 1923.

Tanaka Jun'ichiro, *Nihon Eiga Hattatsu-shi*, vol. 1 (Tokyo: Chuo Koronsha, 1957).
A standard source for Japanese film history, the first volume (*Katsudo Shashin Jidai*, 'The Age of Moving Pictures') of a four-volume series covers the early cinema period and contains much valuable documentary material with a linking commentary. Inevitably it remains little known in the west, along with other works covering early Japanese film, such as Tsukada Yoshinobu's *Nihon Eigashi no Kenkyu* (Tokyo, 1980) which covers the 1897–8 period exclusively.

Tosi, Virgilio, *Il cinema prima di Lumière* (Torino: ERI, 1984).
Fine account of the development of the first moving pictures, concentrating particularly on the chronophotographic work of Marey and Demenÿ and how their scientific ambitions were carried on by a number of scientists, doctors and anthropologists in the first years of cinema. A revised edition has been published in Mexico.

Toulet, Emmanuelle, *Cinématographe, invention du siècle* (Paris: Decouvertes Gallimard, 1988) [English edition, *Cinema is 100 Years Old* (London: Thames and Hudson, 1995)].
Profusely illustrated and attractive colour pocketbook outlining the story of the first films for the general reader, with an appendix including extracts from the memoirs of a number of pioneers. There is a noticeable French bias.

Vardac, A. Nicholas, *Stage to Screen: Theatrical Method from Garrick to Griffith* (Cambridge Mass.: Harvard University, 1949; Da Capo reprint, 1987).
This classic study of the relationship between nineteenth-century stage practice and the early cinema is still useful, especially for its material on melodrama, stage realism and the pantomime in relation to the film medium.

Von Zglinicki, Friedrich, *Der Weg des Films.* Vol. 1: *Textband;* Vol. 2: *Bildband* (Berlin: Rembrandt Verlag, 1956; Oms Press reprint, 1979).
A monumental 680 pages of text presents worldwide coverage of all pre-cinema topics, the invention of cinema, and the silent film to the beginnings of sound. More than half the book is devoted to Victorian and pre-Victorian material, and it is the central German-language source containing much information not included in French and English publications.

Waldekranz, Rune, *Sa foddes filmen: Ett massmediums uppkomst och genombrott* (Stockholm: Bokforlaget Pan/Norstedts, 1976).

Only language has kept this thorough and intriguing study of the evolution of photography, magic lanterns, pantomime, popular melodrama theatres, panoramas and the invention and first years of the cinema from becoming better known. While it cites many unique examples of work drawn from northern Europe, Waldekranz is especially good on the relationship of theatre and film in the Victorian period.

INDEX

Names

This index gives all names cited in the *Technical Essay* and *Who's Who*. It generally records both personal mentions of a name and that name when used as the title of a firm, but restricts itself to mentions of the individual only in the case of the ubiquitous Edison and Lumière. Those names with an entry in the *Who's Who* are given in bold. Prefixes to surnames (de, van, von) are always given first. A separate index below lists all motion picture devices cited in the text.

MOTION PICTURE DEVICES

Cameras, projectors and other motion picture equipment mentioned in the text are listed here, with the inventor, engineer or promoter associated with the machine given in parenthesis. Such names where the person does not have an entry in the *Who's Who* (that is, they only appear in the index above) are given in italics. Machines renamed either by their originator (e.g. Animatographe/Theatrograph) or by a user (e.g. Cinématographe/Fregoligraph) are cited under each name. Details may be traced through the page numbers given in the name index.

New Kinematograph (Haydon & Urry)

Oko (Proszynski)
Omnigrapho (Segreto)

Panoptikon (Latham)
Perfection Cinematograph (*Oulton*-Wray)
Petite (Hughes)
Phantascope (Jenkins)
Phantascope (Rudge)
Pholimeograph (*Heinze*)
Phonoscope (Demenÿ)
Photographon (*Ruhmer*)
Photorama (Lumière)
Photo-Rotoscope (Hughes)
Phototachygraphe (Grimoin-Sanson)
Photothéagraphe (Parnaland)
Photozoötrope (Joly)
Pleograf (Proszynski)
Power's Peerless Projector (Power)
Praxinoscope (Reynaud)
Projecting Kinetoscope (Edison)
Projectograph (Kuhn-Webster)

Projectoscope (Edison)

Reliance (Paul)
Royal Biograph (Joly)

Schnellseher (Anschütz)
Spirograph (*Brown-Joy*-Urban)
Stroboscope (Akimov)

Tachyscope (Anschütz)
Thaumatograph (Messter)
Théâtre Optique (Reynaud)
Theatrograph (Paul)
Triograph (Lumière)

Veriscope (Rector)
Vitagraphe (*Clément et Gilmer*)
Vitaphotoscope (Wolff)
Vitascope (Armat-Edison)

Wundertrommel (Anschütz)

Zoöpraxiscope (Muybridge)